Multiethnic Coalitions in Africa

Business Financing of Opposition Election Campaigns

Why are politicians able to form electoral coalitions that bridge ethnic divisions in some countries and not others? This book answers this question by presenting a theory of pecuniary coalition building in multiethnic countries governed through patronage. Focusing on Sub-Saharan Africa, the book explains how the relative autonomy of business from state-controlled capital affects political bargaining among opposition politicians in particular. While incumbents form coalitions by using state resources to secure cross-ethnic endorsements, opposition politicians must rely on the private resources of business to do the same. This book combines cross-national analyses of African countries with in-depth case studies of Cameroon and Kenya to show that incumbents actively manipulate financial controls to prevent business from supporting their opposition. It demonstrates that opposition politicians are more likely to coalesce across ethnic cleavages once incumbents have lost their ability to blackmail the business sector through financial reprisals.

Leonardo R. Arriola is Assistant Professor of Political Science at the University of California, Berkeley. He is the Vice Chair of the African Politics Conference Group, a research network affiliated with the American Political Science Association, for 2011–2013. He has received grants and fellowships from the National Science Foundation; the Kellogg Institute for International Studies at Notre Dame; the Center for Democracy, Development, and the Rule of Law at Stanford; the Fulbright Program; and the U.S. Department of Education. His work has appeared in journals such as *Comparative Politics* and *Comparative Political Studies*. He received the African Politics Conference Group's award for best article published on African politics in 2009.

*To my mother, Silvia, and my grandmother, Josefina,
and to the memory of my father, Leonardo,
and my grandmother, Florinda.*

Cambridge Studies in Comparative Politics

General Editor
Margaret Levi *University of Washington, Seattle*

Assistant General Editors
Kathleen Thelen *Massachusetts Institute of Technology*
Erik Wibbels *Duke University*

Associate Editors
Robert H. Bates *Harvard University*
Stephen Hanson *The College of William and Mary*
Torben Iversen *Harvard University*
Stathis Kalyvas *Yale University*
Peter Lange *Duke University*
Helen Milner Princeton University
Frances Rosenbluth *Yale University*
Susan Stokes *Yale University*
Sidney Tarrow *Cornell University*

Other Books in the Series

(*continued after index*)

Multiethnic Coalitions in Africa

Business Financing of Opposition Election Campaigns

LEONARDO R. ARRIOLA
University of California, Berkeley

CAMBRIDGE
UNIVERSITY PRESS

CAMBRIDGE UNIVERSITY PRESS
Cambridge, New York, Melbourne, Madrid, Cape Town,
Singapore, São Paulo, Delhi, Mexico City

Cambridge University Press
32 Avenue of the Americas, New York, NY 10013-2473, USA

www.cambridge.org
Information on this title: www.cambridge.org/9781107605435

First published 2013

Printed in the United States of America

A catalog record for this publication is available from the British Library.

Library of Congress Cataloging in Publication data
Arriola, Leonardo R. (Leonardo Rafael)
  Multiethnic coalitions in Africa : business financing of opposition
  election campaigns / Leonardo R. Arriola.
      p.   cm.
  Includes bibliographical references and index.
  ISBN 978-1-107-02111-2 (hardback) – ISBN 978-1-107-60543-5 (pbk.)
    1. Opposition (Political science) – Africa, Sub-Saharan.   2. Electoral coalitions – Africa,
  Sub-Saharan.   3. Campaign funds – Africa, Sub-Saharan.   4. Africa, Sub-Saharan –
  Ethnic relations – Political aspects.   5. Africa, Sub-Saharan – Politics and government –
  1960–   6. Kenya – Politics and government.   7. Cameroon – Politics and
  government.   I. Title.
  JQ1879.A5A77   2012
  324.70967-dc23   2012008619

ISBN 978-1-107-02111-2 Hardback
ISBN 978-1-107-60543-5 Paperback

Contents

Figures

Tables

Preface and Acknowledgments

This book is about interethnic cooperation. It explores cooperation during elections in the places least likely to exhibit it, that is, in countries where ethnicity defines national politics. Early research on democracy in ethnically divided societies suggested that multiethnic coalitions either could not be sustained (Horowitz 1985; Rabushka and Shepsle 1972) or had to be institutionally constrained to remain stable (Lijphart 1969, 1977). Since then, political scientists have accumulated considerable knowledge on the factors that affect the success of ethnic parties (Chandra 2004b), the emergence of particular ethnic cleavage structures (Posner 2005), and the manipulation of ethnic labels for partisan advantage (Ferree 2010). We have made less progress, however, in understanding the question that is central to democracy in multiethnic societies: Under what conditions can politicians forge political bargains that span ethnic cleavages? It is in this context that I seek to explain how opposition politicians build multiethnic electoral coalitions in African countries.

My hope is that the theory and evidence presented in the following pages will be of interest to scholars who study the democratization process in multiethnic societies, the political economy of developing countries, and the dynamics of African politics. The explanation I provide could not have been developed without the cooperation of the politicians, party officials, businesspeople, and scholars I interviewed in Cameroon, Ethiopia, Kenya, and Senegal. They generously shared their knowledge of the cut and thrust of politics in their countries. What I learned from them forced me to abandon the preconceived notions I carried with me into the field. Instead, the explanation I advance in this book has been informed by the lessons imparted through their personal narratives. But because the relationship between money and politics remains a sensitive issue in these countries, I have chosen to withhold their names in these acknowledgments and in most of the interviews cited throughout the book for reasons of security. I am indebted to these individuals, and my first thanks go to them.

I began this book as a doctoral dissertation in the Department of Political Science at Stanford University. I had the great fortune to be advised by extraordinary scholars – David Laitin, Jim Fearon, Beatriz Magaloni, and Alberto

Díaz-Cayeros. I am grateful beyond words for the intellectual guidance and professional mentoring they offered. Their incisive feedback obliged me to be more precise in my reasoning and to be more rigorous in my analysis. Their own research has inspired me to make this book better. I intend to emulate their example throughout my career.

Much of what I learned about political science at Stanford I learned from a wonderful community of graduate students, several of whom read preliminary drafts of this project. In particular, I would like to thank Claire Adida, Dan Butler, Martin Dimitrov, Catherine Duggan, Desha Girod, Nahomi Ichino, Kimuli Kasara, Alex Kuo, Bethany Lacina, Matt Levendusky, Karla López de Nava, Kenneth McElwain, Nora Ng, David Patel, Vidal Romero, Kay Shimizu, Alberto Simpser, and Clint Taylor. Along the way I was also lucky to have the friendship of Tania Castro, Netsanet Demissie, Pepa Guerrero, Barak Hoffman, Alice Kada, Christina Lee, Jeanette Lee-Oderman, Alicia Londoño, Judit Sarossy, Lahra Smith, Solange Taylor, and Eliana Vásquez.

I have received invaluable counsel during my time in the Department of Political Science at the University of California, Berkeley. I especially want to thank Pradeep Chhibber, David Collier, Ruth Collier, Steve Fish, Taeku Lee, Jonah Levy, Peter Lorentzen, Bob Powell, and Jason Wittenberg. I have learned a great deal from these wonderful colleagues and friends. Their insights have enriched my work. I also thank the Berkeley graduate students who provided excellent feedback and assistance at various stages: Matthew Gichohi, Chelsea Johnson, and Mark Rosenberg. I received outstanding assistance from the students who participated in Berkeley's Undergraduate Research Apprentice Program (URAP): Shaibya Dalal, Andrew Feher, Laura MacArthur, Ian Scott, Kevin Showkat, Nancy Ta, and Ian Tholen.

During the course of my research for this book, I benefited from the constructive comments offered on different drafts and presentations by Jennifer Brass, Larry Diamond, Kent Eaton, Karen Ferree, Clark Gibson, Antoinette Handley, John Heilbrunn, Martha Johnson, Edmond Keller, Eleonora Pasotti, Dan Posner, Armando Razo, Kathryn Stoner-Weiss, Scott Straus, Nicolas van de Walle, and members of the Working Group on African Political Economy (WGAPE). I owe special thanks to Jed DeVaro for all his help and support.

I thank Lewis Bateman, the senior editor for political science and history at Cambridge University Press, for his advice and patience. I especially appreciate the feedback from the Cambridge reviewers. Their comments enabled me to significantly improve the manuscript.

I am grateful for the resources that enabled me to undertake the research associated with this book. I received financial support from the Soros Fellowship for New Americans, the Ford Foundation Predoctoral Diversity Fellowship, the Fulbright Program, and the Council of American Overseas Research Centers. At Stanford I received grants and fellowships from the Center for Democracy, Development, and the Rule of Law (CDDRL); the Humanities and Sciences Dean's Office; and the Freeman Spogli Institute for International Studies. The Department of Political Science and the Institute of International Studies (IIS) at the University of California, Berkeley, provided the financial and institutional support needed to transform a dissertation into a book.

This book was ultimately made possible by the loving and unconditional support of my first teachers. My paternal grandmother, Florinda Castro, was a daughter of the twentieth century's first revolution. She taught me from her experience to understand the quotidian consequences of politics and encouraged me to become a teacher, her own deferred dream. My maternal grandmother, Josefina Nava, is a model of resilience who taught me to meet adversity with humor. I wish to be as brave as she. My parents, Silvia and Leonardo, worked tirelessly so that I could have a better life in their adopted country. They taught me to love books, to explore new horizons, and to appreciate the educational opportunities that I was so privileged to receive. This book is the culmination of their efforts. It is for them.

List of Abbreviations

AEUP	All Ethiopia Unity Party
AREAER	Annual Report on Exchange Arrangements and Exchange Restrictions
ARN	Action pour le Redressement National
BAO	Banque de l'Afrique Occidentale
BBWA	British Bank of West Africa
BDP	Botswana Democratic Party
BEAC	Banque des États de l'Afrique Centrale
BIAO	Banque Internationale de l'Afrique Occidentale
BOCCIM	Botswana Confederation of Commerce and Manpower
CAPME	Centre d'Assistance aux Petites et Moyennes Entreprises
CCCE	Caisse Centrale de Coopération Economic
CCIMA	Chambre de Commerce, d'Industrie, des Mines et de l'Artisanat
CCM	Chama Cha Mapinduzi
CCOM	Caisse Centrale de la France d'Outre-Mer
CFA	Communauté Financière Africaine
CFAO	Compagnie Française de l'Afrique Occidentale
CFD	Coalition des Forces Démocratiques
COBAC	Commission Bancaire de l'Afrique Centrale
CPDSG	Central Province Development Support Group
CPP	Convention People's Party
CRRN	Coalition pour la Réconciliation et la Reconstruction Nationale
CUD	Coalition for Unity and Democracy
DAC	Democratic Angola Coalition
DP	Democratic Party
EPRDF	Ethiopian People's Revolutionary Democratic Front
ESAF	Enhanced Structural Adjustment Facility
FAO	Food and Agriculture Organization
FFA	Front des Forces Alternatives
FOGAPE	Fond d'Aide et de Garantie des Crédits aux Petites et Moyennes Entreprises

FORD	Forum for the Restoration of Democracy
FORD-K	Forum for the Restoration of Democracy-Kenya
FORD-P	Forum for the Restoration of Democracy-People
GCP	Ghana Congress Party
GEMA	Gikuyu-Embu-Meru Association
GICAM	Groupement Inter-Patronal du Cameroun
IBAC	International Bank of Africa Cameroon
ICDC	Industrial and Commercial Development Corporation
IFC	International Finance Corporation
IFI	international financial institution
IMF	International Monetary Fund
IPPG	Inter-Party Parliamentary Group
KAM	Kenya Association of Manufacturers
KANU	Kenya African National Union
KCB	Kenya Commercial Bank
KNCCI	Kenya National Chamber of Commerce and Industry
KPC	Kenya People's Coalition
LDP	Liberal Democratic Party
MCP	Malawi Congress Party
MDI	Mouvement pour la Démocratie et l'Interdépendance
MDP	Mouvement pour la Démocratie et le Progrès
MDR	Mouvement Démocratique pour la Défense de la République
MLDC	Mouvement pour la Libération et la Démocratie au Cameroun
MMD	Movement for Multiparty Democracy
NAC	National Alliance for Change
NAC	Nyasaland African Congress
NAK	National Alliance Party of Kenya
NARC	National Rainbow Coalition
NBFI	non-banking financial institution
NBK	National Bank of Kenya
NCEC	National Convention Executive Council
NCNC	National Council of Nigeria and the Cameroons
NCOPA	National Coordination of Opposition Parties and Associations
NDI	National Democratic Institute
NDP	National Democratic Party
NDP	National Development Party
NLM	National Liberation Movement
NNDP	Nigerian National Democratic Party
NPC	Northern Peoples' Congress
NPK	National Party of Kenya
OAU	Organization of African Unity
OED	Operations Evaluation Department
ONC	Oromo National Congress
PAL	Parti de l'Alliance Libérale
PDCI	Parti Démocratique de la Côte d'Ivoire

PDG	Parti Démocratique de Guinée
PPI	Parliamentary Powers Index
PRGF	Poverty Reduction and Growth Facility
PSP	Parti Progressiste Soudanais
RDPC	Rassemblement Démocratique du Peuple Camerounais
SAA	Syndicat Agricole Africain
SCOA	Societé Commerciale de l'Ouest Africain
SDF	Social Democratic Front
SDP	Social Democratic Party
SNH	Société Nationale des Hydrocarbures
SNI	Société Nationale d'Investissement
Syndustricam	Syndicat des Industriels du Cameroun
TANU	Tanganyika African National Union
UAC	United Africa Company
UDC	Union Démocratique du Cameroun
UFDC	Union des Forces Démocratiques du Cameroun
UGCC	United Gold Coast Convention
UNACOIS	Union Nationale des Commerçants et Industriels du Sénégal
UNC	Union Nationale Camerounaise
UNDP	Union Nationale pour la Démocratie et le Progrès
UNIGES	Union des Groupements Economiques du Sénégal
UNITA	Union for the Total Independence of Angola
UPC	Union des Populations du Cameroun
UPR	Union pour la République
US	Union Soudanaise
USAID	United States Agency for International Development

The Puzzle of Opposition Coordination

> You cannot fight fairly against a candidate who is in power if you are divided, especially in Africa.
>
> Blaise Compaoré, president of Burkina Faso, 2005[1]

Democracy seems to break down all too easily in multiethnic societies. While electoral competition can generate democracy's most desirable attributes, this competitive mechanism is widely thought to fail wherever politicians and their parties become identified by ethnicity. Democracy obviously can collapse if the competition between ethnic parties degenerates into a violent confrontation over control of the state. But democracy usually disintegrates through subtler means. It begins when incumbents face too little competition rather than too much. Incumbents who confront an ethnically divided opposition effectively have insufficient competition. And if they do not fear losing elections, incumbents do not have much incentive to be responsive to their citizens, to craft better policy, or to respect institutional constraints. Electoral competition in multiethnic societies, to be meaningful, requires opposition coordination across ethnic cleavages.

The potential impact of opposition coordination is readily apparent in the countries of Sub-Saharan Africa, where opposition politicians have routinely divided along ethnic lines when challenging incumbents through multiparty elections. In Gabon, President Omar Bongo, Africa's longest-serving ruler, died in 2009 after having defeated an ethnically fragmented opposition in three elections since the transition to multipartism in 1990. Because the personalized clientelistic networks used by Bongo to stay in power were disrupted by his death, the election held to replace the deceased president offered an unparalleled opportunity to bring about the country's first democratic alternation.

---

[1] Compaoré made the statement on the eve of the 2005 presidential election in Burkina Faso. He went on to win 80% of the vote against 12 opposition candidates. See Tanguy Berthemet, "Blaise Compaoré: 'La crise ivoirienne inquiète le Burkina,'" *Le Figaro*, 12 November 2005. Author's translation from the French version.

Yet, his son and designated successor, Ali Bongo Ondimba, managed to keep the incumbent regime in power by winning 42% of the vote against an opposition that split its support between two rivals who each garnered a quarter of the vote.[2]

An ethnically divided opposition fumbled a similar opportunity in Zambia. The Movement for Multiparty Democracy (MMD) became the dominant ruling party in that country after winning the 1991 election and each subsequent contest over the next twenty years. In the 2006 presidential election, President Levy Mwanawasa was reelected with 43% of the vote against two opposition candidates who divided the remaining votes between them. In the election called following Mwanawasa's sudden death in 2008, his designated successor, Rupiah Banda, kept the MMD in power with 40% of the vote against two challengers who split the opposition vote. That a divided opposition would enable the ruling party to retain the presidency was known in advance. They were the very same candidates who had competed two years earlier.[3]

A similar problem occurred in Kenya, where an opposition splintered by ethnicity permitted the country's long-ruling incumbent, President Daniel arap Moi, to hold onto power throughout the 1990s. As head of the Kenya African National Union (KANU), which had ruled the country since independence, Moi enjoyed considerable advantages in competing for office, but these were offset by a narrowing base of support. Nevertheless, in the 1992 presidential election, Moi won reelection with only 36% of the vote because his three principal rivals divided the country's largest ethnic groups among them. In the 1997 presidential election, Moi again won reelection with 40% of the vote against four opposition candidates who commanded blocs of their coethnics' votes.[4] A repeat of this scenario was expected in the 2002 presidential election for which Moi had handpicked his successor.

But the Kenyan opposition did not divide along ethnic lines in the run up to the 2002 election. Mwai Kibaki, who had lost two previous bids for the presidency, unexpectedly managed to assemble a multiethnic electoral coalition that would go on to defeat the ruling party, bringing about the country's first democratic transfer of power and one of the few seen in Africa since the transition to multipartism began in the early 1990s. Kibaki, however, was an unlikely standard-bearer for the opposition. Derided by civil society activists as

---

[2] André Mba Obame, an ethnic Fang and a former minister in Bongo's regime, won 26% of the vote in the 2009 presidential election. Pierre Mamboundou, an ethnic Punu and long-time opponent of the regime, won 25%.

[3] In the 2006 presidential election, Michael Sata, an ethnic Bemba and former member of the MMD, won 29%. Hakainde Hichilema, an ethnic Tonga and opposition party leader, won 25%. In the election to replace the deceased Mwanawasa in 2008, Sata won 38% of the vote. Hichilema won 20%.

[4] The Kenyan opposition candidates who divided the 1992 vote were Kenneth Matiba, an ethnic Kikuyu, 26%; Mwai Kibaki, Kikuyu, 20%; and Oginga Odinga, Luo, 18%. The opposition candidates in 1997 were Mwai Kibaki, Kikuyu, 31%; Raila Odinga, Luo, 11%; Michael Wamalwa, Luhya, 8%; and Charity Ngilu, Kamba, 8%.

a reluctant reformer and attacked by his political rivals as an ethnic chauvinist, he had neither the reputation nor the party required to mount a campaign that would attract votes from a cross section of the electorate. Indeed, since the reintroduction of multiparty politics in Kenya in 1991, no opposition politician had built a party organization that could challenge the ruling party on a national scale.

What Kibaki did have in 2002 was money. To overcome his electoral disadvantages, he pursued a pecuniary coalition-building strategy. His campaign advisors, a group of prominent businessmen and former parastatal directors, were able to raise funds among the Kenyan business community.[5] That money was then used to secure public endorsements from politicians representing the country's major ethnic groups, beginning with local notables and moving up to national actors. Opposition politicians were, in effect, paid to leverage their own reputations in mobilizing their coethnics' votes on behalf of Kibaki. This pecuniary strategy ultimately enabled Kibaki to engineer the electoral coordination of Kenya's once-fragmented opposition.

Opposition politicians in African countries face the same electoral disadvantages as Kibaki wherever voters are ethnically mobilized and parties are organizationally weak. However, not all opposition politicians have been able to employ his seemingly simple pecuniary strategy for building electoral coalitions – the coalitions needed for meaningful democratic competition in multiethnic societies. What impedes the coordination of electoral opposition across ethnic clevages? When are coalitions formed among politicians who might otherwise compete with each other for votes? Under what conditions can politicians agree to share power in societies divided by ethnicity?

This book engages such questions in the context of Africa's incomplete democratization. Although the formal elements of democracy – elections, parties, and legislatures – have been widely adopted in the region, these institutions have not brought about their desired effects in most countries. Two decades of experimentation with multiparty competition have not necessarily rendered governments more accountable, obliged their leaders to become more responsive to citizens, or induced their legislatures to more vigorously restrain the actions of executives. What underlies these deficiencies in African countries is the absence of an opposition that coordinates across ethnic cleavages. The competitive mechanism of democracy is ineffectual without it.

In the following pages, I introduce the problem of electoral coordination among ethnic-based opposition parties and why it matters for Africa's ongoing democratization. I then briefly review the relevant explanations found in the political science literature. To better account for the variation in opposition coalition formation across African countries, I provide an alternative explanation that focuses on the autonomy of business from state-controlled capital. I demonstrate in this book that opposition politicians are more likely to pursue

---

[5] Author interviews, Nairobi, 21 July 2008; 29 July 2008; 5 August 2008; 6 August 2008; 15 August 2008.

a pecuniary coalition-building strategy where the state's capacity to act as a gatekeeper for capital has been eroded by liberalizing financial reforms. Under such conditions, opposition politicians can tap the resources of business – the only viable source of campaign funding in poor countries – to amalgamate ethnically defined constituencies into national coalitions.

THE PROBLEM OF OPPOSITION COORDINATION IN AFRICA

Political parties in Africa have struggled to coordinate across ethnic cleavages since they were first mobilized to agitate for independence after the Second World War. The dynamic between a hegemonic ruling party and a fragmented opposition began to take hold before formal independence was even achieved (Kilson 1963; Schachter 1961; Wallerstein 1961). The parties that won control of territorial legislatures in the elections leading up to independence were soon able to dispatch rival parties organized on an ethnic or regional basis. In pre-independence Ghana, Apter (1964a, 279) observed that a fragmented opposition enabled the Convention People's Party (CPP) to become politically ascendant, which meant that "local parties could be annihilated by the CPP one by one."[6] Just a year after most West African countries achieved independence, Wallerstein (1961) was already asking, "What Happened to the Opposition?" He found that opposition parties were represented in parliament in only two of the twelve countries surveyed.[7]

Apter argued during Africa's post-independence decade that opposition politicians would gradually learn to coordinate through repeated elections and thereby generate the competition required for democracy (Apter 1964b, 467–470).[8] But Zolberg (1966) showed instead that incumbents could use their resources to coopt or eliminate their disordered rivals, and do so with minimal violence. The disappearance of a legal opposition by the mid-1960s was among the first signs that Africa's political development would be hindered by the absence of organizations that could effectively coordinate political actors and resources on a national scale (Bienen 1967).

Persistent opposition coordination failure became a feature of politics even in African countries that approximated peaceful multiparty competition. In Botswana, where multiparty elections have been regularly held since 1966,

[6] Apter noted that the opposition attempted to build a united front against the CPP on at least two occasions, though they failed each time. In 1952, the Ghana Congress Party (GCP) was designed to be a broad-based party that would merge the United Gold Coast Convention (UGCC) and the National Democratic Party (NDP), but J.B. Danquah ultimately refused to dissolve his UGCC. In 1954, the Volta Charter was negotiated as a common platform for parliamentary elections, but it was never signed by the participating parties.

[7] Wallerstein found that dominant ruling parties had become established in Ghana, Senegal, Sierra Leone, and Togo, and that no legal opposition party existed in Côte d'Ivoire, Dahomey, Guinea, Mauritania, Mali, Niger, and Upper Volta. Opposition parties had parliamentary representation only in Ghana and Nigeria.

[8] The actual purpose of Apter's 1962 paper was to convince independence-era leaders that multiparty competition was essential for democracy.

the ruling Botswana Democratic Party (BDP) has consistently held at least a two-thirds majority in the National Assembly, which elects the country's president.[9] Much of the BDP's dominance is linked to the opposition's own persistent fragmentation. The cost of coordination failure has been plain in repeated elections, but the main opposition parties have insisted on fielding competing candidates in most constituencies (Molomo and Molefe 2005; Molutsi 2004). In the 2004 elections, for example, the BDP won 77% of parliamentary seats partly because opposition parties split the anti-incumbent vote. The opposition parties won only 13 seats among the 57 contested. Had they coordinated their candidates, the combined opposition would have picked up 12 additional seats, thus denying the BDP its two-thirds majority for the first time (Sebudubedu and Osei-Hwedie 2010).

When multiparty politics were finally reintroduced across the continent in the early 1990s, the opposition in most countries emerged as fragmented as it had been in the early 1960s. African party systems repeated the pattern from forty years earlier: the incumbent's ruling party overawed a weak and fragmented opposition (Bogaards 2004; Mozaffar and Scarritt 2005; Olukoshi 1998; Rakner and Svasand 2002; Rakner and van de Walle 2009; van de Walle 2003). Incumbents, of course, achieve this dominance by using fraud and coercion to reduce the uncertainty associated with holding elections. They actively work to dismiss their opponents as "drunkards, embezzlers and lunatics," as President Robert Mugabe said of his opponents during Zimbabwe's 1990 election,[10] or as "amateurs and opportunists," as President Paul Biya said of his rivals on the eve of Cameroon's 1992 election.[11] However, a recurrent theme in case studies of African party systems is the failure of opposition politicians themselves to coordinate at the ballot box in countries that vary in constitutional arrangements as well as social conditions (Crook 1997; Joireman 1997; Konings 2004; Marty 2002). And incumbents whose governments neither promote the public good nor respect citizen preferences are able to retain power, in part, because they do not confront a coordinated electoral opposition that presents a viable alternative to the political status quo.

The formation of coalitions that aggregate blocs of votes, either as catch-all parties or multiparty alliances, should be a natural strategy for opposition politicians seeking national office in multiethnic societies; otherwise, if too many compete, they enable the incumbent to remain in the office by dividing the opposition vote. Yet, the opposition politicians who challenge incumbents across Africa appear incapable of building national parties, cultivating broad-based constituencies, or forging the electoral alliances necessary to pool their

---

[9] The National Assembly is elected through first-past-the-post single member constituencies. Candidates are required to attest at registration that, if elected, they would vote for their party's presidential candidate.

[10] Quoted in Sylvester (1990, 388).

[11] Quoted in Derald Everhart, "Cameroon President Facing Opposition Challenge in Capital," *Associated Press*, 11 October 1992.

votes. Their fragmentation is all the more noteworthy because the same set of opposition politicians often faces off with the same incumbent over multiple election cycles. These politicians repeatedly fail to coalesce despite having regular interactions that enable them to communicate their political preferences and to demonstrate their relative strength based on vote shares from prior elections. Even when the regime in power has transgressed against them and their constituents, opposition politicians have had a difficult time selecting a single candidate around whom a national electoral coalition might be mobilized.

Although an intuitive strategy for counterbalancing the advantages enjoyed by an entrenched incumbent, the coordination of opposition across ethnic cleavages is difficult to bring about because it involves considerable uncertainty for individual politicians. Opposition politicians may have a common goal of unseating the incumbent, but they do not necessarily have identical preferences over which candidate should do so. As Przeworski (1991, 67) reminds us, "the struggle for democracy always takes place on two fronts: against the authoritarian regime for democracy and against one's allies for the best place under democracy." To be sure, the costs associated with political change are often distributed more equally than the rewards. The gains that could be realized through opposition coordination are unlikely to be shared equally, though each member of a coalition would have to shoulder some of the cost for bringing it about. The coalition candidate for the presidency or the premiership undoubtedly takes the largest prize in an election, while other coalition partners share the remaining spoils and usually on an unequal basis. It is in this respect that coalition bargaining often breaks down among the opposition. Every politician understands that power-sharing promises made before an election are cheap talk. A politician may receive either no compensation or less than what was promised even after having rallied votes for a coalition's candidate. This frustrated politician would have no means of enforcing those promises once the winner is installed in office.

The difficulty of forming opposition coalitions in African countries is clearly observed when the region is placed in a comparative context. Presidential elections are particularly useful for gauging the presence of a coordinated opposition, since any challenger could become a focal candidate for anti-incumbent forces seeking an alternation in power. Figure 1.1 shows that this potential is usually not realized in African presidential elections. Between 1985 and 2005, 45% of all presidential elections held around the world resulted in alternation, meaning that an incumbent or a ruling party's designated candidate was obliged to hand power over to an opposition candidate. But African elections have resulted in such an outcome only 26% of the time, a rate far lower than in comparable regions where presidential systems are commonplace and the democratization process remains ongoing. In Latin America, 66% of elections led to turnover, as they have 50% of the time in Eastern Europe and the former Soviet Union.

Electoral coordination among opposition politicians could have significantly increased the relatively low rate of alternation shown for African elections in

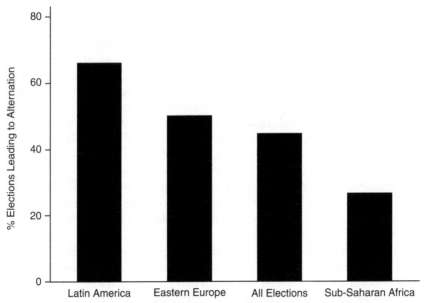

FIGURE 1.1. Alternation in presidential elections across regions, 1985–2005. Note: The sample includes 278 presidential elections held between 1985 and 2005. Of these elections, 106 were held in Sub-Saharan Africa, 85 in Latin America and the Caribbean, and 48 in Eastern Europe and the former Soviet Union.
Source: Author's data set.

Figure 1.1. The outcome might have been different in an estimated 40% of 74 presidential elections that were contested by the opposition but won by the incumbent between 1985 and 2005. If the top three opposition challengers had formed an electoral coalition or arranged for the strategic withdrawal of candidacies, their combined vote share would have been greater than the incumbent's own in nine of those elections.[12] Their combined vote share would have brought them within ten percentage points of the incumbent's in another twenty-two elections. And this would be no small feat in a region where incumbents win reelection with a margin of victory that averages more than 40%.[13] Opposition coordination might have led to alternation in some of these twenty-two elections if a more competitive race encouraged greater voter turnout or vote switching in favor of an opposition coalition that presented itself as a viable alternative government.

But wherever opposition politicians have managed to overcome their divisions, the impact of their coordination has been tangible. Bratton and van de

[12] For countries with runoff systems, the vote shares are from the first round.
[13] The incumbent margin of victory – the difference between the first- and second-place candidates – appears to be unusually high in Africa when compared across regions. The average margin of victory for reelected presidents or their designated successors is 34.5% around the world. That margin falls to 19.8% in Latin America and 9.6% in OECD countries.

Walle (1997) find that the transition from a one-party to a multiparty system was less prolonged in countries with a relatively cohesive opposition: of the sixteen countries with a cohesive opposition, fifteen held founding elections. Howard and Roessler (2006) further show that opposition coalitions can result in liberalizing electoral outcomes in competitive authoritarian regimes. The problem, however, is that there is no explanation for how those coalitions emerge in the first place.

The objective of this book is to explain how opposition politicians are able to forge multiethnic electoral coalitions in some African countries but not others. Opposition coalitions typically attract scholarly or journalistic attention when they lead to an alternation in power, as in Senegal in 2000 or Kenya in 2002. However, as illustrated in Figure 1.2, opposition politicians in several African countries have managed to overcome their fissiparous tendencies to coordinate in the run-up to executive elections, though they do not always win. Multiethnic opposition coalitions are defined in this book as those in which a coalition endorses a single candidate for executive office, represents more than one ethnic group or region, and forms prior to the election in a plurality system or prior to the first round in a runoff system. I find that such electoral coordination has occurred in a number of African countries: 32 opposition coalitions have been formed in the 85 contested executive elections held between 1990 and 2005. These opposition coalitions account for over half of the executive turnover – 15 of 27 cases – seen in region during the same time period.[14]

Figure 1.2 further shows that the frequency of opposition coordination varies considerably across African countries. Opposition politicians in some countries are regularly able to overcome the uncertainty associated with making power-sharing promises before elections. Multiethnic opposition coalitions were formed for at least two elections in the countries shaded in dark gray, an opposition coalition formed for one election in the countries shaded in light gray, and no such coalition formed in countries marked with diagonal lines. The fact that Figure 1.2 suggests no obvious pattern in terms of colonial legacy or authoritarian background underscores our lack of knowledge concerning the institutionalization of electoral opposition or party systems in African countries where democracy has yet to be consolidated. The existing literature offers no convincing explanation for why electoral opposition becomes institutionalized more slowly in some countries than others or for whether the erratic nature of opposition in some countries will stabilize over time.

---

[14] All elections examined in this book are listed in Appendix D. I coded the multiethnic opposition coalitions that formed during ninety-nine executive elections held between 1990 and 2005. The fourteen elections boycotted by the opposition are excluded from the analysis. Parliamentary races from Botswana, Ethiopia, Mauritius, and South Africa are included in the sample. I reason that their inclusion is justified because each party's candidate for president (Botswana and South Africa) or prime minister (Ethiopia and Mauritius) is known before the election. Moreover, the powers of the prime ministers in these countries are as expansive as those of their counterparts in presidential systems. Cox (2005, 80) notes that the incentive to form broad national parties can be as strong in parliamentary systems as in presidential ones "to the extent that parliamentary elections revolve around the prospective prime ministers."

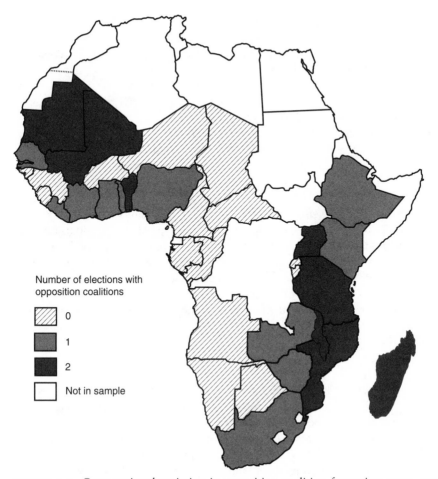

FIGURE I.2. Cross-national variation in opposition coalition formation, 1990–2005. Note: There were nearly three multiparty elections held per African country, on average, between 1990 and 2005. Information on specific elections in each country is listed in Appendix D.

Source: Original Africa map designed by Daniel Dalet (http://d-maps.com).

EXISTING EXPLANATIONS FOR OPPOSITION COORDINATION

The apparent difficulty that opposition politicians face in forming multiethnic coalitions could be easily attributed to the imperfect democratization of African countries. Despite the political liberalization that swept across the region in the early 1990s, executive authority remains highly personalized and unconstrained in most countries. African incumbents tend to rule through hybrid regimes that combine democratic and authoritarian traits. And they have the means with which to manipulate elections to extend tenure (Bratton and Posner 1999; Gandhi and Lust-Okar 2009; Gandhi and Przeworski 2006; Schedler 2006).

These incumbents can predetermine an election's outcome by influencing the vote count, by using violence to repress their opponents, or even by tailoring the composition of their opposition. In Côte d'Ivoire, for example, President Henri Konan Bédié neutralized his chief rival in the 1995 presidential election by having his candidacy barred on allegations that he was not an Ivorian citizen. In Zambia, President Frederick Chiluba employed the same tactic to disqualify his main rival, who also happened to be his predecessor, from running against him in the 1996 presidential election.

Focusing on incumbent chicanery, however, provides limited insight into the conditions under which opposition politicians might become credible challengers. How can we explain the variation in opposition coordination across countries or within countries over time when nearly every incumbent in the region takes measures to prevent such an occurrence? It remains to be shown how opposition politicians manage to forge cross-cleavage alliances under less than ideal conditions. I review here the most plausible hypotheses based on scholarship that has examined the effects of ethnic mobilization, patronage politics, electoral institutions, and economic interests. Each explanation highlights an important structural factor that impinges directly on the choices made by politicians over their electoral strategies, that is, whether to coalesce or to fragment in their pursuit of elected office.

Ethnic Mobilization

The fragmentation of opposition parties could be directly attributed to the ethnic divisions found in most African countries. Scholars have long argued that democracy is conflict-prone and unstable where ethnic identity becomes the primary basis for political organization (Horowitz 1985; Lijphart 1969, 1977; Rabushka and Shepsle 1972; Snyder 2000). Ethnic-based politicking is thought to stimulate the escalation of communal demands, encouraging politicians who compete for the control of ethnic constituencies to engage in outbidding (Horowitz 1985; Rabushka and Shepsle 1972). With their immediate rivals being other coethnics, politicians can seek to gain electoral advantage by advocating increasingly extreme positions. This intragroup competition makes bargaining across cleavages problematic, since politicians may seek to protect their flanks by driving a hard bargain with their counterparts from other groups. Once locked into polarized positions, politicians are unable to strike the delicate balance between maintaining the support of their own coethnics and making concessions to politicians from other ethnic groups (Berman et al. 2004; Ottaway 1999).

These theoretical expectations seem to be borne out by the African record. Empirical studies of electoral mobilization in the region show that partisan support largely reflects ethno-regional identity (Ferree 2004; Norris and Mattes 2003; Posner 2005; Wantchekon 2003). Opposition parties are at a particular disadvantage in this regard because they tend to be based on ethnically defined constituencies that do not approximate an electoral plurality. This can be seen in the ethnic fractionalization scores for political parties. These scores can serve as a proxy for ethnic diversity among a party's voters; higher scores indicate greater diversity.[15] Using the Afrobarometer survey conducted in 2005–2006, I calculated the scores based on the ethnic self-identification and voting preferences reported by respondents in fifteen African countries.[16] The scores show that, when compared with incumbents, opposition politicians lead parties that appeal to a narrower range of the electorate in all but two countries, Ghana and Namibia. In the remaining thirteen countries, the average fractionalization score is 0.686 among opposition parties versus 0.845 among incumbent parties, which represents a 20% difference.[17] This pattern suggests that part of the electoral advantage enjoyed by African incumbents comes from the fact that they can draw support across a larger range of ethnic groups.

The literature suggests that competition among ethnic-based parties is perceived as a zero-sum contest in which gains by one group's politicians are interpreted as losses for all others. This is especially true in the case of the presidency, which is the only office that matters in Africa's weakly institutionalized political systems. Reynolds (1995, 95) finds that in African countries "a directly elected president tends to be pressured into ethnic or regional exclusivity." Manning (2005, 723–724) similarly argues that the prize represented by the executive – in political and economic terms – is so large as to give "little incentive for parties to form electoral coalitions that might preclude their own leaders from a shot at the highest position." Politicians have no incentive to negotiate over the selection of a single opposition candidate because the executive office is a winner-take-all proposition.[18] Politicians and their constituents understand that this single office is the most important instrument for redistribution. Losing it means losing out on resources. Each group will therefore have a clear collective preference for placing its own candidate in that office.

An ethnic-based explanation for opposition fragmentation suggests that African politicians choose to campaign independently because they cannot bargain over an indivisible prize that every ethnic group wants to control. But this

---

[15] The ethnic fractionalization score measures diversity by reflecting the likelihood that two people chosen at random from the party will be from different ethnic groups.

[16] The Afrobarometer surveys use nationally representative samples with an average sample size of 1,200 respondents. The data are available at http://www.afrobarometer.org/.

[17] I calculated the opposition figure as a weighted average based on the distribution of preferences reported by Afrobarometer respondents among all opposition parties within each country. The countries included in this calculation are: Benin (opposition 0.449; incumbent 0.857); Botswana (opposition 0.871; incumbent 0.902); Ghana (opposition 0.738; incumbent 0.549); Kenya (opposition 0.767; incumbent 0.863); Madagascar (opposition 0.779; incumbent 0.810); Malawi (opposition 0.614; incumbent 0.840); Mali (opposition 0.859; incumbent 0.863); Mozambique (opposition 0.605; incumbent 0.776); Namibia (opposition 0.701; incumbent 0.603); Nigeria (opposition 0.491; incumbent 0.857); Senegal (opposition 0.640; incumbent 0.705); South Africa (opposition 0.638; incumbent 0.880); Tanzania (opposition 0.764; incumbent 0.868); Uganda (opposition 0.671; incumbent 0.902); Zambia (opposition 0.776; incumbent 0.858).

[18] The severity of this problem is magnified if we accept Horowitz's (1985) psychosocial explanation in which groups are not merely mobilizing for the acquisition of material resources; they seek to gain status and legitimacy. The status gained through control of the state provides a group with the psychological satisfaction of being politically superior.

explanation tends to overpredict coordination failure by underestimating the ability of opposition politicians to deal with social heterogeneity. Despite the conventional wisdom, African politicians have often been able to successfully arrive at interethnic power-sharing bargains. Although formal democratic institutions were abolished in most countries soon after independence in the 1960s, the representatives of different ethnic groups engaged in regular power-sharing negotiations that helped to avert violent conflict over control of the state (Hyden 1983; Rothchild and Olorunsola 1983). Those bargains were secured, in part, by treating the presidency as a divisible office. A president could essentially allocate shares of executive power by appointing politicians from different ethnicities to the cabinet or other positions backed by executive privilege (Arriola 2009). The distribution of those positions was sufficient to accommodate the communal demands of politically relevant ethnic groups during much of the one-party era from the 1960s through the 1980s. Many of the individuals who peacefully negotiated those appointments have been competing for office as candidates since the 1990s. It seems unlikely that opposition fragmentation can be simply attributed to the inability or unwillingness of such politicians to strike cross-cleavage bargains when they have been doing so for decades. Then and now, politicians mobilize their ethnic constituencies precisely so they can negotiate with their counterparts from other groups over the distribution of national offices.

Patronage Politics

Scholars might instead focus on patronage politics to explain why multiethnic opposition coalitions are infrequently formed. While the distribution of offices may serve as a balm for interethnic political competition, this form of patronage also enables African leaders to retain power. The strategic cooptation of politicians is one of the central mechanisms by which the political status quo has been preserved in African countries (Bayart 1989; Coleman and Rosberg 1964; Jackson and Rosberg 1982; Kilson 1963). During the one-party era, patronage provided an informal and flexible mechanism for regulating political interactions across a range of regimes, including those in Côte d'Ivoire (Zolberg 1969), Tanzania (Bienen 1970), and Zaire (Young 1986). The persistence of patronage politics into the multiparty era is thought to explain both the emergence of dominant parties as well as the lack of turnover in executive elections (Osaghae 1999; van de Walle 2003, 2007). Patronage has allowed entrenched incumbents to divide their opponents through selective incentives, enticing politicians to strike out on their own with the intention of later being invited into the incumbent's government. This strategy may work: I find that between 1990 and 2005, at least one in three African executives has appointed a member of the opposition to the ministerial cabinet within the six months following an election.[19]

---

[19] Among the ninety-nine elections in this time period, I find that executives appointed an opposition party leader or member to their cabinets after thirty-eight of those elections. Executives appoint, on average, nearly four opposition members to these cabinets.

The impulse among African politicians to access patronage is driven not by corruption or venality, but by a political culture that emphasizes a leader's responsibility to engage in redistribution. The Africanist scholarship suggests that leadership is popularly associated with the personalized role of politicians in channeling resources to their followers (Daloz 1999; Ekeh 1975; Médard 1982). Because the state in Africa has historically failed to provide citizens with public goods, norms of political legitimacy have evolved to exalt leaders who nourish and provide for their followers. These norms are not bounded by regime type, for even under democracy politicians are expected to facilitate the consumption of their supporters (Basedau et al. 2007; Bratton et al. 2005; Schaffer 1998; Schatzberg 2001). According to the Afrobarometer survey data from 2005–2006, nearly three quarters of respondents in fifteen African countries "often" or "always" expect their politicians to offer "gifts" during election campaigns.[20] Politicians must make a concerted effort during those campaigns to publicly dispense money, food, or other goods to signal that they acknowledge their social obligation to engage in redistribution – because that is what will be expected from them in office (Nugent 2007). These campaign handouts may be trivial in value, but they have become part of a routinized practice that symbolizes the implicit contract between politician and voter.

The redistributive pressure faced by all African politicians represents a special challenge for those in the opposition. While incumbents can exploit their control of public resources to offer the gifts expected during campaigns, their opposition counterparts must secure private resources to do the same. Where opposition party labels carry little to no information – because they often change from one election cycle to the next – an opposition politician's ability to hand out gifts while campaigning can serve as an indicator of personal leadership. Being able to afford such redistribution enables a politician to project an image of success in an environment that otherwise offers limited economic opportunities. Chabal and Daloz (1999, 34) claim that wealth distinguishes successful from failed politicians in African countries: "Aspirants to political office require both credibility and the means to fulfill their ambition. They must be rich enough to become convincing." This explains why politicians like Abdoulaye Wade, the opposition candidate who was victorious in Senegal's 2000 elections, make a concerted effort to stress their personal wealth: "I was

---

[20] Respondents were specifically asked how often politicians offer gifts to voters during election campaigns. The average percentage of respondents claiming to "often" or "always" expect gifts was calculated using the following countries: Benin (85%); Botswana (55%); Ghana (72%); Kenya (95%); Madagascar (66%); Malawi (70%); Mali (85%); Mozambique (65%); Namibia (45%); Nigeria (85%); Senegal (85%); South Africa (54%); Tanzania (53%); Uganda (85%); Zambia (94%). What is noteworthy in this list is that there is no obvious relationship between the proportion of citizens holding such expectations and a country's party system, institutional arrangements, or democratic experience. Countries that have undergone alternation, like Benin and Senegal, for example, appear to have politics that are as clientelistic as Uganda, which has had far less competitive politics.

very rich.... I owned the most important legal firm in Dakar, and I came back from Abidjan with a lot of money. Everybody knew it; my visible signs of wealth were known" (quoted in Mendy 2001, 36).[21]

Given these redistributive dynamics, a patronage-based explanation for opposition fragmentation would suggest that bargaining among opposition politicians collapses because the incumbent's resource advantage traps him or her in a prisoner's dilemma. The opposition is stuck in a noncooperative equilibrium because office-seekers will attempt to maximize their individual payoffs by negotiating with the incumbent over patronage rather than bargaining with opposition counterparts over the formation of an electoral alliance (Ndegwa 2001; Scarritt 2006; van de Walle 2003). This dilemma would persist even if opposition politicians could agree in principle to form a single party or multi-party coalition, since each politician could still seek to do better by sidling up to the incumbent. In explaining African political transitions as a tipping game, van de Walle (2006) points out that opposition coordination is unlikely to be achieved when it represents a risky proposition for potential regime defectors as well as opposition politicians. Defecting too early can result in reprisals against former regime members, while lining up behind a losing candidate can relegate a politician to oblivion.

But the prisoner's dilemma is not a satisfactory framework for understanding the full range of electoral strategies available to the opposition.[22] Although opposition politicians are commonly depicted as being singularly focused on getting themselves coopted by incumbents, there is a nonnegligible chance that some ambitious politicians will be left out of the executive's coalition. Incumbents with limited resources cannot afford to coopt all those who would join their regimes, particularly if they are already balancing the demands of oversized coalitions, as is often the case in African countries. In Senegal, for example, after a particularly violent election in 1988, President Abdou Diouf sought to consolidate his position by coopting the opposition leader, Abdoulaye Wade. The two men struck a bargain in which Wade would be made vice president – an office that did not yet exist. But high-ranking members of Diouf's party refused to cooperate and successfully maneuvered to veto the plan (Mendy 2001; Thiam 2001). Such internal constraints on an incumbent's patronage distribution suggest that office-seeking politicians cannot depend solely on cooptation as an electoral strategy; they must consider a full range of strategies for acquiring a share of power. Being excluded from government should be sufficient inducement for opposition politicians to consider forming an electoral coalition of their own (Riker 1962).

---

[21] Author's translation from the French.

[22] The prisoner's dilemma, as a model, offers no clear prediction about whether or not coordination will occur. In repeated play, cooperation can be sustained through tit-for-tat strategies that threaten to revert to noncooperation as long as actors expect future interactions, which is a reasonable expectation among politicians who regularly participate in multiparty elections.

Electoral Institutions

The scholarship on electoral institutions has convincingly shown that the incentive for politicians to coordinate nationally depends on the strength of electoral rules (Cox 1997; Duverger 1954; Riker 1982b). The findings from this literature suggest that multiethnic opposition coordination should be more likely to occur in executive elections held under the plurality system. Because the single candidate with the most votes will win in a first-past-the-post presidential election, the candidates who are near-certain losers should abandon their campaigns in favor of forming pre-electoral alliances with one of the two front-runners, either the incumbent or the strongest opposition candidate. Opposition politicians, however, should be more likely to fragment in presidential elections held under the runoff system. The incentive to coalesce is weakened in such a system because, if none secures an absolute majority in the first round, two candidates will advance to the runoff. Minor candidates will then be more likely stay in the race to vie for a second-place finish or to use their vote shares to negotiate over the terms of an endorsement during the runoff.

Further research has shown that the impact of electoral rules on national party systems is conditioned by their interaction with other factors. On the one hand, opposition coordination should be less likely to occur in countries with a larger number of social cleavages, particularly if groups are large enough to meet the threshold for winning office on their own (Amorim Neto and Cox 1997; Ordeshook and Shvetsova 1994).[23] On the other hand, opposition coordination should be more likely to occur in countries with greater levels of government centralization, whether measured in terms of fiscal resources or presidential powers (Chhibber and Kollman 2004; Hicken and Stoll 2008).

But there is controversy in the literature over whether electoral systems actually produce their expected effects in African countries. A dominant ruling party with a large legislative majority has emerged in countries using all types of electoral rules (Bogaards 2004; Mozaffar and Scarritt 2005; van de Walle 2003). Mozaffar et al. (2003) find that the distinct nature of ethnic fragmentation in African societies results in party system patterns that contradict theoretical expectations, though Brambor et al. (2006) show that African party systems are jointly shaped by electoral rules and ethnic cleavages, just as theory would predict. Other scholars claim that African party systems are influenced by electoral rules, but only when the level of democracy or the quality of elections is above a certain threshold (Lindberg 2006; Mylonas and Roussias 2007).

The rules that structure competition undoubtedly factor into the calculus of presidential aspirants in African countries, but an explanation based on

---

[23] Since ethnicity was activated as the politically relevant cleavage during Africa's colonial and authoritarian periods, a sociological theory of party systems would predict that parties would once again emerge to represent ethnic groups with the return of electoral politics in the early 1990s (Lipset and Rokkan 1967).

electoral institutions alone cannot account for the variation in the formation of multiethnic opposition coalitions. Two of the conditions that should discourage presidential aspirants from coalescing are found in most African countries: most use the runoff system and have multiple geographically concentrated ethnic groups. Nevertheless, opposition politicians who compete under the runoff system do not seem to be any less likely to coalesce. About two-thirds of African countries use this electoral formula, and about two-thirds of multiethnic opposition coalitions are also found in those countries. There is no obvious effect in this respect.

The research on electoral institutions suggests that we should see more multiethnic opposition coalitions emerge in African countries than we actually do. Presidential aspirants, for example, should be induced to coordinate by the very diversity of their societies. With the average ethnic group constituting only 12% of an African country's population (Fearon 2003), most politicians could not hope to meet the threshold for winning at the national level, or to advance to the second round in a runoff system, without securing cross-cleavage endorsements. This coalescing logic is reinforced by the centralized nature of political power in African countries. Minor candidates can do better for themselves by allying with one of the front-runners, thereby increasing the likelihood that they gain some share of power as an appointee of whichever candidate they endorse. Moreover, regardless of electoral formula, opposition candidates competing for office in weakly institutionalized democracies could raise the incumbent's cost of committing fraud, placing election results beyond doubt, by coordinating through oversized coalitions.

Economic Interests

An explanation for the emergence of multiethnic opposition coalitions could be derived from the scholarship that attributes regime outcomes to distributional conflicts. If opposition coalitions are based on mostly poor voters, as would have to be the case in most African countries, then the leading theories of democratization offer two relevant hypotheses that point toward a polity's latent potential for continued political liberalization. One view based on Boix's (2003) model would suggest that these coalitions are more likely to form at lower levels of income inequality and asset specificity. Rich elites in control of the state will accept the poor's mobilization as the potential costs from redistribution decline and their ability to protect their own assets increases. A second view, based on Acemoglu and Robinson's (2006) model, would suggest that opposition coalitions should be more likely to emerge at intermediate levels of income inequality. The rich elites in control of the state are willing to permit the poor's mobilization in this scenario because their redistributive demands are unlikely to be too high. The rich face no such dilemma where inequality is low because the poor have little incentive to mobilize for greater redistribution. Under high inequality the rich will move to repress the mobilization of the poor because their redistributive demands will be perceived as more threatening.

This analytical approach offers clear expectations regarding the behavior of specific societal groups vis-à-vis the democratization process, but it is inadequate for understanding political change in most African countries. Case studies from the region indicate that challenges to the status quo more often result from intraelite rivalries than from intergroup conflicts (Clark and Gardinier 1997; Villalón and VonDoepp 2005). It is the distributive conflict among elites that structures political life. The formation of a multiethnic opposition coalition is therefore more likely to reflect the effort of elites to gain advantage in that ongoing conflict. In any case, the level of inequality in most African cases is inconsistent with what would be expected by either of the hypotheses described above. It is simply too high, being on par with the more notoriously unequal levels typically found among Latin American countries (van de Walle 2009). The instances of opposition coordination cannot be distinguished from those of opposition fragmentation on the basis of inequality alone. The average Gini coefficient is 0.47 among the former and 0.46 among the latter.[24]

An alternative explanation that can be adapted to the African context would attribute the emergence of multiethnic opposition coalitions to the distributional consequences of trade. Here, the axis of conflict over redistribution is based on factors of production rather than social class. This approach builds on the fundamental insight from neoclassical trade theory that greater exposure to international trade will raise the income of a country's relatively abundant factor but lower the income of its relatively scarce factor. Rogowski (1989) draws out the political implications of the Stolper-Samuelson theorem to predict the type of cleavages that should arise. Exogenous developments that raise the opportunity costs of protection, for example, should lead the owners of abundant factors to demand greater trade liberalization, while the owners of scarce factors seek to maintain the policies that protect them. Frieden (1991) and Hiscox (2002) use the Ricardo-Viner model to refine these expectations, showing that the cleavages associated with trade's distributional consequences depend on the degree to which factors are mobile between exporting and importing sectors. Those who employ a factor that is costly to move between sectors face greater opportunity costs if they do not obtain their preferred policy.

An explanation based on this approach would lead us to expect an urban–rural cleavage to emerge in African countries because they are relatively abundant in land but relatively scarce in capital and labor. This is consistent with the African experience. Most governments in the region have historically pursued policies that favored capital and labor at the expense of agriculture (Bates 1981; World Bank 1981). Because most of these governments have also been reluctant to reform their policies (van de Walle 2001; World Bank 1997), one could well expect agricultural interests to support opposition coalitions with a pro-liberalization platform. Capital and labor are unlikely to join such

---

[24] The data for this comparison are from the UNU-WIDER World Income Inequality Database (WIID), Version 2.0c, May 2008. The reader should note that the Gini coefficient is available for only about half of the African sample.

coalitions because, having been heavily subsidized, they are sure to face high costs from any reform that requires a move from import-competing to export-ing sectors, at least in the short term.

While this explanation allows the expected welfare changes from increased trade to be mapped onto the political preferences of distinct actors, it provides an insufficient framework for understanding how such preferences could be organized as opposition coalitions. Global developments in trade have pro-vided farmers in all African countries with incentives to mobilize in support of political change, yet there is no evidence that this has occurred in any country. Bratton and van de Walle (1997) find that the protest movements that precip-itated regime transitions in Africa in the early 1990s were exclusively urban affairs. Since then, no mass party has organized farmers or peasants as a voting bloc in any country. And no politician has sought to become the representative of agricultural producers as an interest group. On the contrary, the conditions associated with agriculture in most African countries would predict the sector's political fragmentation. Farmers face severe collective action problems because they are mostly impoverished small landholders who are also geographically dispersed (Economic Commission for Africa 2004; Jayne et al. 2003). The cost of collective action declines when farmers organize themselves on an ethnic or social basis. But this strategy creates new divisions that, in turn, result in con-flict between groups competing for land, as has repeatedly occurred in the cash crop-producing areas of several African countries (Berry 2009; Boone 2009). Multiethnic opposition coalitions are unlikely to be formed by agricultural interests under such circumstances.

An explanation derived solely from trade-related interests incorrectly predicts the behavior of the sector most likely to solve the collective action problem – urban industry. According to this approach, industrial entrepreneurs should be expected to pursue their economic interests by lobbying the incumbent govern-ment. Small in number and located in and around the capital city, many of these entrepreneurs have built their firms in cooperation with members of the govern-ment serving as either patrons or partners (Iliffe 1983; Kennedy 1988). For these individuals, remaining allied to the government should be the most effective strat-egy for preserving the rents enjoyed by industry under protectionist policies. But I show in this book that the policies that enabled African governments to favor certain sectors also allowed them to discriminate in the allocation of privileges among individuals and firms within those sectors. The economic interests and political preferences of urban-based entrepreneurs are therefore not homoge-neous. Entrepreneurs whose interests have not been protected by the incumbent have subsequently developed a preference for greater economic liberalization, if not political alternation. And they have the means to invest in the formation of an opposition coalition that will overturn the status quo.

To summarize, the existing explanations in political science do not fully capture the dynamics influencing the electoral strategies of African politicians. They do, however, reveal important insights for which a complete theory of opposition coalition formation must account. We know that African politicians with ethnic constituencies are pragmatic in their willingness to share executive power across cleavages. But opposition politicians are at a disadvantage in securing the resources needed to maintain the support of coethnics, leaving them vulnerable to cooptation by the incumbent. We also know that politicians have an incentive to coalesce as an electoral strategy because most ethnic constituencies do not meet the threshold for winning national office. And there are economic actors who may have an interest in supporting such coalition building to institute a change in policy or an alternation in power.

ARGUMENT OF THE BOOK

This book presents a theory of pecuniary coalition building in multiethnic societies. I argue that multiethnic opposition coalitions are most likely to emerge in African countries where incumbents have lost the capacity to command the political allegiance of business. Opposition politicians are able to tap the private resources of the business sector only where liberalizing reforms permit entrepreneurs to defect from incumbent regimes without fear of financial reprisals. The ability of opposition politicians to pursue a pecuniary coalition-building strategy that amalgamates blocs of votes into national coalitions – and thereby achieves the coordination required to stimulate meaningful electoral competition – is thus directly linked to the business sector's autonomy from state-controlled capital.

Coalition building is a distinct problem for the opposition in Africa's inchoate democracies. The region's ethnically divided societies also happen to have patronage-based political systems in which electoral support is secured through the provision of money, favors, or goods. Coalition building is necessarily a resource-intensive electoral strategy in polities where the relationship between politicians and voters is structured through clientelistic linkages (Chandra 2004b; Kitschelt and Wilkinson 2007).

Since most politicians lack a constituency large enough to propel them to national power, those who seek to become competitive must purchase the endorsements of politicians from other ethnic groups. The incumbent in most African countries is able to deploy public resources to purchase those cross-ethnic endorsements. But the opposition politician who wants to become a coalition *formateur*, the candidate of a multiethnic coalition, must rely on private resources to do the same. This is the constraint on opposition coalition bargaining.[25] It is this asymmetry in the access to resources between incumbent and opposition – not the nature of ethnic cleavages or the specific arrangement of political institutions – that drives patterns of coalition formation across African countries.

---

[25] I use the term formateur, meaning the one who forms, to refer to any politician who conducts negotiations over the formation of an electoral coalition. This term is borrowed from the parliamentary practice of selecting a party to lead the negotiations that result in the formation of a coalition government after elections are held or a government is dissolved. The formal rules governing the selection of a formateur vary across parliamentary systems (Diermeier and Merlo 2004).

The resource asymmetry between incumbent and opposition underscores the credible commitment problem in interethnic coalition bargaining in patronage-based polities. The politician looking to become a coalition formateur can make a number of power-sharing promises in exchange for the endorsement of politicians from other ethnic groups. In return for those promises, the formateur expects coalition partners to deliver the votes of their coethnics. Here is where the problem arises: coalition partners understand that they will have no means of enforcing pre-election promises once the formateur is installed in office. The prospect of being left with no compensation poses a considerable risk for any politician whose position depends on the delivery of resources to constituents. This risk lowers the incentive for politicians to choose a coordinated electoral strategy over an independent run for office.

The commitment problem can be sidestepped, I argue, when formateurs compensate their partners upfront. Incumbents in Africa can readily provide that compensation through public funds and offices. Opposition politicians, however, have few options in raising private funds. Their supporters are too poor to make individual contributions and their parties are too weak to offer real organizational support. The only possible source of funding for the opposition in these circumstances is the business sector. Recognizing this fact, incumbents will inevitably take steps to prevent entrepreneurs from supporting their opponents. They can do so by leveraging the state's gatekeeping role in finance. Previous studies of electoral competition in African countries have overlooked these dynamics, particularly the central role of business in supplying resources to the opposition.

I seek to explain in this book why opposition politicians choose to coalesce or fragment when competing in elections rather than why the opposition wins or loses those elections. To examine the ability of opposition politicians to pursue a pecuniary strategy in coalition building, I develop the causal sequence in four parts. First, I explain how African leaders sought to reduce the autonomy of business through financial reprisal regimes that shaped the business–state relationship from the 1960s onwards. Second, I show that exogenous economic and political shocks obliged incumbents with vulnerable fiscal bases to relinquish those financial controls in the 1990s. Third, I establish that the liberalization of capital empowered entrepreneurs to diversify their campaign contributions, if not defect completely to the opposition, without fear of financial reprisals. Fourth, I show that financial liberalization enabled opposition politicians to undertake pecuniary coalition building by offering upfront payments for cross-ethnic endorsements. Multiethnic opposition coalitions in Africa's patronage-based polities are underpinned by such exchanges.

IMPLICATIONS OF THE ARGUMENT

How opposition politicians form electoral coalitions remains an open question for scholars interested in the processes of party system development and democratic consolidation, and the interplay between the two. While systematic findings have been accumulated on how politicians organize themselves to compete within districts before elections (Cox 1997; Duverger 1954) or to negotiate the formation of governments after elections (Laver and Schofield 1990; Laver and Shepsle 1990; Martin and Vanberg 2003), the coordination of politicians across districts – either by merging as parties or uniting in electoral alliances – remains "the understudied issue" (Cox 1999, 147).

Studying the electoral coordination of opposition politicians in regions like Africa is, at root, about understanding the institutionalization of opposition as an integral part of democratic consolidation. A coherent opposition is implied in nearly every modern definition of democracy.[26] Lipset (1967, 40) calls democracy "a system of institutionalized opposition in which the people choose among alternative contenders for public office." Dahl (1971, xviii) similarly claims that "one is inclined to regard the existence of an opposition party as very nearly the most distinctive characteristic of democracy itself." Yet, in countries where the future of democracy is uncertain, the institutionalization of opposition remains a poorly understood phenomenon, theoretically and empirically.

The competitive model of democracy depends on a strong, unstated, assumption of symmetry between political actors. It is assumed that incumbent and opposition have comparable, though not necessarily equal, capacities to vie for office, which, in turn, generates the normatively desirable outcomes associated with democracy. "The existence of an opposition – in essence, an alternative government – restrains incumbents," according to Lipset (2000, 48). The competition between these substitutes is thought to generate the following: accountability, by enabling voters to reject a government that does not meet their expectations (Downs 1957); responsiveness, by inducing a government to craft policies most voters prefer (Dahl 1971); and compliance, by providing an institution that extends the time horizon of political actors (Przeworski 1991).[27] But incumbents have little incentive to uphold these normatively desirable outcomes associated with democracy when their opposition does not represent

---

[26] There is, of course, no consensus on the definition of democracy. Scholars holding a minimalist view claim that the essence of democracy involves holding regular elections for high office under mass suffrage (Przeworski 1999; Schumpeter 1942). Advocates of a maximalist view argue that democracy "cannot be reduced to the regular holding of elections or equated with a particular notion of the role of the state" (Schmitter and Karl 1996); conditions such as civilian control of the military are necessary for a regime to be considered democratic (Karl 1990). But what can be said is that nearly all definitions integrate elections – and implicitly competitive elections – as a component, so the puzzle of opposition coordination is of interest regardless of which definition is employed. Moreover, if we are interested in understanding how opposition coordination comes about as one element in democratic consolidation, we can gain greater leverage by examining a range of regimes that do not necessarily fall under a comprehensive definition of democracy.

[27] The accountability, responsiveness, and compliance associated with democracy might emerge under conditions of fragmented opposition, as has happened in countries such as Japan and Sweden, where ruling parties have stayed in office continuously for decades (Pempel 1990). But this is rare. These cases are notable precisely because they are exceptional.

an electoral threat. *A priori* there is no reason to believe that out-of-power politicians, when presented with the opportunity to openly and freely compete for office, will necessarily work together to mount a veritable challenge.

It is not obvious that greater electoral experience will lead to the emergence of a coherent opposition in countries where democracy remains unconsolidated. It was not long after Huntington (1991) identified the global expansion of democracy that scholars observed countries holding regular multiparty elections without necessarily moving toward greater individual liberties or developing stronger institutional constraints. Many now consider these hybrid regimes to be a distinct regime type; they are not merely undergoing an extended transition from one regime type to another (Diamond 1996; Karl 1995; Levitsky and Way 2002; Zakaria 1997). The growing empirics on these hybrid regimes suggest that they behave in ways that differ systematically from the behaviors of either autocracies or democracies.[28]

Political scientists remain unable to explain how democratic consolidation unfolds in such hybrid political systems. O'Donnell's (1996, 39) lament – "There is no theory that would tell us why and how the new polyarchies that have institutionalized elections will 'complete' their institutional set, or otherwise become 'consolidated'" – is echoed without amendment ten years later by Epstein et al. (2006, 564), who note that "we have little information as to the factors that would lead partial democracies to either slide down to autocracy or to move up to full democracy." Explaining how opposition politicians in these regimes coordinate their electoral strategies may help to illuminate how democratic practices are consolidated through the competition for office.

My purpose in this book is to advance our understanding of the conditions in which politicians in multiethnic societies might develop the coherent opposition required for the institutionalization of democracy. Our state of knowledge on democratization processes in multiethnic societies does not seem to have progressed much since Lijphart (1977, 47–48) originally argued that "the ideal of a vigorous opposition, which can be realized to a large extent in homogeneous societies, cannot be used as a standard for evaluating the political performance of plural societies." The troubled democratic record in such societies suggests that the kind of mass organization required for vigorous opposition is infeasible because existing political parties are incapable of bridging social cleavages.[29]

This book adds to a growing literature that questions the presumed infeasibility of democracy in multiethnic societies (Birnir 2007; Chandra 2004a; Fish and Brooks 2004). *Pace* Lijphart, the evidence explored in the following chapters suggests that the effort undertaken by opposition politicians to build

---

[28] Mansfield and Snyder (1995) find that these regimes are more likely to engage in armed conflict with other countries. Bates et al. (2000) demonstrate that partial democracies have a greater tendency to experience political instability and ethnic conflict. Epstein et al. (2006) establish that partial democracies are over four times less stable than autocracies or democracies.

[29] See LeBas (2006) for a notable exception. Her study of Zimbabwe shows how unions can provide a critical organizational infrastructure for opposition.

cross-cleavage coalitions does reflect "vigorous opposition" and thereby serves as an indicator of democratic consolidation in multiethnic societies. While it may be apparent that an incumbent regime will respect democratic norms only when compelled to do so, it is less obvious how its opponents can coordinate across cleavages to bring that about. I suggest that it is the political control of financial resources, and not the ethnicized nature of society, that impedes their coordination.

ORGANIZATION OF THE BOOK

The theory of pecuniary coalition building is developed in subsequent chapters. I specifically isolate the choices made by key actors – incumbents, business entrepreneurs, and opposition politicians – under contrasting conditions of financial repression and liberalization. I trace their choices through each link in the causal chain to identify the conditions in which African incumbents liberalize finance, business diversifies its political contributions, and opposition politicians use upfront payments to make power-sharing promises more attractive to their coalition partners. Through this approach, I am able to explain the emergence of two distinct opposition equilibria across Africa: recurrent coordination failure where business fears reprisals from the incumbent and recurrent coordination where business enjoys greater financial freedom.

Both qualitative and quantitative methodologies are used to corroborate the logic of pecuniary coalition building. This combination of approaches allows me to thoroughly examine the sequence of events, testing specific theoretical predictions and offering a substantive interpretation of the evidence at each link in the causal chain.

I conduct quantitative analyses of cross-sectional time-series patterns with original data on commercial banks, chambers of commerce, and electoral coalitions. These analyses contribute to our stock of knowledge concerning basic but important questions relating to the study of Africa's political economy, including the development of financial institutions, the determinants of economic reform, and the changing nature of business–state relations. These findings should be of broad interest to scholars and policymakers with a focus on developing countries undergoing political and economic transitions.

I employ the Millian method of difference in examining Cameroon and Kenya as case studies. These two countries take on similar values on important background conditions but differ on the dependent variable: there is persistent opposition fragmentation in Cameroon versus progressive opposition coordination in Kenya. This structured case comparison provides considerable inferential leverage by permitting me to illustrate the mechanism at work, to eliminate alternative hypotheses at each link in the causal chain, and to gauge whether the explanatory variables are having their hypothesized effects. The case studies ultimately show how the coefficients identified in the cross-national analyses can influence the behavior of key actors on the ground.

The quantitative tests and case studies developed throughout the book are based on information gathered from unstructured interviews, archival research, and data from government and civil society sources. But readers should note that much of the political behavior predicted by a theory of pecuniary coalition formation cannot be directly observed by the researcher: incumbents do not announce that they are relinquishing their control over capital, entrepreneurs are reluctant to reveal how much they contribute to political campaigns, and politicians do not necessarily want to admit that money plays a central role in their coalition-building efforts. There are neither freedom of information laws in most African countries nor off-the-shelf data sets on political donations in their elections. As a result, the findings presented in the following chapters are based, in part, on proxies that I have constructed. While these proxies may be imperfect indicators for the behaviors associated with a pecuniary coalition strategy, they are based on intuition gained from two years of fieldwork spent visiting party offices, interviewing politicians and businesspeople, and observing election campaigns.

I proceed in Chapter 2 by introducing the theory of pecuniary coalition building with a focus on the choices made by incumbents in restricting the access to capital, business entrepreneurs in realigning politically, and opposition politicians in bargaining over cross-ethnic endorsements. I introduce the cases of Cameroon and Kenya and discuss how their contrasting trajectories can be explained through the argument advanced in this book. These cases are explored in greater detail in Chapters 4 through 7.

In Chapter 3, I discuss the historic origins of state-controlled capital in African countries. I describe the establishment of discriminatory financial practices during the colonial era and the systematic development of those institutions as financial reprisal regimes after independence. I explain how nationalist politicians during the colonial era allied with merchants and traders to overcome the limitations of their weak parties, and, after independence, sought to prevent them from supporting their rivals.

I investigate the origins of the political control of banking in Africa in Chapter 4. Focusing on the size of the commercial banking sector, I show that banking was expanded only in countries where the first post-independence president emerged from a cash crop–growing community. These presidents had little to fear from the accumulation of resources by their coethnics. The provision of finance served as a form of constituency service or inducement that reinforced links between the president and his political base. By contrast, commercial banking was restricted in countries where the first post-independence president's coethnics were not cash crop growers. Because such leaders feared the accumulation of resources among other communities, lest they use those resources to organize opposition around their rivals, they sought to limit the number of banks. The statistical analysis shows that countries with founding presidents from cash crop constituencies acquired five to seven additional banks, on average, when compared with those that did not.

Chapter 5 examines the question of financial liberalization. It remains a puzzle why incumbents would relinquish the financial controls that enabled them to restrict the autonomy of business. This chapter shows that the state control of finance in Africa was a self-undermining institution vulnerable to exogenous shocks. The rationing of credit on political criteria led to decreasing productive investment that, besides reducing economic growth and government income from taxes, undermined the solvency of the entire financial system. Incumbents with vulnerable fiscal bases were compelled to undertake liberalization when they could no longer afford to sustain their patronage-based regimes without the support from international financial institutions. A statistical analysis of two dependent variables – structural adjustment compliance and private credit provision – confirms that financial liberalization was more likely to occur in nonrentier states and states with founding presidents from cash crop communities.

Chapter 6 extends the analysis by demonstrating that business responds politically to changing regulatory conditions in finance. Contrary to the conventional threat hypothesis associated with the political mobilization of business, this chapter demonstrates that business in Africa is more likely to defect from its alliance with the incumbent when the state ceases to act as a financial gatekeeper. By disrupting the traditional business–state relationship, financial liberalization determines the timing and the orientation of business' political alignment. The chapter explores an observable implication of the argument through the organization of its sectoral leadership, namely, the chamber of commerce presidency.

Chapter 7 focuses on the bargaining episodes that took place in the run-up to presidential elections held in Cameroon in 2004 and Kenya in 2002. It shows that their divergent outcomes – opposition fragmentation in Cameroon and opposition coordination in Kenya – can be traced back to the financial conditions found in those countries. The case studies show how opposition politicians jockeyed for position to establish themselves as potential formateurs, structured their intraopposition bargaining, and exercised financial leverage in their negotiations. In Cameroon, an opposition protocoalition fragmented when no politician could secure the support of business. In Kenya, by contrast, an opposition politician bankrolled by business was able to act as a coalition formateur by offering upfront payments for cross-ethnic endorsements.

Chapter 8 provides a cross-national test of the book's main argument concerning the relationship between financial liberalization and the formation of multiethnic opposition coalitions. Based on a data set of multiethnic opposition coalitions in African elections held between 1990 and 2005, the test employs the indicators from previous chapters as explanatory variables – the number of commercial banks (Chapter 4), the availability of credit to the private sector (Chapter 5), and the tenure of the chamber of commerce president (Chapter 6). A binary logistic regression analysis confirms that the nature of the financial system significantly influences the opposition's likelihood of forming a coalition.

Chapter 9 concludes by discussing the argument's implications for the broader comparative study of economic reform and democratic consolidation in countries undergoing prolonged transitions. While there is considerable controversy over the democratic impact of economic liberalization in developing countries, I suggest that such reforms will induce greater accountability by incumbents over the longer term by facilitating the emergence of real electoral competition where none existed previously.

2

A Theory of Pecuniary Coalition Formation

> If only they would act the way I did when I was in opposition....
> Kwame Nkrumah, prime minister of Ghana, 1958[1]

I present in this chapter an analytical framework for understanding how resources affect the formation of multiethnic opposition coalitions in Africa. I argue that the availability of private resources influences the capacity of politicians to coordinate electoral campaigns that span ethnic cleavages. My claim in this regard is straightforward and unremarkable: money is crucial for politicians who seek to become nationally competitive candidates. What is innovative about this claim – and has not been systematically explored in previous research – is the role that money plays in securing cross-ethnic endorsements.

In patronage-based polities across Africa, politicians must be able to pay upfront for the cross-ethnic endorsements that make up electoral alliances. Incumbents do so easily through the distribution of public resources. Opposition politicians, for their part, must secure private resources, and I argue that they are more likely to do so where the state has relinquished its gatekeeping role vis-à-vis financial capital. Otherwise, incumbents can manipulate the state's financial controls to deter individual entrepreneurs from supporting their preferred opposition candidates. The opposition's ability to create multiethnic electoral alliances is thus shaped by the extent to which business depends on state-controlled capital.

The argument presented in this chapter complements existing research on electoral authoritarianism, which has shown how entrenched incumbents use constitutional as well as extraconstitutional measures to minimize the risk of electoral defeat (Gandhi and Lust-Okar 2009; Levitsky and Way

[1] Nkrumah expressed his frustration with the opposition in a 1958 interview – just one year after Ghana's independence – with Gwendolyn Carter, a pioneering scholar of African politics. Carter (1960, 144) would go on to observe, "Of all the roles in the process of government, that of 'the loyal opposition,' either within parliament or within a mass nationalist party, is the most difficult to learn and perform. Yet no other is more essential to the functioning of genuinely responsible government. Nkrumah himself knows this."

2002; Schedler 2002). Political scientists have established in what ways and to what extent incumbent regimes can exploit their resource advantage to mobilize political support, as demonstrated by Lust-Okar (2005) in Morocco and Jordan, Magaloni (2006) in Mexico, Scheiner in Japan (2006), and Beck in Senegal (2008). The scholarship on Africa, in particular, has shown how the centralization of executive power permits incumbents to combine resources and repression in order to hold on to power (Bratton and van de Walle 1997; Villalón and VonDoepp 2005).

The behavior of the opposition under such constraints remains understudied. Political scientists cannot explain why a coherent opposition arises in certain countries and not in others when nearly every authoritarian incumbent takes measures to prevent such an occurrence. We lack a clear conception of the strategic choices available to the opposition and their supporters when incumbents are known to manipulate the parameters of democratic contestation. And establishing a plausible account of how opposition politicians manage to forge electoral coalitions is a necessary first step toward understanding the conditions that might, over time, provide for the consolidation of democracy in multiethnic societies.

Because studies of democratization under diversity have been largely concerned with the impact of social cleavages and political institutions, they have largely ignored how the control of economic resources has influenced the evolution of multiparty competition in the countries that transitioned through the third wave of democratization. The lack of scholarship on the relationship between electoral coordination and access to resources in this context is surprising when opposition politicians themselves point to their material endowments, or lack thereof, to explain their inability to effectively challenge incumbents. Musikari Kombo, a politician involved in negotiating the opposition coalition for Kenya's 2002 presidential election, has claimed that "with the re-introduction of multiparty democracy the resource disparity between struggling opposition and the entrenched ruling party was glaring. This undermined the development of opposition political parties who had no access to state resources and, therefore, could not effectively organize."[2]

Scholars have overlooked the role of business in supplying vital resources to the opposition in multiethnic developing countries. Yet, the unrealized potential for business to influence the balance of power between incumbent and opposition has been repeatedly noted during periods of transition. Examining the newly independent states of Africa and Asia in the 1960s, Shils (1971, 58) found "few rich indigenous businessmen willing to support opposition parties" because government control of the economy gave them sufficient cause to remain allied to the ruling party. Writing more than twenty-five years later,

---

[2] Musikari Kombo, then minister for local government, made this statement to the Stakeholders' Forum on Management and Financing of Political Parties, organized by the Centre for Governance and Development and the National Democratic Institute at the Stanley Hotel, Nairobi, 18 August 2004.

Widner (1997, 66) again found this pattern among Africa's democratizing states, noting that "the very limited extent of economic liberalization means that business and other potential funders of political parties remain hostage to the incumbent government." In this respect, the political consequences of financial liberalization – in enabling business to define its interests separately from the regime in power – deserve greater scrutiny.

I proceed in this chapter by briefly reviewing the theoretical and empirical literature from which I derive the intuition for pecuniary coalition building. I move on to discuss the commitment problem faced by formateurs when organizing multiethnic coalitions in patronage-based polities. I then develop the logic for pecuniary coalition formation and derive testable implications for the behavior of the relevant actors – incumbents, entrepreneurs, and opposition politicians. Using this framework, I introduce the two case studies, Cameroon and Kenya, that are used throughout the book to trace the mechanism linking financial liberalization to opposition coordination.

ECONOMIC RESOURCES AND DEMOCRATIC CONTESTATION

Literature on democracy has long associated the dispersal of economic resources with the historical emergence of political contestation in the advanced industrialized democracies. Moore (1966, 14) argues that an independent economic base is a necessary condition for social coalitions to transform themselves into a "coherent opposition" that can impose limits on the exercise of power. Dahl (1971, 61) similarly claims that "public contestation, and hence polyarchy, is unlikely to exist in a country with highly centralized direction of the economy, no matter what the form of ownership."[3] According to Riker (1982a, 7), "No government that has eliminated economic freedom has been able to keep democracy, probably because, when all economic life is absorbed into government, there is no conceivable financial base for opposition."

The impact of resources on democratization has been extensively documented to explain the variation in levels of democracy among post-communist states. Fish (2005) attributes Russia's stalled democratization to the lack of economic liberalization and the abundance of natural resources, both of which have reinforced economic statism. McMann (2006) shows that individuals in Russia and Kyrgyzstan are more likely to become politically active if they

---

[3] The role of economic elites has been stressed in this relationship between resources and contestation. It has been argued that the protections associated with democracy emerge as a byproduct of the bargaining between state rulers who need revenue to keep themselves in power and elites who seek to protect their wealth (Bates 2001; Tilly 1992). Rulers can maximize revenue by offering political rights in exchange for greater taxation, permitting economically independent elites to impose constraints on the exercise of power over the long term (Levi 1988; North and Weingast 1989; Root 1994). But in contrast to earlier periods, the leaders who took over postcolonial states had little need to bargain over revenue because prevailing development paradigms afforded them direct control over capital through administrative controls or outright ownership; or, foreign aid provided sufficient funds to sustain their regimes (Bates 2001).

are economically autonomous from the state. Complementing these findings, Radnitz (2010) shows that the "colored revolutions" leading to regime change have been more likely to erupt in the former Soviet states where a capitalist class was empowered by economic reform.

The impact of resources on electoral coordination, more specifically, has been established under a wide range of conditions, from national to constituency levels. To explain why "desertion and treason" were rare in the German Socialist Party at the turn of the twentieth century, but frequent among its British, French, and Italian counterparts, Michels (1962, 138) attributes party cohesion to resources: "Financial dependence upon the party...enshackles the organization as with iron chains." Sklar (1963) finds that Nigeria's pre-independence political parties became competitive at the regional level by forming alliances with indigenous business associations that could finance their campaigns. In the United States, where electoral victories are associated with campaign war chests, studies of congressional races show that challengers, more so than incumbents, significantly increase their vote share through greater campaign spending (Abramowitz 1988; Ansolabehere and Gerber 1994; Gerber 2004; Jacobson 1978, 1990).[4] This finding on the effectiveness of campaign spending by challengers has been replicated in settings as varied as Britain (Johnston et al. 1989), Canada (Eagles 1993), France (Palda and Palda 1998), and Korea (Shin et al. 2005).

Taken as a whole, this literature makes clear that resources are essential for political coordination. They not only facilitate the emergence of opposition to government; they are also a requisite for meaningful electoral competition. But it remains to be shown, theoretically and empirically, whether this relationship holds in societies where the principal axis of conflict runs along ethnic rather than ideological or class lines. The theory I delineate in the next sections suggests that it does.

THE FORMATEUR'S COMMITMENT PROBLEM

Politicians who compete for national power in multiethnic societies intuitively understand that they cannot hope to win office based on the votes of their coethnics alone; they need votes from a cross section of groups. But the fissiparous tendencies often found within diverse societies are difficult to aggregate into cohesive partisan movements when political support is conditioned by redistribution, as occurs in patronage-based polities. The ability of politicians to secure multiethnic support in these circumstances is constrained by the fact that they cannot expect to successfully solicit votes from citizens who are not their coethnics. As Posner (2005, 105) explains, "politicians' promises to share

---

[4] The extensive literature on campaign spending in U.S. elections has produced conflicting results. That challengers benefit more than incumbents from increased campaign spending has become a consensus view, yet some work has also shown that spending can benefit incumbents as well as challengers (Erickson and Palfrey 1998; Gerber 1998; Green and Krasno 1988) or that spending has little impact at all (Erickson and Palfrey 2000; Levitt 1994).

the spoils of power with members of other groups are not likely to be viewed as credible. And absent an ability to commit credibly to sharing the spoils of power with members of other groups, cross-ethnic coalitions will be very difficult, if not impossible to build."

To overcome the dilemma identified by Posner, the politician who seeks to become a formateur, the candidate of a multiethnic coalition, can recruit other politicians who have the requisite ethnic identities to solicit votes on her behalf. A formateur can offer these politicians a power-sharing pact that specifies the division of spoils from a victorious electoral campaign. A formateur can promise that, once in office, she will use state offices to reward her coalition partners from other ethnic groups. Such appointments might include the vice presidency, a number of cabinet seats, or the control of certain parastatal companies. In patronage-based polities, these appointments enable politicians to transform public resources into club goods or private services for their constituents. In return for such concessions, the formateur expects her coalition partners to deliver the votes of their respective ethnic constituencies.

The obstacle to negotiating such pre-electoral bargains is not in establishing how offices or spoils are to be divided, but in sequencing the costs and rewards. Politicians must pay the cost of being part of the formateur's coalition before the election is held, regardless of whether they win or lose. Coalition partners will not receive their reward until after the ballots are counted. Under these conditions, politicians must consider the formateur's incentive to engage in time-inconsistent behavior, that is, to renege on the power-sharing promises made before the election (Shepsle 1991; Myerson 2008). Once in office, the formateur might decide to offer her coalition partners less than what was originally promised or nothing at all. Such a scenario could easily arise. A formateur eager to create a winning coalition might promise control of a particularly influential or lucrative cabinet position to more than one politician. Or, having mobilized an oversized coalition, a formateur might discover the day after the election that she has more promises to fulfill than posts to fill.

Politicians must consider that they will have no means of enforcing any power-sharing promises if the formateur does choose to renege after being installed in office. Given the weakly institutionalized conditions in which politicians vie for office in democratizing countries, politicians cannot expect to rely on institutional mechanisms to enforce a pre-electoral agreement. Punishing the formateur for reneging is particularly difficult in patronage-based polities that invest executives with discretionary authority in government appointments. African executives, for example, typically control appointments to nearly all levels of government, ranging from the capital to provincial towns. African legislatures, meanwhile, are among the weakest in the world, having little capacity to check or overturn executive actions.[5] African courts are unlikely to enforce

---

[5] The Parliamentary Powers Index (PPI) developed by Fish and Kroenig (2009) indicates that African parliaments have among the lowest average scores (0.38) in their global sample, being not much different from those in the Middle East (0.34).

a political bargain negotiated verbally through closed-door negotiations even if they have the judicial independence to do so. Additionally, politicians cannot expect to use social mechanisms such as moral suasion against a reneging formateur. If the electorate is ethnically divided, a formateur is unlikely to lose votes among her own coethnics or those of the politicians who were satisfactorily compensated.

Endorsing a formateur represents a high-risk political investment. Politicians must assess the return on that investment because rallying votes on behalf of a formateur will require their time, effort, and money. And this investment is effectively locked in for the duration of the campaign. Under these circumstances, politicians may prefer to withhold their support. If they have little reason to trust that power-sharing promises will be honored after the election, these politicians may be better off competing for office on their own. Even if they lose at the national level, those who compete independently may still derive political dividends from having cemented control over their coethnics' votes, which may include discouraging their rivals at the local level and positioning themselves for future bargaining at the national level.

THE PECUNIARY STRATEGY

The interaction between ethnicity and resources offers pragmatic politicians a solution to the commitment problem associated with pre-electoral coalition bargaining. Politicians who compete for office in patronage-based polities must acquire the means not only to pay for mundane electoral expenses associated with advertising, equipment, and staff, but also to offer cash or goods to mobilize their coethnic constituents on election day. If they are to remain in office, these politicians are expected to deliver favors and channel resources well after the election. Politicians can retain their positions as the putative leaders of their constituencies only through the continuous provision of resources.

This political demand for resources can be exploited by a would-be formateur. A formateur can take advantage of the *de facto* market for endorsements created by the interaction between ethnic mobilization and patronage politics. A formateur can transform the incentive structure for other politicians by supplementing the power-sharing promises normally associated with coalition bargaining with upfront payments for cross-ethnic endorsements. These pre-electoral payments raise the appeal of a formateur's power-sharing promises despite the possibility of an electoral loss or the possibility that promises might not be fulfilled. The payment, often in the form of monies or other fungible assets, can be thought of as a wage for the duration of the campaign or a one-time cash payment consumed by the politician. For their part, the politicians who require resources to maintain their leadership positions have an incentive to auction the blocs of votes they control.[6]

---

[6] The role of money in leadership selection is not exclusive to the African cases I examine in this book. This mechanism can be illustrated with multiple examples from the United States. In the U.S. Congress, for example, politicians secure leadership posts by strategically making campaign

The pre-electoral payment can also function as a signaling device for the formateur. The very act of offering an upfront payment for an endorsement can reveal information about a formateur's expected behavior. It enables a formateur to communicate that she has the resources on hand to sustain a nation-wide campaign and is therefore a viable candidate for executive office. And it enables the formateur to communicate how she intends to treat coalition partners during and after the campaign. Crucially, this signal permits a formateur to amass the early endorsements needed to induce bandwagoning among politicians. A politician may be more likely to endorse a formateur who has already proven the capacity to rally others, since no one wants to waste costly support on a candidate who seems likely to fail.

Would-be formateurs, incumbent and opposition alike, can pursue this pecuniary strategy to compete across ethnically divided constituencies. Incumbents in patronage-based polities have a special advantage, of course. They can readily abuse their control of state coffers to compensate the politicians who can deliver blocs of their coethnics' votes for their reelection campaigns. Opposition politicians are particularly vulnerable to an incumbent's inducement in this regard because, otherwise, they have limited opportunities for securing the large sums needed to retain their leadership positions among their constituents.

Opposition politicians face a distinct problem in accumulating the cross-ethnic endorsements that would constitute a viable electoral coalition. In contrast to incumbents who can use state resources for their reelection campaigns, opposition politicians who seek to become formateurs are typically unable to afford the pecuniary strategy. It is this resource asymmetry between incumbent and opposition that shapes patterns of electoral coordination in patronage-based polities.

I argue that opposition politicians in African countries rely on the private resources of business to pursue a pecuniary coalition-building strategy. Because they lack the organizational options that facilitated electoral coordination in other time periods or regional contexts – for example, civic associations and labor unions – opposition politicians in Africa need the business sector to fund their electoral coordination. There are few nonethnic organizations in these countries that are sufficiently influential or independent to broker electoral agreements among politicians. Because the middle class is so small in these poor countries, business entrepreneurs are the only members of society with the wherewithal to serve as financiers for opposition campaigns. An opposition formateur backed by business is more likely to have the war chest needed to make upfront payments for cross-ethnic endorsements.

The fundamental problem for the would-be opposition formateur is that business in Africa has historically been dependent on state-controlled capital.

contributions to their peers in exchange for their votes (Heberlig et al. 2006; Green 2008). At the constituency level, politicians in Chicago, Philadelphia, New York, and other large cities have been known to hand out "walking-around money" or "street money" to influential community leaders who can deliver blocs of votes (Karlan 1994; Sabato and Simpson 1996).

From independence in the 1960s through the economic crises of the 1980s, the state in Africa functioned as a gatekeeper for capital by acquiring a majority stake in most commercial banks, restricting entry into banking, channeling credit through administrative directives, providing subsidized loan programs, imposing capital account restrictions, and limiting access to foreign exchange. These controls constituted a financial reprisal regime that permitted African leaders to command the allegiance of business. By the time multipartism reemerged in the early 1990s, incumbents already had acquired the capacity to stave off potential electoral challenges by, almost imperceptibly, starving the opposition of coordination resources.[7] Such was the not-so-veiled threat made by Lansana Conté, the former president of Guinea, to business leaders in his country: "I know that among you there are people who are funding political parties. I know them all, but that does not interest me, because there is no opposition leader who will come and beat me here in Guinea."[8]

My claim is that financial liberalization, a process that occurred in some African countries in tandem with political liberalization, has brought about the dispersal of economic power that democratic theorists associate with the emergence of contestation. The gradual dismantling of financial reprisal regimes under external pressure throughout the 1990s has reshaped the strategic context in which opposition politicians compete for power. African leaders with vulnerable fiscal bases were compelled to undertake financial reform when they could no longer sustain their patronage-based regimes without external assistance. They were obliged to bargain away their financial controls in exchange for continued access to donor aid and loans from the international financial institutions. Reforms such as the privatization of state-owned banks and the elimination of credit controls effectively signaled the incumbent's waning control over capital throughout the 1990s.

Financial liberalization has been politically consequential in African countries because it eliminated the state as a gatekeeper for capital. This externally driven process provided business a political safeguard heretofore unknown. Unlike reforms in contracting, licensing, and taxation – the other areas in which state and business interact – financial liberalization places into private hands what had become a state function. And unlike other areas of potential reform, financial liberalization takes on the property of nonexcludability. Incumbents lose the power to use discretion in regulating the access to capital. Business no longer has to fear that the incumbent might unexpectedly cut off credit lines or that state-owned banks might abruptly call in their loans. Where multinational and local banks move in to replace state-owned banks, an incumbent

---

[7] No incumbent, whether autocrat or democrat, voluntarily allows rivals to acquire the resources needed to mount a challenge. Attempts to impose constraints are also made in established democracies. In the United States, both major parties have sought to limit the ability of the other to receive financing from their respective economic bases, e.g., corporations and labor unions.

[8] "Excerpt from speech by Guinean President Lansana Conté in Conakry on 12 January," BBC Monitoring Africa, 15 January 2004.

can no longer exact reprisals on business without first infringing against those privately owned banks. A vulnerable incumbent cannot afford to do so without putting a regime's external assistance in jeopardy. Financial liberalization has thus translated into greater autonomy for business, enabling entrepreneurs to renegotiate their political alliances. In Africa, the political realignment of business has permitted opposition politicians to secure the resources required for electoral coordination.

Business is central to the formation of opposition coalitions in this argument not because it is innately democratic, but because it seeks to protect its own interests. Business entrepreneurs are individuals whose primary vocation involves commercial activities aimed at private accumulation, whether as industrialists, merchants, or traders.[9] They choose to become involved in politics because the state's intervention in the market determines the rate at which profits can be accumulated, if at all. In many African countries, the individuals who populate the state and business can be one and the same.[10] However, the entrepreneurs who seek to maximize wealth through commerce can be distinguished from the politicians who aim to maximize power through control of the state.[11] Since the interests of wealth and power are often at odds, entrepreneurs have clear incentives to influence the institutional context in which they seek to maximize profits, whether by participating in the selection of political leaders or shaping the policies enacted by those leaders.

In countries where incumbents have managed to delay or subvert financial liberalization, incumbents can manipulate the state's control over capital

[9] There has been considerable debate in the literature over the origin and composition of the indigenous capitalist class in African countries (Beveridge and Oberschall 1979; Marris and Somerset 1971; Marsden 1990; Schatz 1977). Individuals have historically entered this vocation through a variety of routes, though there are distinct subregional patterns. Entrepreneurs in West Africa, with a longer history of international trade, often moved from rural agriculture into urban commerce. Cash crop farmers and traders used their surplus revenue to invest in other sectors of the economy, transforming themselves into entrepreneurs involved in food processing, retailing, light manufacturing, and transportation. In other parts of the continent, entrepreneurs also emerged through straddling, using contacts and resources from their work as civil servants in colonial or post-independence governments to launch themselves in commerce (Cowen and Kinyanjui 1977). For example, related to this latter pattern, there is disagreement over the nature of indigenous capitalism in Kenya, a case noteworthy for the presence of white settler and Asian merchant communities. See Leys (1974), Swainson (1980), Khadiagala and Schatzberg (1987), Himbara (1994), Chege (1998), and Vandenberg (2003).

[10] Entrepreneurs focused on profit maximization often consider politicking to be a drain on their time and resources. In their survey of Kenyan businessmen just two years after independence, Marris and Somerset (1971) found that, while many had actively supported the nationalist movement, most preferred to avoid politics even when asked to stand for office. Similarly, most of the entrepreneurs profiled by Forrest (1994) in his study of Nigerian capitalism did not seek to become politicians. But, if they did enter politics, they usually had prosperous firms before doing so.

[11] The boundary between state and business was policed more actively in some countries than in others. In the 1970s, Ghana, Nigeria, and Zambia prohibited civil servants from moving into the private sector. Kenya, however, allowed civil servants to have businesses while remaining in government.

to induce business into denying resources to the opposition. But if financial liberalization were adopted in a way that increased the well-being of business entrepreneurs by removing the obstacles they face in accessing capital, such an improvement would be sufficiently profitable that they would want to invest in ensuring its continuity. In other words, they would be willing to pay to protect their new gains. Business could secure those new gains by financing challengers to the incumbent. Bankrolling the emergence of a viable opposition over the medium to long term would make it more difficult to return to the status quo ante. In competitive races where the support of business could prove decisive, entrepreneurs could exchange campaign financing for policy promises from either the incumbent or the opposition. In this way they could ensure the financial system's open access, regardless of who is in power.

There are clear testable implications associated with the argument described above, each of which is examined in subsequent chapters. First, incumbents should create financial reprisal regimes that correspond to the level of threat posed by business. Second, incumbents should relinquish their financial reprisal regimes only under duress. Third, business entrepreneurs should be more likely to offer campaign contributions to opposition candidates after financial liberalization has been enacted. Fourth, opposition politicians should be more likely to successfully create multiethnic electoral coalitions under conditions of financial liberalization. Taken together, these implications suggest we should observe two equilibria among African countries: opposition coordination under financial liberalization and opposition fragmentation under financial repression. The causal process leading to these outcomes is summarized in Figure 2.1.

The theory of pecuniary coalition formation suggests that the variation in a state's control of capital should map onto the electoral behavior of opposition politicians. Figure 2.2 provides a first test of this hypothesis with data on commercial banking for two sets of countries defined by whether a multiethnic opposition coalition formed at least once for national elections held between 1990 and 2005. A coalition is defined here as an electoral alliance in which politicians from different ethnic or regional groups endorse a single candidate for executive office. Countries that had one or more multiethnic opposition coalitions formed in that time period are identified as having a "coalescing opposition," and countries with no such coalitions are identified as having a "fragmenting opposition."[12]

Figure 2.2 shows a growing divergence in access to commercial banking between countries with a coalescing versus a fragmenting opposition. There

---

[12] The countries with a fragmenting opposition are Botswana, Burkina Faso, Cameroon, Central African Republic, Chad, Congo Republic, Gabon, Guinea, Guinea-Bissau, Namibia, Niger, and Sierra Leone. Two groups make up the countries with a coordinating opposition: countries with one opposition coalition are Côte d'Ivoire, Ethiopia, Gambia, Ghana, Kenya, Nigeria, Senegal, South Africa, Togo, Zambia, and Zimbabwe; countries with two or more opposition coalitions are Benin, Madagascar, Malawi, Mali, Mauritania, Mauritius, Mozambique, Tanzania, and Uganda.

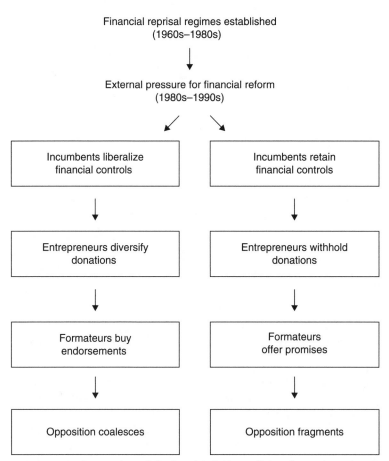

FIGURE 2.1. A causal model of multiethnic coalition formation: the state control of capital and electoral coordination.

is little difference between the two samples prior to 1990, but a widening gap becomes evident as financial reforms are gradually enacted by a select number of African governments. The opposition has been more likely to coordinate across ethnic cleavages in countries where the access to finance capital has been significantly liberalized. A coalescing opposition is found in countries where the banking sector added four commercial banks, on average, between 1985 and 2000. A fragmenting opposition emerged in countries where the access to finance remained relatively unchanged, adding less than one bank, on average, during the same time period.[13]

---

[13] The number of commercial banks was calculated using annual volumes of *Africa South of the Sahara* (Europa Publications Limited 1971–2006).

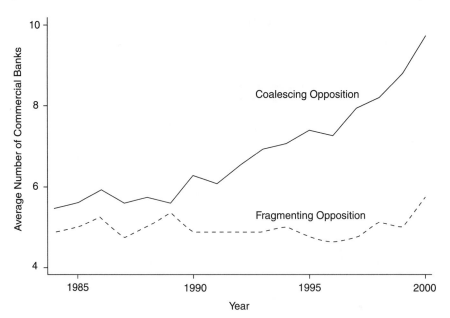

FIGURE 2.2. Access to commercial banking and opposition behavior.
Source: Author's calculations based on annual entries in *Africa South of the Sahara*.

Appendix A shows country-specific trends in the size of the commercial banking sector between 1985 and 2000. Countries are listed in descending order by the number of banks in 2000. Appendix A also shows the number of elections held for executive office and the number of multiethnic opposition coalitions formed in each country between 1990 and 2005. One of the obvious trends concerns the relationship between banking sector growth and the incidence of opposition coalition formation. While the top and bottom quartiles in banking size held nearly the same number of elections, the incidence of coalition building in the top quartile is twelve times the average rate of the bottom quartile. Measured by rate of change, the nine countries in which the number of banks more than doubled had four times as many coalitions being formed, on average, than the nine countries in which the number of banks remained the same or contracted.[14]

THE CASE STUDIES: CAMEROON AND KENYA

I have selected Cameroon and Kenya for in-depth comparison in this book because the two countries demonstrate divergent patterns of opposition

---

[14] The number of banks more than doubled in countries that tended to be former socialist economies: Benin, Burkina Faso, Ethiopia, Guinea, Guinea-Bissau, Madagascar, Mozambique, and Tanzania. The number of banks either remained constant or contracted in the mainly Francophone countries that belong to one of the two regional monetary unions: Cameroon, Central African Republic, Chad, Cote d'Ivoire, Gabon, Niger, Senegal, and Togo. It should be noted, however, that the contraction in banking among these countries preceded the 1994 CFA devaluation.

behavior over time despite sharing important institutional and sociological conditions. Although both countries underwent the legal transition from a one-party to a multiparty system in the early 1990s, opposition politicians in Cameroon have fragmented along ethno-regional lines in every presidential election since then. Their counterparts in Kenya, by contrast, eventually managed to forge a multiethnic opposition coalition that could present a viable challenge to the incumbent.

This divergence in opposition behavior is noteworthy because the two countries share a remarkably similar narrative from the 1960s through the 1980s. In neither country did the leader who first came to power at independence enjoy unquestioned political authority.[15] President Ahmadou Ahidjo in Cameroon and President Jomo Kenyatta in Kenya were compelled to shore up their regimes by using both coercion and cooptation to build national coalitions (Collier 1982). After Cameroon became independent in 1960, Ahidjo sought to overcome potential challenges to his authority that could be mounted by parties that controlled ethno-regional constituencies.[16] He managed to create a one-party regime by the end of the decade by progressively absorbing smaller parties and eventually merging them to form the ruling Union National Camerounaise (UNC) (Le Vine 1971). Likewise, Kenyatta struggled to assert the primacy of his Kenya African National Union (KANU) when he took control of government after independence in 1963. He had to absorb an opposition party mounted by smaller ethnic groups that feared being dominated by the country's larger groups, and he had to crush an opposition party that had been formed by radical defectors from his ruling party. By 1970, Kenyatta had created a *de facto* one-party state (Bienen 1974).

Once Ahidjo and Kenyatta became ensconced in power, their governments enjoyed considerable stability through the end of the 1970s (Bayart 1989; Takougang and Krieger 1998; Throup and Hornsby 1998; Widner 1992). Most politically relevant ethnic groups were represented at the highest levels of leadership in the ruling party and the ministerial cabinet. Realignments in the relative balance among factions within the ruling party could be brought about with little disruption to the political order. Neither country suffered through a successful military coup or a prolonged regional insurgency. Conflicts over resources were typically resolved through political or bureaucratic mechanisms.

The two countries became models of stability by regional standards. Each achieved a peaceful transition in the presidency within the ruling party – and across ethno-regional groups. In Cameroon, Ahidjo, an ethnic Fulbe Muslim

---

[15] Armed anticolonial rebellions were organized in both Cameroon and Kenya. In Cameroon, the Union des Populations du Cameroun (UPC) led an uprising to demand immediate independence in southern regions inhabited by the Bamileke and Bassa from the mid-1950s through the mid-1960s. In Kenya, the Mau Mau rebellion took hold among landless Kikuyu in the early 1950s and ran through the end of the decade.

[16] Ahidjo faced a special challenge in that Cameroon emerged at independence as a federation of French and British UN trust territories rather than as a unitary state. He dissolved the federation by having his ruling party enact a unitary constitution in 1972.

from North Province, retired for health reasons in 1982 and handed power over to his prime minister, Paul Biya, an ethnic Beti Christian from South Province. In Kenya, after Kenyatta, an ethnic Kikuyu from Central Province, died in 1978, he was succeeded by his vice president, Daniel arap Moi, an ethnic Kalenjin from Rift Valley Province. Both Biya and Moi survived challenges to their rule from factions within their parties, mainly from their predecessors' coethnics, and coup attempts by elements within their militaries.[17]

By the time Biya and Moi were forced to open the political system to multiparty competition, each had already secured his tenure through a mix of cooptation and coercion. In fact, they responded to the demand for democracy with nearly identical strategies, managing the transition to multiparty politics without submitting to a national conference or conceding major constitutional reforms, as had been demanded by pro-democracy activists in each country. Only minimal legal changes were carried out at the earliest stages of the democratization process, enabling these leaders to retain many of the political and economic instruments that had been honed under the one-party system.

Standard explanations based on ethnic divisions, political repression, level of development, or international exposure cannot account for the differences that emerged between Cameroon and Kenya's opposition as the 1990s progressed. The two countries can hardly be differentiated on the basis of aggregate measures for such explanations. Their divergence cannot be easily attributed to social diversity. They have comparable levels of ethnic fractionalization: the score is 0.887 for Cameroon and 0.852 for Kenya (Fearon 2003). National politics in each country is structured around five large ethno-regional groups. In Cameroon, politicians can be described as representatives of the Anglophone, Grand North, Grand South, Littoral, and West constituencies (Kofele-Kale 1986; Sindjoun 1998).[18] In Kenya, national politics revolves around the alignments of the Kalenjin, Kamba, Kikuyu, Luhya, and Luo ethnic groups (Bates 1989; Throup and Hornsby 1998).[19]

---

[17] Biya's position was particularly delicate. Ahidjo had insisted on remaining the ruling party's chairman. Once his health recovered, he apparently plotted with his allies in the party and the military to oust Biya.

[18] Cameroon's Anglophone provinces are the North West and South West, which account for about 17% of the national population. The Grand North comprises the provinces of Adamawa, North, and Far North, which together make up 33%. Ahidjo's coethnics, the Fulbe, historically dominated this region, although other various groups (Mundang, Tupuri, Massa, etc.) are numerically larger. The Grand South comprises the provinces of Center, East, and South, representing 26% of the population. Biya's coethnic Beti are concentrated in these three provinces. Littoral is a province that accounts for 14% of the population and is inhabited by the Sawa, or coastal peoples, such as the Duala, Bassa, and Bakoko. West is a province that makes up 10% of the population and his inhabited by the Bamileke, one of the country's largest ethnic groups, and the smaller Bamoun. There is a large Bamileke presence in other provinces, including Center and Littoral. These population estimates are from Cameroon's 2005 census.

[19] The Kalenjin, found mainly in Rift Valley Province, constitute 13% of Kenya's total population. The Kamba are located in Eastern Province and constitute 10%. The Kikuyu of Central Province constitute 17%. The Luhya are concentrated in Western Province and constitute 14%. The Luo of Nyanza Province constitute 10%. These population figures are from Kenya's 2009 census.

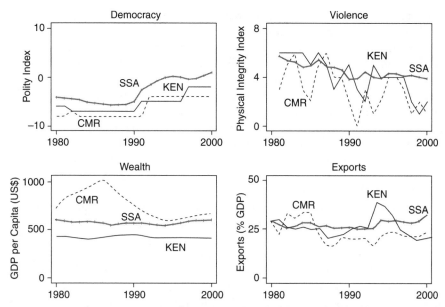

FIGURE 2.3. The cases compared: Cameroon and Kenya. Note: The panels present indicators for Cameroon (CMR) and Kenya (KEN) along with the regional average for Sub-Saharan Africa (SSA).

Sources: Polity IV Project (2009); Cingranelli and Richards Human Rights Dataset (2007); World Bank World Development Indicators (2009).

The panels in Figure 2.3 show that Cameroon and Kenya not only look alike according to a battery of political and economic indicators, but that they also tend to trend with the African region as a whole. Their divergence in opposition outcomes cannot be tied to the quality of democracy, which only marginally improved in either country after 1990. Cameroon's average Polity score is –8 from 1985 to 1991; Kenya's is –7 for the same period. From 1992 to 2000, the two countries have an identical average Polity score of –4 (Marshall and Jaggers 2009). The violent abuse of human rights, as measured by the physical integrity index in which lower scores reflect greater abuse (Cingranelli and Richards 2007), has worsened in both countries over time, oscillating in tandem with political events. There is no marked difference between the two countries in this regard. Additionally, their divergence cannot be explained the level of development. Per capita income rose in Cameroon after it became an oil exporter in the late 1970s, but the country then entered a period of continuous economic decline in the latter half of the 1980s. Kenya simply stagnated economically from the early 1980s through the 1990s (World Bank 2009). If the level of exports provides an indicator of integration into the global economy, then the two countries also appear to be equally reliant on trade with the rest of the world.

I argue that the more compelling explanation has its origins in the financial reprisal regimes created by founding leaders. The financial sector in each country became an instrument of regime maintenance designed to subdue the business sector. By regulating access to finance – through state ownership in banking, administrative credit directives, interest rate ceilings, and capital account restrictions – these leaders could be assured the political cooperation of the entrepreneurial class. In this way, Ahidjo in Cameroon and Kenyatta in Kenya could control the accumulation of resources that might enable their rivals to coordinate challenges to their authority. Even if the political instruments of their authoritarian regimes failed, they could rely on the financial controls needed to secure the allegiance of entrepreneurs, the individuals most capable of funding and organizing collective action outside the ruling party.

The financial reprisal regimes of Ahidjo and Kenyatta differed as a function of the perceived threat posed by business in each country. Their perceptions of that threat depended on whether the entrepreneurs most likely to accumulate resources came from their own ethnic groups, since the various groups over which they governed had unequal rates of capital accumulation. The business sector tended to be dominated by individuals who began either as prosperous farmers or as traders in cash crop–growing regions and were then able to leverage their surplus to enter other areas of commerce.

In Cameroon, the problem for Ahidjo was that his coethnic Fulbe, located in the northern half of the country, produced none of the major exports. Southern ethnic groups like the Bamileke produced those cash crops. Ahidjo thus sought to more tightly control and monitor the access to capital lest the southern groups acquired sufficient influence to challenge his authority. Moreover, if his own coethnics were to accumulate resources, he would have to use more interventionist measures to ensure that they did so, since they were unlikely to successfully compete with groups from the south. Cameroon's financial reprisal regime was therefore characterized by a greater reliance on restrictions in banking entry, including state ownership. For example, the country's first commercial bank to be majority owned by private indigenous shareholders would not be established until more than 25 years after independence. Even then, it took a member of the ruling party to establish that bank.

Kenyatta felt less threatened by business in Kenya because his own coethnic Kikuyu emerged as the country's principal indigenous entrepreneurs. Inhabiting the fertile regions of the country's center, the Kikuyu were among the first ethnic groups to take on the production of coffee and tea. Although Kenyatta's government adopted most of the financial controls found in other African countries, he had less need to strictly regulate the access to capital. With one of their own in power, the Kikuyu were unlikely to support a rival politician. And their own accumulation would also make them powerful allies in sustaining Kenyatta in power. His financial reprisal regime was therefore relatively relaxed when compared to Ahidjo's in Cameroon. Entry in banking and access to credit were more open. Members of the business community were allowed to establish their own private banks and nonbanking financial institutions.

The financial reprisal regimes in Cameroon and Kenya were sustained over time because, once instituted, they conditioned the expectations of both politicians and entrepreneurs. After Ahidjo and Kenyatta passed from the scene, their successors sought to preserve the nature of the financial systems they inherited. While similarly concerned with extending their own tenures, neither Biya in Cameroon nor Moi in Kenya made any effort to change the basic operation of the financial systems they inherited. By that time, the entrepreneurs in each country had already accommodated themselves to the existing equilibrium in business–state relations. Cameroon's entrepreneurs understood that they needed to actively nurture their links to the ruling party, regardless of who was in power, if they were to continue accessing the loan finance that kept them in business, particularly since the state had become a shareholder in every single bank in the country. Their counterparts in Kenya enjoyed greater freedom in this respect, having options between state-owned and private banks. Political links were important in Kenya, too, if entrepreneurs sought preferential treatment for subsidized loans or loan forgiveness, but they were unlikely to be completely locked out of the market for credit without those links.

But Cameroon and Kenya were battered in the 1980s by exogenous economic and political shocks. With the onset of economic crisis, it became increasingly difficult for the leader of either country to sustain a financial reprisal regime without external resources, including conditional loans and foreign aid. As the Cold War wound down, the international financial institutions and Western donors that supported these governments began to demand fiscal discipline. This specifically required dismantling the financial controls long used by these leaders to subdue the business community.

The leaders of Cameroon and Kenya struggled to retain their financial reprisal regimes at the same time they were forced to contend with the demand for democracy that swept across Africa in the early 1990s. Whether they were able to retain their financial reprisal regimes would not only affect the political alignment of business under multiparty competition; it would also determine the ability of the opposition to successfully achieve electoral coordination. It is here that the Cameroon and Kenya narratives diverge. In Cameroon, Biya could leverage his country's oil rents to put off the external demands for reform and thereby maintain his control over the financial sector. In Kenya, however, Moi had a much more vulnerable fiscal base, since his country remained largely a cash crop exporter. He was forced to liberalize the financial sector in order to access the conditional loans that would keep his patronage-based government afloat.

Despite the legalization of multiparty politics in Cameroon, Biya retained his influence over the country's financial sector. Entrepreneurs, regardless of partisan preference, were obliged to retain their links to the ruling party in order to secure their continued access to credit and loans – in short, to stay in business. As a result, opposition politicians could not acquire the resources needed to pursue a pecuniary coalition-building strategy. The pauperization of the opposition has inevitably diminished competition in Cameroon. This is

TABLE 2.1. *Presidential Candidates in Cameroon (Vote Share)*

Candidate	1992	1997	2004
Paul Biya (RDPC)	39.98	92.60	70.92
John Fru Ndi (SDF)	35.97		17.40
Bello Bouba Maigari (UNDP)	19.22		
Adamou Ndam Njoya (UDC)	3.62		4.47
Henri Hogbe Nlend (UPC)		2.50	
Samuel Eboua (MDP)		2.40	
Garga Haman Adji (ADD)			3.73
Others		2.60	3.41
Effective Number of Candidates	3.05	1.15	1.86

Notes: The principal opposition parties (SDF, UNDP, and UDC) boycotted the 1997 presidential election. Party acronyms: Rassemblement Démocratique du Peuple Camerounais (RDPC); Social Democratic Front (SDF); Union Nationale pour la Démocratie et le Progrès (UNDP); Union Démocratique du Cameroun (UDC); Union des Populations du Cameroun (UPC); Mouvement pour la Démocratie et le Progrès (MDP); Alliance pour la Démocratie et le Développement (ADD).

reflected in Table 2.1, which shows the vote shares for presidential candidates between 1992 and 2004. As long as no opposition politician had the financial wherewithal to act as a coalition formateur, Biya could easily win reelection against a fragmented field in two contested presidential elections and a boycotted election in 1997 in which opposition leaders found it more feasible to withdraw altogether rather than coordinate on a single challenger.[20] The continuous fragmentation of Cameroon's opposition since then appears to have undermined popular support for its leaders.

In Kenya, Moi was compelled to relinquish the instruments of financial control in exchange for international assistance. As a result, the number of private banks expanded, the largest-state owned bank was progressively privatized, and the provision of private credit rose throughout the decade. It was in this liberalized environment that Kenyan entrepreneurs began to defect from the ruling party, making it possible for opposition politicians to obtain the resources to pursue a pecuniary coalition-building strategy. Table 2.2 shows that Kenya's presidential field was more fragmented than Cameroon's at the onset of multiparty competition in 1992. Yet, after two failed attempts, the opposition managed to coordinate around the candidacy of Mwai Kibaki, who had become the favored candidate of the business community in 2002.

I have argued through this abridged narrative that the divergent electoral behavior of opposition politicians in Cameroon and Kenya can be attributed to

---

[20] It is quite likely that Biya lost the 1992 presidential election, as many informed observers have argued. The point remains, however, that a fragmented opposition made it easier for the regime to steal that election.

TABLE 2.2. *Presidential Candidates in Kenya (Vote Share)*

Candidate	1992	1997	2002
Daniel arap Moi (KANU)	36.30	40.12	
Uhuru Kenyatta (KANU)			31.30
Kenneth Matiba (FORD-A)	26.00		
Mwai Kibaki (DP)	19.50	31.09	62.20
Oginga Odinga (FORD-K)	17.50		
Raila Odinga (NDP)		10.92	
Michael Wamalwa (FORD-K)		8.29	
Charity Ngilu (SDP)		7.71	
Simeon Nyachae (FORD-P)			5.90
Others	0.70	1.88	0.60
Effective Number of Candidates	3.73	2.27	2.05

Notes: Uhuru Kenyatta was Daniel arap Moi's designated successor as the ruling party's candidate in the 2002 presidential election. Party acronyms: Kenya African National Union (KANU); Forum for the Restoration of Democracy–Asili (FORD-A); Democratic Party (DP); Forum for the Restoration of Democracy–Kenya (FORD-K); National Development Party (NDP); Social Democratic Party (SDP); Forum for the Restoration of Democracy-People (FORD-P).

differences in the financial influence of incumbents. Table 2.3 summarizes the argument as applied to the two cases. The causal mechanism is traced through each case in greater detail in subsequent chapters. The extent to which the state originally controlled the financial sector is established in Chapter 4, while the degree to which financial liberalization was enacted is shown in Chapter 5. The alignment of business is explored in Chapter 6, and the resulting opposition bargaining is discussed in Chapter 7.

CONCLUSION

This chapter has presented a theory for explaining opposition electoral strategies in Africa's multiethnic societies. This argument underscores the resource asymmetry that characterizes the competition between incumbents and challengers in patronage-based political systems. Incumbents can raid the state treasury to bankroll their reelection campaigns. But opposition politicians can neither rely on subsidies from the state nor solicit contributions from an impoverished citizenry. Few politicians are wealthy enough to fund national parties on their own.

I argue that opposition politicians are more likely to form multiethnic electoral coalitions where incumbents have relinquished their control over financial capital. Under conditions of financial liberalization, business entrepreneurs are more likely to provide opposition politicians with the resources needed to secure cross-ethnic endorsements. Conversely, opposition politicians are less

TABLE 2.3. *The Pecuniary Theory Applied to the Cases*

	Cameroon	Kenya
State Control of Capital: *Does the incumbent repress or liberalize the financial sector?*	Incumbent retains control over banking and credit.	Incumbent loses influence over banking and credit.
Alignment of Business: *Do entrepreneurs remain allied to the incumbent or defect to the opposition?*	Most entrepreneurs remain allied to incumbent.	Entrepreneurs increasingly defect to opposition.
Opposition Bargaining: *Are upfront payments used to supplement power-sharing promises?*	No opposition politician has resources to act as a coalition formateur.	A formateur uses business funding to pay for political endorsements.
Opposition Electoral Behavior	Fragmentation	Coalition

likely to coalesce where incumbents can use their financial gatekeeping power to induce the allegiance of business.

The background provided for the case studies of Cameroon and Kenya emphasizes the role of financial reprisal regimes in subduing the business sector politically. In shifting attention away from ethnic or institutional explanations, the case studies suggest that opposition politicians fail to present a serious challenge to African incumbents, not because they are polarized by ethnic conflicts or intimidated through political violence, but mainly because they are unable to secure resources in countries where incumbents have politicized the access to financial capital. By doing so, incumbents can neutralize their rivals by simply pressuring business into starving the opposition of campaign financing.

3

The Emergence of Financial Reprisal Regimes

> Those of you who have capital or who own property, do not try to use your
> wealth as a weapon with which to oppress your brothers....
>
> Julius K. Nyerere, president of Tanganyika, 1962[1]

The theory of pecuniary coalition formation suggests that the central problem
for today's opposition politicians is the fact that business cannot freely serve
as a campaign financier in many African countries. This chapter examines the
historical origins of this dynamic. I argue that two features of the late colonial period – the position of the state in mediating access to capital and the
role of resources in mobilizing nationalist campaigns – shaped the relationship
between politicians and entrepreneurs over subsequent decades. These features
provided Africa's post-independence leaders with the capacity and motivation
to create financial reprisal regimes, that is, to transform the access to financial capital into a privilege that could be extended or withdrawn at a leader's
discretion.

I present in this chapter a narrative that reinterprets the historical record
to highlight the interest of African leaders in suppressing the ability of business to act politically. While standard accounts of the late colonial period
emphasize the role of the "new men" – Western-educated clerks, lawyers, and
teachers – in leading the nationalist cause across Africa (e.g., Kilson 1970;
Lloyd 1966), indigenous entrepreneurs also "constituted a major force in the
rise of nationalism" (Markovitz 1977, 232). Indigenous entrepreneurs forged
close ties with nationalist politicians as they sought to advance their respective
interests vis-à-vis the colonial state. Just as entrepreneurs required political
intervention in order to expand their restricted participation in commerce,

---

[1] Nyerere made the statement in his inaugural address as president of Tanganyika, which later
became Tanzania. In a 1963 speech delivered soon after his inauguration, he further noted: "We
aim at building a classless society for one reason. In no state is there enough wealth to satisfy the
desire of a single individual for power and prestige ... [E]ach person tries to get more wealth, simply so that he will have more power, and more prestige, than his fellows" (Nyerere 1967, 182).

politicians needed resources to build the movements they hoped would one day take control of the state. Merchants and traders played a crucial linkage function in this respect: they facilitated the coordination of nationalist parties across ethnic, linguistic, and regional cleavages. Nnamdi Azikiwe, who led one of Nigeria's first nationalist parties, made this relationship explicit when addressing his party's annual convention in 1957: "If some of us had not accumulated wealth in the dim and distant decade when the oppressor was in his heyday, it would have been impossible to found this great Party, and it would have been an idle dream to achieve the measure of political success that has come our way" (quoted in Sklar 1963, 230).

The relationship between accumulated wealth and political success, as recognized by politicians like Azikiwe in the 1950s, helps to illuminate the role of business as a campaign financier after the transition to multiparty politics in the 1990s. Malawi is a case in point. Prior to independence, the main nationalist party, the Nyasaland African Congress (NAC), was a weak political organization incapable of competing against a better funded rival supported by mining interests and white settlers (Cohen 2008). With each branch raising is own funds and spending them according to local preferences (Rotberg 1965), the NAC was unable to coordinate mass support despite the prevalence of latent anticolonial grievances. Nationalist politicians led by Hastings Kamuzu Banda were able to sustain a territory-wide campaign under the banner of the Malawi Congress Party (MCP), the successor to the NAC, only after being bankrolled by the colony's indigenous entrepreneurs. It was the resources provided by the founders of the African Chamber of Commerce that enabled the MCP to successfully coordinate political support (McCracken 1998; Power 2010). This pattern was repeated in the early 1990s, when the country's business community financed opposition to the long rule of the MCP under Banda. Once again, the country's main opposition party was "literally born in the Chamber of Commerce" with the backing of business facilitating electoral coordination in an otherwise ethnically fragmented polity (Posner 1995, 137).

While the demonstrated import of business resources for political organization motivated African leaders to seek control over capital, it was the state apparatus inherited at independence that enabled them to determine who could accumulate capital and under what terms. Africa's post-colonial leaders had little need to bargain over the state's access to revenue because, as a result of the economic development paradigms prevailing at the time, they enjoyed direct control over productive resources or could access the foreign aid needed to sustain their regimes. These leaders could easily manipulate the state's financial gatekeeping to constrain the autonomy of entrepreneurs, thereby insulating themselves from political challenges financed by business, the segment of society with the greatest capacity to do so.

This chapter proceeds by showing how indigenous entrepreneurs became politicized prior to independence. It details their mounting grievances over financial discrimination under colonialism as well as their linkage function as part of the nationalist movement. It then explains how, after independence, leaders used the state to reinforce business' dependence on politically mediated capital. The chapter concludes with a reevaluation of the received wisdom concerning the business–state relationship in Africa.

THE COLONIAL FOUNDATION OF STATE–CAPITAL RELATIONS IN AFRICA

The enduring nature of state–capital relations in Africa was established under colonialism during the first half of the twentieth century. At the turn of the century, as the colonial state was being extended from the coast to the interior of the continent, European trading firms lobbied their governments for greater intervention in managing commerce. Facing increasing competition in overseas trade along with declining commodity prices, these firms, which had begun to amalgamate their operations through the formation of limited liability companies, sought to eliminate competition from African merchants in order to secure control of additional linkages in the trade networks that spanned colonial territories (Austen 1987; Bauer 1954b; Gann and Duignan 1975; Hopkins 1987).

Responding to the demands of European trading firms, colonial authorities began restricting the participation of African merchants in various areas of commerce in the years leading up to the First World War (Fry 1976; Hopkins 1966; Nwabughuogu 1982). While the colonial state did not act as a mere agent of metropolitan business – indeed, the two sides were occasionally at odds over economic policy – their shared interest in the exploitation of their newly acquired territories aligned their actions vis-à-vis African participation in commerce (Hopkins 1987). Because both colonial authorities and European firms were interested in securing the land and labor necessary to export raw materials to their home markets, the colonial state elaborated a discriminatory regime of market access that benefited European trading firms at the expense of their African counterparts.[2] This intervention enabled select expatriate firms, such as the United Africa Company (UAC) and John Holt in British colonies or the Societé Commerciale de l'Ouest Africain (SCOA) and the Compagnie Française de l'Afrique Occidentale (CFAO) in French colonies, to secure a dominant position in their territories.

Colonial officials enacted policies that amounted to official discrimination in commerce, while permitting oligopolies to be formed among European firms through informal agreements, including price fixing and market-sharing accords. An array of controls in licensing, finance, and taxation was used to regulate African ventures. These restrictions limited the geographic areas in which traders could operate, the access of land-holding farmers to wage labor,

---

[2] Fourchard (2003) shows how French administrators in Ouagadougou and Bobo-Dioulasso used zoning rules to systematically marginalize African merchants and traders in the acquisition of commercial real estate for the benefit of European firms and Lebanese merchants.

and the ability of traders to engage in the wholesale marketing of commodities (Iliffe 1983; Kennedy 1988). And force was used to unravel African supply networks, including the arrest and exile of influential indigenous merchants, whenever necessary (Gertzel 1962).

The level of restrictions imposed on indigenous participation in commerce varied in important ways across colonial empires. The continental powers such as France, Belgium, and Portugal, in reflecting their own patterns of economic development, allowed for greater state intervention in their colonial economies and offered their respective firms greater protection against competition (Gann and Duignan 1975), though the British, of course, did not pursue a pure lais-sez-faire commercial policy in their own colonies (Pedler 1975). Restrictions on indigenous commerce also varied among the colonies of the same imperial power, since colonial policy was not only shaped in metropolitan capitals by politicians and bureaucrats with competing agendas, but was also implemented by administrators who enjoyed wide discretion in far-off outposts. Colonial measures against indigenous merchants were less severe in West Africa because those territories lacked white settler communities or mineral wealth. Among the territories of East and Southern Africa, it was the representatives of white settlers and mining interests who lobbied colonial authorities for additional restrictions on African commerce.

For all colonial powers, the control of finance became a key instrument for restricting African commercial activities. Since businesses are unlikely to survive or expand without access to credit, formal regulations aimed at limiting the access of indigenous entrepreneurs to finance, regardless of creditworthiness, inexorably limited their participation in business. In the Gold Coast, which was renamed Ghana at independence, colonial legislation from 1906 stipulated that only banks incorporated outside the colony could engage in banking (Stockwell 2000). Such a law not only constrained the accumulation of capital by African merchants – the most likely candidates to establish local banks – but it also kept them dependent on the two British-owned banks that serviced the colony until the legislation was revoked in 1949. Elsewhere, the amount of credit that Africans could borrow was regulated ostensibly for the purpose of protecting the indigenous population from indebtedness. In Kenya, the Credit to Natives Ordinance of 1926 imposed limits on the amount of credit that could be extended by foreigners to Africans; the limit of 200 shillings was not abolished until 1960 (Kitching 1980). Fears of incipient nationalism led the French administration in Senegal to encourage banks and companies to favor the expatriate Lebanese merchant community with credit over indigenous entrepreneurs (Amin 1969). A similar motivation led Belgian authorities in the Congo to legally prohibit Africans from having access to formal credit. The 1917 decree that imposed penal sanctions for lending money to Africans was not revoked until 1953 (Jewsiewicki 1977; Lemarchand 1964). As a whole these financial controls, as Kennedy (1988, 30) notes, "acted as a brake on commercial endeavour" because indigenous merchants could not expand their operations without loan capital.

Compounding the impact of formal regulations, European-owned banks operating in the colonies pursued informal discriminatory practices that limited the amount of capital available to African entrepreneurs. As the expansion of trade at the turn of the century stimulated the demand for financial intermediation – the first bank in British-controlled West Africa was founded in Lagos in 1890[3] – banks were established in the colonies mainly to facilitate financing for the trade conducted by European trading houses between metropolitan markets and their sources of raw materials in the colonies.[4] Because these banks were partly owned by the European trading houses, or linked by overlapping membership on their boards of directors, they restricted credit facilities to African entrepreneurs to ensure that they would not emerge as a source of commercial competition (Austen 1987; Uche 1999). The banks did provide some Africans with short-term advances for small-scale trade related to the cultivation and transport of cash crops, but they generally refused to extend longer-term facilities such as loans for investing in capital equipment or acquiring property, especially since indigenous land tenure systems often meant that merchants and traders lacked mortgageable security (Kennedy 1988).

Financing options for indigenous entrepreneurs were further reduced by active collusion among expatriate banks. In West Africa, the British Bank of West Africa (BBWA) and the Banque de l'Afrique Occidentale (BAO) reached an agreement as early as 1913 not to open new branches in the colonies of the other's metropole (Austin and Uche 2007).[5] With the onset of the global depression of the 1930s, BBWA and Barclays Bank – the two main banks operating in Britain's West African colonies – agreed to limit competition between them by coordinating their rates as well as their branches. Neither bank would open a branch in a new territory without giving notice to the other. The two banks codified their collusion with a contract entitled "Cooperation between banks in West Africa" in 1945; it remained in force until 1957 (Fry 1976; Stockwell 2000).[6] In the same time period, the three principal banks of East Africa, Barclays, Standard, and National and Grindlays, regulated their cartel through a "Summary of Banking Arrangements" (Mittelman 1978).

---

[3] British bankers were initially reluctant to establish a presence in West Africa despite having already set up banks in several other colonies in Asia and the Middle East. The initiative to set up a bank originally came from shipping companies that ran steamships between Liverpool and the West African coast. Without banks, firms had to actively manage the amount of cash kept on hand for planting and harvesting seasons. In French West Africa, the Banque du Senegal was established in 1853 and taken over by the government-owned Banque de l'Afrique Occidentale (BAO) in 1901. The BAO also served as the monetary authority for French West Africa (Fry 1976).

[4] Banks also provided colonial government a valuable service by handling payments for their civil servants, collecting customs revenue, and acting as an agent of the monetary authority.

[5] BBWA agreed to limit itself to existing branches in Côte d'Ivoire (Austin and Uche 2007).

[6] The 1945 agreement stipulated that six months notification was required in writing before a change or cancellation came into effect.

THE ARTICULATION OF INDIGENOUS BUSINESS GRIEVANCES

Financial discrimination by colonial authorities and expatriate banks fueled the political grievances of African merchants and traders. Their critiques mainly focused on the local population's restricted access to banking as well as what were perceived to be artificially inflated rates that banks imposed on their transactions. One specific area of dispute concerned the fact that European banks invested private deposits and public savings collected in the colonies in metropolitan capitals rather than using those funds to increase lending to members of the indigenous business sector (Austin and Uche 2007; Wickins 1986).

Because they had no access to the alternative markets for capital or credit – and because company-based mechanisms failed to meet their growing needs[7] – African entrepreneurs sought redress from colonial authorities. Indeed, the lack of credit was among the first economic grievances to galvanize political action among the nascent indigenous business sector in African colonies. In 1912, when BBWA absorbed the Bank of Nigeria, the only other bank in the colony of Nigeria, the local business community published a pamphlet, "An appeal from the native traders of Lagos to the financiers of Great Britain," to condemn BBWA's excessive rates and discriminatory practices (Fry 1976). By the 1920s, African merchants were seeking to form their own banks as a means of pooling their resources to expand beyond small-scale activities in retailing, contracting, and transport.

Banks took on a political significance among indigenous business. After Winifred Tete-Ansa, a merchant born in the Gold Coast colony, established the Nigerian Mercantile Bank in 1931, he appealed for support from the merchant community by calling on them to release themselves from "economic bondage, always bearing in mind that every independent nation must have its own Economic Freedom and that without your own Banking Institution which can be recognized abroad, you cannot attain that freedom" (quoted in Hopkins 1966, 145).[8] Significantly, the chairman of the Nigerian Mercantile Bank was Dr. Crispin Curtis Adeniyi-Jones, the president of the Nigerian National Democratic Party (NNDP), which had become a focal organization for indigenous business opposition to colonial policies. Although the NNDP did not seek to challenge the colonial system as a whole, the party demanded changes in the functioning of the colonial economic system by expanding economic opportunities for Africans, including the establishment of indigenous banks.

African entrepreneurs increasingly sought an institutional solution to their financing problems because they correctly understood that state intervention had not only endowed expatriate banks with their privileged position, but

---

[7] Expatriate firms like British American Tobacco and the European trading houses guaranteed bank credit to African traders as a means of extending their networks.

[8] But, as occurred with Tete-Ansa's previous attempt to start an indigenous bank in 1924, the Nigerian Mercantile Bank failed in 1936. The first successful indigenous bank in British West Africa was the National Bank of Nigeria established in 1933 (Hopkins 1966).

was also the source of the nonmarket constraints that impeded their commercial expansion. Colonial governments and expatriate banks had become closely linked over time. In Britain's West African colonies, for example, BBWA became the government's local banker, acting as the sole agent of the West African Currency Board and being the sole depository of funds for all government agencies until 1955 (Fry 1976). Just as British MPs were routinely recruited to serve as directors for companies engaged in colonial trade, colonial administrators often served on the boards of expatriate banks. When the governor of Nigeria, Lord Milverton, retired from his post in 1951, he joined BBWA's board of directors. That same year Lord Harlech, a former secretary of state for the colonies, became BBWA's chairman.[9]

The existing colonial institutions proved incapable of accommodating or channeling indigenous demands. The cartels organized by European firms, such as the Joint West African Committee and the Association of West African Merchants, provided them an effective mechanism for negotiating with the colonial administration and lobbying the colonial office, but they excluded African merchants by definition. Africans were not permitted to join European-based chambers of commerce in most colonies until after the Second World War. In the Gold Coast colony, representatives from business were nominated from the chambers to sit as *ex officio* members of the Legislative Council, but the prohibition on African membership to the chambers persisted in practice until independence (Stockwell 2000).

After the Second World War, authorities in some colonies sought to respond to the grievances of African entrepreneurs by taking steps to loosen restrictions on indigenous access to credit. In 1947, colonial officials in the Gold Coast established an informal committee, which included legislative council members and African commercial representatives, to explore the promotion of local participation in trade. In identifying access to credit as one of the principal obstacles to indigenous enterprise, the committee recommended establishing a state bank, which eventually led to the creation of the Bank of Gold Coast in 1953 (Uche 2003). In Nigeria, public lending agencies began offering loans to entrepreneurs beginning in 1946 with four regional development boards providing such loans by the end of the decade (Kilby 1969). In Uganda, the colonial administration established the Uganda Credit and Savings Bank to provide credit to small-scale entrepreneurs who might not otherwise meet the security demanded by expatriate banks (Gerschenberg 1972). In Kenya, after 1950, colonial authorities began providing funds to Local Native Councils for loans to African traders (Swainson 1980). A separate program was initiated in 1956 to provide credit for those working in commerce and industry (Himbara 1994, 83).

But the colonial state's attempts at ameliorating financial discrimination proved to be insufficient. These palliative measures neither abolished

---

[9] BBWA's previous chairman had been Alfred Milner, who was a member of the House of Lords and governor in South Africa.

discriminatory banking practices nor repealed administrative restrictions. Moreover, existing constraints became all the more restrictive on indigenous entrepreneurs as state intervention expanded and deepened through Depression-era policies that had been reinforced during the war-time effort of metropolitan governments. By the end of the 1940s, it had become common knowledge among Africans seeking to enter into merchant ventures or expand their commercial activities that they operated in, according to P.T. Bauer (1975, 652), "closely controlled economies in which people's livelihoods came to depend largely on political and administrative decisions."

This was certainly the analysis among Africans who subsequently moved from business into politics.[10] Oginga Odinga, the nationalist politician who went on to become Kenya's first vice president, drew a straight line from his commercial frustrations to the colonial government.[11] In a chapter of his autobiography, entitled "Independence through Business?," Odinga recounts working with John Paul Olola, the founder of the Kisumu Native Chamber of Commerce, to establish the Luo Thrift and Trading Corporation in 1947. Recalling being stymied by the formal regulations and informal demands invoked by colonial officials, Odinga summarizes the experience of African entrepreneurs of his time: "We found, as the years went by, that we had more to contend with than just routine business difficulties. Far from encouraging African economic ventures, the government seemed set on producing obstacles.... Invariably when we applied for loans we were turned down" (Odinga 1967, 88–89).

A POLITICAL SOLUTION TO THE CREDIT PROBLEM

The nascent African business community, chafing under a restrictive colonial system, opted for a political solution to their mercantile grievances after the Second World War. Embracing nationalism as a mechanism for addressing their commercial grievances, entrepreneurs joined an elite stratum of society that sought to steer their colonies toward independence. Across the continent, merchants and traders endorsed nationalist movements that explicitly linked economic opportunity to state control (Bates 1983; Freund 1984; Kilson 1958; Wallerstein 1970).[12]

---

[10] Wallerstein (1970, 412, FN 4) notes that several African politicians, including Patrice Lumumba, had initially tried their hand at business before being frustrated by administrative obstacles.

[11] The first indigenous political organizations that formed in Kenya, while being localized and finding expression through ethnic associations, were mainly economic associations aimed at lobbying the colonial administration for economic issues, including land rights and taxes (Nyangira 1987). The leadership that would later make up the Kenya African National Union (KANU), of which Odinga was a part, would emerge from these early associations.

[12] Indigenous entrepreneurs were, of course, a heterogeneous group, and their political preferences surely reflected those differences. Lewis (1965) thought that wealth was the primary axis of differentiation, suggesting that poorer merchants and traders tended to support the more radical parties, while their richer counterparts aligned themselves with the more establishmentarian elites, modern and traditional.

Evidence for the influence of indigenous entrepreneurs on nationalist mobilization is reflected in the extent to which their grievances were prioritized even though many of their specific concerns were not those of the broader agrarian population. The commercial grievances once represented by the earlier, more accommodationist and urban-based, generation of nationalist organization that emerged in the interwar period, such as the National Congress of British West Africa in the 1920s, were taken up as the policy positions of a more radical generation that sought to mobilize mass support for outright independence after the Second World War. Demands for the removal of trading preferences reserved for metropolitan firms and the establishment of banks to assist Africans in commerce were written into the program of nearly every nationalist party.

The representation offered by nationalist parties in the Gold Coast colony is an exemplar of the significance attached to the grievances of merchants and traders. The same month that British colonial officials allowed an informal committee to explore the promotion of African business, August 1947, the colony's commercial and professional classes formed the United Gold Coast Convention (UGCC) to campaign for self-government. The UGCC's founding president, J. B. Danquah, who had been on the board of directors of a failed indigenous bank, lobbied for the establishment of a state-owned bank to provide credit to Africans. The goal of a state-owned bank was then adopted as a key campaign promise by the UGCC's rival, the Convention People's Party (CPP) led by Kwame Nkrumah.[13] Although the CPP is typically depicted as the more radical counterpart to the UGCC, Nkrumah also sought the support of the indigenous business community. His CPP became the party of the "aspirant businessman" for whom nonmarket restrictions, especially in the area of credit, blocked their entry into many sectors of the economy (Rathbone 1973). The head of the African chamber of commerce, which was formed in 1953 to contest the allocation of merchant seats to the Gold Coast's reformed legislative assembly, was a member of the CPP (Austin 1964).[14]

African entrepreneurs became prominent members of the parties that articulated the nationalist agenda. These first parties were often founded by members of the urban professions – functionaries, lawyers, and teachers – who emerged as a result of the educational and commercial changes associated with the initial economic modernization of African colonies (Coleman 1954; Hodgkin 1957, 1961).[15] But merchants and traders similarly engaged in the work of

---

[13] Riots that erupted in Accra in 1948 pushed colonial officials in the Gold Coast to accept the creation of the bank, but they were then vetoed in London by the Colonial Office and the Bank of England. See Stockwell (2000) for a discussion of this period.

[14] Nkrumah had previously been the UGCC party secretary before founding the CPP.

[15] The standard characterization of African nationalism in many ways corresponds closely to the notion of blocked elites described by Anderson (1983). Of course, the very same economic changes that allowed urban-based elites to emerge also provided most Africans with incentives to support political change, as has occurred more generally with the rise of nationalism (Gellner 1983). In other words, the masses did not need to be convinced or to be duped (Lonsdale 1968).

party building and representation because they too confronted constraints on their advancement. In his encyclopedic study of the first Nigerian party system, Sklar (1963) shows that entrepreneurs were a core constituency for each of the colony's three regional parties and were incorporated into nearly every level of organization. Nnamdi Azikiwe, who led the National Council of Nigeria and the Cameroons (NCNC) and was himself an entrepreneur, publisher, and banker, recruited the support of entrepreneurs by proclaiming "that the struggle for Nigerian freedom had many fronts, and that political freedom was not enough; economic freedom must be won also..." (quoted in Sklar 1963, 168).[16] The founders of the Action Group, led by Obafemi Awolowo, were mostly merchants and bankers who had experienced nonmarket impediments to their business in and around Lagos, the colony's commercial and administrative capital. Ahmadu Bello's Northern Peoples' Congress (NPC), though often caricatured as a party of traditional authorities, was also rooted in that region's business community, which cooperated with traditional authorities to advance their mutual interests vis-à-vis the colonial state as well as other regions. Businessmen formed the largest contingent within the executive committee for each of these parties: 28% of the NCNC; 21% of the Action Group; 26% of the NPC (Sklar 1963, 480–494).[17]

The Nigerian party system was not anomalous in Africa. The participation of entrepreneurs in nationalist parties far exceeded their proportion in the population of most colonies, as gauged by the number who were elected as parliamentarians on the eve of independence. In Dahomey, later renamed Benin, entrepreneurs constituted 21.6% of representatives serving the Parti Dahoméen de l'Unité in 1960 (Le Vine 1968). That same year, 25.6% of legislators elected under the banner of the Sierra Leone People's Party had business-related occupations (Kilson 1964). Approximately 20% of legislators elected as members of the Kenya African National Union or the Kenya African Democratic Union between 1957 and 1968 had previously been engaged in business and trade (Rouyer 1975). In Uganda, 33.3% of Kabaka Yekka's representatives in the 1962 National Assembly were identified as businessmen, as were 24.3% of the Uganda People's Congress and 8.3% of the Democratic Party (Jorgensen 1981). In Zambia, 21% of the candidates nominated by the United National Independence Party owned businesses or farms (Baylies and Szeftel 1984).

A colony's level of economic development and the range of economic opportunity permitted by its administration predictably shaped the participation of African entrepreneurs in nationalist parties. An entrepreneurial class capable of political action might seem less likely to emerge in territories dominated by

---

[16] Azikiwe was specifically referring to his experience in seeking service, namely, overdraft facilities, from an expatriate bank in pre-independence Nigeria. Based on that experience, he moved to create his own bank and include the nationalization of banks in the NCNC manifesto in 1951.

[17] Sklar (1963) also shows that approximately 31% of local leadership and candidates for each party was made up of businessmen, the largest occupational group.

European trading and mining companies or by white settler communities.[18] In the Belgian Congo, 10% of those elected to the House of Representatives in 1960 were identified as having been *commerçants* (Bustin 1963). Nevertheless, even in situations like that in the Belgian Congo, contemporary observers saw that "the early manifestations of national consciousness have been associated with the growth...of a new class of prosperous business men" (Hodgkin 1957, 116).

THE LINKAGE ROLE OF BUSINESS

African entrepreneurs did not merely support nationalist aspirations; they provided the resources that gave those movements organized expression. They were well placed – quite literally – to facilitate, if not subsidize, their expansion. Having successfully adapted to the exigencies of the money economy introduced through colonialism, merchants and traders straddled the multiple terrains that these politicians had to engage. They knew how to negotiate with European officials and traditional chiefs, move between coastal ports and inland villages, and adapt to rural and urban realities (Hunter 1962). Entrepreneurs were especially important in this last respect. The economic changes that had accelerated during the interwar period helped to create the urban centers that became focal points for nationalist mobilization (Coleman 1954; Hodgkin 1957; Mazrui and Tidy 1984). At these centers of administration and commerce, entrepreneurs could link together distinct segments of society and extend those linkages into the interior through personalized commercial networks.

Empowered by their unique socioeconomic position, entrepreneurs became pivotal actors on behalf of parties that sought to become truly national organizations capable of wresting control of the state from a retreating colonial administration. And they were pivotal in addressing the linkage problem in two specific respects: they provided parties an informal mechanism through which they could connect to various communities across large territories and they furnished parties with the resources to compete when confronted with rivals for power.

Nationalist politicians had been obliged to seek mass support once European powers consented to extensive institutional reforms in their colonies after the Second World War, including the establishment of territorial legislatures with elected representatives and nearly universal suffrage (Collier 1982). The British government began endowing some of its colonies with constitutions for internal self-government in the early 1950s (Hargreaves 1982; Pratt 1982), while the French government gradually expanded rights for its colonial citizens, beginning with the 1946 constitution of the Fourth Republic and culminating with the Loi Cadre in 1956 (M'bokolo 1982; Person 1982). These institutional

---

[18] The ideology of party leaders also certainly mattered. In Tanzania, where Julius Nyerere imbued his Tanganyika African National Union (TANU) with a socialist orientation, only 8% of party leaders came from business at independence (McGowan and Wacirah 1974).

changes presented an opportunity for nationalist politicians to immediately influence the internal affairs of their colonies while positioning themselves to take future control of the state itself.

But the abrupt installation of electoral institutions created a challenge for which most nationalists were ill suited. Their parties were typically loose coalitions of pre-existing associations – urban-based tribal clubs or district-level parties – that lacked any centralized or coherent organization. In Côte d'Ivoire, for instance, the Parti Démocratique de la Côte d'Ivoire (PDCI) led by Félix Houphouët-Boigny was "an organization for the masses rather than a mass organization" (Zolberg 1969, 185). He attempted to turn this "bourgeois organization" into a veritable political machine in the 1950s (Rapley 1993, 46), but its prospects continued to depend on the loyalty of local elites, modern as well as traditional, rather than on the reputation of the party itself.[19] One challenge in this regard emerged when the native civil servants who had acted as local branch leaders for the party began to withdraw under pressure from the French colonial administration. Houphouët-Boigny then found his organizational solution among ethnic Dioula traders, who were already the principal intermediaries between farming communities and foreign trading houses. Their dispersal throughout Côte d'Ivoire ensured that the party would be able to coordinate support across communities. According to Zolberg (1969, 186–187),

These men are linked to one another through a network of commercial channels through which other communications can flow as well. Thus, economic skills and the influence they provide can easily be adapted to political use. A Dioula general secretary can make a farmer's vote a condition for obtaining cash advances before the beginning of the cocoa or coffee trading season.

Scholars studying political mobilization in other African colonies in the decade preceding independence described the dynamic captured by Zolberg with remarkable narrative consistency. Dioula traders, whose routes spanned several countries in West Africa, played a similar linkage role when Sékou Touré sought to extend his Parti Démocratique de Guinée (PDG). Touré would invoke his lineage from Samory Touré, a nineteenth century warrior–trader from whom the Dioula also claim descent, to secure their support in extending the PDG through the trading routes they controlled in Guinea's interior (Morgenthau 1964, 234–244). Across the continent, in Uganda, Apter (1961) found that petty traders, despite operating on a small scale, were essential agents of nationalist coordination in rural areas, turning their shops into party offices where communication, organization, and fundraising could occur.

Each small trading stall and *duka* now became a focal point of organization. Farmers who bought their grains and implements at these *dukas* or came to repair their bicycles

---

[19] PDCI was essentially on offshoot of the Syndicat Agricole Africain (SAA), an organization formed to represent the interests of indigenous planters who, according to Rapley (1993, 32), "were capitalists first and planters second."

remained to discuss matters of cotton and coffee prices. The result was that an increase in economic transactions also meant an increase in political organization. (Apter 1961, 240–1)

If entrepreneurs were the human cogs that permitted a party machine to operate across a colony's territory, then it was their money that fueled the machine. The resources needed to run a party were continually in short supply, leading party leaders to worry about their ability to retain control of the fissiparous tendencies found within their organizations. The majority of farmers and workers in these agrarian-based economies certainly had little to spare, so parties could not rely on voluntary membership subscriptions to fund daily operations or electoral campaigns. Even the nationalist movements that appeared to approximate the mass party ideal could not count on such subscriptions. Julius Nyerere had to turn to "private financing" from local notables as he sought to extend his Tanganyika African National Union (TANU) into the rural areas of Tanzania (Bienen 1970, 61).[20] Nkrumah's CPP, the leading party in pre-independence Ghana, drew more of its funding from merchant contributions rather than from membership subscriptions (Austin 1964).[21] The source of political funding for these nationalist parties reinforces the fact that the dichotomy between mass and cadre parties made early on by scholars such as Morgenthau (1964), following Duverger (1954), had no empirical basis, which Zolberg and Bienen originally established when they found that the mass parties had little to no organizational skeleton – just like the cadre parties to which they were compared.

Entrepreneurs, when compared to clerks and teachers, were the social category most likely to afford donations to the nationalist cause.[22] Politicians actively sought out their support as party patrons because their money magnified the linkage service they provided. In pre-independence Mali, merchants and traders had a prominent position on the executive committee of Modibo Keita's Union Soudanaise (US), the colony's leading party, because they linked the party through their commercial networks to every town and rural marketplace. Their influence in such places was enhanced by the fact that they were also the primary donors to mosques and madrasahs – the

[20] Bienen (1970, 62) notes that TANU had no stable source of funding prior to independence. The party was so short of money before taking power that "a TANU branch secretary received less than a domestic servant."

[21] It may well have been constant money problems that led parties to accept contributions from the very expatriate firms they criticized. Austin (1964, 172) thought that the CPP almost certainly received financial backing from some European firms and Lebanese merchants. Stockwell (2000, 146) has since found evidence that the CPP received funding from the United Africa Company (UAC), a London-managed subsidiary of Unilever. The CPP's opponents, namely, the National Liberation Movement (NLM) led by Kofi Busia, also received financial support from the UAC, the British Bank of West Africa, and the Ashanti Goldfields Corporation.

[22] Katzin (1964, 191) provides the example of a newly opened bank branch in Nigeria in 1961. She notes that traders were the largest group among its depositors, more than double the number of teachers and clerks combined.

very places where politics were discussed (Amselle 1977; Morgenthau 1964). Echoing the description offered by Zolberg in Côte d'Ivoire and Apter in Uganda, Snyder (1965, 74) points out that, in Mali, Dioula traders, who sought to displace the French in commerce, "willingly became an important means of communicating US ideas.... [They] had considerable prestige and personal wealth and often extended credit to rural peoples; thus they wielded economic power." What is more, the influence of the Dioula enabled the Union Soudanaise to gain ground in rural areas against its main rival, the Parti Progressiste Soudanais (PSP).

In Nigeria, Azikiwe cultivated the support of entrepreneurs in the 1950s to help stave off dissent within the ranks of his NCNC. During one of the party's earliest internal crises, businessmen affiliated with the NCNC raised a fund to enable Azikiwe to pacify rebellious party members (Sklar 1963). And it was this colony's particularly competitive politics that led parties to attach themselves to indigenous banks that could serve as *de facto* campaign war chests. Azikiwe financed the campaigns of his NCNC through the African Continental Bank. By the mid-1950s, the party owed the bank £50,000, or more than $1 million in today's terms (Sklar 1963). Azikiwe used this command over party finance – he was the only private shareholder of the African Continental Bank – to supplement his control over the NCNC's weak party structure, which otherwise offered few mechanisms for keeping wavering party members in line.[23] Similarly, the Action Group was allied to three indigenous banks, including the National Bank of Nigeria, the country's oldest bank. With both the chairman and manager of the National Bank of Nigeria being vice presidents of the Action Group's Lagos branch, the party was able to have access to unsecured loans to fund its campaigns.

BUSINESS DEPENDENCE ON STATE CONTROLLED CAPITAL

The momentous transfer of power from European colonial administrators to African nationalist leaders did little to alter the fundamental nature of the state–capital relationship. Over half a century, the colonial state had established and elaborated a model in which political power was used to discriminate in the allocation of economic rights. At independence, the nationalist politicians who took charge of the state would take up this model and adapt it to their own needs, adjusting the criteria by which the state granted or withdrew access to land, labor, and capital. In this respect, the investment made by indigenous entrepreneurs in their alliance with nationalist politicians

[23] Azikiwe's effort to gain political advantage through finance came to a head in the mid-1950s, when banking moved to the center of conflict between Azikiwe, as a nationalist leader, and British colonial authorities. Colonial authorities launched an investigation into improprieties involving the Eastern Region's government, controlled by Azikiwe's party, and African Continental Bank, also owned by Azikiwe. While the position of African Continental Bank was dubious, the British campaign seemed aimed at undermining Azikiwe politically as much as it was intended to ensure financial rectitude (Uche 1997).

seemingly produced its intended payoff: independence would enable them to enjoy the same privileges once reserved for metropolitan firms or settler communities.

But the alliance between entrepreneurs and politicians was itself transformed by independence. Their roles were effectively reversed. While nationalist politicians had previously relied on the organizational and financial resources of business to advance their office-seeking goals, it was now entrepreneurs who depended on the politicians for access to the finance capital required for them to prosper commercially. The adoption of the one-party system, which became the modal form of government in the region by the mid-1960s, enabled nationalists-turned-presidents to deploy public resources to manufacture whatever mass political support they desired; they no longer needed the private resources of business for electoral coordination.

African nationalists took over a state apparatus that endowed them with tremendous economic power vis-à-vis society, including the indigenous business community. They had pragmatic as well as ideological reasons for choosing to retain the state, rather than turn to the market, as the principal mechanism for allocating access to resources. To begin with, the state inherited at independence had been explicitly designed to appropriate land, control labor, and channel capital. Once stripped of their racist orientation, the panoply of colonial-era regulations now available to the nationalists in charge of the state were too convenient to be dismantled; they provided ready-made tools for improving the lives of their citizens through the reallocation of resources, directly and immediately. The motivation to use such instruments was reinforced by the apparent success with which the state had imposed additional controls to overcome the economic challenges presented by the Great Depression and Second World War (Bauer 1954a; Meredith 1986).[24]

Nationalists turned to state intervention because it was the dominant paradigm for economic development at the time of independence in the 1960s. Import substitution industrialization, in particular, offered a template for accelerating the modernization process through the centralized coordination of investment and production. African governments, counseled by foreign economic advisors, considered the local private sector to be too weak to serve as an effective engine of development. The state itself would have to act as that motor by expanding its regulatory capacity, making large-scale investments, taking ownership of strategic assets, and protecting strategic sectors (Kennedy 1988; Sender and Smith 1986). Implementing this development model in its entirety would require the state to become an owner and purveyor of financial capital. And the international conditions prevailing in the 1960s and 1970s made it possible for governments to easily tap external resources in the form of aid and loans.

---

[24] By the end of the Second World War, Britain had instituted control boards for the purchase of all commodities in its colonies. Additional exchange controls had also been imposed on transactions with countries outside the sterling area.

Africa's new leaders – empowered by the inherited state apparatus and encouraged by contemporary development thinking – actively used the structures of resource control previously employed under colonialism. They initially used this power to fulfill their pre-independence bargain with entrepreneurs. Their governments not only abolished racial barriers for accessing capital after independence, but they carried out an unprecedented expansion of credit provision to the private sector.[25] Existing credit facilities were augmented as new mechanisms for state finance were created. Regimes espousing conflicting ideologies – ranging from the socialist ideals claimed in Ghana, Uganda, and Zambia to the capitalist line maintained in Côte d'Ivoire, Kenya, and Nigeria – enacted surprisingly similar policies, including state-owned banks and subsidized loan programs. By the mid-1970s, most had also undertaken indigenization programs that targeted banking as a key sector and included loan provisions to facilitate the acquisition of foreign-owned firms by African entrepreneurs (Kennedy 1988; Wilson 1990).[26]

Kenya provides a representative example of government efforts to expand the availability of credit. In the year immediately following independence, the Kenyan government established the Industrial and Commercial Development Corporation (ICDC) to provide three-year loans to indigenous entrepreneurs, especially those acquiring businesses from noncitizens through the government's program for the Kenyanization of trade. Between 1964 and 1975, more than 3,000 traders and industrialists received loans through the ICDC (Ochieng' 1989). Additionally, the government took a controlling interest in one of the largest foreign-owned banks, which was subsequently renamed the Kenya Commercial Bank. This bank increased lending to Kenyan nationals by 225% in the year after the government acquired its stake (Swainson 1980).[27]

REINTERPRETING THE BUSINESS–STATE RELATIONSHIP

Africanist scholars inspired by Marxist analytical approaches interpreted the tight embrace between politicians and entrepreneurs after independence as the consolidation of an elite ruling class. A dominant class representing an alliance of politicians, bureaucrats, and entrepreneurs was thought to have secured a hold over public institutions in order to serve private accumulation; they sought to control the apparatus of the state to monopolize access to the

---

[25] Licensing was the other mechanism used by African governments to promote indigenous participation in commerce. Licensing typically was used to restrict participation in areas such as retail trade, light manufacturing, and transport to indigenous merchants and traders. In Kenya, for example, the Trade Licensing Act of 1967 excluded noncitizens from trading in rural areas and specified a list of goods, often staples, that were restricted to indigenous traders. The Trade Licensing Act was amended in 1975 to require that all goods manufactured by foreign firms in Kenya were to be distributed through government-licensed traders (Swainson 1980).

[26] Indigenization was generally conceived of as a policy for reinforcing the economic independence of African countries by transferring foreign-owned assets to African control.

[27] The Kenyan government also placed restrictions on borrowing by foreign firms in 1974.

scarce goods of modernity. Invoking Michels, Sklar (1963, 1979) claimed it was "the fusion of elites" that fundamentally shaped the development of the Nigerian political system. Taking exception to ethnicized depictions of Nigerian politics, he saw elites cooperating across cleavages to protect their power and wealth at the expense of urban workers and rural farmers. Markovitz (1977, 1987) argued that these same elites constituted an "organizational bourgeoisie" that imposed a social order that maximized their political and economic power. According to Markovitz (1977, 261), business was an essential partner in that process: "virtually every government in every country, whether military or civilian, has increasingly sought the support of business as a political interest group.... African business must be counted a basic force in the consolidation of power." Bayart (1989) offered his own account in Gramscian terms, describing how elites striving for political hegemony employed "mechanisms of reciprocal assimilation" to forge a ruling class that cut across social cleavages.

These Marxist-influenced frameworks depicted state–capital cooperation as the inevitable manipulation of the state by capital. From this perspective, governments were thought to serve the interests of a rising indigenous bourgeoisie due to the structural dependence of the state on capital, as theorized more generally by scholars such as Block (1977) and Lindblom (1977).[28] This logic suggested that governments would be obliged to adopt policies in accordance with the preferences of the business sector because the material well-being of society, in terms of growth and employment, depends on the investment decisions made by individual entrepreneurs. And since this result would be produced structurally, business had no need to organize or lobby to bring about its preferred policies.[29] The expansion of credit programs and the establishment of state banks thus merely reflected the influence of a rising national bourgeoisie that sought to cement its control over society's productive resources (Wilson 1990). This became the standard narrative for countries such as Nigeria (Diamond 1987; Joseph 1984; Sklar 1963), Kenya (Kitching 1980; Leys 1974), and Côte d'Ivoire (Fauré and Médard 1982; Rapley 1993).

This class-based analysis, which became received wisdom among Africanist scholars by the late 1970s, usefully highlighted two intertwined stylized facts: first, that access to political power had become necessary for private accumulation; and second, that politicians and entrepreneurs had managed to establish

---

[28] Scholars informed by the dependency thinking of the time would claim that the indigenous bourgeoisie merely served as an intermediary for the interests of foreign capital. But the dependency framework was later shown to be inadequate for dealing with empirical realities on the ground. This is reflected in the intellectual trajectory of Leys (1974, 1978, 1982), who initially saw Kenyan entrepreneurs as junior partners of multinational capital in an economic system designed to keep their country dependent. He then updated his position based on new facts and saw Kenyan entrepreneurs as an independent class of actors.

[29] Przeworski and Wallerstein (1982) subsequently amended the logic of structural dependency, noting that almost any level of taxation is compatible with continued private investment. It is only when changes in taxation are anticipated, but not yet implemented, that investment might be reduced, thereby making the state dependent on capital during such periods.

a cooperative relationship toward that end. This analytical framework could seemingly explain how such a dynamic had been brought about without the aid of political institutions to constrain the inevitable conflict over the distribution of power and wealth, meaning that the entrepreneurs either controlled or bought off the politicians.

This Marxist-influenced analysis was flawed, however, because it mischaracterized the fundamental nature of the relationship between state and capital in Africa. The notion of structural dependence was, in reality, inverted: it was capital that was dependent on the state. African business had no structural power because the state, in supplanting the expatriate banks after independence, had effectively become the principal source of finance capital for indigenous entrepreneurs. The politicians in charge of this financier state understood the Keynesian insight: "It is not the ownership of the instruments of production which it is important for the state to assume. If the state is able to determine the aggregate amount of resources devoted to augmenting the instruments and the basic reward to those who own them, it will have accomplished all that is necessary" (Keynes 1964, 378). By exploiting their influence over the distribution of commercial credit and bank loans, politicians could directly control entrepreneurs.

Controlling business was a central concern for African leaders who headed brittle coalitions after independence (Bates 1981; Herbst 1990; Iliffe 1983; Kennedy 1988; Lewis 1965). Since entrepreneurs had already demonstrated a capacity to assist in the coordination of opposition during the late stages of colonialism – in a way that neither workers nor farmers had – nationalist politicians sought to avoid the replication of their own coalition-building strategy. The politicians who took control of the state feared, as Boone (1990, 429) explains, the emergence of an autonomous business sector free to accumulate resources that could then be deployed to mobilize challenges to their authority or to support their rivals for power. Even under the single-party system, when there were no outside alternatives for entrepreneurs to rally around, business resources could be used to orchestrate opposition within the ruling party. Nkrumah, who originally became the nationalist standard-bearer in Ghana by forming alliances with members of an aspiring commercial class, articulated precisely this logic to explain why he sought to constrain his erstwhile allies: "Any Ghanaian with a lot of money has a lot of influence; any Ghanaian with a lot of influence is a threat to me" (quoted in Esseks 1971, 61).[30]

African leaders had little need to invest in building new political institutions, as has often been suggested in the literature (Bienen 1967; Jackson and

[30] Nkrumah reportedly made this remark to one of his cabinet ministers, Kojo Botsio. Esseks (1971) notes that Nkrumah initially adopted policies that enabled indigenous entrepreneurs to compete with expatriate firms in a mixed economy. But once he had secured his hold on the state, and was guaranteed sufficient external resources from foreign sponsors, he began reneging on larger promises, such as the establishment of a bank for indigenous contractors, and increasingly diverted resources to the parastatal sector.

Rosberg 1982), because the economic institutions they inherited and honed sufficiently protected them from opposition. They could readily use the state's gatekeeping position in finance to constrain the economic, and thus political, autonomy of entrepreneurs.[31] Business could be compelled to ally with government as long as they depended on the state for the financing needed to sustain and expand their commercial activities. In this respect, African leaders pursued a strategy followed in many other post-colonial societies, where, as Chaudhry (1994, 6) observes, "the most intrusive policies of the state were aimed, not at supplementing private capital to promote international competitiveness, but rather at creating a national bourgeoisie which would support the state, if not mirror the ethnic, religious, sectarian, and tribal characteristics of the new political and military leadership."

Entrepreneurs, for their part, willingly accepted the Faustian bargain offered by their leaders, exchanging political loyalty for access to loan capital, because it represented their best option. While expatriate banks had largely retained orthodox lending requirements that few indigenous entrepreneurs could fulfill, and indigenous private banks remained too small and weak to meet local demand, the government offered a ready supply of cheap loans for a credit-starved business sector. In Cameroon, even as President Ahmadou Ahidjo progressively dismantled the federal institutions that once protected minority Anglophone interests in a largely Francophone country, the leading entrepreneurs from that region remained loyal to the ruling party because their access to credit had become politicized. The first indigenous bank of that region, Cameroon Bank, had become an auxiliary of the ruling party by providing preferential treatment to its members. "Loans were canceled as bad debts at the first sign of insolvency, while other portfolios were repayable in ninety years in a country where the average life expectancy did not exceed half that figure" (Kofele-Kale 1987, 159).

The multiple financial channels ostensibly created by African governments in support of indigenous business – state-owned banks, subsidized credit schemes, and sectoral loan programs – constituted a financial reprisal regime designed to insulate leaders from political challenges. Through a mix of inducements and constraints (Collier and Collier 1979), leaders could motivate the cooperation of specific segments of business by rewarding them with targeted credit facilities. They could divert financing to coopted entrepreneurs who willingly became their allies.[32] Or, without having to resort to coercion, they could

---

[31] The financial power of African states was augmented by their broader statist economic policies. Governments not only provided finance capital to the private sector; they also directly controlled whole segments of the economy, expanding the state's role as owner of the factors of production as well as consumer of goods and services produced by the private sector (Sandbrook 1985).

[32] The benefits of politicizing finance were recognized even before independence in some countries. In Nigeria, regional development boards channeled loans to supporters of whichever party controlled the regional government (Harnett-Sievers 1995; Sklar 1963). In Kenya, when the Local Native Councils made up of local notables were empowered to extend loans to indigenous businesses, many of those loans went to the notables themselves (Kitching 1980).

discipline errant entrepreneurs by threatening to cut off their access to those facilities. This arrangement served both sides. For leaders, financial institutions provided corporatist-like structures to regulate the relationship between their governments and business, the segment of society most likely to mount or support a rival to their rule.[33] It thus enabled them to neutralize business as a source of opposition. For entrepreneurs, the financial reprisal regime, while raising the costs of political opposition, permitted them to secure the capital required to expand their participation in the market, making them unambiguously better off economically.[34]

Boone (1992) provides one of the best documented cases of how financial controls worked in tandem with a larger set of statist economic measures to induce the political cooperation of business. Her study of Senegal shows how Léopold Sédar Senghor's regime consolidated its hold on power by using contracts and licenses alongside credit to tightly bind the business class to the ruling party. Besides distributing rent-generating privileges, Senghor's government instituted multiple facilities for allocating short-term credit, long-term loans, and investment capital to entrepreneurs affiliated with his party. This lending amounted to free money for the politically connected because the government only selectively enforced repayment. Entrepreneurs who depended on the government's discretion for continued access to subsidized credit or free loans had little incentive to disrupt the status quo by encouraging outside rivals for power or backing rebel factions within the ruling party – just as Senghor had intended.

While nearly all African leaders developed a financial reprisal regime to bring business into the state's embrace, the mix of inducements and constraints varied from country to country.[35] At one extreme, the leaders of socialist governments, such as those that dominated Ethiopia and Tanzania up to the late 1980s, were more likely to impose constraints on credit to business and divert capital to the parastatal sector.[36] Yet, in Uganda, President Milton Obote, whose government pursued socialist economic policies that favored the parastatal

---

[33] African single-party regimes attempted to approximate the corporatist ideal-type by regulating the relationship between the state and functional interest groups through formal organizations and peak associations (Callaghy 1984; Shaw 1982). In practice, however, they achieved mixed results, since not all developed the state capacity required to sustain such arrangements (Nyang'oro and Shaw 1989).

[34] The manipulation of financial controls, along with economic controls more generally, can lead to plunder rather than accumulation, as occurred in Zaire (e.g., MacGaffey 1987). But it was mainly the politicians who plundered in cases like Liberia, Uganda, and Zaire, since the application of economic controls in those cases had essentially forced entrepreneurs out of the formal economy. Such instances thus perhaps reflect the extent to which leaders sought to weaken, if not eliminate, a country's business class as a whole.

[35] The exact mix of constraints and inducements would most likely follow Iliffe's (1983) typology of business-state relations in African countries: anticapitalist, parasitic, and laissez-faire. For case studies that reflect this variation, see the chapters in Berman and Leys (1994).

[36] Kennedy (1988) suggests these states were also more likely to accord preferential access to foreign firms or expatriate merchants because they were perceived as being less likely to become politicized.

sector, still created loan facilities that were targeted at entrepreneurs linked to his ruling party (Mamdani 1976).[37] At the other extreme, governments that promoted capitalist development, as in Kenya and Nigeria, were more likely to offer credit-based inducements to business. Nonetheless, even among these countries, measures were taken to reinforce the state's gatekeeping position. In Côte d'Ivoire, where private sector growth was encouraged, President Félix Houphouët-Boigny took conscious steps to ensure that the state, through its commercial banks and other financial institutions, became the principal source of credit for business (Boone 1993; de Miras 1982).

CONCLUSION

The theory of pecuniary coalition building underscores the resource constraints encountered by opposition politicians in forging electoral alliances in patronage-based, multiethnic polities. This chapter has presented essential background for understanding the argument's causal logic by explaining how the access to capital first became politicized in African countries. Financial reprisal regimes were established by Africa's founding leaders to coopt and control the segment of society that had already proven its capacity to mobilize opposition: business.

---

[37] Mamdani (1976) suggests that part of Obote's objective in targeting credit was to offset the influence of the Baganda bourgeoisie and Asian commercial community.

4

The Political Control of Banking

> The winning of political freedom for Nigeria will be meaningless and will be lacking in reality if Nigerians are unable to win economic freedom at the same time. Any country which is free politically but whose banking operations are controlled from outside its territorial limits is not truly free.
>
> Nnamdi Azikiwe, premier of Nigeria's Eastern Region, 1959[1]

Independence represented a critical juncture at which Africa's founding leaders chose the political strategies that would set their countries on distinct trajectories of financial system development. The previous chapter suggested that these leaders were concerned with regulating the access to capital for fear that such resources could be turned against them. This chapter now nuances that claim by demonstrating that African leaders responded differently to the perceived threat of capital accumulation, depending on whether it would benefit their own constituents or those of rival politicians. I argue that a leader's constituency type, exporter versus nonexporter, affected the severity of that perceived threat and thereby the extent to which leaders would seek to directly control commercial banking. Limiting the number of banks provided these leaders with a mechanism for institutionalizing executive discretion over the flow of capital.

My claim is that founding leaders who emerged from constituencies that directly profited from increased access to the financial sector were more likely to use inducements to bind business to their regimes. Their constituencies were composed of ethnic groups that grew cash crops for export; they could readily amass a bankable surplus that would enable them to enter other sectors of the economy. The leaders from these groups provided a form of constituency service by allowing the number of commercial banks to expand over time. The easy accumulation among such groups, however, posed a threat to leaders

---

[1] This passage comes from a speech delivered by Azikiwe (1961) at the opening of a new branch of the African Continental Bank, which had been used to finance the election campaigns of his party, the National Council of Nigeria and the Cameroons (NCNC). Azikiwe would go on to become Nigeria's first president once the country was declared a republic in 1963.

whose own coethnics did not produce cash crops and would therefore not immediately benefit from increased access to financial services. I maintain that founding leaders from nonexporting constituencies – whose economic activities focused on subsistence agriculture or the production of food crops for domestic consumption – responded to that threat by limiting entry into commercial banking. Fearing that resources accrued by protocapitalists from other groups could be used to mobilize opposition, these leaders were motivated to closely control banking and impose constraints on credit provision.

By delineating a mechanism by which post-independence political incentives induced African leaders to structure banking, I offer an alternative to the standard view represented by the law and finance literature, namely, that financial development is determined by a country's colonial history (La Porta et al. 1998). According to this account, former British colonies should be expected to have a larger number of commercial banks than former French colonies. The British common law tradition is thought to facilitate financial development by affording greater protection to creditors, investors, and shareholders, while the French civil code tradition discourages such development by empowering the state vis-à-vis private firms. In the African context, moreover, France had set an example for its colonies by nationalizing the country's major banks in 1945. The regulatory institutions established at the same time were not only expressly designed to prevent banks from acting contrary to state policy, but they were also later adopted wholesale when France's colonies became independent (Alibert and Sathoud 1975).[2] The state's role in the provision of credit had also been actively promoted in France's colonies prior to independence.[3]

I proceed in this chapter by first explaining why the post-independence extension of banking was expected to produce unequal rates of capital accumulation among exporter and nonexporter constituencies. I then describe the political rationale of independence-era leaders who sought to control access to finance through the commercial banking sector. Using data on the number of commercial banks in African countries from 1945 through 2000, I provide empirical evidence that challenges the standard, pre-independence, explanations offered

[2] The nationalization of France's largest banks at the end of 1945 was mainly intended to promote the efficient allocation of resources in accelerating the country's postwar recovery, though the move was partly motivated by the desire to punish collaborationist firms (Kuisel 1983). The institutions tasked with controlling banking were the Conseil National du Crédit, the Commission de Contrôle des Banques, and the Association Professionnelle des Banques. Headed by the minister of finance, the Conseil National du Crédit was responsible for structuring the organization of banking and allocating credit among banks and sectors. The actual policing of banks was delegated to Commission de Contrôle des Banques, while the Association Professionnelle des Banques coordinated agreements among banks on sectoral and technical issues (Wilson 1957).
[3] France established the Caisse Centrale de la France d'Outre-Mer (CCOM), which later became the Caisse Centrale de Coopération Economic (CCCE). This agency channeled funds to private enterprises as well as development projects through existing private banks and facilitated the creation of local state banks. On the eve of independence, it had become the most important source of credit in less developed economies such as Madagascar and the equatorial states of Chad and Congo (Thompson and Adloff 1960, 1965).

to account for the cross-national variation in financial development. I show instead that the cross-national and diachronic differences among African countries are best explained through the political incentives of post-independence leaders. Banking systems implanted by founding leaders from exporter constituencies, when compared to their nonexporter counterparts, permitted the entry of five to six additional banks. This is a considerable difference in small, developing economies.

UNEQUAL CAPITAL ACCUMULATION ACROSS CONSTITUENCIES

Foreign-owned banks largely made up the banking sector in African colonies prior to independence, and they proved to be remarkably capable of adapting to the economic as well as political empowerment of Africans. Despite facing the loss of a privileged relationship with colonial authorities – and having become a target of criticism by the very nationalist politicians who were expected to take power – foreign-owned banks chose to expand rather than contract their operations as the end of colonial rule approached (Engberg and Hance 1969; Kahler 1981). As Figure 4.1 illustrates, between the end of the Second World War and the eve of independence, the average number of banks in African territories doubled from 2.38 in 1945 to 4.77 in 1965.[4] London-based Barclays Bank and Standard Bank, for example, opened new offices throughout British-held territories in East and West Africa and proceeded to extend their branch networks within each colony from administrative capitals to rural market towns.[5] Crédit Lyonnais and Société Générale, headquartered in Paris, followed a similar pattern, albeit at a slower pace, in the French territories of West and Equatorial Africa. By the mid-1950s, bank offices had been opened even in previously ignored hinterland territories like Bechuanaland, Oubangui-Chari, and Upper Volta.

Rising commodity prices fueled Africa's pre-independence banking expansion. Banking in Africa had originated with the demand for financing of the commodity trade, providing the credit modalities that facilitated the purchase, transport, and shipment of cash crops. The potential for harnessing African deposits, however, had become apparent even before the Second World War. In French West Africa, the number of African savings accounts continued to grow despite the onset of the Great Depression, surpassing the number of European savings accounts by 1936 (Coquery-Vidrovitch 1977).[6] After the

---

[4] These figures represent the number of commercial banks within each country and not the number of branches operated by these banks. The bank numbers are estimated at five-year intervals from volumes of *Rand McNally International Bankers Directory* (Rand McNally and Company 1945–1965) and *Africa South of the Sahara* (Europa Publications Limited 1971–2006).

[5] Engberg and Hance (1969) note that by the mid-1960s, 76% of all bank branches in former British colonies were in towns with fewer than 10,000 inhabitants; in former French colonies, nearly 60% of branches were outside the top three urban areas.

[6] The French government had sought to encourage savings among farmers by instituting *sociétés de prèvoyance* in West and Equatorial Africa during the interwar period. Headed by local

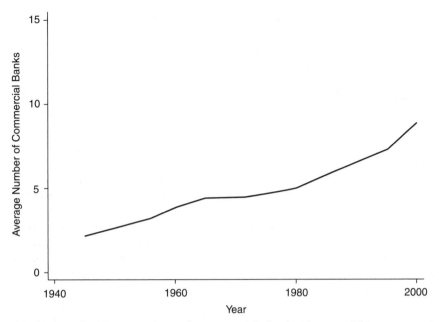

FIGURE 4.1. Average number of commercial banks in 27 African countries, 1945–2000.
Source: Author's calculations based on annual entries in *Rand McNally International Bankers Directory* and *Africa South of the Sahara.*

Second World War, following increasing world prices for crops such as cocoa, coffee, and groundnuts, the rising real incomes of cash crop farmers presented a new opportunity for expatriate banks (Fieldhouse 1986; Gann and Duignan 1975; Thompson and Adloff 1975). In the case of Kenya, the expansion of banking in the decade leading up to independence was directly attributed to "the growing importance of African farming and trading enterprise and of the rising African wage bill" (McWilliam 1962, 26). More generally, as newly independent African governments transferred accounts to their central banks, the foreign-owned banks sought to compensate for the loss of official colonial deposits by opening branches that would attract the accumulated savings of Africans associated with the production and trade of cash crops (Alibert and Sathoud 1975; Crick 1965; Decker 2005; Uche 1998).

Banks such as Barclays expected their reputational advantage as long-solvent institutions to facilitate their growth among potential African depositors despite

colonial administrators, these credit and cooperative associations were locally funded and operated. Their functions included extending credit to farmers and managing communal granaries. However, the *sociétés* failed to realize their intended goals. African farmers resisted participating in a forced savings program, referring to their mandatory dues as a *petit impôt*, or a little tax. Moreover, colonial administrators who enjoyed wide discretion in the allocation of credit inconsistently and poorly managed the program (Mann and Guyer 1999).

the emerging competition from indigenous and state-owned banks (Ackrill and Hannah 2001; Vander Weyer 2000). Chronicling the history of the British Bank of West Africa (BBWA), Fry (1976, 204) notes that during "these years of deliberate expansion the Bank's commercial deposits increased so massively that they easily offset the loss of governmental deposits when these were transferred to the new African banks."[7] In cocoa-exporting Gold Coast, for example, BBWA tripled the number of its branches between 1952 and 1962, while Barclays quadrupled the size of its own branch network in the same period. Across East African territories, which produced coffee, cotton, and sisal, the number of deposits nearly doubled between 1950 and 1963. At the same time, the number of bank branches quadrupled in Kenya and tripled in Tanzania and Uganda (Engberg 1965).

As the slope in Figure 4.1 indicates, banking expanded across Africa between 1945 and 1965. It was in this period that the relationship between banking and commodity production became physically cemented. Banks systematically extended their branch networks according to the geography of cash crop production (Engberg and Hance 1969). They were, in this way, replacing the withdrawing European trading companies that had provided credit services for African produce buyers and traders from the turn of the century through the Second World War. Up to that point, banks had financed the commodity trade indirectly by extending credit facilities to trading companies like Lever Brothers and United Africa Company, which then offered credit to their own brokers in cash crop growing regions (Crick 1965; Fry 1976; Newlyn and Rowan 1954). These trading companies effectively maintained the credit system in rural areas where their commodities were produced. As one contemporary commentator observed, "the African trader's best source of credit is probably the large expatriate importer. The United Africa Company, for example, has 5,000 credit customers in Ghana and 30 percent of its business is done on credit terms.... In turn, most of the big African traders give credit, on a smaller scale, to their own African customers" (Hunter 1962, 139).

The system of indirect credit came undone in the 1950s as wartime marketing boards were institutionalized as the sole legal buyers of commodities on behalf of colonial and then African governments.[8] The marketing boards, however, did not fully replace the credit system previously sustained by the trading firms. Exploiting this gap in financial services, expatriate banks expanded their operations strategically by moving into areas where they could take deposits from, and extend credit to, farmers and traders in relatively prosperous cash crop–growing regions. These foreign-owned banks made their location

[7] Fry (1976) suggests that the metropolitan banks, such as the British Bank of West Africa (BBWA), exploited the fact that some of their African clientele preferred to do business with expatriate bank managers rather than indigenous bank staff. BBWA was renamed the Bank of West Africa in 1957 and then acquired by Standard Bank in 1965.

[8] Marketing boards had been set up to deal with the exigencies of the wartime economy. Among the British colonies, for example, the Ministry of Food took over the purchase of cocoa in 1939. By 1942, the West African Produce Control Board was created to take over the marketing of cocoa, palm oil, and groundnuts (Meredith 1986).

choices by recognizing the inequalities that Arthur Lewis saw when touring West Africa's newly independent countries: "An area which has seventy inches of rain, and grows cocoa, coffee or bananas has a per capita income perhaps five times as high as that of an area in the same country, 200 miles away, which has only thirty inches of rain and lives at subsistence level" (Lewis 1965, 24).

African nationalists, too, recognized the political import of the inequalities between cash crop exporting and nonexporting communities, increasingly magnified by their unequal access to credit. These growing differences were inevitably a source of tension within the coalitions organized to agitate for independence. As Morgenthau (1964, 332) notes in her study of early party mobilization in Francophone Africa, when compared to the inland savannahs of West African countries, "[m]uch more economic activity took place in the coastal and forest belt.... This caused trouble both for parties and for nations." But politicians sought to downplay these inequalities in the interest of holding together the nationalist coalitions that might propel them to power. They managed to do so, in part, by promising to make credit available for Africans as a whole, as Nnamdi Azikiwe does in the epigraph to this chapter. Politicians of all ideological stripes claimed that post-independence governments would intervene in the financial sector to correct market failures through the state ownership of banks and the administrative allocation of credit according to development priorities. And these politicians were true to their word: they actively involved their governments in the financial sector after independence. However, it was the political imperative of staying in office, and not the nationalist goal of making credit widely available, which largely guided their interventions.

A POLITICAL RATIONALE FOR CONTROLLING BANKING

I argue that politics shaped the post-independence development of African commercial banking. Africa's founding leaders feared that an emerging business class might use their resources to orchestrate opposition to their regimes – just as they had supported the nationalist movements that had challenged colonial authorities. Having inherited state instruments that allowed for the control of capital, these new leaders sought to structure the financial systems of their countries to produce a compliant business class and thereby reinforce their hold on power. The degree to which they sought to directly control banking, in particular, reflected the threat posed by capital accumulation among distinct constituencies, exporters versus nonexporters. Employing the notion of inducements and constraints, as defined by Collier and Collier (1979),[9] I claim that founding leaders from cash crop exporter constituencies relied on inducements to coopt the business class, while their counterparts from nonexporter constituencies used constraints to render business incapable of acting autonomously.

---

[9] Collier and Collier (1979) originally employed the notion of inducements and constraints to distinguish the strategies used by different Latin American regimes to control labor.

Founding leaders from exporter constituencies established commercial banking systems with relatively open entry as an inducement for business' support. Since they expected to derive political benefits from the accumulation of capital among their own constituents, these leaders sought to shore up their support by following a policy of banking expansion. Cash crop farmers not only were more likely to accumulate a bankable surplus because they grew lucrative commodities, but they were also better positioned to use formal credit to enter other sectors of the economy. Traders who operated among these groups were similarly able to take advantage of short-term loans to purchase stocks, pay for imports, and carry billings. These farmers and traders, enjoying access to privately owned banks without the intervention of the state, had little incentive to seek alternative leadership within their own groups or to defect in support of politicians from other groups, particularly since they might well expect politicians from other groups to pursue policies favoring their own constituencies while passing along the costs to them.

Founding leaders from nonexporter constituencies, those engaged in subsistence agriculture or the production of food crops, sought to constrain business by restricting entry into the commercial banking sector. Anticipating that the proto-capitalists among cash crop growers might use their resource advantage to support a rival politician, leaders from nonexporting constituencies had every reason to restrict access to banking. A small number of banks, especially if state owned, would permit these leaders to determine who could access capital and on what terms. And these leaders could translate that financial discretion into political advantage. Their ability to allocate credit and loans would mean they could determine which individuals could accumulate wealth *ex ante*, ensuring that the interests of business would be aligned with those of the regime, as often occurred in post-colonial settings in other parts of the world (Chaudhry 1997). Rather than attempting to expropriate the wealth of business *ex post*, vigorously guarding the gate to capital markets would provide leaders with a more effective, and less costly, means of minimizing the likelihood of future political threats emanating from business.

The logic advanced above is consistent with comparative research suggesting that banking systems reflect configurations of state–capital relations (Boone 2005) and the influence of political institutions (Haber et al. 2008). It builds on a literature showing that African leaders have pursued distinct strategies to control differently endowed groups. Bates (1981) explains how leaders sought to reinforce their hold on power by catering to urban and industrial interest groups as well as offering favorable prices to agricultural exporters from their own ethnic bases. Boone (2003) shows that central governments developed alternative arrangements for governing different regions, depending on whether local elites controlled land and labor through pre-existing social structures. Azam (2005) provides a model in which regimes face different constraints in committing to redistribution, and therefore securing peace, depending on whether the group in power happens to be rich or poor. Kasara (2007) finds that incumbents adjust taxation according to the information and control they can exert through local intermediaries, which means they can afford to impose higher taxes on their own coethnics.

My contribution to this literature is in establishing that African leaders have systematically manipulated commercial banking systems for political ends as a function of their relationship to different types of constituencies. Controlling entry into banking provided these leaders a simple and direct mechanism for institutionalizing executive discretion over the flow of capital. The granting of bank charters was not only a political act, but also one that could be easily adapted according to a leader's constituency type. The pre-independence expansion of banking had visibly occurred along a commodity-based geography – and geography overlaps with ethnic identity and agricultural production in most African countries (Posner 2004; Scarritt and Mozaffar 1999) – so politicians well understood whether their own constituencies would profit from the extension of financial services after independence. In this context, banks were effectively transformed into government agents in policing the accumulation of wealth among business.

While all African leaders could employ the full panoply of instruments to manage the allocation of scarce credit – capital controls, foreign exchange quotas, and sector-specific interest rates – regulating entry into the commercial banking sector conferred special advantages. As Zysman (1983, 77) explains, "credit allocation is a universal tool, one that eliminates the need to find specific authority to influence specific decisions or to control an agency that has formal authority over a specific policy instrument." Control over banks enhanced their discretion in this respect, politically as well as administratively. Unlike with fiscal decisions, a leader had no need to negotiate with the party or the legislature because the country's finance ministry could usually grant banking charters as a regulatory or technical issue under its own jurisdiction. Restricting banking entry further permitted leaders to delegate the task of controlling credit to the banks without having to build and sustain a large administrative apparatus, as they would have to do in the case of taxation. The banks, whether private or public, could be made responsible for carrying out political directives in channeling credit to privileged individuals or prioritized groups.

In manipulating the banking system to accord with their political needs, Africa's founding leaders took steps that had a lasting impact on the financial development of their countries and, by extension, on the relationship between entrepreneurs and politicians. The rules and practices established to constrain business after independence created a considerable degree of path dependence over subsequent decades. These constraints, once in place, set in motion a dynamic that became self-reinforcing over time by shaping expectations, and payoffs, on both sides of the business–state relationship. Successive leaders in charge of the state, regardless of how they came to power, would find that exerting control over capital was politically advantageous. These leaders would quickly learn that restricting business' access to finance provided an effective means of neutralizing a potential source of opposition. And, since the policy instruments needed to control that access were already in place, it proved relatively costless for new leaders to simply continue utilizing them.

Entrepreneurs operating under conditions of restricted financial access would have an incentive to continue relying on personalized political relationships. Because capital markets have historically been small and weak across much of Africa, with only a handful of countries having stock markets, business has had to rely on commercial banks for financial capital. In this context, the political mediation of banking rewarded individual opportunism at the cost of collective action by business as a whole. Entrepreneurs understood that they were more likely to secure a line of credit by cooperating with, rather than challenging, whoever was in office. Moreover, concerted action by entrepreneurs to demand financial reform was made even less likely by the increasing complexity of the relevant regulations, especially when they could be tailored by governments to discriminate among different types of economic actors or sectors.

POLITICAL CONSTITUENCIES AND COMMERCIAL BANKING SECTOR SIZE

The argument outlined earlier suggests a straightforward hypothesis: African countries where founding leaders emerged from exporter constituencies should have a larger number of commercial banks when compared with countries where founding leaders emerged from nonexporter constituencies. Table 4.1 provides the data needed to test this claim, listing the founding leaders and commodity exports for African countries that gained independence before 1970.[10] Constituencies are classified as exporters or nonexporters by establishing whether the leader's ethnic group produced one of the country's two largest commodity exports, in terms of total dollar value, at independence.[11] Leaders whose coethnics produced such commodities are coded as having an exporter constituency. For example, Kenya's independence leader, Jomo Kenyatta, is coded as having an exporter constituency because his Kikuyu coethnics were among the country's main coffee growers (Bates 1989). Leaders whose coethnics did not participate in the production of such crops are coded as having a nonexporter constituency. Cameroon's independence leader, Ahmadou Ahidjo, is coded as having a nonexporter constituency because his northern

---

[10] Limiting the sample to countries that achieved independence before 1970 excludes the Portuguese colonies. Their armed struggle for independence, animated by socialist ideology and Soviet aid, overdetermined their stance on commercial banking: Angola and Mozambique immediately nationalized banking and reduced commercial banking to one institution. Guinea-Bissau had only one bank at the time of independence.

[11] The two largest commodity exports were identified for each country through the Food and Agriculture Organization (FAO) of the United Nations (http://faostat.fao.org/). The identified commodities are from the years 1961 to 1965. See Appendix B for secondary materials consulted to determine whether the leader's coethnics participated in the production of these crops.

TABLE 4.1. *Commodity Exports, Independence Leader, and Constituency Type by Country*

Country	Independence Leader	Commodities	Constituency
Benin	Hubert Maga (1960–63)	Palm kernels	Nonexporter
Botswana	Seretse Khama (1966–80)	Cattle meat	Exporter
Burkina Faso	Maurice Yameogo (1960–66)	Cotton, shea nuts	Nonexporter
Burundi	André Muhirwa (1962–63)	Coffee, cotton	Exporter
Cameroon	Ahmadou Ahidjo (1960–82)	Cocoa, coffee	Nonexporter
Central African Republic	David Dacko (1960–66)	Cotton, coffee	Nonexporter
Chad	François Tombalbaye (1960–75)	Cotton, millet	Exporter
Congo, Republic	Fulbert Youlou (1960–63)	Sugar, palm kernels	Nonexporter
Côte d'Ivoire	Félix Houphouët-Boigny (1960–93)	Coffee, cocoa	Exporter
Gabon	Léon M'Ba (1960–67)	Cocoa, coffee	Exporter
Gambia	Dawda Jawara (1965–94)	Groundnuts	Exporter
Ghana	Kwame Nkrumah (1957–66)	Cocoa	Nonexporter
Guinea	Ahmed Sékou Touré (1958–84)	Coffee, bananas	Nonexporter
Kenya	Jomo Kenyatta (1963–78)	Coffee, tea	Exporter
Madagascar	Philibert Tsiranana (1960–72)	Coffee, vanilla	Nonexporter
Malawi	Hastings Kamuzu Banda (1964–94)	Tobacco, tea	Nonexporter
Mali	Modibo Keïta (1960–68)	Groundnuts, cotton	Nonexporter
Mauritius	Seewoosagur Ramgoolam (1968–82)	Sugar	Exporter
Niger	Hamani Diori (1960–74)	Groundnuts, millet	Nonexporter
Nigeria	Abubakar Balewa (1960–66)	Cocoa, groundnuts	Exporter
Rwanda	Grégoire Kayibanda (1962–73)	Coffee	Exporter
Senegal	Léopold Sédar Senghor (1960–80)	Groundnuts	Exporter
Sierra Leone	Milton Margai (1961–64)	Palm kernels, coffee	Nonexporter
Tanzania	Julius Nyerere (1964–85)	Sisal, cotton	Nonexporter
Togo	Sylvanus Olympio (1960–63)	Cocoa, coffee	Exporter
Uganda	Milton Obote (1962–71)	Coffee, cotton	Nonexporter
Zambia	Kenneth Kaunda (1964–91)	Tobacco	Nonexporter

Note: The data on commodity exports for the years 1961–1965 are from the Food and Agriculture Organization (FAO) of the United Nations. The data are available at http://faostat. fao.org/. See Appendix B for additional secondary sources used to code constituency type.

Fulbe ethnic group did not cultivate either of the country's main crops, cocoa and coffee; they were produced by southern ethnic groups such as the Bamileke and the Beti-related Bulu and Ewondo (Joseph 1977).

An informed student of African politics would note one distinct pattern regarding ideology in Table 4.1. The region's most prominent socialists from the 1960s through the 1980s – Kenneth Kaunda, Modibo Keïta, Milton Obote, Kwame Nkrumah, Julius Nyerere, and Ahmed Sékou Touré – seem to be over-represented among the leaders identified with nonexporter constituencies. This begs the question of whether the leftist orientation of these leaders was endogenous to the economic profile of their constituencies. That would be too strong a claim to sustain here, particularly when leaders with exporter constituencies, such as Jomo Kenyatta and Léopold Sédar Senghor, espoused principles of African socialism to varying degrees. Indeed, socialist principles were rarely fully implemented even by the most avowed leftists (Arrighi and Saul 1968; Jackson and Rosberg 1982). One could speculate, nevertheless, on how the worldview of socialist leaders may have been originally shaped by the economic position of their constituencies. Being raised in communities that derived little benefit from the cash economy under colonialism, either because they relied on subsistence agriculture or were largely pastoralist, would have certainly influenced these men intellectually as well as professionally. The socioeconomic dislocations that emerged in the decades preceding independence would have prompted them to question the rationality of maintaining the economic institutions implanted by their colonizers. These leaders would have been receptive to a state-led model that promised to correct structural constraints, redistribute resources, promote egalitarianism, and reduce dependence on international markets. Moreover, the preference of these leaders for centralizing control over the means of production may have reflected their life experiences. Because they were from economically marginal regions, many of these men ascended professionally through the civil service instead of commerce. Their formative experiences working within the state would have informed their views of how the bureaucracy, rather than the market, could be deployed to develop society's productive potential.

Beyond ideology, the less obvious classifications in Table 4.1 can be used to illuminate the argument's underlying logic. Consider the case of Nigeria, where Abubakar Tafawa Balewa became the country's prime minister at independence.[12] Balewa, a northerner, is coded as having an exporter constituency despite the conventional association of Nigeria's southern ethnic groups with economic influence. Southern groups were, of course, in direct contact with the Atlantic trade for far longer, and they cultivated the country's predominant cash crop, cocoa, in the southwest. Nevertheless, Table 4.1 identifies Balewa as having an exporter constituency because the groundnut trade constituted

---

[12] Balewa's party, the Northern Peoples' Congress (NPC), was the senior partner in the coalition that formed Nigeria's first post-independence government along with Nnamdi Azikiwe's National Council of Nigeria and the Cameroons (NCNC).

the economic engine of his natal region from the time of the First World War through the 1970s. The Lagos-Kano rail line, after opening in 1912, permitted the groundnut export to flourish by connecting northern inland areas to international markets (Hogendorn 1978; Shenton 1986). At independence in 1960, Nigeria had become the world's top producer of groundnuts, a position it held through the early 1970s. Groundnuts constituted the country's second-largest export after cocoa during this time period. Between 1961 and 1971, the groundnut trade equaled approximately 80% of the total dollar value of cocoa exports. It exceeded the total value of cocoa exports in 1963 and 1966.[13]

Balewa's party, the Northern Peoples' Congress (NPC), represented the merchants and traders whose livelihoods were tied to the groundnut trade. Many of these individuals had not only expanded into other sectors of the economy, but also formed an integral part of the NPC (Sklar 1963, 324–336). Their accumulation of capital posed little threat to Balewa or to other NPC leaders.[14] To the contrary, because the NPC was pitted against other regional parties in a contest for national power, greater economic opportunities for northern entrepreneurs could only have been seen as advancing the NPC's political prospects.[15] The two sides developed a symbiotic relationship as a result: politicians expected entrepreneurs to cultivate mass support for their party and entrepreneurs relied on politicians for expanded economic opportunities. And the party did ensure that its members were favored as British colonial authorities relaxed political and economic restrictions. In the early 1950s, after regional elections enabled the NPC to take control of the Northern Region's House of Assembly, the Groundnut Marketing Board recognized two NPC financiers, Alhassan Dantata and Ibrahim Gashash, as its very first indigenous licensed buying agents (Loimeier 1997, 91–92).[16] Additional licenses for local traders were allocated to NPC supporters (Clough and Williams 1987, 179). After independence, the NPC continued expanding its merchant members' access to capital by having the regional government finance individual loans and offer overdraft guarantees through existing commercial banks. This was achieved by diverting taxes collected on the region's agricultural output by the state-controlled marketing system (Forrest 1994, 199; Hogendorn 1978, 142). The NPC's continued service to northern entrepreneurs, in Sklar's assessment (1963, 494), would effectively transform the Bank of the North, the Loans Board of the

---

[13] All statistics are from the FAO of the United Nations (http://faostat.fao.org/).

[14] The fact that Balewa did not head the NPC, despite being prime minister of the national government, reinforces the point that he was an agent of northern interests. Balewa served as the party's vice president, while Ahmadu Bello, the premier of the Northern Region, remained president.

[15] Each of Nigeria's original three regions was dominated by a different party: the Action Group became the Yoruba party of the Western Region, the National Council for Nigeria and the Cameroons was the Igbo party of Eastern Region, and the Northern Peoples' Congress the Hausa-Fulani party of Northern Region.

[16] The Groundnut Marketing Board had previously set the requirements for licensed buying agents so that only foreign firms could afford to qualify.

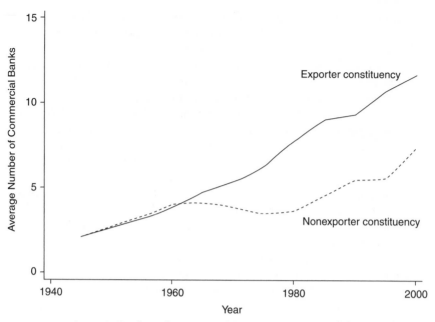

FIGURE 4.2. Average number of commercial banks by leader's constituency type. *Source:* Author's calculations based on annual entries in *Rand McNally International Bankers Directory* and *Africa South of the Sahara.*

Northern Region Development Corporation, and the Northern Amalgamated Merchants' Union into the party's "unofficial apparatus" of power.

Figure 4.2 provides a simple cross-national test of the hypothesis, showing the average number of commercial banks according to a founding leader's constituency.[17] The trend lines between 1945 and 2000 unambiguously corroborate the logic of the argument in two ways. First, the divergence in the trend lines occurs when expected – after 1960. This suggests that whatever difference eventually emerged among Africa's commercial banking sectors, its origin is unlikely to be found in the pre-independence period. The trend lines are virtually indistinguishable from 1945 to 1960, when banking decisions were being made in London, Paris, and Brussels during the colonial period. In 1945, the average number of banks is 2.1 in countries where leaders from exporter constituencies eventually took power; it is also 2.1 among countries with leaders from nonexporter constituencies. By 1960, the average rises to 3.8 for exporters and 4 for nonexporters. The marked divergence between the two trend lines

---

[17] The bank numbers are estimated at five-year intervals from volumes of *Rand McNally International Bankers Directory* (Rand McNally and Company 1945–1965) and *Africa South of the Sahara* (Europa Publications Limited 1971–2006). This count is limited to commercial banks. It does not include central banks, development banks, or specialized banks in areas such as agriculture or housing.

begins only after 1960, as African countries were becoming independent and banking decisions were being repatriated to their respective capitals.

Second, the post-1960 divergence in the trend lines moves as expected. Additional commercial banks appear to enter the sector nearly unabated where independence leaders had little to fear from the accumulation of capital among their own exporter constituencies. The sector's growth is arrested, however, among countries where leaders from nonexporter constituencies sought to restrict the number of new banks in order to exercise greater control over access to finance. Although there was almost no difference in the average number of banks between the two types of countries in 1960, within a decade of that watershed year, the countries led by exporter-friendly leaders had already begun to expand with an average of 5.4 banks versus 3.8 banks in countries headed by nonexporter leaders. The commercial banking sector was virtually frozen among this latter set of countries for the first twenty years after independence; their average remained 3.7 by 1980.

The data in Table 4.1 indicate, moreover, that there is no direct relationship between colonial legacy and the number of commercial banks, as would otherwise be suggested by the legal traditions argument (La Porta et al. 1998). The eleven former British colonies are nearly equally divided between five leaders from exporter constituencies and six from nonexporter constituencies. The leaders in former French colonies appear to be less likely to have emerged from exporter constituencies: only five of the fourteen had such constituencies at independence. In Chad, François Tombalbaye's Sara coethnics participated in the production of cotton (Lemarchand 1980); in Côte d'Ivoire, the Baoule coethnics of Félix Houphouët-Boigny cultivated coffee and cocoa (Woods 2003); in Gabon, the Fang coethnics of Léon M'Ba harvested cocoa (Rich 2007); in Senegal, Léopold Sédar Senghor's Serer participated in groundnut production along with the more dominant Wolof (Cruise O'Brien 1998); and in Togo, Sylvanus Olympio's Ewe also harvested cocoa (Amenumey 1989). The relative paucity of Francophone leaders from export constituencies could be due to the influence of centralizing institutions, which may have enabled ambitious politicians from peripheral regions to become involved in nationalist parties at the center (Collier 1982). Such institutions would certainly interact with the unfortunate geography of these colonies. A cursory glance at a colonial map shows that France's possessions were more irregularly shaped than Britain's, with territories stretching into less fertile areas of the continent's interior. This, too, would increase the number of groups that did not participate in cash crop production. Consider the shapes of Mali and Niger. The founding leader in each of these countries emerged from a nonexporting constituency.

Figures 4.3 and 4.4 make clear that colonial legacy cannot explain either the cross-national or the diachronic variation seen in African commercial banking. The number of banks does grow more quickly after 1960 in former British colonies. But the divergence between exporter and nonexporter constituencies persists across both colonial systems. These patterns suggest that, regardless of the institutions inherited at independence, founding leaders had

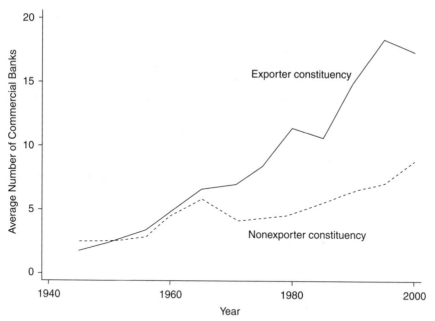

FIGURE 4.3. Average number of commercial banks in former British colonies.
Source: Author's calculations based on annual entries in *Rand McNally International Bankers Directory* and *Africa South of the Sahara*.

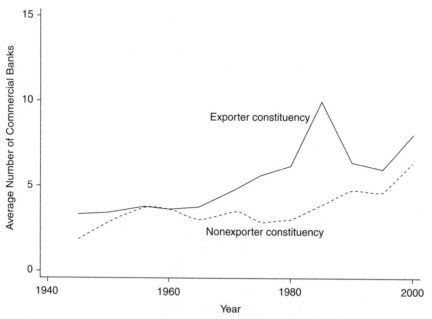

FIGURE 4.4. Average number of commercial banks in former French colonies.
Source: Author's calculations based on annual entries in *Rand McNally International Bankers Directory* and *Africa South of the Sahara*.

the same incentives to manipulate banking for political advantage. Even the timing of the divergence is consistent with a political explanation: exporters and nonexporters begin to diverge earlier among the former French colonies, most of which became independent in 1960, than among former British colonies, which transitioned into independence five years later on average. One marked difference between the exporter constituencies in Figures 4.3 and 4.4 is the temporary spike that occurred among the Francophone countries. In the late 1970s, the banking sector had begun to expand at an accelerated rate as foreign-owned banks such as Citibank began to enter markets in Côte d'Ivoire, Gabon, and Senegal. But, coinciding with the onset of economic crisis, this expansion proved to be unsustainable and their banking sectors contracted to their previous size by the end of the decade, though they remained larger, on average, than nonexporter banking sectors.[18]

POLITICAL CONSTITUENCIES AND COMMERCIAL BANKING OWNERSHIP

The argument made here has a corollary for the structure of banking ownership. If a political calculus led Africa's founding leaders to manipulate the size of the commercial banking sector, it must have also shaped their incentives to influence the ownership of individual banks. Leaders could more effectively transform banks into auxiliaries of executive power if the state assumed a stake in their ownership. Leaders who were threatened by the accumulation of wealth among exporter constituencies would want to have the state acquire a sufficiently large share of their ownership in order to exercise direct influence over lending decisions. Indeed, these leaders intuitively understood the proverbial admonition: "the borrower is servant to the lender." And a complete takeover of banks would be unnecessary to achieve this end, since partial state ownership, combined with local incorporation, would be sufficient to permit the government to appoint members to the board of directors.[19] Leaders with exporter constituencies were less threatened by capital accumulation, so they had less reason to promote state ownership in banking.

While the financial dirigisme of the 1960s and 1970s entailed state ownership of banking, few African countries undertook the complete nationalization

---

[18] The temporary spike in the number of commercial banks among these countries may be related to their membership in the Franc zone. They may have sought to manipulate their monetary union's currency convertibility and pooled foreign exchange, underwritten by the French treasury, in order to stimulate the distribution of credit, though this proved to be unsustainable under deteriorating economic conditions (Collier 1991; Engberg 1973; Stasavage 2003).

[19] Besides legally requiring the heads of banks to be citizens, several governments also instructed banks to incorporate locally, which made it more difficult for assets to be moved from the local subsidiary to the overseas head office. Leaders could then try to blackmail banks by threatening to block the repatriation of profits. In 1974, Mobutu Sese Seko threatened to close Barclays Bank's local subsidiary and confiscate its deposits in order to extract $11 million to finance his "Rumble in the Jungle," the world title fight he hosted in Kinshasa between Muhammad Ali and George Foreman (Ackrill and Hannah 2001).

of the banking sector. Cases such as that of Tanzania stand out because they were relatively rare. In his Arusha Declaration of 1967, Tanzanian President Julius Nyerere, a leader from a nonexporter constituency, announced the immediate nationalization of seven foreign and two local commercial banks. Their assets were transferred to the state-owned National Bank of Commerce, ostensibly to accelerate the expansion of the financial network to marginalized areas (Mittelman 1978; Temu and Due 2000). But most African leaders, including the avowed socialists, were less radical. In Uganda, another leader from a nonexporter constituency, President Milton Obote, followed on his own blueprint for socialist transformation, the Common Man's Charter of 1969, by requiring the banks to incorporate locally with a paid-up capital to be held in securities defined by the government (Gerschenberg 1972). This had the immediate effect of inducing a round of amalgamation among the commercial banks. Six months later, Obote announced that his government would acquire a 60% share in the commercial banks as well as in a broader set of enterprises (Jorgensen 1981).[20]

If founding leaders from nonexporter constituencies, such as Nyerere and Obote, were threatened by the potential capital accumulation of exporter groups, the rate of state ownership in commercial banking should be considerably higher among their countries than those first headed by leaders from exporter constituencies. Figures 4.5 and 4.6 bear out this observable implication with two measures of state ownership in commercial banking in 1985, a year by which most African countries had had sufficient time since independence to shape the banking sector according to domestic preferences. Although all African countries began independence with largely foreign-owned banking systems, both measures indicate that countries headed by nonexporter leaders at independence went on to pursue a larger state presence in banking. Figure 4.5 shows that, by 1985, the governments of countries founded by nonexporter leaders acquired shares in over two-thirds of banks, while exporter-led countries did so in only about one in four banks.[21] This result is partly driven by the fact that countries with nonexporter leaders at independence also developed smaller banking sectors. In 1985, these countries had an average of about five banks with the state holding shares in three of those banks. At the same time, exporter-led countries had grown to an average of nine banks with the state taking ownership in just two of those banks. Figure 4.6 further shows that governments with nonexporter leaders at independence tended to become

---

[20] After the 1971 coup, Idi Amin announced that his government would lower the state's participation in commercial banks from 60% to 49%. He reversed himself within the year, having thought the better of it.

[21] A difference-of-means test indicates that there is no meaningful difference in the degree of state ownership by colonial origin in 1985. The former British colonies have an average of 40.8%, while the former continental colonies have a higher average of 50.7%. But the continental colonies do show a greater tendency for state participation more generally: 61% of banks have state ownership in former continental colonies versus 36% among former British colonies. A difference-of-means test confirms that this difference is statistically significant.

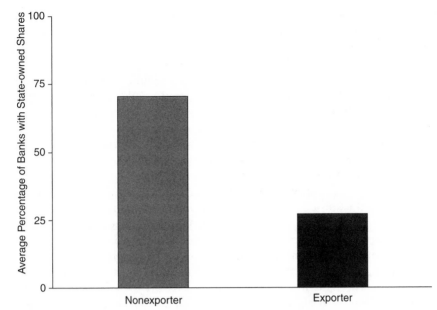

FIGURE 4.5. Average percentage of commercial banks with state-owned shares in 1985.
Source: Author's calculations based on entries in *Africa South of the Sahara.*

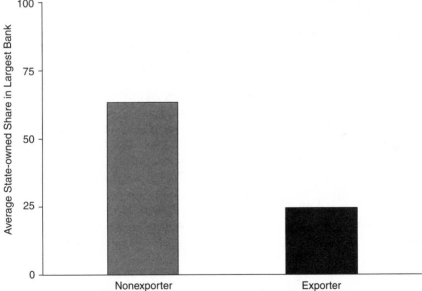

FIGURE 4.6. Average state-owned share in largest commercial bank in 1985.
Source: Author's calculations based on entries in *Africa South of the Sahara.*

majority shareholders in the largest commercial bank found in their countries in 1985: they acquired 63% of shares, on average, versus the 25% average among countries with exporter leaders.

The differing rates of state intervention among African governments cannot be attributed to state capacity or to the source of bank capital. From independence through the 1980s, nearly all governments could leverage the funds controlled through state marketing boards – which had monopsonistic powers in the purchase of agricultural crops as well as monopolistic powers in their sale (Bates 1981) – to acquire a greater stake in commercial banking. Yet, as is evident in Figures 4.5 and 4.6, the incentives for governments to do so depended instead on the origin of the country's founding political leadership. Even where the relative importance of agricultural revenue for capitalizing commercial banks declined over time, as occurred among those countries that became rentier states, the potential threat posed by business was more likely to influence state ownership in banking. Among the countries listed in Table 4.1, rentier states can be identified as those in which fuel and minerals grew to represent more than one-third of merchandise exports. Based on this definition, the rentier states originally founded by exporter leaders are Botswana, Gabon, Nigeria, and Togo; those founded by nonexporter leaders are Cameroon, Congo Republic, Guinea, Niger, Sierra Leone, and Zambia. In 1985, the rentier states founded by exporter leaders had an appreciably lower participation rate in commercial banking when compared with rentier states founded by nonexporter leaders. The former acquired shares in 30% of banks, on average, while the latter did so in 67% of banks. This reflects the same pattern illustrated in Figure 4.5 for the entire sample of African countries.

The data, on the whole, suggest that African countries founded by leaders from nonexporter constituencies moved to expand the state's participation in commercial banking while simultaneously restricting the size of the banking sector. This pattern is consistent with broader empirical findings from the finance literature. Government ownership in banking is generally associated with slower financial development cross-nationally over time (La Porta et al. 2002). The ownership structure of banks has further been shown to influence the provision of credit, which declines with greater banking concentration and a larger share of state-owned banks (Beck et al. 2004).

DATA AND METHODS FOR ASSESSING COMPETING EXPLANATIONS

I have argued that Africa's independence-era leaders transformed the main institutions of finance – commercial banks – into instruments of regime consolidation. Because this political explanation for the cross-national variation in African banking runs counter to the received wisdom on financial systems and economic institutions, I also assess alternative explanations based on claims regarding the impact of legal traditions, colonial settlement, and ethnic diversity. I test these competing claims by estimating a random effects model in which the dependent variable is the number of commercial banks found in a country. The units of analysis are country-years from 1970 to 2000 for the set of African countries listed in Table 4.1.[22]

The main explanatory variable of interest denotes whether a country's founding leader emerged from an exporter constituency, as reported in Table 4.1. This dichotomous variable takes on a value of 1 in such cases; it is 0 otherwise. The political hypothesis developed in this chapter suggests that African countries where founding leaders emerged from exporter constituencies should have a larger number of commercial banks. These leaders recognized that liberal credit flows would accrue to entrepreneurs from their own political bases; therefore, they adopted relatively easy access to banking as an inducement for their support. Their counterparts from nonexporter constituencies, however, sought to control the flow of credit because their own supporters were unlikely to be its beneficiaries; they needed to turn credit into a constraint on entrepreneurial autonomy to forestall future political challenges.

Another dichotomous variable denotes whether a country is a former British colony. The dominant explanation in this field, the legal traditions hypothesis, suggests that the legal institutions implanted through colonialism should drive subsequent patterns of financial development. Financial systems are more likely to expand and deepen in countries that inherited English common law because it provides greater protection for creditors and investors (La Porta et al. 1998). Former British colonies in Africa should therefore be expected to have larger commercial banking sectors when compared with former continental colonies that inherited versions of the Napoleonic civil code.

Estimates for the mortality rate among early European settlers as well as the size of the European population in 1950 are included as proxies for the nature of pre-independence institutions. The colonial settlement hypothesis suggests that early settler mortality determined the type of economic institutions implanted by the metropolitan powers (Acemoglu et al. 2001). Institutions designed to protect property rights are thought to have been established wherever Europeans could migrate, while extractive institutions were created where they could not survive. This explanation is consistent with the literature on banking in Africa (Crick 1965; Newlyn and Rowan 1954). According to Wickins (1986, 63), "the development of banking was to a considerable degree in direct proportion to the size of the European population." Larger banking sectors should therefore be found in African countries with lower settler mortality or a larger European population on the eve of independence.

Ethnic fractionalization, as a measure of social cleavages, is used to test the hypothesis that countries with greater diversity are less likely to build developmental institutions (Easterly and Levine 1997). This line of thinking

---

[22] The random effects model is appropriate for this type of analysis because it captures some of the unobserved heterogeneity across countries. In this case, the use of the random-effects versus fixed-effects estimator is driven by the fact that the main explanatory variable of interest is time invariant. Additionally, robust standard errors clustered by country are estimated to correct for heteroskedasticity and autocorrelation.

suggests that competition for resources induces fear of exploitation among ethnic groups, since each seeks to maximize its share in redistribution while the costs are borne by all groups. If one group cements its hold on the state, it may simply expropriate the resources of other groups. This competitive dynamic is thought to lead groups to withhold their contributions to the common pool of the state, diminishing the state's capacity to build institutions and provide public goods. Since banks have characteristics of developmental institutions, this logic would suggest that banking sector size is inversely related to ethnic diversity.

To control for the effects of variables not distinguished as one of the primary hypotheses discussed earlier, I include measures for per capita income, country population, landlocked status, the Polity score as a proxy for level of democracy, and decade dummies for the 1980s and 1990s. I assess alternative economic sources for the size of the commercial banking sector by controlling for exports, manufacturing, mineral and oil extraction, and foreign aid. I estimate the impact of political instability by controlling for the number of years a leader has been in power and the number of coups experienced in a country.

A description of all variables, including their summary statistics, is found in Appendix C.[23] The explanatory variables are lagged for the following analysis.

EMPIRICAL ANALYSIS OF COMMERCIAL BANKING SECTOR SIZE

Table 4.2 reports the main results from the random effects regression analysis of the number of commercial banks in African countries. The estimated coefficients in Models 2 through 8 reveal that countries with founding leaders from exporter constituencies have, on average, four to seven more commercial banks than countries where founding leaders emerged from nonexporting regions, holding all else constant. This result is robust to the inclusion of relevant political and economic controls. And it does not depend on the coding or inclusion of any specific country. The substantive size and level of significance for the coefficient on exporter constituency remains stable whether potential outliers like Nigeria are dropped from the sample or controversially coded cases are recoded.

The results indicate that the nature of business–state relations established at independence have had a powerful and lasting impact on the development of commercial banking in African countries. This political explanation can better account for much of the difference in commercial banking sector size between African countries than the conventional explanations for financial and economic development. A founding leader's constituency type explains a greater share of cross-national variation than colonial legacies, settler mortality, or ethnic diversity. Comparing Models 1 and 2 shows, for example, that the inclusion of this variable alone increases the overall R^2 by more than 20%.

---

[23] All independent variables are lagged one year.

TABLE 4.2. *The Determinants of Commercial Banking Sector Size*

	Model 1	Model 2	Model 3	Model 4
Exporter constituency		6.415*** (1.714)	5.376*** (1.408)	6.539*** (1.771)
British colony	3.348** (1.571)	2.467** (1.052)	3.394** (1.381)	2.300** (1.108)
Settler mortality, log			1.198 (0.930)	
Europeans in 1950, log				−0.055 (0.431)
Ethnic fractionalization	32.809** (14.825)	55.613*** (15.734)	49.954*** (14.007)	57.260*** (16.553)
Ethnic fractionalization, square	−32.394** (14.413)	−44.887*** (13.605)	−42.551*** (12.541)	−46.105*** (14.196)
GDP per capita, log	1.303*** (0.395)	1.262*** (0.360)	3.038*** (0.618)	0.897** (0.368)
Population, log	4.423*** (1.019)	4.762*** (0.961)	4.946*** (0.910)	4.892*** (1.028)
Landlocked country	−3.348** (1.480)	−1.626* (0.908)	−0.398 (0.928)	−1.697* (0.954)
Polity score	−0.042 (0.030)	−0.044 (0.030)	−0.057* (0.032)	−0.035 (0.031)
1980s decade	0.580 (0.395)	0.484 (0.387)	0.593 (0.383)	0.585 (0.404)
1990s decade	0.910* (0.545)	0.726 (0.530)	0.916* (0.509)	0.497 (0.566)
Constant	−76.111*** (17.069)	−93.579*** (18.538)	−111.594*** (22.454)	−93.341*** (19.053)
Number of observations	731	731	644	682
Number of countries	27	27	24	25
R^2 within	0.2126	0.2131	0.2095	0.2109
R^2 between	0.6262	0.8217	0.8771	0.8075
R^2 overall	0.5948	0.7326	0.7744	0.7255

Notes: The dependent variable is the number of commercial banks. All independent variables are lagged one year. Robust standard errors, clustered by country, in parentheses.
*** $p < 0.01$, ** $p < 0.05$, * $p < 0.10$, two-tailed tests.

TABLE 4.2. *The Determinants of Commercial Banking Sector Size (continued)*

	Model 5	Model 6	Model 7	Model 8
Exporter constituency	4.043***	6.209***	6.530***	6.638***
	(1.041)	(1.249)	(1.740)	(1.687)
British colony	1.425**	2.616***	2.440**	2.689**
	(0.714)	(0.867)	(1.066)	(1.050)
Ethnic fractionalization	37.947***	56.101***	56.125***	53.047***
	(9.617)	(13.140)	(15.955)	(15.164)
Ethnic fractionalization, square	−29.778***	−45.757***	−45.147***	−42.506***
	(8.196)	(11.740)	(13.771)	(13.025)
GDP per capita, log	2.049***	1.370***	1.290***	1.575***
	(0.340)	(0.341)	(0.358)	(0.361)
Population, log	4.074***	4.791***	4.763***	4.660***
	(0.519)	(0.767)	(0.964)	(0.907)
Landlocked country	−0.398	−1.406**	−1.615*	−1.504
	(0.663)	(0.677)	(0.925)	(0.939)
Polity score	0.034**	−0.043	−0.051*	−0.022
	(0.016)	(0.029)	(0.031)	(0.027)
1980s decade	0.506**	0.405	0.535	0.125
	(0.208)	(0.379)	(0.389)	(0.387)
1990s decade	0.206	0.619	0.818	0.074
	(0.285)	(0.485)	(0.538)	(0.524)
Exports, % GDP	0.020*			
	(0.011)			
Manufacturing, % GDP	0.001			
	(0.030)			
Oil exporter		1.240		
		(1.225)		
Mineral exporter		0.219		
		(0.247)		
Leader years in power			−0.026*	
			(0.015)	
Number of coups				0.607***
				(0.193)
Constant	−82.929***	−94.731***	−93.854***	−94.096***
	(10.253)	(14.500)	(18.636)	(17.795)
Number of observations	656	731	731	731
Number of countries	26	27	27	27
R^2 within	0.2885	0.2071	0.2157	0.2300
R^2 between	0.7750	0.8576	0.8218	0.8425
R^2 overall	0.6851	0.7597	0.7336	0.7456

Notes: The dependent variable is the number of commercial banks. All independent variables are lagged one year. Robust standard errors, clustered by country, in parentheses.
*** $p < 0.01$, ** $p < 0.05$, * $p < 0.10$, two-tailed tests.

The coefficient for former British colonies in Model 1 suggests that such countries have 3.3 more banks than countries colonized by the continental powers, holding all else equal. The magnitude of this variable is somewhat diminished when controlling for a leader's constituency type at independence. The British effect drops to approximately 2.5 banks once controlling for a founding president's constituency type, as indicated in Model 2. Under most other model specifications, the coefficient for former British colonies is about one-half the size of the coefficient for exporter constituency.

The politics surrounding independence-era leaders also appears to have a greater impact on banking sector development than do the legal or economic institutions implanted through colonialism. The settler mortality variable, in this respect, performs unexpectedly. The positive sign on the coefficient for this variable in Model 3 suggests that a larger banking sector emerged in countries where European settlers experienced higher rates of mortality, though it fails to attain statistical significance. In any case, this result is contrary to theoretical expectations based on the work of Acemoglu et al. (2001), who find that countries with higher rates of settler mortality in colonial times have a greater risk of expropriation today. The commercial banking sector should therefore be unlikely to expand under such conditions. An alternative specification in Model 4 substitutes settler mortality with the size of the European population prior to independence, since cross-national differences in banking may reflect the varying rates of European immigration to African colonies in the interwar period and following the Second World War. But the coefficient for this variable is negative and fails to attain statistical significance.

The results in Table 4.2 further show that social diversity is not an impediment to financial development. The direction of the relationship between ethnic fractionalization and commercial banking sector size moves contrary to the expectations described in the literature (Easterly and Levine 1997). The coefficients for ethnic fractionalization and its quadratic indicate that more diverse African societies acquire more commercial banks, though at a decreasing rate. The estimated coefficients in Model 2 suggest that increasing ethnic fractionalization from 0.35 to 0.89, a move from the 10th to the 90th percentile, would be associated with nearly six additional banks, holding all else constant.

The economics-related variables show that the commercial banking sector is larger in wealthier and more populous countries, as would be expected. Both GDP per capita and population size are consistently positive and statistically significant. The landlocked variable performs less consistently, losing significance under certain model specifications. Model 5 indicates that among the variables reflecting a country's potential demand for credit, namely, levels of exports and manufacturing, only the former appears to be associated with a larger banking sector. Model 6 shows that the controls for oil and mineral exporters fail to attain statistical significance.

Regime type appears to have no clear impact on the development of com-mercial banking across African countries. The coefficient on the Polity score, a standard measure for level of democracy, does not consistently attain statistical significance, and its sign moves in opposite directions in differ-ent models. But the measures for political stability, the number of years a leader has been in power and the number of coups experienced by a coun-try, do attain statistical significance. The banking sector appears to contract with each additional year a leader is in power, but the coups that unseat leaders are associated with a subsequent increase in the number of banks. These results, taken together, reinforce the argument made in this chapter regarding the political underpinnings of banking in African countries. While entrenched leaders may seek to constrain the ability of business to under-take autonomous political action, unexpected changes in leadership may provide entrepreneurs with an opportunity to recalibrate the business–state relationship.

CAMEROON AND KENYA: DIVERGENT BANKING NARRATIVES

The causal logic developed thus far can be traced through the cases of Cameroon and Kenya. The governments of both countries early on established relatively market-friendly reputations, at least when compared with the rest of the con-tinent. However, they also adopted the dirigiste policies recommended by the development paradigm of the 1960s, including import substitution industriali-zation. That meant that their economies were partly managed through institu-tions designed to channel resources according to state priorities. Although such interventions had been justified by the desire to expand mass participation in the market economy, it also permitted these governments to assume a role in mediating business' access to capital.

Despite having comparable economic orientations, the leaders of these two countries followed distinct strategies vis-à-vis business. And these can be traced through their governments' treatment of commercial banking. Figure 4.7 shows that Cameroon and Kenya had similarly sized banking sectors prior to independence, but they diverged considerably over the next four decades. In 1960, there were seven banks in Cameroon and nine banks in Kenya. Over the next twenty years, by 1980, Cameroon's banking sector had been reduced to five banks while Kenya's had expanded to 14 banks. Obvious explanations cannot account for this divergence. In this time period, both countries were multiethnic societies governed by stable one-party systems, and both economies mainly exported cash crops that exposed them to similar oscillations in world prices. These explanatory variables are effectively held constant across the two cases for at least twenty years after independence. In fact, the contraction of Cameroon's banking sector leading up to 1980 is all the more noteworthy because the country had begun to export oil by that point in time.

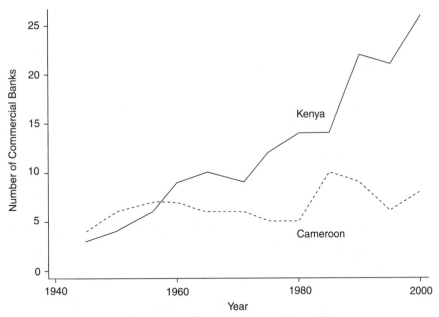

FIGURE 4.7. Commercial banking sector size in Cameroon and Kenya.
Source: Author's calculations based on annual entries in *Rand McNally International Bankers Directory* and *Africa South of the Sahara.*

Kenya's experience as a British colony with a large white settler community might offer a plausible account. But this too is an insufficient explanation because, as noted earlier, the foreign-owned banks, British as well as French, had begun to expand their operations in most colonies throughout the 1950s in order to service African populations. Figure 4.7 indicates that this was the case in both Cameroon and Kenya: additional banks were entering both countries up to 1960, after which they began to diverge. What is more, given the exodus of European capital in the run-up to independence in Kenya, one might have expected its new leaders to have been concerned with imposing stronger controls on banking, as had been done in British colonies like Ghana and Tanzania within five years of independence.[24]

The political explanation advanced here would link the source of the divergence in Figure 4.7 to the relationship between independence leaders and the cash crop exporters in their countries. Capital accumulation was a political threat to Cameroon's independence leader in a way that it

---

[24] Kenya's commercial banks were forced to temporarily restrict credit in 1960, when nearly 20% of deposits were withdrawn. The World Bank's mission to Kenya noted, "As a result of the current crisis of confidence, private capital has become increasingly scarce and is unlikely to be available again until conditions in East Africa warrant a favorable reappraisal of the risks of investing there" (World Bank 1963, 38).

was not to his counterpart in Kenya. The case study evidence corroborates this claim.

Cameroon: Restricted Banking Entry

Cameroon's first president, Ahmadou Ahidjo, was an ethnic Fulbe whose group resided in the northern half of the country. At independence, the Fulbe were not engaged in the production of the country's main exports, cocoa and coffee. Not only did southern groups cultivate these crops, but one of them, the Bamileke, had also become economically ascendant as rich planters who expanded into other areas of commerce (Warnier 1993). From the end of the Second World War, when the Bamileke began to compete for land and labor with French plantation owners, "it was only a question of time before the Bamileke replaced the whites as the dominant entrepreneurial group in Mungo," the country's most productive cash crop–growing region (Atangana 1998, 26). When the Bamileke subsequently began to seek political influence to match their economic prosperity in the 1950s, their politicization led them to support a radical nationalist party, the Union des Populations du Cameroon (UPC). This put them into direct conflict with the French colonial administration, which banned the UPC in 1955, and later with Ahidjo, who continued to repress the UPC as the territory's prime minister and then as the country's president (Joseph 1977).[25]

When Ahidjo took power of an independent Cameroon in 1960, the ability of the Bamileke to accumulate resources was well established. Their potential to use those resources to mobilize opposition represented a threat to the single-party system Ahidjo sought to build under the banner of his Union Nationale Camerounaise (UNC) (Bayart 1989; Konings 2007; Takougang and Krieger 1998; van de Walle 1993). While he could restrain them through an array of economic controls, including licensing and taxation, the most powerful instrument at his disposal was the financial system. Rather than simply seeking to tax Bamileke entrepreneurs *ex post* – by which time they could have already acquired too much influence – Ahidjo could direct credit so as to mold the composition of the business community *ex ante*. It was not so much that Ahidjo sought to starve Bamileke entrepreneurs of credit. It was that he sought to assert his control over banking so that he could determine who among them would accumulate resources and under what conditions. Restricting entry into, and access to, the banking sector permitted him to neutralize a potential source of opposition.

Ahidjo's government developed expansive regulatory powers in banking and pursued extensive state ownership in banking.[26] After having revised the

---

[25] After being banned, the UPC launched an insurrection that was sustained with Bamileke and Bassa support for several years.

[26] Cameroon's membership in the Communauté Financière Africaine (CFA) means that it does not directly control its own monetary policy. This is done in conjunction with the other

country's constitution in 1972 to replace the federal system with a unitary republic, his government enacted a banking sector law ostensibly aimed at standardizing banking operations across the Anglophone and Francophone halves of the country. In practice, this 1973 law provided the government with the instruments to exercise direct control over the allocation of capital by requiring the state to acquire at least one third of shareholding in all banks as well as to restrict foreign shareholding in banks to 65%. The law further required the heads of banks to be Cameroonian nationals (Doe 1995).

Cameroon's government wielded sufficient power over banking to routinely intervene in the lending decisions of banks (Doe 1995; Ndongko 1986; Tamba and Tchambane Djine 1995), whether extending unsecured loans to friends or cutting off credit to foes.[27] At the national level, the government's influence over banking was underpinned by the authority of the finance minister, as chair of the National Credit Council, to regulate banking and allocate credit. This influence was magnified in 1980 with the creation of a new seven-member committee, including four from the finance ministry, to make recommendations on the distribution of government-controlled funds among banks. Parastatals were required to consult with this committee in order to choose banks in which to make deposits. In effect, this meant that political criteria would determine which banks were granted the government's largest accounts.

At the level of individual banks, the state's acquisition of shares meant that the government was represented on the board of directors of nearly every bank in the country by the mid-1980s. The government could monitor compliance with its lending preferences because, in many instances, the government had sufficient shares to appoint civil servants to act as senior bank officers. This monitoring capacity had been reinforced by a 1981 decree that obliged commercial banks to establish their headquarters in Yaounde, the national capital; previously, most banks had been based in Douala, the country's main port and economic hub.

The strategy of restricted banking access was largely retained after Ahidjo stepped down in 1982 and was succeeded by Paul Biya. Cameroon had become an oil exporter by the time Biya assumed power, and the banking sector was allowed to expand accordingly. The state, following the precedent

member states of the Banque des États de l'Afrique Centrale (BEAC), a multinational central bank. The six member countries of the CFA zone in Central Africa are Cameroon, Central African Republic, Chad, Congo Republic, Equatorial Guinea, and Gabon. France is also a member.

[27] The 1973 law also empowered the state to appropriate bank assets. One provision required banks to transfer 10% of their deposits to the Société Nationale d'Investissement (SNI), a government holding company, in order to provide parastatals with additional capital. Another provision imposed a 1% tax on all bank credits to be paid by borrowers to finance support for small- and medium-sized enterprises. Additionally, in 1976, the government required banks to contribute 10% of their profits to the Fond d'Aide et de Garantie des Crédits aux Petites et Moyennes Entreprises (FOGAPE), which would guarantee loans and take equity shares.

established by Ahidjo, continued acquiring a stake in every new bank that was established. As an ethnic Beti from the southern half of the country, Biya did seek to recalibrate the distribution of resources among Cameroon's major groups. He redirected credit flows toward his coethnics, all while limiting the access of his predecessor's Fulbe allies and the Bamileke entrepreneurs who dominated commerce. Nearly a decade would pass before Biya's government permitted privately owned banks to be established without state participation. Even then, those bank charters were mainly distributed to members of his ruling party.

Despite the brief expansion in banking in the 1980s – many of these state-owned banks had become insolvent by the end of the decade – Bamileke entrepreneurs continued experiencing difficulties in acquiring sufficient credit through the formal system.[28] It was due to such ongoing problems with established commercial banks that "the Bamileke have tried to create their own bank, but they have unfortunately suffered the failure that is known" (Dongmo 1981, 253). Indeed, the government would not grant a charter to a privately owned Bamileke bank until 1997. This lack of access to financial capital helps to explain why Bamileke entrepreneurs are reputed to rely so heavily on informal rotating credit mechanisms such as tontines or njangis (Brenner et al. 1990; Warnier 1993). While these informal mechanisms enable them to survive commercially, tontines are unlikely to provide Bamileke entrepreneurs with sufficient capital to undertake the expansion and diversification of their businesses in a sustainable way. But this is as Ahidjo had intended.

Kenya: Open Banking Entry

Kenya's leader at independence was not politically threatened by capital accumulation. Jomo Kenyatta, to be sure, personified the constituency most likely to benefit from increased financial intermediation. His coethnic Kikuyu were "capitalist farmers" who had managed to achieve considerable gains despite the restrictions imposed by a colonial administration aimed at protecting the interests of European settlers (Swainson 1980). Kikuyu entrepreneurs had begun to expand beyond small-scale agriculture and trade before the Second World War, and the gradual relaxation of colonial restrictions since then, including the removal of the ban on the African cultivation of coffee and tea in the 1950s, only accelerated that process. Bank deposits from the indigenous population grew tenfold in the decade leading up to independence due to the rapid growth of cash crop production from mainly Kikuyu-owned farms (Maxon 1992). When the British colonial government finally withdrew from Kenya, it was mostly wealthy Kikuyu who took over from departing settlers

---

[28] The Bamileke, nevertheless, probably constitute the country's largest market for formal bank lending. Three banks consulted by Dongmo (1981) in Douala claimed that the Bamileke represented some 75% of their clientele for short-term credit.

the large-scale farmland that had been developed for export production (Leys 1974).

Kenyatta became the founding leader of Kenya in 1963 as the head of a nationalist organization that had been founded, in part, to articulate the economic grievances, including the lack of credit, of cash crop farmers and traders.[29] That he would go on to use the power of the state to support capital accumulation among this class of Kikuyu was therefore expected (Bates 1989; Holmquist et al. 1994; Throup 1987). Facilitating their access to credit would enable Kenyatta to consolidate his political position within his own group and vis-à-vis other groups. While his ruling party, the Kenya African National Union (KANU), represented a multiethnic alliance, it was a fractious grouping of politicians with autonomous ethnic bases and conflicting economic ideologies. The distribution of economic resources, public and private, underpinned Kenyatta's ability to remain at the center of this alliance (Throup and Hornsby 1998). In this respect, the expansion of banking enabled Kenyatta to induce the active support of his coethnics, since they would be its primary beneficiaries, and thereby strengthen his hand more generally. If Kenyatta did not trust that he could rely on the party or the state to control his coalition, he had at least secured the support of the group most capable of organizing outside those structures.

Kenyatta's government permitted private banking to operate largely unimpeded, imposing credit and interest rate controls that were relatively mild in comparison with those of other African countries, though they did introduce distortions.[30] Beyond allowing additional private banks to enter the sector, Kenyatta sought to expand access to credit by creating state-owned banks, though without attacking existing private banks (Brownbridge 1998; Nasibi 1992). In a single year, 1968, two state-owned banks were founded: the National Bank of Kenya (NBK) was created to extend credit to African-owned businesses as well as to facilitate financing for the acquisition of land by African farmers, while the Co-operative Bank of Kenya was established to provide services to cooperatives in agricultural production. In 1970, the government went on to acquire 60% of the shares in National and Grindlays Bank, which had operated throughout the colonial period as one of the three largest banks, and renamed it the Kenya Commercial Bank (KCB); the remaining shares were acquired by 1976. KCB and NBK were among the country's largest banks by the end of the 1970s along with two foreign-owned banks, Barclays and Standard Chartered. While KCB went on to become the single

---

[29] While the landless Kikuyu who made up the Mau Mau rebellion against colonial rule were not originally part of Kenyatta's nationalist coalition, their mobilization obliged Kenyatta to also address their concerns, at least rhetorically (Kanogo 1987).

[30] Throughout the 1970s, government regulations segmented financial markets by setting interest rates below inflation and then assigning rates by type of banking institution. Non-banking financial institutions (NBFIs) were permitted to charge higher interest rates than commercial banks, while being restricted from engaging in other banking services. Commercial banks responded by establishing NBFIs as a means of escaping interest rate restrictions.

largest bank with over 20% of the market, private banks continued to play a central role in commercial banking.[31]

Kenyatta's banking policies were not without controversy precisely because they were understood to be politically motivated. Just one month before Kenyatta's death, in August 1978, a debate ensued in the Kenyan parliament in which the ruling party's backbenchers attacked a bill to permit Barclays Bank to incorporate locally, facilitating the transfer of assets and liabilities from Barclays Bank International to its new bank in Kenya.[32] The bill's opponents charged that the local incorporation was intended to favor Kikuyu entrepreneurs, particularly members of the Gikuyu-Embu-Meru Association (GEMA), who were planning to buy the bank.[33]

Assuming the presidency upon Kenyatta's death in 1978, Daniel arap Moi continued his predecessor's liberal stance toward banking. While Moi did attempt to redirect resources to his coethnic Kalenjin by providing them with privileged access to resources and bringing them into business networks – just as Kenyatta had done for the Kikuyu – he did not constrain the growth of banking.[34] Between 1978 and 1992, when Moi was forced to adopt a multi-party constitution, the number of commercial banks had grown from 14 to 23, a faster rate than that under his predecessor.

Rather than restrict access to credit through the control of banking, Moi sought to redirect its flow for political ends. After Moi assumed the presidency, KCB and NBK apparently took on more pronounced political roles. The two state-owned banks were obliged to increasingly circumvent commercial criteria to extend credit to parastatals, politicians, and their allies (Brownbridge 1998). The government decreed in the 1980s that KCB would open a branch in every district of the country without regard to local conditions, claiming that such a move would decentralize access to development resources. Grosh (1990, 38) points out that such an expansion could permit the government to furtively deliver money to anywhere in the country in a way that would "circumvent the budget process where such inter-regional transfers receive more scrutiny and debate."[35] NBK similarly became a vehicle for channeling resources to

---

[31] By the end of the 1970s, KCB would control a large share of lending across a range of economic sectors. As a share of lending by all banks in Kenya, KCB loans represented 29% of those in agriculture, 21% in mining, 32% in manufacturing, 25% in construction, and 17% in trade. See "Hefty Profits for Kenya Banks," *Weekly Review* (Nairobi), 8 August 1977, p. 22.

[32] "Barclays Bank Bill Sails Through Storm," *Weekly Review* (Nairobi), 28 July 1978, p. 23.

[33] GEMA Holdings, though a business association, was considered politically consequential because many of its directors and members were not only the president's coethnics, but they also tended to be from Kiambu, the president's home area.

[34] KCB's executive chairmen had all been Kikuyus during its first decade of existence: John Njoroge Michuki (1970–79), Phillip Ndegwa (1980–82), and George Saitoti (1983).

[35] Benjamin Kipkorir, who served as KCB's executive chairman from 1983 through 1991, notes in his memoir that he had to actively dispel the notion that he would favor his coethnic Kalenjin, especially since he had been appointed to the position by Moi. He recalls that some held "the view that since the bank had long been led by members of the Kikuyu community, who had accordingly been seen to have benefited from it, that now that I was in charge, it would hereafter

high-profile members of the ruling party who "had no intention of ever repaying," according to Micah Cheserem (2006, 127), the country's reformist central banker in the 1990s. By the mid-1990s, the list of NBK's unserviced loans was a who's who of the ruling party that represented a cross section of the country's ethnic groups.[36]

Moi sought to secure his support among Kenya's business class by influencing the behavior of privately owned banks, many of which were linked to Kikuyu entrepreneurs as well as members of the ruling party (Widner 1992). Political criteria were inevitably used in the distribution of banking licenses and the supervision of banks. Cheserem (2006, 70) admits that the central bank and the ruling party had become "closely inter-linked" by the time he assumed his post in 1993. Small local banks associated with politicians were not only permitted to violate prudential norms and regulations – allowing directors or clients to take large unsecured loans – but were also favored with the investment of parastatal deposits, as occurred with Trade Bank, the bank partly owned by Nicholas Biwott, Moi's longtime advisor and former government minister. At best, this scheme amounted to subsidized loans for politically connected bank owners who could then turn around and lend the parastatal deposits to themselves or to their friends; at worst, it amounted to free cash whenever those loans were not repaid and the government chose not to pursue defaulters. This politicized allocation of parastatal deposits among private banks also provided the government with a useful weapon to punish errant allies: small banks with insufficient capital could be forced into bankruptcy if the government chose to withdraw its deposits without notice. Kenyan entrepreneurs were thus able to continue accessing capital, but it came at the price of political loyalty.

CONCLUSION

The commercial banking sector, as depicted in this chapter, is a vehicle for charting the evolution of the business–state relationship in Africa. While the banking sector was manipulated in all countries to conform to the political interests of their leaders, I have shown that a founding leader's constituency type had a systematic impact on the development of commercial banking over subsequent decades. Leaders who emerged from groups that were cash crop exporters were more likely to permit the expansion of commercial banking to induce the cooperation of business, while their counterparts from nonexporter constituencies imposed constraints on business by restricting the size of the banking sector. In this way, the financial system served as an instrument for managing the evolving business–state relationship in countries where

---

be the financial institution from which my Kalenjin community would obtain free loans" (Kipkorir 2009, 266–267).

[36] For a list of names, see "Millionaire Debtors," *Africa Confidential*, vol. 39, no. 25, 18 December 1998.

formal political institutions were insufficiently developed to regulate political conflict. By permitting leaders to align the interests of entrepreneurs with their own, banks became an auxiliary mechanism for building and sustaining the one-party state from the 1960s through the 1980s. It enabled these leaders to inhibit the emergence of opposition among those most capable of mobilizing it – that is, business.

5

The Liberalization of Capital

Let me emphasise that I want Zambian businesses to expand and to prosper. But for goodness sake, I do not propose to create Zambian capitalism here.

Kenneth Kaunda, president of Zambia, 1968[1]

The state control of capital proved to be a self-undermining institution in Africa. Because the discretionary allocation of credit encouraged inefficient investments as well as strategic defaults by the politically well connected, the region's financial systems were left vulnerable to solvency crises and exogenous shocks. After the economic downturn of the late 1970s and early 1980s, African leaders found that they could no longer sustain their financial influence without external resources. But, with the end of the Cold War, those resources became increasingly difficult to secure, as Western donors and the international financial institutions (IFIs) began to condition their aid on the implementation of liberalizing reforms.

If the manipulation of finance had been central to the governing strategies of African leaders, why would they undertake reforms aimed at diminishing their discretion? Focusing on the bargaining between African leaders and the IFIs, this chapter shows that reform outcomes have depended on the nature of a country's financial reprisal regime, namely, on whether business–state relations were conditioned on incentives or constraints, as discussed in previous chapters. The governments that induced the cooperation of business by facilitating their access to capital, as in Kenya, were more likely to comply with external demands for reform. Financial liberalization was less threatening to these governments because they were already less invested in using the financial system to subdue business. Liberalizing reforms posed considerably higher costs for governments that relied on constraints in managing business–state relations, as in Cameroon. The enactment of reforms in such cases would have

---

[1] This passage comes from Kaunda's pronouncement of the Mulungushi Declaration (1968), a set of economic reforms aimed at nationalizing the means of production, including the use of capital controls and credit restrictions.

required dismantling the controls that permitted leaders to secure the allegiance of business.

This chapter further shows that, beyond the extent to which governments directly controlled capital, leaders with vulnerable fiscal bases were compelled to liberalize their financial sectors. The leaders of economies dependent on cash crop exports were more likely to adopt reform conditionalities than the leaders who could tap into oil and mineral resources to parry the external pressure to reform. The leaders of rentier states could sustain their regimes by leveraging their resources to secure hard currency, all without having to relinquish their control over capital.

These findings on the sources of financial liberalization address a potential endogeneity in the central argument of the book. The theory of pecuniary opposition coalition formation treats financial liberalization as exogenous to the strategic interaction among the actors – the incumbent, business, and the opposition. However, it could be reasonably asked whether pre-existing coordination within the business community enabled it to campaign for economic reforms, thereby producing financial liberalization and, as a byproduct, the electoral coordination of the opposition. If that were the case, a causal link between financial liberalization and opposition coordination could not be drawn as is done in this book. Yet, as will be demonstrated in this chapter and the next, the business class in most African countries lacked the wherewithal to successfully bargain with incumbents over reform. Entrepreneurs generally chose to pursue individual solutions in reaching accommodation with the regime in power rather than pursuing collective action to confront it.

The following section summarizes the patterns of financial dirigisme and liberalization across African countries. The standard explanations for the adoption of liberalizing reforms, namely, the intensity of crisis, the influence of interest groups, and the prevalence of patronage, are reviewed. I then turn to explaining the logic that attributes financial liberalization to the manner in which African leaders have used the financial system to manage business–state relations. The competing explanations are assessed through cross-national quantitative analyses of two reform outcomes – the compliance with structural adjustment loans and the level of private credit provision. The results indicate that financial liberalization has been more likely to take place in African countries where exporter leaders first molded the financial system, after the onset of financial crises, and in nonrentier states. Leaders with larger patronage coalitions are also shown to be less likely to liberalize the financial sector.

The causal mechanism, once corroborated by the statistical findings, is traced through the Cameroon and Kenya case studies. In Cameroon, President Paul Biya sought to hold onto the constraints that had conditioned the business–state relationship since independence. To this end, he was able to rely on the country's oil reserves to forestall financial liberalization. Oil rents were sufficient to keep his regime afloat without assistance from the IMF or the World Bank. Moreover, the country's oil enabled Biya to secure special favors from the French government, which was interested in propping up a regional ally who controlled an important fuel source. In Kenya, by contrast, President Daniel arap Moi's cash-strapped government, lacking significant fuel or mineral exports, was obliged to bargain with the IFIs for continued aid. To preserve the business–state equilibrium, he had to ensure that the financial system could continue furnishing the credit on which the support of business had been conditioned.

SELF-UNDERMINING FINANCIAL DIRIGISME

African governments, regardless of avowed ideology, became the principal financiers of their economies after independence. The establishment of state-owned commercial banks, coupled with the nationalization of private banks, endowed governments with nearly pharaonic powers in finance: they held, on average, a majority interest in over 50% of the banking sector and a minority interest in another 40% by the end of the 1970s (Popiel 1994). This concentrated ownership structure enabled governments to politicize the allocation of credit and selectively enforce regulations. An array of administrative instruments, many of which were inherited from the colonial period, buttressed the discretionary allocation of capital: credit controls, capital and current account restrictions, foreign exchange quotas, and sector-specific interest rate ceilings.[2] Governments in Francophone countries, for example, often determined who was creditworthy by requiring prospective borrowers to seek official pre-approval for loans (Honohan and Beck 2007). The importance of government connections in finance was reinforced through subsidized loan schemes, including indigenization programs, access to which depended on political rather than economic criteria (Kennedy 1988).

The economic shocks produced by declining terms of trade and rising interest rates in the late 1970s exposed the vulnerability of politicized finance.[3] The continuous diversion of credit to risky or unproductive investments at nonmarket rates not only depleted the funds available for loans, but also encouraged greater reliance on political channels for access to a shrinking capital base. Many of the politically connected entrepreneurs who borrowed on discounted terms could not repay those loans, or, more cynically, defaulted because they understood that the government would prevent creditors from prosecuting them. This politicized rationing of credit helped to provoke 41 systemic banking crises in 33 African countries during the 1980s and 1990s (Laeven and Valencia 2008). The largest portfolio losses involved state-owned banks in

---

[2] Governments also manipulated banking to give themselves a soft budget constraint. The seigniorage revenue earned through high reserve requirements – on average 20–25% in Africa versus 5–7% in industrial countries – effectively enabled governments to tax the banking sector in order to finance their own budget deficits (Seck and El Nil 1993). This strategy came at a cost to society: banks could have used the capital held in reserve to make productive loans rather than subsidizing the patronage distributed by governments.

[3] The terms of trade for Africa's nonoil exporters declined by more than one third between 1977 and 1993 (UNCTAD 1999, 10).

countries such as Tanzania and Zambia, though the failures of private banks in Kenya and Nigeria were also linked to politicized lending.

Africa's financial crises were to a large extent the product of internal political dynamics rather than external economic factors. Mehran et al. (1998) find that financial crises were exacerbated by "political interference in the operations of financial institutions." According to Gulde and Patillo (2006, 135), "politically motivated lending to public enterprises and political insiders, as well as a blind eye from supervisors, created the problem of rampant nonperforming loans, insolvent banking systems, and financial crises." Honohan and Beck (2007) note that banking crises in Africa, unlike those in other parts of the world, have been produced by government intervention – discretionary regulation and politicized lending – rather than boom-and-bust cycles, which have typically been the cause of such crises in other parts of the world.

With their economies in crisis, African leaders were obliged to negotiate with the World Bank and the IMF (Callaghy and Ravenhill 1993; Leonard and Straus 2003 van de Walle 2001). These leaders may have derived political benefits from manipulating finance, producing the collusive business–state relations that were intended, but they were unable to sustain that equilibrium without external support once their economies stagnated. Financial distress in Africa, however, had coincided with an international shift in development thinking that brought interventionist policies into doubt. Once the Berg Report (World Bank 1981) crystallized this new development thinking, attributing the source of economic problems to the statist policies pursued by governments, the IFIs progressively linked the disbursement of aid and soft loans to the implementation of liberalizing measures. African governments, increasingly dependent on foreign aid and international loans, therefore came under pressure to relinquish their direct control of capital.

Compounding the impact of economic shocks, the political shock represented by the end of the Cold War undercut whatever immunity African leaders previously enjoyed. Donor governments became less willing to subsidize their erstwhile allies, insisting that African leaders needed to stanch the financial hemorrhaging that brought their governments into crisis in the first place. That meant eliminating the instruments used to subsidize budget deficits, unprofitable parastatals, and politically connected firms. For example, because the government of Senegal shares a common currency with other West African countries in the Communauté Financière Africaine (CFA) zone, it could not finance its deficit by printing more money. However, it could pass its expenditures through parastatals that enjoyed guaranteed credit lines with local banks (Berthelemy 1997). Increasingly bankrupt, African governments seemingly had little alternative but to give up such instruments: 30 of 45 countries accepted IFI-sponsored stabilization and structural adjustment programs by the early 1990s (Popiel 1994). Reform conditionalities were attached to between a third and a half of all aid to Africa (van de Walle 2001).

Financial liberalization, though coming later to Africa than other parts of the world (Pill and Pradhan 1995), became a central component of reform programs imposed on the region's governments. Reforming the financial sector became a priority for donors due to its potential role in accelerating growth.[4] The IMF's stabilization programs were crafted to bring about macroeconomic balance in the short term through prudential monetary policies and liberalized exchange rates, while the World Bank's structural adjustment programs were designed to promote growth in the long term by liberalizing interest rates, eliminating credit controls, privatizing commercial banks, and strengthening banking regulation.[5] Nearly two-thirds of the World Bank loans made to African governments in 1980–1995 included conditions related to financial policies and institutions.[6]

Although stabilization measures were often delayed and structural adjustment programs were fitfully implemented (Easterly 2005; Pitcher 2004; van de Walle 2001; World Bank 1997), African financial systems began to exhibit considerable variation by the mid-1990s. Studies of the relevant institutional and policy changes largely agree on which countries led or lagged in reform (Gelbard and Pereira Leite 1999; Gulde et al. 2006; Honohan and Beck 2007; Mehran et al. 1998; Reinhart and Tokatlidis 2000). The reformers moved toward a liberal regulatory framework and greater openness in capital flows, allowing the market to determine interest rates, lending rates, and exchange rates. In these countries, the central bank, and bank supervision in general, became more insulated from political interference. The laggards continued to employ direct instruments of monetary policy, including controls on credit, interest rates, and current and capital account convertibility. Between these two extremes, a diverse set of countries partially liberalized the financial sector, but still retained direct controls in areas such as foreign exchange.

The move toward financial liberalization is corroborated by trends in banking ownership. In 1990, the state still held a majority share in some 60% of banks. But the banking sector's ownership structure changed as liberalization created greater competition through more open-entry policies. By the mid-1990s, governments controlled more than 50% of banks in only one third of African countries. Government control of banks was reduced throughout the decade in countries such as Kenya, Mozambique, Senegal, Tanzania, and Uganda (Mehran et al. 1998). A large part of this restructuring has been associated with growing foreign participation, as foreign banks entered African markets by acquiring state-owned banks. The banking systems in two of every five countries are now mainly foreign owned, that is, foreign banks control more than 60% of total assets (Honohan and Beck 2007).

---

[4] The financial repression hypothesis became increasingly accepted. It suggested that the removal of controls would stimulate growth by freeing the market to allocate capital, encouraging deposit rates, savings, and investment to rise in tandem (McKinnon 1973; Shaw 1973).

[5] Restructuring banking sectors without improved regulation often compounded problems. See Lewis (1994).

[6] Conditions related to financial policy were included in 75 of 116 loans made by the World Bank to African countries between 1980 and 1995 (Dollar and Svensson 2000).

EXISTING EXPLANATIONS: CRISES, GROUPS, AND RENTS

To account for the cross-national variation in financial liberalization, the literature on reform offers alternative explanations based on the intensity of crisis, the mobilization of interest groups, and the availability of rents from aid and resources. I briefly review these explanations before assessing their impact empirically later in this chapter.

The crisis hypothesis has been a consistent theme in the case study literature (Callaghy and Ravenhill 1993; Haggard and Kaufman 1995; Krueger 1993; Widner 1994; Williamson 1994). The standard narrative suggests that leaders undertake whatever reforms are necessary to keep their regimes in power because the onset of an economic crisis might lead to elite defections or popular protests. One variant of this argument claims that crises disrupt the balance of power among interest groups, providing governments the political flexibility needed to ignore distributive demands in changing the status quo. Explaining variation in reform according to this logic requires linking the adoption of reform to the timing and magnitude of crises: the greater the economic shock, the greater the likelihood of reform.

But the empirical support for this crisis hypothesis has been mixed. In his review of structural adjustment across the continent, van de Walle (2001) concludes that crisis is insufficient to account for the lack of reform seen in most African countries. He finds, instead, that reform implementation was largely constrained by internal clientelistic dynamics. With regard to financial liberalization in particular, however, Abiad and Mody (2005) find that economic and political shocks are significantly associated with policy change. Defining crisis broadly, they examine a cross-national sample of countries to show that the likelihood of reform increases under a range of such shocks, including a balance of payments crisis, a recession, a decline in U.S. interest rates, an IMF program, or a new government. But, given that African countries experienced many of these conditions simultaneously, yet still varied in their reform outcomes, it remains unclear which factors have been important enough to compel leaders to relinquish their use of economic controls. The Abiad and Mody sample of 35 countries includes only three Sub-Saharan African countries – Ghana, South Africa, and Zimbabwe – that are not necessarily representative of the region.

The interest group hypothesis shifts the focus of analysis from the government to the economic actors most likely to be affected by reform. Because policy changes have redistributive consequences and their costs are often concentrated, it is assumed that interest groups will play a central role in determining the course of reform. Interest groups – usually business associations, labor unions, or other sectoral groups that have solved their collective action problems – are thought to mobilize to block reforms that threaten privileges enjoyed under protectionist policies. Interest groups may also organize in favor of reform, though this is a less common claim because the potential beneficiaries of liberalization tend to be widely dispersed. In either scenario, the government is forced to bargain with interest groups over the content of policy.

There is little support for the interest group hypothesis in studies of reform (Bates and Krueger 1993).[7] Africanist scholars generally find no evidence to suggest that any constituency effectively mobilized for or against economic reform. The groups most likely to mobilize to defend their privileges generally sought private solutions to persistent economic crisis, regardless of the government's response. Bates (1999a, 90) reminds us that, despite facing increasing interventions and distortions in the economy, "Africa's middle class remained largely silent." The sector most likely to solve the collective action problem, business, has been too weak to pressure government on policy. While it retained sufficient autonomy to inform the policymaking process in select countries (Handley 2008), business in most cases neither opposed nor promoted the enactment of any policy reform. Business associations, if they were not mute on the question of economic reform, often lacked the wherewithal to bring it about (Brautigam et al. 2002; Heilbrunn 1997; Kraus 2002; Rakner 2001; Taylor 2007). This pattern is particularly apparent with regard to financial liberalization. The business sector has been too weak to pressure the government over policies concerning credit, interest rates, or banking (Brownbridge and Harvey 1998; Mkandawire 1999b). Stasavage (1997) observes that member countries of the two CFA zones failed to develop fiscal discipline, in part, because they lacked a class of private bankers that could lobby their governments for prudential policies.

An alternative hypothesis suggests that African governments have little incentive to undertake reform as long as they continue benefiting from the rents provided by foreign aid. Donors may have imposed stricter conditions on certain reluctant reformers, but such pressure was not imposed on select countries in which donors had other interests at play. Van de Walle (2001) finds that the continuing flow of aid resources lowered the incentives for African governments to undertake economic reforms. Stone (2004) shows that the enforcement of IMF loan conditionality was undermined by the interests of donors who intervened on behalf of their allies. This has been most apparent in the case of French intervention. France's political and economic relations with its former colonies enabled African governments to delay reform much longer than non-CFA countries such as Ghana and Kenya. The CFA central banks, subsidized by France, could continue injecting liquidity into failing commercial banks by refinancing their nonperforming loans at concessional rates into the early 1990s (Popiel 1994; Stasavage 1997).[8]

The literature on rentier states suggests that resource rents enable leaders to resist the pressure to reform, whether from domestic groups or foreign donors.

---

[7] Evidence from the United States shows that, while most of the lobbying done in Washington is on behalf of individual business firms and peak associations (Baumgartner and Leech 1998, 2001), there are few issues that provide sufficient cause for cross-sectoral mobilization (Hart 2004; Smith 2000).

[8] It was only after the 50% devaluation of the CFA franc in 1994 that the monetary unions moved to replace their direct instruments of monetary policy with indirect ones.

Rents from oil and minerals provide leaders with a considerable degree of fiscal autonomy, providing a revenue stream that is independent of the broader population's productivity, while localized production allows for close monitoring (Chaudhry 1997; Dunning 2008; Humphreys and Bates 2005; Jensen and Wantchekon 2004; Karl 1997). Since they have not had to bargain away rights for revenue, as in the historical European model, leaders of extractive economies can leverage the state's influence to induce the cooperation of economic actors. Business, to be sure, often chooses to link its own productive activities to extractive sectors as a way to maximize profits. And once business owners' incomes become tied to government contracts or the foreign firms that manage extraction, their interests become aligned with the incumbent's, creating a greater incentive to maintain the system.

BUSINESS–STATE RELATIONS AND FINANCIAL REFORM

While the statist policies of the 1960s had dovetailed with the political interests of African leaders – providing a justification for their active use of economic controls – the free market prescriptions advocated by the IFIs in the 1980s and 1990s were antithetical to those interests. These reforms were politically unpalatable because they entailed dismantling the instruments that had enabled leaders to exercise discretionary control over capital accumulation. These leaders did not want to lose the ability to selectively reward their allies with credit or to punish their enemies through exclusion. Some were forced to relent, nevertheless. But even if they were assured more aid in exchange for those reforms, these leaders would be gambling that their additional resources would offset the loss of financial control. What kind of leader would take such a risk?

I focus on the nature of Africa's financial reprisal regimes to explain the cross-national variation in liberalization. As discussed in previous chapters, founding leaders sought to shape the business–state relationship to reflect the political threat posed by uneven capital accumulation. Where these leaders had exporter constituencies – the cash crop producers most likely to benefit from financial intermediation – the business–state relationship was managed largely through incentives rather than constraints. These governments cultivated the political support of business by facilitating access to capital, including subsidized loans. I argue that such governments were more likely to undertake financial liberalization because it would not fundamentally undermine the pre-existing equilibrium in business–state relations. Abolishing credit controls or reducing state participation in banking represented a relatively low threat because these governments already exerted little effort in policing capital accumulation among entrepreneurs. Such reforms, moreover, provided potential rewards by enabling governments to secure the donor grants and IFI lending that would permit these governments to sustain themselves in the near term.

The business–state relationship, however, was conditioned on constraints in countries where financial reprisal regimes were first implemented by leaders from nonexporter constituencies. In these cases, governments would go on to subdue business by strictly regulating the access to capital through political criteria. These governments, I maintain, were less likely to comply with external demands for financial liberalization precisely because it would eliminate the controls that underpinned the business–state relationship. Abolishing controls on access to credit or privatizing state-owned banks would reduce the incentive for business to remain allied to a government that could no longer act as a gatekeeper.

The argument made here is consistent with the general intuition from the Africanist scholarship on reform, which has shown that leaders have refused to enact policies that diminish their discretionary authority over the distribution of resources (Bienen and Herbst 1996; Herbst 1990; Lewis 1996; van de Walle 2001). These leaders have sought to protect themselves by selectively liberalizing those sectors in which their instruments of control were no longer viable or useful. This might explain why some governments loosened their grips over credit controls and interest rates, while shielding public enterprises and the civil service, where their abilities to directly hand out jobs and contracts remained a useful form of patronage. In the specific case of financial liberalization, Mkandawire (1999b) argues that reforms were possible in some African countries because the elimination of such controls touched a relatively small number of people. He suggests that restructuring the state-dominated banking sector actually benefited a regime's elite allies by enabling them to avoid repaying their outstanding loans to failed banks.

Whether reform patterns are influenced by the nature of business–state relations can be assessed with data on private credit provision. Credit to the private sector is the preferred indicator of depth and liberalization in the literature on financial development among other monetary aggregates such as the ratio of broad money to GDP or interest rates (Pill and Pradhan 1995). Beck et al. (2004) show that access to credit declines with greater banking concentration, more government regulation, and a larger state share in banking. The availability of private credit thus mirrors the very nature of business–state relations, suggesting the degree to which financial transactions might be subjected to political manipulation.[9] Previous studies indicate that patterns of private credit provision among Africa's reformers have approximated those seen in the developing countries of other regions, whereas pre-reform credit patterns have persisted, if not declined, among reform laggards (Honohan and Beck 2007; Reinhart and Tokatlidis 2000). Liberalizing countries generally have attained higher levels of private credit as a share of GDP than those countries in which reforms lagged.

---

[9] Gulde et al. (2006) point to a strong correlation between private credit provision and indices for the legal rights of creditors. Since legal systems are generally underdeveloped in Africa, banks are often reluctant to lend because courts are unable to enforce contracts. The World Bank's *Doing Business* (2005) surveys confirm that banks in African countries do not lend, in part, because of difficulties in prosecuting defaulters.

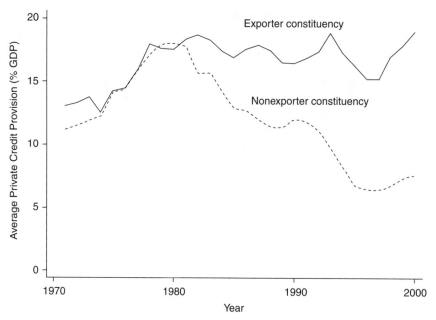

FIGURE 5.1. Average private credit provision by founding leader's constituency type. *Source:* Data on credit to the private sector are from Beck, Demirgüç-Kunt, and Levine (1999).

Figure 5.1 shows average private credit provision by founding leader's constituency type from 1970 through 2000. While there was virtually no difference between the two sets of countries prior to 1980, the trendlines indicate a widening gap after that year. The timing of this divergence is significant, reflecting distinct political responses to the onset of the region-wide economic crisis.[10] Private credit provision remained relatively constant where founding leaders emerged from exporter constituencies. However, private credit provision entered a continuous decline from 1980 to the late 1990s in countries where founding leaders were from nonexporter groups.

The divergence between the two sets of countries in Figure 5.1 is likely due to their distinct strategies for managing business–state relations. First, the marketing boards of exporter-led governments tended to pay cash crop farmers higher producer prices than their nonexporter counterparts (Bates 1981). This would mean that a greater proportion of agricultural revenue was retained in private hands and deposited in commercial banks, which could, in turn, make those funds available to other clients as credit. Second, exporter-led

---

[10] There is no considerable difference between the two types of countries in their rates of economic growth at this juncture. Average GDP growth in 1980–1984 is 2.8% for exporter constituency countries; it is 2.2% for nonexporter constituency countries. The difference is not statistically significant according to a difference-of-means test.

governments were shown in Chapter 4 to have a larger commercial banking sector as well as a smaller state presence in banking ownership. These governments therefore had less leverage in diverting funds from private credit provision for noninvestment purposes. Nonexporter governments, by contrast, created state-dominated banking sectors that could be directed to respond to political needs instead of market demands. And these governments apparently chose to respond to the onset of the economic crisis by slashing the provision of credit to the private sector rather than enacting reforms that would have led to the loss of financial control.

ASSESSING THE SOURCES OF FINANCIAL REFORM

Empirically identifying the sources of reform is complicated by the lack of transparency that characterizes policymaking in most countries. Governments publicly announce reforms without implementing them, unexpectedly reverse reforms previously enacted, and surreptitiously counteract reforms through regulatory measures. In Zimbabwe, for example, Mehran et al. (1998, 13) observe that although "the supervisory authority has apparent power to act alone, in practice – as with other central banking activities – it finds itself subject to overall control from the minister of finance, at whose pleasure the governor often exercises the office." There is a large gap between what governments say versus what they do, so testing the competing explanations for financial reform requires measures that reflect a government's actual rather than reported behavior. Since no single measure can accurately capture the multiple aspects of financial sector reform, I employ two dependent variables in the empirical analysis of this chapter.

The first dependent variable is a dichotomous measure of reform implementation required for compliance with structural adjustment loans. The data come from the Dollar and Svensson (2000) cross-national data set of internal evaluations made by the World Bank's Operations Evaluation Department (OED) for loans issued between 1980 and 1995. The OED evaluation is a particularly good proxy for financial liberalization because nearly two-thirds of the loans made to African governments included conditions related to financial policy.[11] Moreover, the OED evaluation captures whether the policy objectives of reform were met, and not simply whether loan conditionalities were implemented. Countries successfully complied with reform requirements in approximately 59% of the sample.

The second dependent variable is private credit provision. The data for the 1980–2000 period are from the database of Beck et al. (1999) of financial indicators. It is measured as a share of GDP and excludes credit to governments and parastatals. As noted earlier, credit to the private sector has been shown to

---

[11] Dollar and Svensson (2000) assembled a global sample of more than 300 loans made between 1980 and 1995. Here, I limit the sample to African countries; these constitute about 40% of all observations. I thank the authors for sharing their data.

be lower under greater government regulation and a larger state share in banking (Beck et al. 2004). In this respect, higher levels of credit provision should reflect patterns of financial liberalization after 1980.

The analysis employs explanatory variables for each of the hypotheses discussed in this chapter. To reflect the nature of business–state relations in a country, the exporter constituency variable is used to indicate whether a country's independence-era leader had an exporting cash crop constituency, as coded in Table 4.1. Countries where founding leaders from exporter constituencies originally designed the financial system are expected to be more likely to pursue liberalization than countries that were first led by leaders from nonexporter constituencies.

The number of cabinet ministers is used to reflect the size of a leader's patronage coalition. Van de Walle (2001) has previously used cabinet size as a measure of consumption by political elites in order to show that African governments protected themselves from austerity measures despite ongoing economic crises. Leaders with larger cabinets may be expected to more vigorously put off reform if their tenure depends on satisfying all groups represented within their oversized coalitions (Arriola 2009).

The crisis hypothesis is tested through dichotomous measures that indicate whether a country experienced a banking, currency, or debt crisis within the previous five years. Greater financial liberalization is expected with the onset of any of these crisis types, since each signals the government's waning control over instruments of finance. These data come from Laeven and Valencia (2008). As a related measure, total debt service, as a share of gross national income, is included to capture a government's susceptibility to external pressure. Governments facing higher interest payments may be more likely to cede some economic controls in exchange for continued access to foreign currency.

The interest group hypothesis is assessed through the organizational form of the national chamber of commerce (Coleman 1990; Fedotov 2007; Pilgrim and Meier 1995), since business is the most relevant economic actor with regard to financial liberalization. Countries are coded dichotomously to identify whether a chamber of commerce is governed by private law rather than public law. Membership is voluntary for businesses in private law chambers, which are self-governing organizations established through the cooperative effort of a business community. In public law chambers, membership is mandatory for registered businesses. The chamber serves as a public organization whose operations are subject to government supervision.[12] In this context, private law chambers of commerce should be associated with greater financial liberalization, since a self-organizing business community is more likely to act independently in pressuring a government for policy change.

The impact of rents is captured through the measures for foreign aid as a percentage of GDP and dichotomous indicators for oil and mineral exporters.

---

[12] While the chambers of commerce found in African countries tend to be organized according to the tradition of their former colonizers – Francophone countries, for example, follow the French public law system – there are several exceptions.

A dummy variable indicates whether oil or mineral exports constitute more than one-third of a country's exports. Greater values on these variables should be associated with a lower likelihood of reform.

The control variables are based on those found to be significant predictors of compliance with structural adjustment in Dollar and Svensson's (2000) analysis: length of tenure in office, ethnic fractionalization, and level of democracy. Additional controls include per capita income and population size.

The variables are summarized in Appendix C. All explanatory variables are lagged in the analysis.

EMPIRICAL ANALYSIS OF REFORM

The findings from the empirical analysis are reported in two parts. I first discuss the results from the binomial logistic regression of structural adjustment compliance. I then turn to presenting the results from the random effects models of private credit provision. All models are specified using the same set of explanatory variables.

Structural Adjustment Compliance

Table 5.1 reports the results from the binomial logistic analysis of compliance with structural adjustment reforms. The units of analysis are individual country loans issued between 1980 and 1995. Each loan required a set of reform conditions that African governments were expected to implement, so the dependent variable reflects whether governments fulfilled these policy objectives, as judged by the World Bank. The results in Table 5.1 are reported in log-odds units. Because log odds are difficult to interpret directly, I convert them into predicted probabilities in order to provide a more intuitive discussion of how each of the main independent variables affects reform compliance. Model 1 presented in Table 5.1 correctly classifies 76% of the outcomes.

The results in all models of Table 5.1 are consistent with this chapter's expectation that African countries are more likely to engage in financial liberalization if a founding leader from an exporter constituency originally shaped the business–state relationship. Not only does the coefficient on this variable attain statistical significance at conventional levels, but its impact is also substantively large. Transforming the log odds reported in Model 1 suggests that the predicted probability of complying with the reforms of structural adjustment increases by about 75%: it rises from 0.29 in countries where business–state relations were molded by nonexporter leaders to 0.52 in countries first led by exporter leaders, holding other independent variables at mean or modal values.[13]

---

[13] The simulated values discussed throughout this section were generated through the Clarify program (Tomz et al. 2001). The independent variables in Table 5.1 are set at the mean or modal values reported in Appendix C: cabinet size = 21.524, bank crisis = 0, currency crisis = 0, debt crisis = 0, debt service = 4.832, private law chamber = 1, foreign aid = 12.376, oil exporter = 0, mineral exporter = 0, Polity = -2.861, leader years = 9.912, and ethnic fractionalization = 0.728.

TABLE 5.1. *The Determinants of Structural Adjustment Compliance*

	Model 1	Model 2	Model 3	Model 4
Exporter constituency	1.204**	0.928*	1.247**	1.617**
	(0.530)	(0.559)	(0.568)	(0.665)
Cabinet size	−0.322***	−0.374***	−0.320***	−0.312***
	(0.090)	(0.124)	(0.092)	(0.094)
Banking crisis in previous 5 years	2.580***	2.631***	2.649***	2.832***
	(0.872)	(0.898)	(0.907)	(1.000)
Currency crisis in previous 5 years	1.292**	1.374*	1.396*	1.975**
	(0.640)	(0.745)	(0.768)	(0.777)
Debt crisis in previous 5 years	1.330	1.296*	1.322	1.061
	(0.816)	(0.770)	(0.828)	(0.857)
Debt service, % GDP	0.249**	0.214**	0.249**	0.292***
	(0.097)	(0.098)	(0.097)	(0.105)
Private law chamber of commerce	0.539	0.840	0.634	0.840
	(0.558)	(0.639)	(0.668)	(0.651)
Foreign aid, % GDP	−0.118***	−0.123**	−0.123**	−0.139***
	(0.044)	(0.058)	(0.048)	(0.054)
Oil exporter	−5.742***	−6.471***	−5.670***	−4.979**
	(1.904)	(2.397)	(2.014)	(2.084)
Mineral exporter	−2.284***	−2.360***	−2.392***	−2.753***
	(0.857)	(0.787)	(0.897)	(0.970)
Polity score	0.015	0.032	−0.001	−0.062
	(0.078)	(0.083)	(0.088)	(0.100)
Leader years in power	−0.027	−0.039	−0.029	−0.031
	(0.052)	(0.051)	(0.051)	(0.058)
Ethnic fractionalization	3.284*	3.950**	3.583*	3.894*
	(1.821)	(1.619)	(2.008)	(2.014)
GDP per capita, log		1.359		
		(0.912)		
Population, log			−0.199	
			(0.484)	
Loan amount, log				−1.270*
				(0.709)
Constant	3.273	−3.186	6.084	7.094***
	(2.038)	(4.343)	(6.650)	(2.164)
Number of observations	84	83	84	84
Log likelihood	−39.21	−37.84	−39.16	−36.61
Pseudo R^2	0.3195	0.3338	0.3205	0.3647

Notes: The dependent variable is reform compliance with structural adjustment loans. All independent variables are lagged one year. Robust standard errors, clustered by country, are in parentheses.

*** $p < 0.01$, ** $p < 0.05$, * $p < 0.10$, two-tailed tests.

The leaders of larger patronage-based coalitions, as proxied by cabinet size, appear less likely to carry out the liberalizing reforms required by structural adjustment. Based on the log odds reported for cabinet size in Model 1, the predicted probability of reform compliance in a country first led by a nonexporter leader is estimated to be 0.60 under a 17-member cabinet, at the 25th percentile, holding other independent variables at mean or modal values. Expanding this country's cabinet to 25 ministers, at the 75th percentile, reduces the predicted probability to 0.14. Exporter countries follow a similar pattern: the predicted probability declines from 0.79 under 17 cabinet ministers to 0.28 under 25 cabinet ministers. It remains unclear, however, whether the lack of reform among larger patronage coalitions is due to the refusal of leaders who fear the disintegration of their regimes or the resistance of coalition members who insist on retaining their perquisites.

The crisis variables indicate that banking and currency crises encourage African leaders to comply with structural adjustment reforms. Model 1 in Table 5.1 indicates that the onset of a banking crisis in the five years prior to the signing of a structural adjustment loan raises the predicted probability of compliance in nonexporter countries from 0.29 to 0.80, holding other independent variables at mean or modal values. The log odds reported in Model 1 also suggest that the onset of a currency crisis in the previous five years increases the predicted probability of reform compliance to 0.53. These crises have a similar impact on exporter-led countries; their predicted probabilities rise from 0.52 to 0.92 after a banking crisis and to 0.73 after a currency crisis. The log odds for debt service further show that more indebted countries are more likely to comply with structural adjustment reforms.

The estimated log odds for private law chambers of commerce, while moving in the hypothesized direction, are statistically insignificant. Self-organizing private sectors are no more successful than those with corporatist relationships in pressuring their governments to enact liberalizing reforms.

The results in Table 5.1 indicate that higher levels of foreign aid discourage compliance with structural adjustment reforms, which is in line with the argument that financial statism could not be sustained in most African countries without external support. The estimated log odds on this variable suggest that countries receiving greater foreign aid are less likely to enact the reforms on which that aid is conditioned. This result suggests that donors may need to cut off aid, as discussed in the Kenyan case later, to induce recipient governments to concede to reform. But large aid recipients are most likely receiving external assistance from multiple sources, so the lack of coordination among donors makes the threat of aid withdrawal less credible for governments that refuse to reform (van de Walle 2001).

The rentier variables move in the hypothesized direction: oil and mineral rents enable African leaders to resist complying with structural adjustment reforms. These results corroborate the argument that alternative fiscal

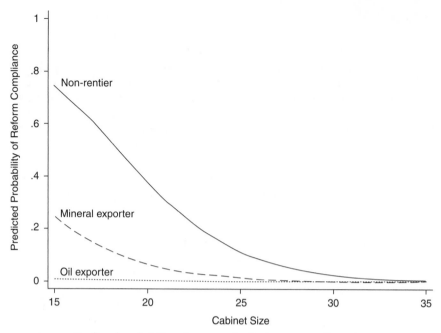

FIGURE 5.2. Predicted probability of structural adjustment compliance by resource type.

resources enable leaders to resist the external pressure for reform.[14] The World Bank's (1997) own report on structural adjustment compliance shows that successful reformers were often resource-poor countries such as Benin, Ghana, and Tanzania, while the nonreformers were rentier states such as Cameroon, Central African Republic, and Gabon. In this analysis, different types of resources appear to influence reform outcomes at distinct levels of magnitude, most likely reflecting their prices on world markets. Recall from the previous example, based on Model 1, that the predicted probability of reform compliance for the nonexporter country is estimated to be 0.29. That predicted probability would plummet to 0.01 if such a country were to become an oil exporter, holding other independent variables at mean or modal values. The impact of mineral resources is less severe, but also consequential. The predicted probability for such a country would drop to 0.07 if it were to become a mineral exporter. Figure 5.2 illustrates these effects in combination with cabinet size.

Among the control variables, only ethnic fractionalization and the loan amount attain statistical significance. More diverse African countries appear

---

[14] Countries are defined as rentier states if fuel and minerals represent more than one-third of their merchandise exports. Being a rentier state is unrelated to a founding leader's constituency type; rentier states emerged under both exporter and nonexporter leaders. Those founded by exporter leaders are Botswana, Gabon, Nigeria, and Togo; those founded by nonexporter leaders are Cameroon, Congo Republic, Guinea, Niger, Sierra Leone, and Zambia.

more likely to implement reform,[15] while countries with larger loans appear to be less likely to fulfill their conditions. The level of democracy, a leader's tenure, per capita income, and population size fail to attain statistical significance.

Private Credit Provision

Table 5.2 reports the results from the random effects analysis of panel data on private credit provision.[16] The units of analysis are country-years from 1980 to 2000, covering the crisis period in which African governments were negotiating with the IFIs over the reforms attached to conditional loans. Employing the same set of explanatory variables from the analysis of structural adjustment compliance, the results presented here largely confirm the impact of the main independent variables of interest. Private credit provision, as a proxy for financial liberalization, rises in countries where founding leaders emerged from exporter constituencies. However, credit declines under governments based on larger patronage coalitions and those that tap oil rents.

African countries where business–state relations were crafted by founding leaders with exporter constituencies appear more likely to carry out the liberalizing reforms required to permit greater access to private credit. This variable attains statistical significance at conventional levels, indicating that such countries did sustain higher levels of credit between 1980 and 2000. The estimated coefficient in Model 3 suggests that private credit provision was 4.9 percentage points higher in such countries, holding all else constant. Consider the average country in which the founding leader was from a nonexporter constituency. Private credit provision in such a country would stand at 8.5% of GDP, holding all other variables at mean or modal values.[17] But it would rise to 13.4% of GDP – a 58% increase – if this hypothetical country had been first led by a leader from an exporter constituency.

Leaders with larger ministerial cabinets appear less likely to carry out liberalizing reforms. The coefficients for this variable across Table 5.2 suggest that five additional cabinet ministers would be associated with half a percentage point decline in the provision of private credit, holding all else constant. This is not trivial change when considering the relatively low rates across African countries. This negative association may reflect the pressure coalition members place on governments for the diversion of funds from the financial sector to parastatals, government agencies, or politically connected firms.

[15] Dollar and Svensson originally found a parabolic relationship between reform compliance and ethnic fractionalization in their global sample. I found no such effect in the African sample used here.

[16] Random effects are used instead of fixed effects for the analysis because the main independent variable of interest is time invariant. Robust standard errors clustered by country are estimated to correct for heteroskedasticity and autocorrelation.

[17] The independent variables in Table 5.2 are set at the mean or modal values reported in Appendix C: cabinet size = 21.524, bank crisis = 0, currency crisis = 0, debt crisis = 0, debt service = 4.832, private law chamber = 1, foreign aid = 12.376, oil exporter = 0, mineral exporter = 0, Polity = −2.861, leader years = 9.912, ethnic fractionalization = 0.728; 1990s decade = 1; log of GDP per capita=5.881; log of population=15.595.

TABLE 5.2. *The Determinants of Private Credit Provision*

	Model 1	Model 2	Model 3
Exporter constituency	0.097***	0.045*	0.049**
	(0.022)	(0.023)	(0.021)
Cabinet size	−0.001*	−0.001**	−0.001**
	(0.001)	(0.001)	(0.001)
Banking crisis in previous 5 years	0.004	0.009*	0.009*
	(0.005)	(0.005)	(0.005)
Currency crisis in previous 5 years	−0.026***	−0.024***	−0.025***
	(0.004)	(0.004)	(0.004)
Debt crisis in previous 5 years	0.015**	0.016***	0.016***
	(0.007)	(0.006)	(0.006)
Debt service, % GDP	0.001	−0.000	−0.000
	(0.000)	(0.000)	(0.000)
Private law chamber of commerce	−0.042**	−0.056***	−0.055***
	(0.019)	(0.020)	(0.019)
Foreign aid, % GDP	−0.001*	0.000	0.000
	(0.000)	(0.000)	(0.000)
Oil exporter	−0.033	−0.114***	−0.112***
	(0.029)	(0.032)	(0.032)
Mineral exporter	0.006	0.007	0.005
	(0.008)	(0.007)	(0.007)
Polity score	−0.000	−0.001	−0.001
	(0.000)	(0.000)	(0.000)
Leader years in power	0.001*	0.000	0.000
	(0.000)	(0.000)	(0.000)
Ethnic fractionalization	0.121**	0.119*	0.117**
	(0.050)	(0.062)	(0.056)
1990s decade	−0.016***	−0.016***	−0.016***
	(0.006)	(0.005)	(0.006)
GDP per capita, log		0.098***	0.094***
		(0.019)	(0.020)
Population, log			0.002
			(0.011)
Constant	0.0532	−0.484***	−0.495**
	(0.0407)	(0.117)	(0.234)
Number of observations	492	491	491
Number of countries	26	26	26
R^2 within	0.1593	0.2955	0.2891
R^2 between	0.4499	0.4921	0.5154
R^2 overall	0.3708	0.4202	0.4371

Note: The dependent variable is private credit provision. All independent variables are lagged one year. Robust standard errors, clustered by country, are in parentheses.
*** $p < 0.01$, ** $p < 0.05$, * $p < 0.10$, two-tailed tests.

The results reported in Table 5.2 show that crises do not have a uniform impact on the provision of private credit. Banking crises are shown to subsequently induce higher levels of private credit provision, while currency crises seem to dampen those levels. The onset of a debt crisis also increases the provision of private credit, though this may reflect greater demand as much as a loosening of state control. A country's debt burden has no effect on private credit.

The estimated coefficients for private law chambers of commerce are statistically significant, but move against the expected direction. Countries with self-organizing business communities are associated with lower private credit provision. This result may reflect the transition made by some of the more economically vulnerable countries of the region. Countries such as Guinea and Tanzania, for example, began to liberalize their economies after pursuing socialist development strategies for decades. It was also during this transition that many of these countries first permitted the establishment of chambers of commerce, which tended to be organized according to the private law rather than the public law model, regardless of colonial background.

The rentier variables perform inconsistently. Foreign aid and mineral exports appear to have no consistent impact on private credit provision, failing to attain statistical significance in most model specifications. The coefficient on oil exporters, however, is statistically significant, indicating that such countries have rates of private credit provision that are 11.2 percentage points lower than nonoil exporters, holding all else constant.

The results in Table 5.2 indicate that more diverse countries as well as wealthier countries have higher levels of credit. However, the political control variables, the Polity score and leader tenure, have no impact on private credit provision.

CAMEROON AND KENYA: DIVERGENT REFORM NARRATIVES

This section turns to tracing the causal mechanism of financial liberalization through the cases of Cameroon and Kenya. Both countries had been buffeted by economic shocks in the 1980s and experienced severe banking crises by mid-decade, but their reform outcomes ultimately depended on the nature of business–state relations implanted at independence and the relative fiscal autonomy provided by resource rents. In Cameroon, Paul Biya sought to put off reforms that might undermine a business–state relationship based on the direct control of banking and credit. He could forestall financial liberalization because oil provided his regime with the hard currency as well as the external support needed to sustain the status quo. In Kenya, by contrast, although Daniel arap Moi sought to maintain the instruments for providing party allies with preferential access to capital, his cash-strapped government was obliged to adopt liberalizing reforms imposed by the IFIs in exchange for additional loans and aid.

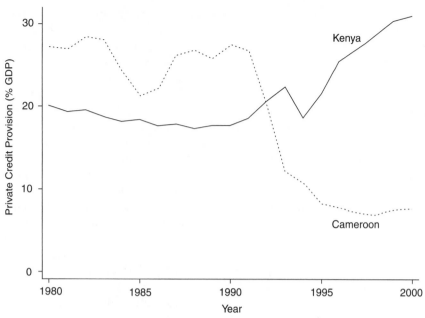

FIGURE 5.3. Private credit provision in Cameroon and Kenya.
Source: Beck, Demirgüç-Kunt, and Levine (1999).

The divergent trajectories of Cameroon and Kenya are evident in Figure 5.3, reflecting distinct patterns of government–business relations. Biya's influence over business in Cameroon was magnified as private credit provision plummeted in the early 1990s, coinciding with the country's transition to multiparty politics. Although the country's economic growth rate recovered to nearly 5% after 1994 – with the 1994 CFA devaluation helping to reinvigorate the economy – there was no concomitant rise in the level of private credit provision. In Kenya, Moi lost his influence over business as financial liberalization unfolded throughout the 1990s. The availability of private credit rose progressively through subsequent reforms and persisted at higher rates despite a recession at the end of the decade.

Financial Control in Cameroon

The economic shocks that began in the 1980s initiated nearly a decade of lost growth in Cameroon. Declining commodity prices coupled with an overvalued currency had made the country's main agricultural exports – coffee, cocoa, and cotton – less competitive in world markets (van de Walle 1991). More critically, the collapse of world oil prices in 1986 plunged the country, a small exporter, into a recession that would last until 1994, during which time the economy shrank at an average annual rate of 3.81%. Nevertheless, despite the severity of the country's economic problems, Biya's government did not relinquish its hold over capital.

A former resident representative of the IMF would observe nearly ten years after the onset of the crisis that Cameroon's finance minister continued to exercise "the effective and real authority" in the allocation of credit (Doe 1995, 105).

After taking office in 1982, Biya initially moved to relax banking regulations by abolishing rules requiring the state to take one-third ownership in all banks as well as bank managers to be Cameroonian nationals. But these 1985 reforms did little to change the relationship that had evolved between the government and commercial banks. As long as banks continued to act in accordance with the government's lending preferences, the finance ministry had no incentive to carry out its prudential oversight responsibilities. Years of politicized lending, however, began to push the entire financial system into crisis. Most commercial banks became insolvent by 1987.

Cameroon resisted seeking support from the IFIs for far longer than most African countries, but the economic reality of the late 1980s forced Biya's government to arrange for its first stand-by loan from the IMF in 1988 and its first structural adjustment loan from the World Bank in 1989. Alarmed by the rapid deterioration of Cameroon's financial system, the IFIs placed financial reform, including bank restructuring, at the center of the short-term stabilization and long-term adjustment recommendations made to Biya's government (Brachet 2008; Doe 1995; Ezé-Ezé 2001). In 1990, the restructuring of Cameroon's banks required 90% of the resources needed to restore the solvency of all six national banking systems in Central Africa (Kamgna and Dimou 2008). The IFIs were especially interested in promoting reforms that would prevent the government from continuing to use banks as an instrument of deficit financing, as had been occurring in all members of the CFA zones (Stasavage 1997). The government had been using its control over banks to demand loans for parastatals and political allies and then refinancing those loans at subsidized rates through the Banque des États de l'Afrique Centrale (BEAC), the regional central bank. But the trick was repeated as the banking system was being restructured: the government assumed the outstanding debts of bankrupt banks and again refinanced them through the BEAC at a subsidized rate.

In consultation with the IFIs, Biya's government responded to the crisis by updating the country's banking laws in 1990, more clearly specifying their responsibilities, broadening their range of services, creating new categories for finance companies and merchant banks, and offering guarantees for investment in the sector.[18] It overhauled the banking sector by liquidating four banks in 1989, namely, Banque Camerounaise de Développement, Banque Paribas-Cameroun, Cameroon Bank, and Société Camerounaise de Banque (World Bank 1996). Six more banks were closed in a second round of liquidation between 1992 and 1997.

---

[18] At the time, however, the government did not abolish the regulations obliging banks to deposit 10% of their assets with the Société Nationale d'Investissement (SNI) or to deposit 10% of their profits with the Fond d'Aide et de Garantie des Crédits aux Petites et Moyennes Entreprises (FOGAPE).

Cameroon, along with the other member states of the BEAC, signed onto agreements between 1990 and 1992 that liberalized finance at the regional level, requiring the elimination of credit controls, the coordination of banking regulations, and the implementation of stricter banking supervision (Brachet 2008). In 1993, the Commission Bancaire de l'Afrique Centrale (COBAC) became the regional banking regulator with the authority to license new institutions, monitor their operations, and impose sanctions. In supplanting national banking regulators, COBAC was more likely to appoint trained professionals rather than political cronies as supervisors.

While the reforms undertaken in Cameroon during the first half of the 1990s helped to shore up the banking sector, these measures did not appreciably weaken the government's overall role in mediating access to capital. The government's implementation of reform was essentially constrained by its own political imperatives. By mid-decade, the World Bank (1996) concluded that "attempts to restructure the financial sector over the last seven years have failed. Any new reforms have little chance of success as long as the environment in which banks operate continues to be plagued by severe structural problems." Although COBAC provided more rigorous banking supervision, the enforcement of its decisions continued to rely on national officials. Undercapitalized banks were allowed to stay in business, while nonperforming loans continued to mount (International Monetary Fund 2000; World Bank 2001).

Most significantly, after nearly ten years of restructuring, the state remained the principal banker to the private sector. Figure 5.4 shows that the state held shares in nearly all of the country's commercial banks, both foreign and domestic, since the 1970s.[19] By 1989, the state was tied to all of the country's eleven commercial banks as a majority shareholder in four banks and a minority shareholder in another seven.[20] The state's minority shareholding averaged 33%, which was sufficient in many cases to provide veto power on bank decisions or policies. By 1999, the state remained a shareholder in four of the country's eight commercial banks, holding a majority stake in two banks and a minority stake in two others. The government could thus continue pressuring banks into extending or denying financial services on the basis of political criteria. And even a minority stake could ensure tangible influence. Consider the experience of Standard Chartered Bank, a London-based bank operating

[19] This tally excludes the state-owned development banks such as SNI, Crédit Foncier du Cameroun, or Crédit Industriel et Commercial, which replaced the FOGAPE.

[20] By 1989, the state was the majority shareholder in Banque Unie de Crédit, Banque Paribas Cameroun, Cameroon Bank, and Société Camerounaise de Banque. It was the minority shareholder in Société Générale de Banques au Cameroun (45%), Banque Internationale pour le Commerce et l'Industrie du Cameroun (39%), Bank of Credit and Commerce Cameroon (35%), International Bank of Africa Cameroon (35%), Standard Chartered Bank Cameroon (34%), Banque Internationale pour l'Afrique Occidentale-Cameroun (25%), and Meridien Bank Cameroon (25%). The estimated figures for state-owned shares listed here include those held by parastatals.

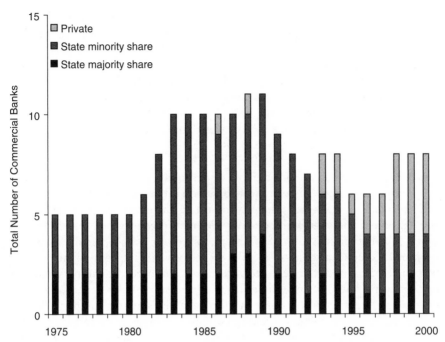

FIGURE 5.4. State-owned shares in Cameroon's commercial banking sector.
Source: Author's calculations based on annual entries in *Africa South of the Sahara.*

in Cameroon. Although Standard Chartered is a large multinational bank, the government was able to use its 34% share to have Ephraim Inoni appointed the bank's chairman in 1993. At the time, Inoni simultaneously served as the assistant secretary general for Biya's office – the equivalent of the president's deputy chief of staff. Inoni stepped down from his post as bank chairman after more than a decade only when Biya designated him to be his new prime minister in December 2004.

Cameroon is only one of three African countries in which the number of commercial banks shrank between 1990 and 2000.[21] Figure 5.4 underscores how the banking sector's contraction from a high of eleven banks in 1989 to a low of six banks by 1997 reinforced the politicization of finance. The contraction in commercial banking effectively led to rationing, since credit to the private sector as a share of GDP simultaneously plummeted from 26% in 1989 to 7% in 1997. As financing options narrowed throughout this period, entrepreneurs understood that they needed to maintain close links with the ruling party that controlled, directly and indirectly, the country's few remaining banks. Only by doing so could they ensure their continued access to a shrinking capital base.

[21] Sierra Leone and Togo are the other two countries.

The ability of Biya's government to put off more comprehensive financial reforms in the 1990s is explained by its access to oil rents. In this respect, Biya was afforded a margin of fiscal autonomy enjoyed by few African leaders. After Cameroon became an exporter in 1978, oil grew to account for two-thirds of its export earnings by the mid-1980s. In the process, the government became less dependent on IFIs or donors by accumulating considerable foreign currency reserves with little external debt. By 1990, the country's debt servicing, as a percentage of GDP, was 15.5% lower than the regional average. Foreign aid to Cameroon, as a percentage of GDP, represented only about 35% of the regional average in 1990 (World Bank 2001).

Oil rents provide Biya considerable discretionary power. Because a quarter of government revenue, on average, is based on oil production, Biya's regime is less dependent on taxes from the private sector. The presidency's direct control over oil rents endows it with considerable fiscal power. When oil production originally came on line, Ahmadou Ahidjo, the country's first president, began a tradition of keeping a share of oil rents off the official budget and placing them in foreign accounts to be accessed directly by the office of the president for infrastructure development. While this tradition supposedly ended with more transparent budgeting procedures in the 1990s, the state oil company, Société Nationale des Hydrocarbures (SNH), continues to operate under the jurisdiction of the secretary general of the president's office. Besides making regular transfers to the treasury, SNH can make cash advances to the government without requiring prior authorization ostensibly for the purpose of funding national security or public enterprises. Cash advances to the government in 2003–2005 averaged nearly a quarter of SNH's total revenue. In 2003, 22% of those cash advances were allocated to the president's office; during the 2004 election year, the presidency's allocation jumped to 38% of all advances (Cossé 2006).

Oil has further enhanced Biya's fiscal position by conditioning Cameroon's relationship with France, which has had a strategic incentive to ensure the continuity of Biya's regime. Although French President François Mitterrand announced in 1990 that French aid to its former colonies would be made conditional on democratization, Stasavage (1997, 149) notes that "when the need for adjustment arose, but bore a perceived risk of unseating governments (and a risk of a restructuring of Franco-African relations that might accompany regime changes), French politicians with a vested interested preferred financing that would assure short-term political stability." While France cut aid to countries like Benin and Mali, where democratization was in full swing in the 1990s, it increased aid for strategic partners like Cameroon, Congo, and Gabon through a special development fund (Martin 1995). The rationale was resource-based. France's state-owned Elf-Aquitaine depended on four African countries for 70% of its supplies: Angola, Cameroon, Congo, and Gabon. Elf-Aquitaine, which was later absorbed by Total, controls 68% of Cameroon's oil production (Cossé 2006).

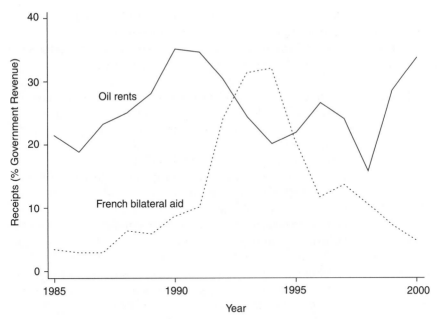

FIGURE 5.5. Oil rents and French bilateral aid in Cameroon.
Sources: Author's calculations based on IMF Cameroon Statistical Appendix; OECD Development Database.

Traditionally Cameroon's largest bilateral donor, the French government chose to shield Biya's regime from having to make politically costly reforms in the early 1990s. France increased its aid to Cameroon just as other donors were withdrawing their support in light of Biya's reluctance to engage in serious reform.[22] Figure 5.5 shows that French bilateral aid was pivotal in offsetting declining government revenue due to falling world oil prices. From 1992 to 1997 – the country's most politically contentious years – France provided Biya's government with 72% of all bilateral aid, turning Cameroon into its second-largest aid recipient after Côte d'Ivoire.

To further shore up Biya's regime, France provided additional bilateral lending through various mechanisms. In 1992, Elf-Aquitaine, long a French policy instrument in Africa, arranged for Biya to receive a $45 million loan (Verschave 2000). In 1993, France provided a FCFA 15 billion loan, or about $53 million, to pay salary arrears to civil servants and provided additional loans when the IMF would not (Konings 1996). Biya later hired the former French ambassador to Cameroon, who had retired in 1993, as his special counselor

---

[22] The United States suspended $14 million in aid to Cameroon in November 1992. See Russell Geekie, "Biya's Anglophone Adversary," Interview with John Fru Ndi, *Africa Report*, v. 38, n. 2, 62–63.

(Stasavage 1997). It is no doubt for such reasons that Elf-Aquitaine's former president, Loïk Le Floch-Prigent, would acknowledge in 1996 that "President Biya cannot hold power without Elf's support in containing the Anglophone community of that country" (quoted in Verschave 2000, 176).

The fiscal autonomy gained through oil rents, and associated French support, enabled Cameroon to resist implementing the more extensive reform conditions tied to IMF and World Bank lending. Cameroon undertook some reforms between 1990 and 1992, but these were "implemented haphazardly in the early stages and lacked government commitment," according to the IMF (2000, 8). Rather than engaging in further liberalization, the government sought to shore up its position by cutting back on spending. In 1993, the government reacted to a decline in revenue by cutting on capital expenditure and slashing salaries up to 70%. The 50% devaluation of the CFA franc in January 1994 prompted the government to secure additional stand-by loans from the IMF, but there was little reform to show for it. None of the four agreements negotiated with the IMF between 1988 and 1996 were implemented.

Biya's government publicly took up the reform process once more in 1996. Not coincidentally, as shown in Figure 5.5, this was also the year in which French bilateral aid was slashed to pre-1991 levels. Biya responded by reshuffling his government in September 1996 to produce a new-look government with Peter Mafany Musonge, a respected Anglophone parastatal director, as prime minister. But it was unclear how much more effective this new pro-reform administration could be. Biya had already appointed, since 1994, two additional ministers to oversee the national budget and the stabilization plan; these portfolios presumably differed from the pre-existing finance and state inspection portfolios. Nevertheless, the cabinet reshuffle helped the government to secure a new structural adjustment facility from the IMF in August 1997. And perhaps not coincidentally, in October 1997, the same month that opposition parties boycotted the presidential election, Paris Club creditors agreed to reschedule and write off part of Cameroon's $2 billion debt over the next three years.

Biya's government appeared to make progress after 1997 in previously neglected reform areas, including financial deregulation, fiscal policy, and parastatal privatization (International Monetary Fund 2000, 2005a). But assessments of progress at this stage were more likely to reflect reduced expectations. World Bank officials essentially admitted defeat when evaluating their relations with Cameroon in the 1990s: "The Bank avoided investment projects which were difficult to implement and costly to supervise; it concentrated on adjustment credits which could be pushed through by a Minister" (World Bank 2001, 12).

FINANCIAL LIBERALIZATION IN KENYA

Falling commodity prices for coffee and tea exports, coupled with rising real interest rates, brought the Kenyan economy into near continuous decline in the 1980s. Kenya began the decade by signing onto its first structural adjustment program with support from the IMF and World Bank. Conditionality-based lending became a major component of government finance, principally for balance-of-payments support, from that point forward. Between 1986 and 1991, the World Bank approved six more loans for reforming different sectors of the Kenyan economy. Yet few reforms were actually enacted during the period. The IFIs continued to tolerate government intervention in the market.[23] In practice, loans were disbursed to the government despite the lack of compliance with prior commitments and even further tightening of certain economic controls (O'Brien and Ryan 2001; Were et al. 2006).

Moi resisted dismantling financial instruments that permitted him to channel resources to regime allies.[24] The state-controlled banks had become a mechanism for decentralized corruption that benefitted the politically well-connected. For example, branch managers working for the Kenya Commercial Bank (KCB) could issue loans at their discretion, which often resulted in collusive local relations between bank officials, businesspeople, and politicians. Benjamin Kipkorir, KCB's executive chairman in the 1980s, therefore encountered political resistance when he attempted to reassign certain branch managers seen as indispensable by their clients. Kipkorir recalls that on one occasion "the matter even reached certain quarters in government that ought not to have concerned themselves with it" (Kipkorir 2009, 291–292).[25] Another example of politicized lending concerns the first financial institution to go into receivership in Kenya, Rural Urban Credit Finance Company. After its chairman, Andrew Kimani Ngumba, incorporated this nonbanking financial institution in 1982, he proceeded to distribute easy loans to voters in the constituency from which he sought to be elected as a member of parliament the following year.[26] Since Ngumba would quickly go on to become an assistant minister for lands, it is unlikely that his unorthodox lending occurred without the ruling party's implicit consent.

[23] The Washington Consensus on reforms did not gel until the late 1980s, when structural adjustment programs were gradually expanded to encourage governments to implement liberalizing policies aimed at reducing market distortions and increasing reliance on market forces. This meant that aid recipients were asked to eliminate state monopolies and lift controls on foreign exchange, credit, and prices (Williamson 1993).

[24] Politicized lending could serve either as punishment or reward. In 1978, when a member of parliament raised questions implicating the state-owned National Bank of Kenya (NBK), Assistant Finance Minister Arthur Magugu responded the next day by publicly revealing the questioner's own checkered financial dealings with the same bank, including defaulting on personal loans and transferring assets between his personal account and companies for which he was listed as a director. The threat was implied, but clear: what the government had once permitted could also be taken away. See "When Is a Banking Secret Not Secret?" *Weekly Review* (Nairobi), 6 October 1978, p. 26.

[25] Kipkorir was unexpectedly dismissed from his post in December 1991, in part, because he had been unwilling to submit to growing political pressure to lend to teetering parastatals or politically connected banks. According to Kipkorir (2009, 296), "I am certain I had said 'No' enough times than the President or the [Finance] Minister could tolerate."

[26] "Rural Urban's Lesson for Banking Industry," *Weekly Review* (Nairobi), 14 December 1984, p. 17; "Rural Urban, First Financial Collapse," *Weekly Review* (Nairobi), 14 December 1984, p. 20.

Moi came under increasing pressure to relinquish the instruments of financial influence as donor priorities shifted with the end of the Cold War. And he lacked the fiscal autonomy to resist that pressure. With his government depending on external support for 45% of its operating budget by 1990, he was forced to bargain with the IFIs throughout the subsequent decade. Many of the reforms that his government would eventually enact were consistent with the pre-crisis equilibrium in business–state relations. Entrepreneurs already enjoyed options for credit provided by both private and state-owned banks. Liberalization served to further expand those options, forcing the government to reduce its participation in banking and eliminate restrictions in areas such as foreign exchange.

Moi was compelled to accept the IFIs' terms for liberalization because decades of politicized lending threatened to undermine the entire financial system. A mounting share of nonperforming loans helped to provoke five banking crises from the mid-1980s through the mid-1990s (Laeven and Valencia 2008). Politically related solvency problems led to the failure of 12 banks and nonbanking financial institutions between 1984 and 1989; 17 more failed in 1993–1994 (Brownbridge 1998). By the end of the 1990s, the banking sector's nonperforming loans had ballooned to more than one-third of gross loans. Two-thirds of those debts were concentrated in the state-owned banks: in 1999, 20% of loans made by KCB were in default, along with 84% of loans made by the National Bank of Kenya (NBK) (Economist Intelligence Unit 2000; International Monetary Fund 2002).[27]

Moi's government responded to this prolonged financial crisis by undertaking a series of reform measures that liberalized the financial system throughout the 1990s. Interest rates were deregulated, foreign exchange controls were eliminated, a flexible exchange rate was adopted, and credit controls were abolished by mid-decade. The central bank's autonomy in implementing monetary policy and supervising the banking sector was reinforced through legislation in 1996; this legislation provided for the security of tenure of the central bank governor. As a result of these reforms, the IMF (1996) recognized that the government had brought about "a major economic transformation," turning Kenya into one of Africa's most open economies. Especially in the financial sector, Kenya became "a regional leader in following best practices" (Mehran et al. 1998, 14).

Along with its financial policy reforms, the government began to divest itself of equity holdings in the banking sector, gradually scaling back its ownership in KCB and NBK through flotations on the Nairobi Stock Exchange that were then acquired by the local business community. The state's equity in KCB, the country's largest bank, was reduced to 70% in 1990 and 60% 1996. The state became a minority shareholder in KCB when it reduced its shareholding to 35% in 1998. A similar, though slower, process was undertaken with the

---

[27] The memoir of Benjamin Kipkorir (2009), KCB's executive chairman from 1983 to 1991, suggests that he was under increasing political pressure to divert funds to troubled parastatals.

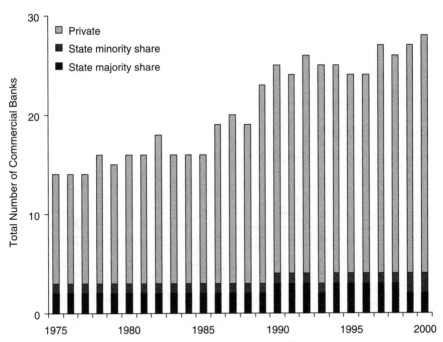

FIGURE 5.6. State-owned shares in Kenya's commercial banking sector.
Source: Author's calculations based on annual entries in *Africa South of the Sahara.*

troubled NBK: the government reduced its shareholding to 80% in 1994 and then to 64.5% by 2000.

The impact of Kenya's financial liberalization can be observed in the size of the commercial banking sector. As shown in Figure 5.6, the number of privately owned banks began to grow steadily throughout the 1990s in parallel with the progressive enactment of reforms and the state's divestment from banking. Compensating for the mid-decade failure of several banks connected to politicized lending, both multinational and local banks entered the sector despite the transition toward a more stringent regulatory regime. By 2000, Kenyan entrepreneurs had more banking options than at any other point in the country's history.

What explains the implementation of such extensive reforms in Kenya throughout the 1990s? The reform process was largely driven by the government's need to access foreign aid. Having become one of the largest recipients of aid funding in Africa – receiving nearly $1 billion in 1989 alone – Moi's government had become dependent on Western donors for budget and balance-of-payments support. Lacking the resource rents available to leaders like Biya in Cameroon, Moi had neither the fiscal autonomy nor the foreign sponsorship necessary to keep his government afloat. What is more, his ruling party had become a coalition held together largely through the distribution of patronage

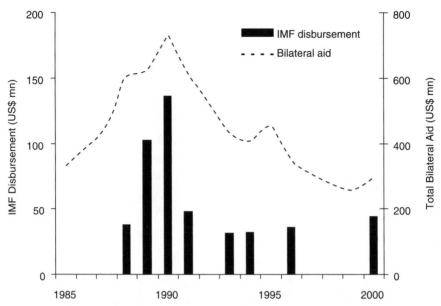

FIGURE 5.7. IMF disbursement and bilateral aid to Kenya, 1985–2000.
Source: Author's calculations based on IMF Kenya Statistical Appendix; OECD
Development Database.

just as demands for democracy were mounting. He understood that he would
lose power without access to external resources.

The financial reforms adopted by Kenya in the 1990s were required by
Western donors as conditions for continued aid. In contrast to the local business
community, which had attempted "over the years to engage the government in
economic policy dialogue, but with little or no success" (O'Brien and Ryan
2001, 508), the donors had the leverage to oblige the cash-strapped regime
to comply. According to Micah Cheserem (2006, 123), the country's central
banker from 1993 to 2001, "economic reforms that the government implemented during my tenure were mainly part of IMF loan conditionalities."

A review of the bargaining between Kenya and the IMF reveals how the
content and timing of reform were determined by the periodic freezing of
donor aid. Donors would periodically withhold the disbursement of aid to
extract additional reforms from Moi's government. This proved to be particularly effective, since IMF approval was required before further multilat-
eral lending or bilateral aid, including debt rescheduling, could be unlocked.
Figure 5.7 shows how total bilateral aid to Kenya moved in tandem with the
intermittent disbursement of IMF loans.

The bargaining between the IMF and Kenya was a protracted affair in the
1990s, as reforms were stalled or rolled back, because Moi sought to preserve
his discretionary authority for as long as possible. The banking-related crises
that erupted after each multiparty election, which are discussed later, underscore

the value that Moi placed on being able to channel funds from the financial system to contend with political challenges. The allocation of credit and loans for political allies had served him as an instrument of regime maintenance. And it acquired greater importance with the transition to multiparty competition. Yet, the banking crises of 1993 and 1998, which these practices provoked, served as critical turning points in ongoing aid negotiations. These crises permitted the IMF to escalate reform conditions in a manner that forced the government to gradually extract itself from banking by the end of the decade.

The decade-long bargaining over aid to Kenya began when, in November 1991, donors suspended $350 million in balance-of-payments support over stalled progress on economic reforms that had been previously negotiated with the IFIs (O'Brien and Ryan 2001).[28] Table 5.3 provides highlights of those back-and-forth negotiations. Donors explicitly conditioned the resumption of aid on the fulfillment of Kenya's commitments under existing agreements with the IMF, which included the liberalization of interest rates, the strengthening of banking supervision, and the introduction of greater competition in the banking sector.[29] But the Kenyan government, anticipating the country's first multiparty presidential elections, undertook no serious reforms until after Moi secured his reelection in December 1992.[30]

Six weeks after the first multiparty election, in February 1993, the government announced a series of liberalizing measures – just in time for the arrival of an IMF review team – that included, among others, permitting exporters to retain their hard currency earnings without having to remit them to the central bank.[31] However, when the IMF proclaimed that the recently enacted reforms had not gone far enough to justify the restoration of aid, Moi reacted by reimposing exchange and price controls in March 1993.[32] Decrying the IMF's demands as "dictatorial and suicidal,"[33] Moi argued that additional reforms would lead to food shortages and social unrest without additional donor aid.[34]

---

[28] The IMF then froze the disbursement of a $63 million loan. See Jane Perlez, "Global Lender Withholds Kenya's $63 Million," *New York Times*, 29 December 1991, 11.

[29] Other measures were the liberalization of import licensing and the decontrol of prices for nonessential goods. See Jane Perlez, "Will Kenya's Bad Habits Jeopardize Its Aid?," *New York Times*, 17 November 1991, 45.

[30] The Kenyan constitution was amended in December 1991 to permit the legal formation of political parties. The 1992 election was the first multiparty election since 1966.

[31] "Asking for More," *The Economist*, 13 March 1993, 51.

[32] Exporters holding foreign currency in "retention accounts" were given 48 hours to transfer them to the central bank at a lower official rate. See Mark Huband, "Aid Crisis as Moi Scraps IMF Plan," *The Guardian* (London), 25 March 1993, 14.

[33] Richard Dowden, "Nairobi Halts IMF and World Bank Reforms," *The Independent* (London), 24 March 1993. See also "Moi Blames IMF, World Bank and Opposition for Kenya's Economic Plight," *BBC Summary of World Broadcasts*, 20 March 1993.

[34] Keith B. Richburg, "Kenya, in Protest of IMF Demands, Reverses Economic Changes," *Washington Post*, 24 March 1993, A27. For a full elaboration of the government's rebuttal, see "Finance Minister's Statement Rejecting IMF and World Bank Conditions," *BBC Summary of World Broadcasts*, 24 March 1993.

TABLE 5.3. *Bargaining between the IMF and Kenya, 1990–2000*

Year	IMF	Kenya
1990	May–Dec.: disburses $136m	
1991	Aug.: disburses $48m	
	Dec.: suspends loans	
1992		
1993	March: requires additional reforms	April: closes down "political banks"
	Dec.: disburses $32m	Oct.: eliminates official exchange rate
1994	Nov.: disburses $32m	May: relaxes foreign exchange controls
		June: relaxes capital controls
		Oct.: sells 20% of shares in NBK
1995	Sept.: suspends loans	
1996	May: disburses $36m	July: increases central bank independence
		July: sells 20% of shares in NBK
		Oct.: sells 10% of shares in KCB
1997	July: suspends loans	Dec.: establishes anticorruption commission
1998		April: sells 25% of shares in KCB
1999		March: tightens banking regulations
2000	Aug.–Oct.: disburses $44m	

The IMF claimed that government actions had compounded existing economic problems: the printing of unbacked Kenyan shillings to finance Moi's re-election campaign had increased the money supply by nearly a third and drove inflation up to 55% in 1993. And as the scale of politicized lending became known after the election, the IMF ratcheted up its demands throughout 1993. In the run-up to the election, the financial system as a whole – the Central Bank of Kenya, state-owned banks, and private banks – had been used to funnel money to ruling party members and allies. The central bank regularly advanced loans and cleared overdrafts to "political banks" (Brownbridge 1998).[35] Most of these banks became insolvent after accumulating a large number of nonperforming loans made to members of the government in their personal capacity or to companies in which they were shareholders. In the case of Trade Bank, many of its nonperforming loans were linked to Nicholas Biwott, a former government minister and the president's close confidant.[36]

The revelation of the Goldenberg financial scandal in mid-1993 reinforced the IMF's demands for greater scrutiny of the banking sector. Goldenberg International, a Kenyan company, had colluded with government officials to

---

[35] Mark Huband, "Kenyan Banks 'Illegally Funded by Government,'" *The Guardian* (London), 23 March 1993, 8.
[36] Mark Huband, "Kenyan Bank Closes Amid IMF Scrutiny,'" *The Guardian* (London), 16 April 1993, 15.

defraud state coffers of some $400 million in 1992, costing approximately 6% of GDP (International Monetary Fund 2008; Republic of Kenya 2005; World Bank 2000). The fraudulent scheme relied on the use of finance-related controls to transfer money from the Central Bank of Kenya to Exchange Bank, a private bank owned by Goldenberg International. Funds were transferred to Goldenberg through falsified claims for the reimbursement of gold exports under a government export promotion program and the purchase of foreign exchange.[37] Export Bank's overdrafts with the Central Bank of Kenya were never repaid.

As the Kenyan economy sunk into recession and the government's fiscal position deteriorated, Moi was forced to capitulate to IMF demands to clean up the banking sector and undertake greater supervision. By April 1993, he was already reversing his stance, promising monetary and economic reforms in exchange for the resumption of aid. The government moved that month to control the money supply, raising interest rates and ordering banks to hold 20% of their cash reserves at the central bank. It then took action to clean up the banking sector, conducting an audit of four banks in June 1993 and closing down at least 14 "political banks," including Trade Bank and Exchange Bank, by the end of the year.[38] A floating exchange rate was effectively adopted in October 1993 with the elimination of the official exchange rate. Consequently, in November 1993, donors agreed to resume aid, including balance-of-payments support, pledging $850 million for the following year. The following month, the IMF disbursed a $32 million loan to the government under the Enhanced Structural Adjustment Facility (ESAF).[39]

The Kenyan government continued enacting reforms demanded by the IMF through 1994 and 1995. In May 1994, commercial banks were allowed to undertake foreign exchange transactions without going through the central bank. Exporters were also allowed to retain their hard currency earnings in local banks without surrendering them to the central bank. Capital controls were further relaxed between June and October 1994: Kenyan exporters were allowed to keep their foreign currency earnings in banks outside the country, while foreign investors were permitted to move capital without approval from the central bank. The government renounced all restrictions on current international transactions by signing Article VIII of the IMF Articles of Agreement in June 1994. The government then sold 20% of its shares in NBK, the most troubled of state-owned banks, on the Nairobi Stock Exchange in October 1994.[40]

---

[37] The government's export compensation program was abolished in September 1993.

[38] "How Not to Seek Approval," *The Economist*, 24 April 1993, 43; Donatella Lorch, "Kenya, Calling for Aid, Fights Falling Economy," *New York Times*, 7 June 1993, 6; Richard Dowden, "Kenya 'Political' Banks Come Under Scrutiny," *The Independent* (London), 9 June 1993; Richard Dowden, "Kenya's Scandal Bank Shut," *The Independent* (London), 22 July 1993, 11.

[39] Robert M. Press, "International Donors Resume Aid to Kenya," *Christian Science Monitor*, 26 November 1993, 7.

[40] "Kenya Banks Go on Safari," *The Banker*, vol. 144, no. 826, 1 December 1994.

While Moi's government had made considerable progress in restoring mac-roeconomic stability to the country by the start of 1995, the reform process slowed down in that year once negotiations began over a new ESAF. On one side, the government sought to restrict the number of conditions demanded by the donors. The ruling party's secretary general, Joseph Kamotho, proclaimed that "[t]heir only agenda is their desire to remove KANU from power.... We shall continue telling the donors that there is no economic or social reason why they should continue withholding further aid to the country."[41] On the other side, the IMF announced that it was reconsidering the release of additional aid due to continued irregularities in the financial system.[42] Having reached a stale-mate with the government, the IMF delayed negotiations on the disbursement of further loans in September 1995. It specifically sought assurances that the government would undertake an inquiry into malfeasance in the Goldenberg case (Were et al. 2006).[43] Up to that point, the government had refused to pur-sue an official investigation, since it was the vice president, George Saitoti, who had authorized the fraudulent transactions in the Goldenberg case in his capac-ity as finance minister at the time. The stalled negotiations meant that only a small part of the $850 million originally pledged by donors in November 1994 had been delivered to Kenya.[44]

The IMF approved a new three-year ESAF loan worth $220 million for Kenya in April 1996 on condition that the government provide the central bank with greater independence and continue its divestment in commercial banking.[45] Gazetted in July 1996 and ratified by parliament later in the year, the amendment to the Central Bank of Kenya Act effectively provided for its operational autonomy in monetary policy and banking supervision. And its governor was given security of tenure. The government then went to the Nairobi Stock Exchange to sell 10% of its KCB shares in September 1996 and 20% of its NBK shares in October 1996.

With the approach of presidential elections scheduled for December 1997, Moi's government once more slowed the reform process.[46] On 20 June 1997, the courts threw out criminal charges against those implicated in the Goldenberg scandal.[47] The IMF responded on 31 July 1997 by delaying

---

[41] "KANU Leader Says Donors Want to Remove KANU from Power," *BBC Summary of World Broadcasts*, 6 May 1995.

[42] David Orr, "Aid May Dry Up as Donors Lose Patience with Kenya," *The Independent* (London), 27 May 1995, 8; "Aid for Kenya. Stop, Go," *The Economist*, 19 August 1995, 37.

[43] The IMF also wanted the government to investigate what happened to millions missing from the reserves of the Central Bank of Kenya. See Donatella Lorch, "Is Kenya Sliding Back Toward Repression?," *New York Times*, 29 October 1995, 3.

[44] James C. McKinley Jr., "Spendthrift Priorities Delay Kenya's Bid for More Aid," *New York Times*, 29 January 1996, 3.

[45] The 1996 ESAF also contained provisions requiring a reduced budget deficit and competi-tive bidding for public procurements. See "IMF Grants Loan for Structural Adjustment," *BBC Summary of World Broadcasts*, 29 April 1996.

[46] Growing demands from civil society for constitutional reforms also distracted Moi from the economy.

[47] "Brutal Seventh," *The Economist*, 19 July 1997, 41.

the second tranche of Kenya's three-year ESAF loan, cutting off budget and the balance-of-payments support.[48] Criticizing the government for failing to remedy conditions that had made financial scandals possible in the first place, the IMF again called on the government to prosecute officials implicated in the Goldenberg case (World Bank 2000). Over the next six months, the IMF reiterated its demands for the pursuit of official accountability in the Goldenberg case along with the creation of an autonomous anticorruption authority.[49]

Moi's government took steps to mollify the IMF by announcing the commencement of hearings into Goldenberg in October 1997,[50] launching the Kenya Anti-Corruption Authority in December 1997, and reducing the state's shareholding in KCB to 35% in April 1998.[51] However, the government's measures were overtaken by the emergence of additional banking scandals linked to politicized lending.[52] The government's fiscal situation worsened throughout 1998 as the banking sector fell into crisis once more, thereby delaying the resumption of aid by adding a new item to the list of IMF concerns. Although the central bank had begun to carry out more rigorous banking supervision, the commercial banking sector continued to be plagued by nonperforming loans linked to politically connected individuals, including Moi's son. Nearly a third of all loans in the banking sector were in default, accounting for 8.8% of GDP, and five private banks collapsed by the end of 1998 (International Monetary Fund 2002).

Fearing that NBK might also collapse under the weight of bad debts, especially after a run on deposits began in November 1998, the government recapitalized the bank with an infusion of $31 million in that month alone.[53] NBK was teetering on the verge of insolvency due to unserviced debts owed mainly by politicians, businessmen connected to the ruling party, and parastatals. A list tabled in parliament indicated that 87 borrowers owed the NBK approximately $131 million.[54] Among those who received unsecured loans for themselves or firms they owned were a former commerce minister, Arthur Magugu ($15.6 million); the local authorities minister, Sam Ongeri ($2.8 million); the

---

[48] Eman Omari, "IMF Acts Tough on Liberalisation," *Daily Nation* (Nairobi), 27 July 1997; Mutahi Mureithi and Paul Redfern, "Shilling Falls as IMF Stops Aid," *Daily Nation* (Nairobi), 2 August 1997; Paul Blustein, "IMF Takes Stance Toward Corrupt Regimes," *Washington Post*, 8 August 1997, 25; "The Big Squeeze," *The Economist*, 9 August 1997, 38.

[49] IMF demands included reducing the budget deficit, completing stalled parastatal privatizations, and increasing independence for the Kenya Revenue Authority. See Mbatau wa Ngai, "Goldenberg Case Blocks Kenya–IMF Deal," East African (Nairobi), 26 October 1998; Washington Akumu, "IMF Team Happy with Progress," *Daily Nation* (Nairobi), 10 March 1999; "Moi, Lord of Kenya's Empty Dance," *The Economist*, 15 May 1999.

[50] "Goldenberg Dates Fixed," *Daily Nation* (Nairobi), 24 October 1997.

[51] "New Era Dawns for KCB as Govt Reduces Stake," *Daily Nation* (Nairobi), 27 April 1998.

[52] "Pay Up, IMF to Debt Defaulters," *Daily Nation* (Nairobi), 1 December 1998.

[53] Mishael Ondieki and Kipkoech Tanui, "'Bad, Doubtful Debts' Behind National Bank of Kenya's Woes," *Daily Nation* (Nairobi), 24 November 1998.

[54] "Big Names That Hold NBK Cash," *Daily Nation* (Nairobi), 27 November 1998.

public works minister, Kipkalya Kones ($1.3 million); and the deputy speaker of parliament, Joab Omino ($640,000).[55]

Aid to Kenya was not resumed until July 2000, when the IMF agreed to extend a three-year loan amounting to $198 million under a Poverty Reduction and Growth Facility (PRGF).[56] By that point, with the economy in recession and agricultural production declining due to prolonged drought, Moi was obliged to reach an accord with donors. The central bank had already taken steps to close gaps in existing banking regulations. To remove political appointees from the boards of directors, it ordered banks to abolish the post of executive chairman in March 2000.[57] And to ensure that banks had sufficient resources to absorb risk, it raised the capital adequacy ratio in September 2000, making the renewal of licenses conditional on banks meeting new capital requirements.[58] But Moi had to surrender even more of his discretionary authority by agreeing to the IMF's terms for renewed lending, which included, among other provisions, enacting legislation to reinforce prudential regulation in banking, selling additional shares of KCB, and strengthening the authority of the anticorruption agency and the auditor-general. His government was further required to submit audited public accounts to parliament and to allow IMF officials to inspect the central bank's balance sheet on a weekly basis.

CONCLUSION

This chapter has shown how financial liberalization across African countries has been shaped by differences in the origin of the business–state relationship as well as the resource rents available to their leaders. The cross-national and case study evidence suggests that liberalizing reforms are a byproduct of the bargaining that ensues between resource-poor countries and their donors. Leaders of nonrentier states are compelled to bargain with the IFIs, conceding reforms in exchange for the resources needed to sustain their patronage coalitions. Leaders of rentier states, by contrast, are less likely to undertake reforms because they benefit from greater fiscal autonomy and foreign support.

This chapter's finding – that financial reforms have been enacted by resource-poor leaders under pressure from the IFIs – sheds light on a crucial link in the book's larger causal argument. While Chapter 4 showed that political factors influenced the extent to which leaders sought to control the financial system, this chapter has established that business played little to no role in limiting that

---

[55] Moi later demoted Simeon Nyachae, the reformist finance minister who allowed those names to be revealed, with a transfer to the industrial development portfolio in February 1999. Nyachae then resigned from the cabinet. See Kipkoech Tanui, "Fighting Graft Cost Me My Job – Nyachae," *Daily Nation* (Nairobi), 18 February 1999.

[56] Gitau Warigi, "IMF Funds: Implications and the Strings Attached," *Daily Nation* (Nairobi), 30 July 1999; "Dancing in Kenya to the Donors' Tune," *The Economist*, 5 August 2000.

[57] "Banks to Get Rid of Executive Chairmen," *Daily Nation* (Nairobi), 3 March 2000.

[58] Washington Akumu, "CBK's Warning on Capital Rules," *Daily Nation* (Nairobi), 1 September 2000.

control. It simply lacked the wherewithal to affect government policy or the course of reform once it began. But if financial freedom is essential for businesspeople in African countries to begin supporting alternative coalitions to the one in power, as is argued in this book, then it seems that the key to opposition electoral coordination was inadvertently secured through international pressure rather than domestic mobilization. The next chapter will show how the resulting differences in levels of financial freedom subsequently determined the political behavior of business.

6

The Political Alignment of Business

> The second decade of independence will see measures to intensify the class struggle and suppress the bourgeoisie....
>
> Ahmed Sékou Touré, president of Guinea, 1968[1]

This chapter explains how the political alignment of business in Africa has continued to be shaped by the state's influence over capital despite the adoption of democratic constitutions in the 1990s. The onset of multiparty competition, if anything, has underscored the political import of the private resources in the hands of entrepreneurs. If the resources of business could be brought to bear on the electoral process, opposition parties would be more likely to mount a viable challenge against incumbents who are able to fund their own reelection campaigns through the state's coffers.

The evidence presented in the following pages shows how African leaders have prevented entrepreneurs from deploying their private resources toward political ends. Incumbents in most countries can leverage the state's financial instruments and regulations to induce the acquiescence, if not active support, of business. Entrepreneurs are often obliged to publicly endorse the incumbent in an election or risk losing access to financial capital. But, in the African countries where liberalizing reforms have been undertaken, entrepreneurs are able to bypass the state in securing credit through multinational banks or locally owned private banks. No longer required to resort to political connections, these entrepreneurs are free to follow their partisan preferences, diversifying their political donations without fear of reprisals from the ruling party. It is under such conditions that business provides the opposition with the resources needed to become a viable alternative to the incumbent.

Providing a direct test for this claim – financial liberalization facilitating the political realignment of business – is problematic because there are no systematic data on the campaign contributions of business. There are no off-the-shelf

---

[1] Quoted in A.K. Essack, "Guinean Lesson for Africa," *Economic and Political Weekly*, vol. 5, no. 52, 26 December 1970.

measures that operationalize the business–state relationship in a way that would confirm whether the relationship is influenced by financial controls or how changes in the relationship might subsequently impact the political alignment of business. In most African countries, campaign contributions, especially for opposition candidates, are made informally and discreetly. Parties themselves rarely comply with laws that require the disclosure of campaign funding sources.

This chapter must take an indirect route by focusing on the national chamber of commerce as the institutional manifestation of the business–state relationship. While a variety of business organizations exist in African countries – for example, employers' associations, manufacturers' associations, and merchants' associations – the national chamber of commerce is of particular interest because it is the one that most closely approximates the kind of "encompassing organization" described by Olson (1982, 48). Representing firms involved in all sectors of the economy as well as firms that vary in size, the chamber encompasses the interests of this diverse membership by pursuing goals aimed at broadly improving the economic environment in which firms operate rather than seeking targeted benefits such as subsidies, as is often done by specialized lobbies. The chamber thus serves to advance the collective interests of business as a class.

If the political alignment of business is conditioned by the incumbent's influence over finance, as I argue, then the relative autonomy of business might be gauged through the behavior of the chamber of commerce. In this regard, I focus on the tenure of the chamber's president as an observable aspect of the business–state relationship. I claim that a business community operating under statist financial controls should prefer longer tenures for chamber presidents so that they can cultivate political connections with the regime in power. I confirm this expectation through a duration analysis of chamber presidency tenure across African countries, which shows that the dismantling of capital controls increases the likelihood of chamber leadership turnover where business is self-organizing rather than state-organized. By disrupting the traditional business–state relationship, financial liberalization appears to diminish an incumbent's ability to prevent entrepreneurs from defecting to the opposition.

I then turn to tracing how financial liberalization has influenced the political alignment of business by providing an alternative interpretation for the narratives conventionally associated with multiparty politics in Cameroon and Kenya. By juxtaposing changes in government policies in banking and finance with the shifting political endorsements of high-profile entrepreneurs, the case studies demonstrate how the removal of financial controls can affect the timing and the orientation of business' partisan support. In Cameroon, where the state's influence over capital persisted well after the transition to multiparty politics, business remained allied to the incumbent through three presidential elections. By contrast, the progressive liberalization of the financial sector in Kenya enabled business to shift its political alignment from the incumbent to the opposition.

THE POLITICAL MOBILIZATION OF BUSINESS

Explanations for the political mobilization of business are often based on some variant of a threat hypothesis: individual firms or sectoral associations take action to defend their material interests against transgressions by state or social actors. This type of account travels relatively easily across time and space. Stoner-Weiss (1997) finds that Russian regions dominated by a few large enterprises were able to coordinate local actors in resisting federal government policies. Schneider (2002, 2004) argues that business in Mexico adopted a strategy of "defensive organization" in creating associations that could negotiate with the ruling party over labor policy. Cammett (2007) shows that a cohesive class identity permitted exporters in Morocco to act collectively in responding to new economic challenges; however, sectoral cleavages among exporters in Tunisia undermined similar efforts.

But the threat hypothesis, by itself, appears to hold little explanatory power in the African context. Business had sufficient cause for grievance. The region's authoritarian leaders had repeatedly committed transgressions against individual entrepreneurs as well as the private sector as a whole. Yet, when the onset of democratization presented an opportunity to replace the very leaders who had brought their economies into crisis – perhaps the most existential form of threat for business – this class of economic actors generally hesitated to act. In most African countries, business neither publicly endorsed the mass movements demanding multiparty democracy nor discreetly financed the campaigns of emerging opposition leaders. In contrast to the supporting role they played during the nationalist mobilization that led to independence, entrepreneurs remained largely silent during what was expected to become Africa's "second liberation." Why did business fail to mobilize politically at this juncture?

Part of the answer can be found in the incentives facing individual entrepreneurs. Many simply had little reason to defect from the status quo because they had become dependent on political connections to survive commercially in the years between independence in the 1960s and the transition to multipartism in the 1990s. Some entrepreneurs achieved success by embedding themselves in the clientelistic networks that sustained authoritarian regimes (Boone 1992; Iliffe 1983; Kennedy 1994; MacGaffey 1987; Tangri 1999). Others had built their enterprises on "straddling" strategies that enabled them to use their positions within the state apparatus or the ruling party to exploit profit-making opportunities (Bayart 1989; Cowen and Kinyanjui 1977; Fauré and Médard 1982; Swainson 1980). Whether they operated under capitalist policies, as in Côte d'Ivoire, or socialist programs, as in Zambia, most entrepreneurs pursued individual solutions to secure the discretionary favors needed to navigate an array of statist controls in financing, contracting, and licensing. The large presence of state-owned enterprises in African economies reinforced the importance of clientelistic connections, since every entrepreneur could then resort to politics to increase the likelihood of securing a credit line, winning a contract, or receiving a license to import goods or export materials (Quinn 1999).

While the importance attached to personalized political connections undermined the incentive for entrepreneurs to act collectively, Africa's authoritarian leaders also imposed limits on the organizational capacity of business. Independent associations were suppressed under the one-party regimes that governed most countries until the late 1980s. And those organizations permitted to operate were compromised: they were designed to serve as corporatist structures that coordinated entrepreneurs and firms in the interest of government rather than business. As a result, most business associations and chambers of commerce failed to act when the interests of business were being threatened by political or economic events. Focusing on the development of business' organizational structures, Heilbrunn (1997) contrasts the political mobilization of business associations in Benin and Togo during the critical period of political transition in the early 1990s. He shows that Benin's decentralized business community, which had retained local autonomy, permitted business not only to distance itself from the incumbent regime, but also to engage in active protest against it. Meanwhile, because the centralized organization of Togo's business community had lent itself to being coopted from the top, it encouraged continued allegiance to the regime in power.

Thioub, Diop, and Boone (1998) show that economic liberalization transformed the business–state relationship in Senegal by facilitating the political mobilization of business. The broad reform program implemented by the Senegalese government in the 1980s and 1990s undercut the ruling party's ability to prevent factions within the commercial sector from acting independently. Once the regime lost control of the instruments with which to control accumulation – allocating import licenses or directing state-subsidized credit – it lacked the means to coopt entrepreneurs. Here, the contrast between the 1960s and 1990s is instructive. The government of Léopold Sédar Senghor had originally been able to use the provision of state credit along with the indigenization of the chamber of commerce, among other instruments, to coopt the Union des Groupements Economiques du Sénégal (UNIGES), a business association that had mobilized to criticize the regime's economic policies. By the 1990s, however, Senghor's successor, Abdou Diouf, could not engineer the same accord between business and the state. He could not so easily neutralize or silence the Union Nationale des Commerçants et Industriels du Sénégal (UNACOIS), a business association mobilized to protect the interests of informal sector merchants and which quickly became one of the most important associations in the Dakar Chamber of Commerce.[2]

Handley's (2008) study of business in economic policymaking in African countries underscores the importance of organization. She finds that it was the autonomous organization of business vis-à-vis the state that enabled entrepreneurs to influence economic policy in Mauritius and South Africa. By contrast,

---

[2] Thioub et al. (1998) note that the group of wealthy merchants who led UNACOIS was able to consistently mobilize an army of street vendors and petty traders in support of their demands vis-à-vis the government because the former are the creditors and suppliers to the latter.

the neo-patrimonial relationships developed between business and state under-cut the potential contribution of entrepreneurs to economic policymaking in Ghana and Zambia, including the extensive reforms undertaken by those governments in the 1980s. In such cases, Handley finds that the state's pronounced role in the economy, particularly through nationalization and Africanization policies, motivated individual entrepreneurs to seek commercial advantage by aligning themselves with those in power rather than coordinating action on a sectoral basis.

THE CHAMBER OF COMMERCE AS CORPORATIST INSTITUTION

Building on these earlier findings concerning African business–state relations, I focus here on the chamber of commerce as one of the corporatist instruments employed by leaders to politically demobilize business. In principle, the chamber of commerce is supposed to serve as an organized lobby that interacts with government to protect the interests of the private sector by educating its members, proposing reforms, and negotiating on economic policies (Coleman 1990; Fedotov 2007; Pilgrim and Meier 1995). In practice, however, the chamber in African countries became a mechanism by which business–state relations could be managed in the interest of whoever was in power.

The ability of leaders to exert influence over business was magnified by whether the chamber of commerce was organized under the private or public legal model. This distinction indicates the legislation that governs a chamber's operations and membership. Under the private law model, the chamber is a self-governing organization and membership is voluntary. Under the public law model, the chamber is subject to government supervision and membership is mandatory for registered businesses. The public law model thus structures the chamber to collaborate closely with the state; in some cases, the chamber becomes a de facto appendage of the bureaucracy.[3]

The chamber of commerce, regardless of legal model, has become a focal institution through which entrepreneurs interact with the state. Most entrepreneurs seek to join the chamber or similar business associations because it provides a mechanism for pursuing their commercial interests. In a survey of entrepreneurs in eight African countries, Goldsmith (2002) finds that, on average, more than two-thirds of respondents belonged to a chamber of commerce or business association. This result is evidently not driven by a public law requirement, since only two of the eight countries were former French colonies.[4] These high levels of participation are not conditioned by firm size.

[3] The chambers found in African countries tend to be organized according to the tradition of their former colonizers. Francophone countries follow the French public law system that is also commonly found among continental European countries. Anglophone countries tend to follow the private law model found in the Great Britain. However, there are notable exceptions. Many former Portuguese colonies follow the private law model.

[4] The eight countries in the Goldsmith sample are Ghana, Kenya, Madagascar, Malawi, Senegal, Tanzania, Uganda, and Zambia.

Goldsmith finds that nearly all firms with more than 100 employees belong to an association, as do some two-thirds of firms with fewer than 100 employees. Whether their own firms are large or small, the entrepreneurs who join business associations are more likely to respond that government works toward addressing the concerns of business.

But why would entrepreneurs support a chamber or association that has been seemingly impotent in improving the environment in which business operates in most African countries? The answer here has to do with the nature of the financial reprisal regimes discussed in previous chapters. In a context where the access to capital is extended or withdrawn at the government's discretion, the chamber of commerce is not simply an instrument of top-down control; it serves as a mechanism for sustaining the political relationships that facilitate bank loans, credit lines, and foreign exchange. In their study of Ghanaian private sector associations, including the Ghana National Chamber of Commerce, Hart and Gyimah-Boadi (2000, 5) found that "[m]ediating negotiations between individual entrepreneurs and bureaucrats responsible for assigning import licenses and foreign exchange allocations constituted the major activity of the associations for the greater part of their histories." In this respect, organizations such as the chamber of commerce are consequential because they serve as brokers for access.

Since the chamber of commerce negotiates the politics of capital access, the identity of the chamber's president is of critical importance for both government and business. African leaders prefer to deal with pliant chamber presidents who are willing to ensure that only regime allies can accumulate capital. It is for this reason that some leaders directly appoint the chamber president, as occurs under the public law system in Cameroon, where that individual has often simultaneously served on the ruling party's central committee or as an elected member of parliament for the ruling party. African entrepreneurs, for their part, want to ensure that the chamber president is someone who will effectively represent their interests. This is often seen in the ethnic identity of the chamber president. Again, in Cameroon, where the Bamileke ethnic group dominates commerce, the president of the Chambre de Commerce, d'Industrie, des Mines et de l'Artisanat (CCIMA) has, with the exception of a single year in the 1970s, been led by a Bamileke since independence.[5]

Two vignettes from Kenya underscore the importance of the chamber's leadership. The first concerns the chamber's initial organization soon after independence in 1963, when "a ferocious and protracted struggle ensued between a state now controlled by an African political elite, and the commercial and industrial bourgeoisie" (Himbara 1994, 59). At the time, the country's chambers of commerce remained organized along racial lines, as Asians and Europeans hesitated in merging their pre-existing chambers with the newer

---

[5] CCIMA has been led over the past 50 years by Paul Monthé (Bamileke), Victor Mukete (Bafaw), Francois Djapou (Bamileke), Noucti Tchokwago (Bamileke), Pierre Tchanqué (Bamileke), Claude Juimo Monthé (Bamileke), and Christophe Eken (Bamileke).

chamber organized by African Kenyans. Part of that reluctance stemmed from growing demands by African entrepreneurs for the indigenization of commerce and industry (Gregory 1993). For the country's president, Jomo Kenyatta, the independent organization of business interests by communities already thought to be hostile to the ruling party was simply unacceptable. Despite the use of the private law system to organize chambers of commerce in Kenya, the minister for commerce and industry, Julius Kiano, was able to compel Asian Indians and Europeans to fold their respective chambers into the Kenya National Chamber of Commerce and Industry (KNCCI) by the end of 1965. Francis Macharia, a Kikuyu like Kenyatta and Kiano, became KNCCI's first president.

Under Macharia's leadership, the KNCCI became the representative for indigenous entrepreneurs who sought better access to financing and licensing in an economy dominated by European settlers and Asian merchants (Swainson 1980).[6] In advocating legislation to promote African participation in commerce, the KNCCI specifically articulated demands for the redistribution of state-controlled capital. The state's Industrial and Commercial Development Corporation (ICDC), for example, operated three different loan programs for African traders and firms.[7] When Marris and Somerset (1971) interviewed Kenyan entrepreneurs who received loans from the ICDC, they found that a quarter of their respondents were active members of the KNCCI and that a quarter had also facilitated the negotiation of their ICDC loans through political contacts.[8] It is perhaps for this reason that one of their respondents, a wholesaler, would note, "I'm a member of the Chamber of Commerce – that's my root.... The Chamber and KANU and business is all I want" (quoted in Marris and Somerset 1971, 68). This incipient politicization of state-subsidized loans was further reflected in their distribution. Marris and Somerset's analysis of the ICDC loans found that 64% of all industry loans and 44% of all commercial loans went to the coethnics of the president, the minister of commerce, and the KNCCI president.

The second Kenyan vignette concerns KNCCI elections that were to be held in 1985. The controversy that erupted that year and persisted for the following two years reflects not only the significance to which factions within business attached to control of the chamber, but also the interest that the government

---

[6] The KNCCI also pushed the government to implement and expand the licensing restrictions that tended to favor those with political contacts. For example, the KNCCI lobbied the government to extend the Trade Licensing Act of 1967, which limited certain trading activities to citizens. But the KNCCI also sought to police those privileges: it demanded that government revise the Ndegwa Commission Report of 1971 that allowed civil servants to run businesses while holding government positions, apparently fearing that those positions would be used to secure unfair advantage over KNCCI members. See Swainson (1980).

[7] ICDC operated the Small Industrial Loans Scheme, the Commercial Loans Scheme, and the Property Loans Scheme.

[8] Marris and Somerset (1971, 69) explain that these political contacts facilitated faster processing of loans rather than larger amounts or better terms. Unfortunately, they do not cross-tabulate the data to show to what extent KNCCI membership overlaps with the use of such contacts.

would have in the composition of its leadership.[9] The government's response to the KNCCI election controversy suggests that President Daniel arap Moi, Kenyatta's successor, supported the move to wrest control of the chamber away from its longtime head, an ethnic Kikuyu. It is precisely at this time that scholars suggest Moi sought to collaborate with the country's Asian business community to counterbalance the influence of Kikuyu entrepreneurs (Throup 1987; Throup and Hornsby 1998).

Routinely reelected to the KNCCI's presidency, often unopposed, Francis Macharia faced his first real contest in 1985. The chamber's governing council, however, moved to postpone those elections over disagreements on voting procedures when Nicholas Gor, a former member of parliament and an ethnic Luo, announced that he would stand in the election. In response, Macharia publicly attacked his rival as a representative of Asian entrepreneurs who sought control of the chamber to advance their own interests, the implication being that those would come at the expense of African entrepreneurs. Gor, it so happened, was a director of the Chandaria Group of Companies owned by Manu Chandaria, one of Kenya's most important Asian industrialists. Moi's minister for commerce and industry, Peter Okondo, intervened in the controversy by ordering the cancellation of the KNCCI's rescheduled elections. This was an unexpected move by the government because the chamber of commerce is a limited company, and its officers are entitled to operate without state supervision. After two years of further delays – including a court injunction that prevented the KNCCI's amended articles of association, including its revised voting procedures, from being registered – Macharia nevertheless managed to be reelected in 1987 with the support of Kikuyu businessmen in Central Province, where the largest number of chamber branches were concentrated.

The preceding vignettes suggest a general implication for the tenure of chamber presidents across African countries. Business communities that operate under statist financial controls are more likely to prefer longer tenures for chamber presidents so that they may develop the personalized connections needed to cultivate favor with the regime in office. Consider, for example, the entrepreneur who must comply with multiple regulations to execute a capital transaction. Because regulations often enable government officials to exercise considerable discretion, they can reduce the likelihood of any transaction being completed successfully. This creates an incentive for the entrepreneur to seek the intervention of an ally who can help circumvent the regulations. And a politically connected chamber president can help facilitate such an intervention.

[9] "No Polls," *Weekly Review* (Nairobi), 26 April 1985, p. 22; "Chamber Row," *Weekly Review* (Nairobi), 10 May 1985, p. 25; "Chamber Warned," *Weekly Review* (Nairobi), 4 October 1985, p. 17; "Chamber Drama," *Weekly Review* (Nairobi), 31 October 1986, p. 19; "Chamber Sets Yet Another Election Date," *Weekly Review* (Nairobi), 20 February 1987, p. 20; "Jumping the Gun," *Weekly Review* (Nairobi), 27 February 1987, p. 16; "Uncertainty Reigns," *Weekly Review* (Nairobi), 3 April 1987, p. 15; "Chamber Elections Hit a New Snag," *Weekly Review* (Nairobi), 3 July 1987, p. 18; "What Was All the Fuss About?," *Weekly Review* (Nairobi), 17 July 1987, p. 20; "A Controversy-Ridden Association," *Weekly Review* (Nairobi), 17 November 1989, p. 24.

A similar dynamic emerges when a government uses administrative mechanisms to allocate credit or foreign exchange, which effectively results in rationing. The entrepreneur who wants access to those scarce financial resources, especially when they are subsidized by the state, also has an incentive to appeal for the intervention of an influential ally. Again, a chamber president with connections to ruling party officials or high-level bureaucrats can help broker that access.

Financial liberalization reduces the need for political mediation. Extending the chamber president's tenure would no longer be necessary under such circumstances, since entrepreneurs could secure their access to capital without the intervention of political allies. Business communities in these circumstances should, in fact, prefer shorter tenures for chamber presidents to ensure that none of their members receives an unfair advantage in the competitive market for loan capital.

Figure 6.1 shows the average tenure for chamber presidents between 1970 and 2005 for a cross section of African countries. The figure reflects the wide variation across the sample. And that variation appears to corroborate the notion that chamber leadership may be related to the nature of business–state relations. At the extremes, the average tenure in Senegal, the country with the longest duration, is twelve times the figure found in Mauritius, the country with the shortest duration. This difference in tenure rates reflects the general perception of these countries. Senegal has been the archetype for the symbiotic business–state relationship (Boone 1992), while Mauritius has been described as a classic reformist economy with an autonomous business community (Brautigam 1999).

Figure 6.2 further shows that a chamber's legal framework does affect average leadership duration. The annual rate of turnover in the chamber presidency for the two legal types is illustrated – the private law chambers found in eighteen countries in the top panel versus the public law chambers found in fourteen countries in the bottom panel. The average turnover rate has been declining from the 1970s through the 1990s in both chamber types, as represented by the dotted black lines. Although the private law chambers seemed to have been more adversely affected by the onset of the region's economic crisis – their average annual turnover rate fell by six percentage points between the 1970s and 1980s – turnover in the chamber presidency has consistently remained higher among the private law chambers. Average turnover among private law chambers was 30% in the 1970s, 24% in the 1980s, and 21% in the 1990s. The corresponding averages for public law chambers were 20% in the 1970s, 19% in the 1980s, and 14% in the 1990s.

The declining rate of turnover among African chamber presidents has obviously meant longer tenures over time. Among private law chambers, a president would serve for an average of 2.6 years in the 1970s, 4.3 years in the 1980s, and 4.7 years in the 1990s. The average duration was higher in public law chambers; their presidents would serve 3.2 years in the 1970s, 6.1 years in the 1980s, and 5.3 years in the 1990s.

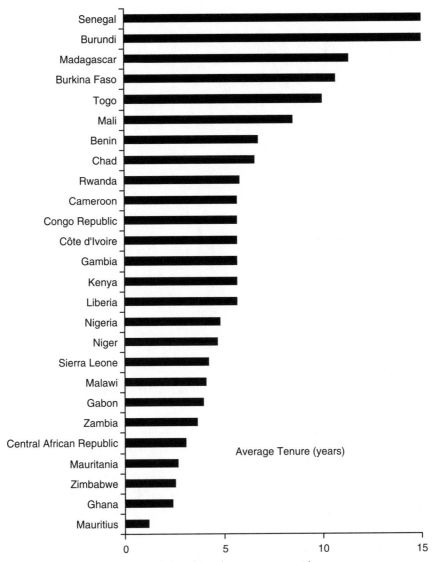

FIGURE 6.1. Average tenure of chamber of commerce president, 1970–2005.
Source: Author's calculations based on annual entries in *Africa South of the Sahara*.

Examining the factors that influence the duration of chamber leadership can provide insight on the very nature of the business–state relationship in Africa. If that leadership is structured to facilitate political interventions in capital transactions – because entrepreneurs are either stymied by regulation or seduced by privileged access to rationed credit – then the chamber president's tenure becomes an observable manifestation of business' more general political autonomy. According to this logic, Figure 6.2 suggests that business' autonomy

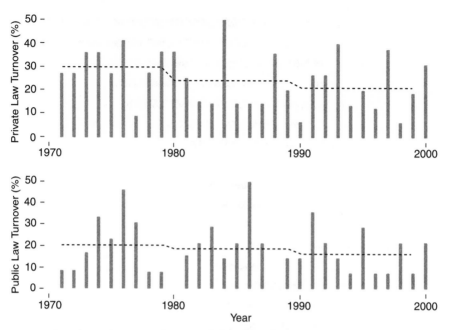

FIGURE 6.2. Annual turnover by type of chamber of commerce.
Note: The gray bars show the annual percentage of chambers that experienced turnover in the presidency. The dotted line represents the decade average for turnover (1970s, 1980s, and 1990s).
Source: Author's calculations based on annual entries in *Africa South of the Sahara.*

began to decline with the onset of the region's economic crisis in the late 1970s, and that most business communities were relatively weaker vis-à-vis the state when multiparty constitutions were adopted in the 1990s. By that point in time, an entrepreneur who had to rely on contacts in the ruling party or state bureaucracy for access to finance was unlikely to publicly support an opposition candidate for office even when presented with the opportunity.

ASSESSING THE DETERMINANTS OF CHAMBER PRESIDENCY TENURE

My claim is that the tenure of chamber presidents provides a means for gauging the political autonomy of business – and thereby the likelihood that entrepreneurs will defect from the incumbent regime. I assess this intuition by estimating a Cox proportional hazards model of duration in the chamber of commerce presidency.[10] The dependent variable is the time until turnover in the chamber

---

[10] The advantage of the Cox model versus other parametric specifications is that it does not impose a particular shape on the baseline hazard. There is no concrete basis for assuming what form that shape should take, since no prior research has been done on the tenure of African chamber

presidency. Volumes of *Africa South of the Sahara* were used to identify presidents of national chambers of commerce as well as to determine the length of their tenures. The sample of African countries used here is larger than the one examined in Chapters 4 and 5. It includes countries for which the analysis of founding leaders was inapplicable because they attained independence after 1970 or were never colonized. The specific claim made in this chapter, however, can be applied broadly to all African countries. Countries enter the sample in 1970 or the first year a national chamber of commerce is formed after independence.

The Cox proportional hazards model is used to generate hazard ratios, which reflect the change in the odds of turnover associated with a one-unit change in the independent variable. A higher hazard ratio indicates a greater likelihood of change in the chamber presidency. Given the logic outlined in this chapter, the hazard ratio can be interpreted as a proxy for the business community's relative autonomy from the regime in power. A higher hazard ratio would suggest that businesses are less reliant on political interventions, since frequent changes in chamber leadership would not be seen as jeopardizing their access to capital. Conversely, a lower hazard ratio would indicate that businesses are dependent on political interventions, preferring to extend the chamber presidency in order to nurture their relationship with the regime.

I have hypothesized that greater financial liberalization should lead to greater turnover in the chamber of commerce presidency. To determine whether this relationship holds, I assess the impact of financial liberalization through two alternate measures that reflect the degree of freedom from government involvement in capital transactions. The first independent variable is credit to the private sector as a share of GDP. As noted in the previous chapter, private credit is a preferred indicator of depth and liberalization in the literature on financial development (Pill and Pradhan 1995). Reflecting a higher degree of financial liberalization, higher levels of private credit provision are expected to increase the hazard ratio for turnover in the chamber presidency.

The second independent variable is the state's control over capital mobility. Based on the IMF's Annual Report on Exchange Arrangements and Exchange Restrictions (AREAER), the Chinn and Ito (2008) measure of capital account openness reflects the extent to which international financial transactions are regulated, including restrictions on capital account and current account transactions, the presence of multiple exchange rates, and the surrender of export proceeds. This continuous measure runs from –2 to 3, with higher values indicating greater financial openness. Business communities that can freely undertake capital transactions across borders, whether borrowing abroad or moving

---

of commerce presidents. Among alternative models, the Akaike Information Criterion suggests that the Gompertz distribution performs marginally better than the Weibull distribution. The results from the Gompertz model, however, are not substantially different from the Cox model, so they are not reported here. A test of the Schoenfeld residuals shows that none of the variables violate the proportional hazards assumption (Box-Steffensmeier and Zorn 2001).

assets offshore, have no need for political connections to conduct their affairs. Greater capital liberalization is therefore expected to increase the hazard ratio for turnover in the chamber presidency.

Chambers of commerce are coded dichotomously by legal framework, private law versus public law, and interact with the two alternate measures of financial liberalization. Countries that allow business to organize under the private law framework, which is a self-governing model, are expected to have higher hazard rates. Because the legal framework determines a chamber's operations and membership, it may be the case that tenure is solely the product of legal regime. Moreover, a self-governing business community may be more likely to exercise its autonomy after the onset of financial liberalization. A business community that operates under the public framework may not act autonomously despite financial liberalization because it continues to be organized from above by the state.

A dichotomous variable identifies countries that use fixed exchange rate regimes. Its coding is based on the classifications by Reinhart and Rogoff (2004), who find that exchange rate practices have often differed from official currency regimes. Previous research has shown that governments often impose capital controls to limit speculative pressure on fixed exchange rates (Leblang 1997). Capital controls are used to sustain a currency peg because short-term capital flows can lead to large changes in foreign reserves, undermining the stability of the exchange rate. Countries with fixed currency regimes are expected to have lower hazard rates for turnover in the chamber presidency.

Variables such as level of democracy, an incumbent's years in power, and ethnic fractionalization are used to assess the impact of political factors on the duration of chamber presidency. More democratic regimes are expected to have higher hazard rates for turnover in the chamber presidency, since democratization may enable business to enjoy greater policy influence. The literature suggests, however, that the effects of democratization may be constrained by economic stagnation (Brautigam et al. 2002; Rakner 2001). Cabinet size is used as a proxy for the size of an incumbent's patronage coalition. Measures for oil and mineral producers as well as foreign aid are included to reflect the possibility that a regime's sources of revenue may undercut the autonomy of business. The potential influence of economic factors is assessed through GDP per capita, the share of manufacturing in GDP, and the share of exports in GDP. Population is added as a measure for country size.

The description, measurement, and source of all variables are listed in Appendix C. All explanatory variables are lagged in the analysis.

EXPLAINING THE DURATION OF CHAMBER PRESIDENCY

Table 6.1 reports the results from a Cox proportional hazards model of duration in the chamber presidency. Hazard ratios are reported for each variable: a hazard ratio above one indicates that higher values for that variable will increase the probability of turnover in the chamber presidency; a hazard ratio below one indicates that higher values will lower the probability of such an event.

TABLE 6.1. *Duration Analysis of Tenure in Chamber of Commerce Presidency*

	Model 1	Model 2	Model 3
Private law chamber of commerce	0.643**	0.350***	0.903
	(0.139)	(0.098)	(0.274)
Private credit, % GDP		0.952***	
		(0.011)	
Private credit × private law chamber		1.062***	
		(0.018)	
Capital account openness			0.719**
			(0.118)
Capital account openness × private law chamber			1.493**
			(0.261)
Fixed exchange rate	0.444***	0.562***	0.504***
	(0.095)	(0.103)	(0.109)
Polity score	0.989	0.985	0.996
	(0.017)	(0.016)	(0.017)
Leader years in power	0.987	0.988	0.991
	(0.010)	(0.012)	(0.011)
Ethnic fractionalization	1.472	1.287	1.201
	(0.631)	(0.418)	(0.561)
Cabinet size	0.990	0.998	0.995
	(0.017)	(0.015)	(0.017)
Oil exporter	0.447**	0.489**	0.453**
	(0.159)	(0.176)	(0.164)
Mineral exporter	1.107	1.250	1.097
	(0.183)	(0.215)	(0.183)
GDP per capita, log	1.895***	1.664***	1.815***
	(0.298)	(0.258)	(0.294)
Manufacturing, % GDP	1.002	1.007	1.009
	(0.010)	(0.009)	(0.010)
Exports, % GDP	0.999	1.006	0.998
	(0.006)	(0.006)	(0.005)
Population, log	1.010	1.096	1.000
	(0.090)	(0.087)	(0.090)
Number of observations	795	657	791
Number of countries	29	27	29
Log likelihood	−482.23	−363.52	−476.64

Notes: The dependent variable is the time until turnover in the chamber presidency. All independent variables are lagged one year. Hazard ratios are reported. Robust standard errors, clustered by country, are in parentheses.
*** $p < 0.01$ ** $p < 0.05$ * $p < 0.1$, two-tailed tests.

The results presented in Table 6.1 broadly corroborate this chapter's hypothesis: the duration of chamber leadership, as an institutional manifestation of business' autonomy, is influenced by the extent to which the state mediates finance. And this relationship is conditioned by a chamber's legal framework. In Model 2, the interaction between private credit provision and private law chamber attains statistical significance at conventional levels. This interaction suggests that higher levels of private credit provision increase the likelihood of turnover in the chamber presidency, but only in countries with private law chambers. Each percentage point increase in private credit provision, as a share of GDP, is associated with a percentage point increase in the likelihood of turnover in the chamber presidency, *ceteris paribus*. If private credit were to be increased by nine percentage points, a one standard deviation change, then the odds of turnover would increase by 9.4% in a country with a private law chamber of commerce, holding all other variables constant.

Greater credit provision, however, appears to have the opposite effect under the public law chamber. The same standard deviation increase of nine percentage points in private credit provision would lower the likelihood of turnover by 36.2%, holding all else constant. This unexpected result may reflect the fact that public law chambers operate in countries where governments can tighten the business–state relationship through other means. A government could attempt to offset the advantage to business from easier access to credit through statutory restrictions or policy-related distortions that oblige entrepreneurs to continue working through political contacts. For example, when compared with their private law counterparts, countries with public law chambers tend to have smaller banking sectors, a greater state presence in banking, and more restricted foreign participation in banking. If credit does become more available, it may well be channeled through a state-controlled bank.

The results in Model 3 also support the business autonomy hypothesis. In Model 3, the interaction between capital account openness and private law chamber attains statistical significance at conventional levels. This interaction shows that greater capital liberalization increases the likelihood of turnover in the chamber presidency under the private law framework. A full point increase in the capital openness index, which is slightly more than a one standard deviation change, would increase the turnover rate by 7.2% under the private law chamber, holding all else constant. But capital liberalization has the opposite effect under the public law model. A one standard deviation increase in liberalization would reduce the likelihood of turnover in the chamber presidency by 28.1%, holding all else constant. Governments that can organize business from above may be able to use other instruments to induce the cooperation of entrepreneurs despite the freedom gained through capital liberalization.

Further supporting the business autonomy hypothesis, Models 1 through 3 show that fixed exchange regimes lower the likelihood of change in the chamber presidency. According to the estimated hazard ratio in Model 2, the likelihood of turnover falls by 43.8% in countries with pegged currencies when compared with those with flexible exchange rates, holding all else equal. The stabilization of the chamber turnover rate in the 1990s, rather than the continuous decline from the 1970s to the 1980s seen in Figure 6.2, may be related to the move from fixed to flexible rates. Thirteen African countries switched from fixed to flexible exchange rates between 1990 and 1995. Another nine accepted

Article VIII of the IMF's Articles of Agreement, committing them to currency convertibility for international transactions (Masson and Patillo 2005).

The results in Table 6.1 show that political variables have little direct impact on the nature of business leadership. The Polity score, the tenure of the country's leader, and ethnic fractionalization are all statistically indistinguishable from zero. These non-results hold when using alternative specifications for regime type.

The patronage-related variables produce mixed results. The dummy variable for oil-producing countries is statistically significant, indicating that the chambers in those countries are less likely to experience leadership turnover. Based on Model 2, the likelihood of turnover in the chamber presidency falls by 51.1% among oil exporters, holding all else constant. A business community that derives rents from its participation in the oil sector, which is state-dominated in most African countries, may need to rely on a politically connected chamber president to sustain those linkages. However, the other patronage-related variables, cabinet size and mineral exporters, do not attain statistical significance.

Wealth appears to encourage turnover in chamber leadership. The hazard ratios on GDP per capita in Table 6.1 show that higher income levels increase the likelihood of turnover in the chamber presidency.[11] A 1% rise in the log of per capita income is associated with a 66.4% increase in the chamber turnover rate, holding all other variables constant. The exact mechanism for this relationship remains unclear, however. Wealthier countries may have more diverse economies that are less likely to be dominated by the state. But, perhaps more to the point, the economic contraction that has characterized many African countries may have also induced business to extend the tenure of chamber presidents in order to facilitate the political contacts needed to survive commercially under adverse conditions. To be sure, the declining turnover rates shown in Figure 6.2 parallel the region's declining income. Between 1976 and 1996, average income in the region fell by about 18%, from $674 in 1976 to $572 in 1996.

CAMEROON AND KENYA: DIVERGENT ALIGNMENT NARRATIVES

This section extends the intuition concerning the relationship between financial liberalization and business autonomy. If business as an interest group responds to the incentives created by statist controls, then one might surmise that individual entrepreneurs will also be strategic in the timing of their political realignments. Entrepreneurs should be more likely to defect from the ruling party to the opposition as incumbents lose the capacity to blackmail them through financial reprisals. This strategic behavior can be shown through the contrasting cases of Cameroon and Kenya. The political alignment of business in each case followed the state's shifting control over capital.

---

[11] Additional controls for banking, currency, and debt crises failed to attain statistical significance.

President Paul Biya in Cameroon and President Daniel arap Moi in Kenya were well ensconced in power by the time they confronted demands for democratization in the early 1990s. Throughout the previous decade, these leaders had taken steps to further insulate their political positions, discouraging political coordination among elites by imposing individually specified privileges. Biya and Moi sought to ensure that elites would not coordinate against them by permitting one faction to gain economically from the regime's transgressions against others.

With the onset of multipartism, the entrepreneurs whose interests had been adversely affected by the incumbent's discrimination had the opportunity to support an opposition candidate who might offer a better economic deal. Select entrepreneurs did provide early support for the opposition movements that came together to push for a political opening in the early 1990s. But precisely for this reason, Biya and Moi also sought to reassert their own influence over business and thereby cut off the opposition's source of electoral financing. Both incumbents succeeded at first, inducing much of the business community to support the ruling party or to remain neutral.

Their abilities to sustain such a strategy through the 1990s, however, ultimately depended on their control of capital. Biya retained his grip over finance in Cameroon, delaying or manipulating reforms. Cameroon's entrepreneurs therefore became unwilling to openly support the opposition because they remained dependent on the incumbent's goodwill for access to capital markets. In Kenya, however, Moi lost his influence over capital when financial reforms were institutionalized by the latter half of the decade. Once the access to capital was effectively liberalized, Kenyan entrepreneurs increasingly defected from the incumbent's coalition to support their preferred opposition candidate by the 2002 election.

Figure 6.3 reflects these contrasting trends with data on capital liberalization. The data are from the Chinn and Ito (2008) index of capital account openness. The left-hand panel illustrates the annual average levels of capital account openness for private law versus public law chambers, while the right-hand panel shows the corresponding figures for Cameroon and Kenya. The two countries evidently mirror the general patterns. If capital liberalization interacts with a chamber's legal framework to influence how a business community structures its leadership, as suggested by the duration analysis in the previous section, then the trends in Figure 6.3 can proxy for the relative autonomy of business from state-mediated capital. In this respect, business autonomy in Cameroon for most of the 1990s was unchanged when compared to the 1980s. Only during a temporary three-year window in 1993–1995 did Biya's government apparently loosen capital controls. While many other African governments were forced to relinquish their control over capital during this same time period, Biya's government could leverage the country's oil production to retain its influence over finance and delay much needed reforms (Doe 1995). By contrast, in Kenya, after an initial tightening of capital controls between 1992 and 1995, the nature of the business–state relationship was transformed by the government's dramatic liberalization of capital after 1995.

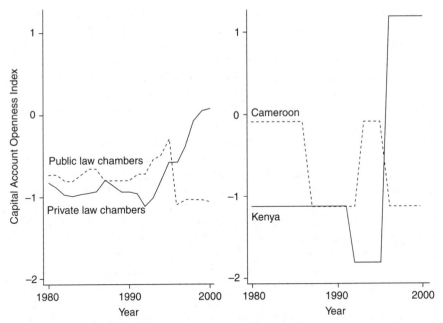

FIGURE 6.3. Capital liberalization in Cameroon and Kenya.
Note: The left-hand panel shows the average level of capital account openness for chamber type – private law versus public law. The right hand panel shows capital account openness for Cameroon and Kenya.
Source: Data on capital account openness are from Chinn and Ito (2008).

Business Alignments in Cameroon

The persistent allegiance of Cameroonian business to Biya and his ruling party is, at first view, puzzling. At the time of the transition to multiparty politics in 1990, Biya confronted a multiethnic pro-democracy movement that seemed on the verge of bringing about a new political order. While some entrepreneurs did initially support that movement, most have since chosen either to publicly endorse Biya's Rassemblement Démocratique du Peuple Camerounais (RDPC) or to remain neutral, at least publicly. This section shows how the business–state relationship in Cameroon, underpinned by the state's continued influence over capital, made it infeasible for most entrepreneurs to defect in support of the opposition.

The business community's enduring alignment with the incumbent is all the more noteworthy for the hostility that grew between the two sides prior to 1990. Throughout the previous decade, entrepreneurs had been subjected to increasing government interference as Biya consolidated his hold on power by reorganizing the economic bases of his regime. While having succeeded Ahmadou Ahidjo to the presidency through a peaceful transition in 1982, Biya was forced to put down a coup attempt in 1984 that had been orchestrated by his predecessor's loyalists (Le Vine 1986). This challenge led Biya to rein in the influence of economic actors who had been favored by his predecessor: traders from Ahidjo's Fulbe ethnic group and entrepreneurs from the Bamileke ethnic group who dominated sectors such as construction, retail, and transport.[12] The commercially prominent Bamileke, who had already become accustomed to dealing with the state to ensure the survival of their businesses (Konings 1996), were a special concern for Biya.[13] He sent that message early on by having high-profile Bamileke businessmen like André Sohaing, who had been a member of the ruling party's central committee since 1975, briefly arrested under charges of colluding with coup plotters (Owona Nguini 1996).

Biya sought to recalibrate the business–state relationship that had existed since independence (Bayart 1989; van de Walle 1993). He did so by reinforcing the state's role as gatekeeper for capital, inducing greater dependence on state-mediated finance. In assuming office at the peak of an oil boom in the early 1980s, Biya could afford to extend his predecessor's policy of subsidizing targeted investments in the private sector.[14] His government liberalized the investment code in 1984 to promote the participation of indigenous entrepreneurs (Ngwasiri 1989) and increased the credit made available through existing state institutions – the Centre d'Assistance aux Petites et Moyennes Entreprises (CAPME) and the Fonds d'Aide et de Garantie de crédit aux Petites et Moyennes Entreprises (FOGAPE) (Owona Nguini 1996). FOGAPE's mission was further expanded in 1984 to buy shares in local enterprises and to grant loans in exchange for equity stock (Jua 1990). In 1985, the government revised banking rules requiring the Cameroonian state to hold at least one third of the equity in banks in order to permit Cameroonian nationals to substitute for the state (Doe 1995).

While Biya seemingly offered greater access to credit to bolster his support among members of the business community – the delinquent debt ratio more than doubled from 5.6% in 1982 to 13.7% in 1985 despite good economic times (Kobou et al. 2008) – this was a targeted and monitored political privilege. Biya sought to counterbalance the commercial strength of Bamileke entrepreneurs by steering financial opportunities toward individuals from his political base among the ethnic Beti and others from Central and South Provinces (Jua 1993; Warnier

---

[12] Bamileke is an umbrella ethnic identity – somewhat akin to the Luhya in Kenya – that combines a number of culturally related groups whose languages are not necessarily mutually intelligible.

[13] Commentators suggest Ahidjo had arranged an implicit bargain with the Bamileke: their economic activities would not be impeded as long as they stayed out of politics. The Bamileke were thus effectively paying for their earlier participation in a rebellion that began in the 1950s and continued for some years after independence. For example, in his autobiography, businessman Victor Fotso (1979) describes a 1971 meeting in which Ahidjo "invited" Bamileke entrepreneurs to integrate other ethnic groups into their business ventures.

[14] The government had multiple instruments for investing in the private sector. The Société Nationale des Hydrocarbures (SNH) was established as a parastatal in 1980 to manage the country's oil resources, but because it is supervised directly from the office of the president, its cash surplus could be invested at the government's discretion. The Société Nationale d'Investissement (SNI), a government holding company, was used to take equity stock, guarantee loans to enterprises, and form joint ventures between parastatals and local firms.

1993). In 1986, James Onobiono, a businessman from Central Province who had joined the ruling party's central committee a year earlier, acquired Bank of America's local branch, renamed the International Bank of Africa Cameroon (IBAC).[15] In doing so, Onobiono established the first commercial bank to be majority owned by private indigenous shareholders in Cameroon. Because Onobiono's takeover would have been impossible without the government's consent – the state had held a 35% stake in Bank of America's operation[16] – it underscored the fact that no Bamileke had achieved such a feat despite that community's obvious interest in commercial finance. The government, under both Ahidjo and Biya, had blocked Bamileke efforts to establish their own banks. In contrast to Onobiono, Victor Fotso, a nationally prominent Bamileke businessman, was rebuffed when he attempted to take over the Cameroonian branch of the Banque Internationale de l'Afrique Occidentale (BIAO) in 1988.

Intervening in financial markets enabled the regime to fortify a corporatist-like arrangement with the business community. This was epitomized by Biya's decision to integrate sectoral representatives into the ruling party's most important body. At the 1985 party conference, as he was easing out his predecessor's supporters, Biya appointed businessmen from different ethnic groups to the ruling party's central committee, including Noucti Tchokwago, a Bamileke who served as president of the national chamber of commerce, Pierre Tchanqué, another Bamileke who would go on to become chamber president in 1988,[17] and Samuel Kondo, a Sawa from Littoral Province who was president of a national employers' association, the Syndicat des Industriels du Cameroun (Syndustricam).[18]

Cameroonian Business Supports Opposition Demands

While Cameroonian business was effectively subdued by the time regime critics were articulating their demands for democracy in the early 1990s,

---

[15] Onobiono's bank was closed down in 1994 by the regional banking authority, the Commission Bancaire de l'Afrique Central (COBAC). See Brian Killen, "Great Success Story Out of Africa," *Sunday Mail* (South Africa), 20 November 1988; "James récupera-t-il sa banque?," *La Lettre du Continent*, no. 221, 27 October 1994; "Affaire IBAC (suite)," *La Lettre du Continent*, no. 224, 8 December 1994.

[16] The state must have sold part of its own shares to Onobiono and his partners, since the state's participation in the bank declined from 35% to 12.5%. My calculations are based on figures reported in the bank listings under Cameroon in the 1986 and 1987 volumes of *Africa South of the Sahara* (Europa Publications Limited).

[17] Pierre Tchanqué is often held up as the model of the entrepreneur who relies on political connections to advance business interests (van de Walle 1993). Tchanqué started a major brewery in 1979 with capital from the state investment company, the SNI. He went on to serve as president of Cameroon's chamber of commerce from 1988 until he died in 1998; he remained a member of the RDPC central committee throughout that time.

[18] The other businessmen were James Onobiono and Joseph Sack. It was also at this 1985 party conference that the Union National Camerounaise was renamed the Rassemblement Démocratique du Peuple Camerounais. See "Biya's Prospects for Survival," *Africa Confidential*, 18 September 1985, pp. 4–6.

Biya's regime could not forestall the mass mobilization in favor of multi-party democracy, particularly after four years of continuous economic contraction. The country had experienced a 6% decline in 1990 alone. To lead the democracy movement, politicians representing the country's major ethno-regional groups formed the National Coordination of Opposition Parties and Associations (NCOPA). [19] John Fru Ndi, the charismatic leader of the Social Democratic Front (SDF), quickly emerged as the one candidate who could appeal to both Anglophones and Francophones, a linguistic divide that has complicated politics since independence. [20] He was joined in NCOPA by nationally recognized politicians such as Samuel Eboua, a Christian Sawa from Littoral Province and a member of Ahidjo's administration, who led the Union Nationale pour la Démocratie et le Progrès (UNDP), a party largely supported by Muslim Fulbes from the northern provinces. Adamou Ndam Njoya, a Francophone who had served as minister of education under Ahidjo, led the Union Démocratique du Cameroun (UDC). Although his political base was limited to his ethnic Bamoun, a relatively small group, Ndam Njoya was nationally respected as having been a reformer in government.

Responding to mounting domestic and international pressure, Biya legalized the creation of political parties in December 1990. [21] But NCOPA's various parties were not satisfied: they remained united in their demand for a sovereign national conference with the power to rewrite the constitution. When Biya refused to convene such a conference, as incumbents in other Francophone countries had already done, NCOPA ratcheted up the pressure by organizing a general strike dubbed Opération Villes Mortes, or Operation Ghost Town, in July 1991. Intended to bring the government into a fiscal crisis by shutting down economic activity and withholding taxes, the strike's observance held for three months in the provincial capitals of South West and Littoral; it lasted nearly six months in the provincial capitals of North West and West, which

---

[19] This opposition coordination was catalyzed by the arrest in February 1990 of a group that had been secretly meeting in Douala to discuss how to promote the transition toward a multiparty system. The "Douala ten," charged with inciting revolt and acts of sedition, were promptly convicted. But contrary to the regime's expectations, the case resulted in the mushrooming of civil society organizations and political parties (Takougang and Krieger 1998).

[20] Fru Ndi originally filed a petition with local authorities in March 1990 to request recognition of the SDF under Article 5 of Law No. 67/LF/19 of 12 June 12 1967. After the government failed to dissuade him, Fru Ndi launched the SDF at a public rally on 26 May 1990, a month after the "Douala ten" case concluded. Fru Ndi's inauguration of the SDF in the North West provincial capital of Bamenda attracted a public rally of some 20,000 people. The regime reacted by deploying the army, which fired on the crowd and killed six.

[21] Two political reforms were enacted on 19 December 1990. Law No. 90/056 established procedures for registering new parties, which would be authorized to operate three months after filing petitions with the minister of territorial administration. This law barred parties from having foreign support or from being ethnically, linguistically, religiously, or regionally based. Law No. 90/052 created conditions for free press and repealed a provision that had previously been used to censor the media.

represented the regional core of SDF support (Krieger 1994). The opposition's strike endured, in part because it enjoyed the support of business.

Certain entrepreneurs allied themselves with the opposition at this early stage of the political transition by supporting the general strike. Given the speed with which mass demonstrations had been organized, it seemed that Biya might be dislodged even before the first multiparty election could be scheduled. The array of groups that had been aggrieved by Biya's interventions throughout the 1980s – Anglophones in North West Province, Bamileke in Littoral and West Provinces, and Fulbe in Adamawa, North, and Far North Provinces – saw an opportunity to help bring about a new political order that might serve their economic interests. The support of business for the opposition's strike was, according to Mbembe (1993, 368), part of "the economic arm of a confrontation in which the stakes, from the beginning, involved the redistribution of spoils of the state."

But the opposition coordination achieved through NCOPA unraveled once negotiations with the government were initiated at the end of 1991. Opposition representatives had agreed not to attend talks called by Biya unless their demands were met beforehand. Defections among opposition party leaders, however, swelled on the very first day of negotiations.[22] The agreement produced through these talks widened the divide within the opposition: it was signed by two of the main opposition parties, the UDC and UNDP, but putative opposition leader Fru Ndi walked out of the talks and refused to let his SDF sign on (Takougang and Krieger 1998).[23] This intraopposition division persisted into subsequent legislative and presidential elections held in 1992. The three main opposition parties – SDF, UNDP, and UDC – failed to form an electoral coalition, splitting the opposition vote and thereby enabling Biya to secure his reelection through a rigged process.[24] The ruling RDPC also subsequently retained a legislative majority with the support of minority parties.

Biya would go on to reconstitute his national coalition over the following decade, while, as one country expert notes, "the opposition parties have been

[22] According to Ngayap (1999), the coalition contentiously split between moderates who were willing to attend the trilateral talks and hardliners who insisted that their conditions be met beforehand. The hardline position prevailed: NCOPA stated on 27 October 1991 that they would not go to Yaounde until the trilateral talks were transformed into a sovereign national conference with the power to address the constitution, the electoral code, and media access for political parties. Ngayap believes that hardliners won the debate within NCOPA because the civil society organizations, more radical to begin with, voted with the minority among the political parties.

[23] The Yaounde Declaration of 13 November 1991 required the opposition to call off the general strike and postpone their demands for a national conference until after elections were held. In exchange, the government would introduce a grace period for the payment of taxes and other arrears caused by the strike, lift the ban on human rights groups, terminate the regional military commands, release prisoners arrested during the strike, and permit political exiles to return.

[24] The rigging of the 1992 presidential election was made easier by the opposition's own fragmentation (Gros 1995). For a discussion of specific irregularities, see the National Democratic Institute's election monitoring report, "An Assessment of the October 11, 1992 Election in Cameroon."

plagued by dissention and disarray, and appear to be less of a threat to the regime today than they were a decade ago" (Takougang 2003, 422). Fru Ndi, the leader of the opposition SDF, progressively lost the support of the Bamileke entrepreneurs who provided much of his party's early electoral financing. While the SDF was initially seen "as the party of the Bamileke ethnic group" (van de Walle 2003, 305), it lost most of that elite backing by the mid-1990s (Konings 2004).[25]

Cameroon's Bamileke Entrepreneurs Realign with Biya

Why did Cameroon's incipient opposition coordination come undone? The answer can be linked to the political alignment of business, namely, Bamileke entrepreneurs. Although certain entrepreneurs initially supported NCOPA and their orchestration of Opération Villes Mortes, the opposition's erstwhile business allies began to rethink their political stance as the general strike dragged on. Many entrepreneurs had been willing to forgo some months of revenue to support the strike if it would bring about political and economic change. However, as it became increasingly apparent that the regime could withstand the economic boycott,[26] business chose to seek an entente with Biya.

Joseph Kadji Defosso, a Bamileke businessman who headed the Groupement des Hommes d'Affaires Camerounais, attempted to mediate between the government and the opposition. This move, in reality, signaled the end of the brief alliance between business and the opposition, as many entrepreneurs began withdrawing their support from NCOPA at this point.[27] According to Pierre Flambeau Ngayap (1999, 194), who participated in the negotiations, Bamileke entrepreneurs estimated their losses from persisting with the strike as being too great: "When they realized that the government was numb to the suffering and the death of the 'villes mortes,' and that it was determined to let the social fabric rot, the Bamileke business elite began to reevaluate the 'opportunity cost' of their support."[28] Business, in effect, made a separate peace with Biya.

---

[25] The outcome of leadership struggles within the SDF in the mid-1990s may well reflect the loss of that entrepreneurial Bamileke support. When Bamileke members, who made up the majority of SDF's Francophone membership, demanded greater representation in the SDF's executive, namely, the post of secretary-general, Fru Ndi responded by stating that "it was unacceptable that a Bamileke would ever become secretary-general of the SDF" (quoted in Konings 2004, 297).

[26] It also became apparent that the regime was willing to use force, if necessary, to bring about a resolution to the political impasse. In May 1991, Biya established three military commands aimed at containing potential rebellions in the provinces where opposition was strongest: Far North–North–Adamaoua; West–North West; and Littoral–South West. Only Biya's core region of Center–South-East was excluded from military command.

[27] Other businessmen involved in the mediation between government and opposition were Victor Fotso, Maurice Kamgaing, Samuel Kondo, Pascal Monkam, and André Sohaing. See Ngayap (1999) and Owona Nguini (1996).

[28] Growing differences between opposition politicians and their business allies were exacerbated when, in September 1991, hardline members advocated extending the general strike to include a boycott of the academic year. Moderate members opposed the move, claiming that it would reduce compliance with the strike as a whole. In the view of Takougang and Krieger (1998), this division was class-based, since the academic boycott would impose greater costs on urban and middle classes. The hardliners won the debate, but the academic boycott proved to be ineffectual.

The political support that business has given to Biya since 1992 has been rooted in the state's control of capital. Business has had to continue relying on political contacts for access to finance because Biya resisted implementing many of the reform conditionalities tied to IMF and World Bank lending. This financial control was further assured by the placement of Biya's co-regionalists in key portfolios within government. Between the time Biya took power in 1982 and 2000, the finance minister was someone from Center or South Provinces for 13 of 18 years.[29] The trade minister was also someone from Center Province for 14 of those 18 years.[30] In this way, Biya guaranteed that his co-regionalists would have an advantage in accessing finance and that capital accumulation by any entrepreneur would be closely monitored.

Biya's most effective instrument in retaining the support of business has been the politicization of commercial banking. As discussed in Chapter 5, the state continued to hold shares in nearly all of the country's commercial banks, both foreign and domestic, throughout the 1990s. While the establishment of privately owned banks in the latter half of the 1990s appeared to signal the banking sector's recovery, compensating for the withdrawal of state-controlled banks, the promise of depoliticized finance was illusory. By 2000, Cameroon had four banks wholly owned by private interests – more than at any time in the previous three decades. Besides the entry of American-owned Citibank, Cameroonian private interests established Amity Bank, Highland Corporation Bank, and Commercial Bank of Cameroon. And it is the ownership of these three indigenous banks that underscores the regime's capacity to continue acting as a gatekeeper for capital. The principal shareholder in each of these indigenous banks can be linked to the ruling party either as a party official or an elected representative.

Lawrence Loweh Tasha, an Anglophone from North West Province, established Amity Bank in 1991. He went on to serve as the RDPC section president for Bui I constituency of North West Province and lead the constituency's party list during the 2002 legislative elections. When Tasha lost control of Amity Bank in 2000, Christophe Sielienou became the majority shareholder. Sielienou, a Bamileke, was elected in 2002 as the RDPC mayor of Kekem in Haut-Nkam Department of West Province.[31]

---

[29] The finance portfolio was held by Etienne Ntsama (Center, 1983–1985), Edouard Koualla (Littoral, 1986), Botoo a Ngon (Center, 1987), Hayatou Sadou (North, 1988–1990), Justin Ndioro (Center, 1991–1992), Antoine Ntsimi (Center, 1993), Jean Marie Ngankou (West, 1996), and Edouard Akame Mfoumo (South, 1997–2000).

[30] The trade portfolio was held by Tori Limangana (Far North, 1983), Edouard Nomo Ongolo (Center, 1984–1987), Joseph Tsanga Abanda (Center, 1988–1990), Rene Owona (Center, 1991–1992), Patrice Ambassa Mandeng (Center, 1993), Pierre Eloundou Mani (Center, 1994–1995), Justin Ndioro (Center, 1996–1997), and Maigari Bello Bouba (North, 1998–2000).

[31] Tasha, who unsuccessfully sought the intervention of the Ministry of Finance for seven years, put the battle over control of Amity Bank in ethnic terms: "Most of these shareholders who are not comfortable seeing me at Amity are Bamilekes." However, the conflict also illustrates the regime's role in allocating access to financial resources, since the bank was ultimately transferred from one political ally to another. See Lazare Kolyang, "Restructuration – L'argent de

Paul Nji Atanga, an Anglophone from Bamenda in North West Province, founded Highland Corporation Bank in 1995. Atanga's unexpected entry into banking – he had not been a prominent entrepreneur beforehand – followed his vocal criticism of Fru Ndi, the opposition politician who also happened to be from Bamenda.[32] While Atanga's bank was forced into liquidation at the end of 2000, when its license was revoked by the Commission Bancaire de l'Afrique Centrale (COBAC), he remained the RDPC section president for Mezam I constituency in North West Province. He later served as a member of Biya's 2004 reelection campaign committee in the same constituency. Atanga was subsequently appointed as a minister for "special duties" in 2007.

The third bank, Commercial Bank of Cameroon, was founded by Victor Fotso in 1997. Fotso, a Bamileke, had been a long-time member of the RDPC central committee, but only took on a public role as a party representative after the transition to multipartism. He became the elected RDPC mayor of Pete-Bandjoun in Khoung Khi Department of West Province.[33]

The government's preponderant role in finance – directly through state ownership and indirectly through ruling party allies – helps to explain why representatives of Cameroon's main entrepreneurial ethnic group have remained aligned with the incumbent through every election since the transition to multipartism. The support enjoyed by Biya among Bamileke entrepreneurs can be explained neither by the success of his economic policies nor by his popularity among voters.[34] Rather, the state's continued control of banking has meant that Bamileke entrepreneurs could not afford to do otherwise. They could not expect to enjoy continued access to capital without rallying behind Biya because finance has remained, along with licensing and taxation, a tool by which the incumbent can discipline business (Gabriel 1999; Jua 1993; Konings 1996; van de Walle 1993).[35]

Amity Bank fait grand bruit," *Mutations*, 30 January 2008; Chris Mbunwe, "Court Halts Sale of Amity Bank," *The Post*, 25 February 2008; "Lawrence Tasha Lowe, Ndzana Ndouga et Christophe Sielienou – Trois pour l'enfer," *Mutations*, 18 June 2009.

[32] The origins of Atanga's commercial success are nebulous. See Jean-Marie Aboganena, "Paul Atanga Nji – jeune homme ambitieux," *Africa International*, no. 292, March 1996, p. 22.

[33] Fotso's two wives are also RDPC representatives: Josephine Fotso is a member of parliament for Bamboutous constituency in West Province, while Julienne Fotso is a deputy mayor for one of Yaounde's boroughs.

[34] In the 2004 election, despite the ruling party's significant advantages, opposition candidate Fru Ndi could still win 45.04% of the vote in West Province, the Bamileke heartland, versus Biya's 49.78%. In Littoral Province, where the port of Douala is located, Fru Ndi managed 32.71% against Biya's 51.52%. Two Bamileke politicians – Djeukam Tchameni of the Mouvement pour la Démocratie et l'Interdépendance (MDI) and Victorin Hameni Bieleu of the Union des Forces Démocratiques du Cameroun (UFDC) – were also presidential candidates for the 2004 election, but they were not considered viable candidates. They received no endorsements from the prominent entrepreneurs of their ethnic group, and they won a marginal number of votes.

[35] Eyoh (1998) claims that elites, rather than join political parties, have increasingly turned to ethno-regional organizations, such as the South West Conference of Chiefs, as a strategy for obtaining access to economic privileges from the state.

Supporting the opposition, even covertly, would risk provoking the kind of harassment that might push businesses into bankruptcy, since the government's influence over local banks allows it to cut off credit lines or to call in unpaid loans. This would explain why Laakam, an elite Bamileke association described as "the closest communal approximation to a Bamileke party" (Takougang and Krieger 1998, 180), disappeared soon after it had been linked to the presidential bid of opposition candidate Fru Ndi in 1992. Considering the situation of Bamileke entrepreneurs, Mbembe (1993, 358) writes, "heavily indebted for the most part and practically dependent on goodwill of the state, the principal businessmen of the West have had no choice but to continue publicly financing the RDPC and supporting Paul Biya's regime."

Cameroon's Bamileke Entrepreneurs Become Ruling Party Stalwarts

The Bamileke sealed their alliance with Biya throughout the 1990s by serving the ruling party as candidates and officials. This represented a marked departure for a group of entrepreneurs who had largely avoided having a visible presence in politics since independence. A select number had been previously connected to the regime through the ruling party's central committee or the government's advisory economic council, but, as noted by Ngayap (1983, 264), more generally "the absence of businessmen from government did not come about naturally." Ahidjo, and later Biya, had arranged it that way under the one-party system of the 1970s and 1980s. But with the return to multipartism in the 1990s, "the widening of the RDPC political class to include the main Bamileke businessmen" had been observed by scholars of Cameroonian politics (Mouiche 2005, 50). The regime now needed these entrepreneurs to deliver the votes of their coethnics, who constitute one of the largest, if not the largest, demographic groups in the country. This was a particularly urgent concern for the ruling party because the Bamileke had turned out en masse for the opposition in the 1992 elections.

Biya turned to entrepreneurs to reconstitute his base of support among Bamileke voters who remained disaffected from the ruling party. Because their wealth gives Bamileke entrepreneurs considerable influence in the constituencies populated by their coethnics, the RDPC began using them, rather than traditional chiefs, to lead the electoral lists in legislative and municipal elections held in West Province, the Bamileke homeland (Mouiche 2005; Nuembissi Kom 2007).[36] Entrepreneurs headed three of eight lists in the 2002 legislative elections. Nationally prominent Bamileke entrepreneurs, including those previously punished by Biya, entered politics as RDPC mayors in

---

[36] Nuembissi Kom (2007) points out that businessman André Sohaing's resources enabled him to displace the local traditional chief to become mayor of Bayangam even though the chief had also been an RDPC stalwart. Opposition parties in Bayangam tried to follow the ruling party's strategy, but could not attract the same quality candidates: the RDPC could recruit businesspeople and retired bureaucrats; the SDF could only attract teachers, peasants, and laborers.

TABLE 6.2. *Political Alignment of Cameroon's Leading Businessmen in 2004*[a]

Entrepreneur	Ethnicity/Province	Ruling Party Affiliation
Fadil, Mohamadou Bayero[b] (Fadoul)	Fulbe/North	Party central committee National reelection campaign
Fotso, Victor	Bamileke/West	Party central committee National reelection campaign Elected office
Kadji Defosso, Joseph	Bamileke/West	Party central committee National reelection campaign Elected office
Kamgaing, Maurice Wafo	Bamileke/West	Local reelection campaign
Kondo Ebelle, Samuel	Sawa/Littoral	Party central committee Local reelection campaign
Mbafou, Claude Joseph	Bamileke/West	Government minister Local reelection campaign
Monthé, Claude Juimo[b] (Paul)	Bamileke/West	National reelection campaign
Mukete, Victor	Bafaw/South West	Party central committee
Pantami, Mamadou	Fulbe/North	Local reelection campaign
Sandji Ndongo, Francois	Beti/Center	Local reelection campaign
Sohaing, André	Bamileke/West	Party central committee Local reelection campaign Elected office
Tanko, Amadou	Fulbe/Littoral	Party central committee Local reelection campaign

[a] This list of businessmen is based on Ngayap's (1983) identification of 32 Cameroonians who led enterprises worth FCFA 50 million.

[b] These men inherited family enterprises from deceased fathers whose names are in parentheses. The ruling party affiliations pertain to the sons.

constituencies that had been opposition bastions at the start of multiparty politics. In West Province, businessmen-turned-mayors have included Victor Fotso in Pete-Bandjoun, Joseph Kadji Defosso in Bana, Marcel Niat Njifenji in Bangangté, Christophe Sielienou in Kekem, André Sohaing in Bayangam, and Pierre Tchanqué in Bazou. Françoise Foning, founder of the Groupement des Femmes d'Affaires du Cameroun, became mayor of a borough in Douala, the country's economic capital.

The 2004 presidential election signaled continuity in the political alignment of Bamileke entrepreneurs. Although opposition politicians had attempted to organize a coalition in the run-up to the election, the country's most influential business leaders instead chose to endorse Biya's reelection. There were no defections: the entrepreneurs who had been linked to the RDPC in the 1980s and 1990s remained allied to the ruling party. Table 6.2 shows that the country's most notable entrepreneurs, many of whom began their careers by securing rent-generating opportunities through political connections, remained closely and publicly affiliated with the RDPC. This list of magnates, half of whom are Bamileke, is based on Ngayap's (1983) original identification of 32 Cameroonians who led firms worth at least FCFA 50 million, or about $235,000, in 1980.[37] Two decades later, 10 of the 23 surviving entrepreneurs, including two additional cases in which sons maintained the political ties established by their deceased fathers, could be found serving as members of the RDPC central committee, representatives of the president's reelection campaign at national or local levels, or as elected officeholders on behalf of the ruling party.[38] Only one entrepreneur could be linked to the opposition by 2004. Mohamadou Catché's small political party, Action pour le Redressement National, participated in the opposition protocoalition. Ten of the 23 could not be linked to any political party in 2004.

Cameroonian entrepreneurs seemingly chose to support Biya and his RDPC despite the government's poor management of the economy over the previous decade – the one issue that would be expected to determine their political alignment. It could be the case that the individuals listed in Table 6.2 reflect a particular class of older entrepreneur dependent on patronage from the ruling party. But the argument advanced in this chapter is more general, suggesting that the government's role as financial gatekeeper compels entrepreneurs to ally with the incumbent, regardless of generation or sector.

This claim can be tested by examining the membership of the Groupement Inter-Patronal du Cameroun (GICAM), the country's most influential employers' association.[39] GICAM represents both domestic and foreign firms from a variety of sectors, including agriculture, finance, manufacturing, mining, telecommunications, and transportation. Comparing GICAM's membership roster to RDPC campaign committees reveals that more than one-third of Cameroonian employers were directly affiliated with the ruling party: 47 of 128 domestic members served on either a presidential campaign committee in 2004, a legislative campaign committee in 2007, or both.[40] It should be noted that, of the 12 individuals listed in Table 6.2, only Samuel Kondo Ebelle is a member of GICAM.

Just one GICAM member, Noucti Tchokwago, a Bamileke who in the 1980s served as president of the chamber of commerce and a member of the RDPC central committee, could be found among the opposition's ranks. Having joined the opposition after the transition to multipartism, Tchokwago attempted to

---

[37] This figure would be the equivalent of half a million dollars in 2005.
[38] Among the nine who died before the 2004 election, four were associated with the RDPC (Fadoul Fadil, Lévis Koloko, Paul Monthé, and Jean Teinkela) and two others with the opposition (Hassan Tanko with UNDP and Daniel Awah Nangah with SDF). Teinkela, who had served as a member of parliament for UNDP, apparently returned to the RDPC before his death.
[39] GICAM was originally established in 1957 as the Groupement Interprofessionnel pour l'Etude et la Coordination des Intérêts Economiques, which was largely made up of foreign businessmen at the time. It became the Groupement Interpatronal du Cameroun in 1992.
[40] The GICAM membership roster is made up of 199 firms. For the purposes of this study, the name of the president or manager listed for each firm was coded either as a Cameroonian national or an expatriate. I found 128 Cameroonians and 71 expatriates.

run as a presidential candidate in 2004, but his candidacy was rejected by the Supreme Court.

Biya's reelection in 2004 was, in fact, endorsed by the leaders of Cameroon's main business organizations, the GICAM and the Chambre de Commerce, d'Industrie, des Mines et de l'Artisanat (CCIMA).[41] André Siaka, the Bamileke leader of GICAM, was a member of Biya's provincial reelection campaign committee in Littoral Province.[42] Claude Juimo Monthé, a Bamileke who was appointed as CCIMA's leader by presidential decree in 1998, was a member of Biya's national reelection campaign committee.[43] Altogether, the incumbent's campaign committees, from the national to the local levels, comprised a who's who of Cameroonian business. Françoise Foning headed the local committee in Douala. In West Province, the traditional Bamileke homeland, Marcel Niat Njifenji led the provincial committee; Kadji Defosso and Christophe Sielienou were members of the departmental committee in Haut-Nkam; Christophe Eken, who would go on to become the new leader of CCIMA,[44] led the local committee in Bafang; and André Sohaing, president of the Groupement des Importateurs Camerounais, was a member of the local committee in Bayangam.[45]

Ten days before the 2004 presidential election, the Bamileke business community organized a campaign rally à *l'américaine* in Douala to have Biya declared as the sole candidate for their coethnics.[46] The rally showcased notable business leaders such as Siaka, the GICAM president, Monthé, the CCIMA president, along with Foning, Kadji Defosso, Njifenji, and Sohaing. Kadji

[41] There are other business groups, but government officials seem to regularly meet with representatives from CCIMA and GICAM, including them in official delegations overseas and in meetings with foreign investors and international financial institutions. In any case, nearly all business factions in Cameroon are allied to the ruling party. A description of some of these factions can be found in "Deux 'patrons des patrons,'" *La Lettre du Continent*, 17 June 1999; "Patrons et propriétaires," *La Lettre du Continent*, 13 January 2000.

[42] Siaka became GICAM's president in 1993 and served until 2008. In this respect, Siaka's public association with the ruling party raises questions about the relationship between the government and foreign firms, which make up a large proportion of GICAM's membership. As noted earlier, 71 of 199 GICAM members are headed by expatriates.

[43] CCIMA, which was founded in 1921 and is headquartered in Douala, is the national chamber of commerce to which all registered business must belong. The organization and functioning of CCIMA were revised by decrees 2001/380 and 2001/381 of 27 November 2001. The country's president appoints CCIMA's leader from among the chamber's elected general assembly. A 12-member electoral commission headed by the commerce minister supervises the election of the executive board and general assembly; seven of the 12 members are government representatives. CCIMA is also subsidized by the state. In 2002, for example, the chamber received FCFA 600 million, or about $828,000 for its operations. See Nicolas Amayena, "Les hommes d'affaires à l'immeuble Etoile," *Cameroon Tribune*, 17 April 2003.

[44] Eken succeeded Monthé as CCIMA president in 2008. Eken, who is owner of a transport company, headed the RDPC's parliamentary list in Haut-Nkam Department of West Province in 2007.

[45] Sohaing, interestingly, was for a long time Cameroon's sole importer of French wines and spirits.

[46] Stéphane Tchakam, "Littoral: les natifs de l'Ouest avec Paul Biya," *Cameroon Tribune*, 1 October 2004.

Defosso, who had vacillated between the opposition and the ruling party at the onset of multipartism, made his pitch to the rallied crowds in practical, rather than hortatory, terms: "As long as there is no war there is hope that our situation will improve. Make the choice of peace."[47] For her part, Foning, who has been derisively labeled "the scarecrow of the RDPC" by her business rivals,[48] was even more pragmatic in her rationale for supporting the incumbent: "Vote for Paul Biya, if you want to continue doing your business in peace."[49]

Business Alignments in Kenya

The Kenyan case illustrates how the political realignment of business closely follows the liberalization of finance. The country's entrepreneurs had an incentive to support the opposition at the start of multiparty politics in the early 1990s, yet the fear of financial reprisals prevented most from doing so. Daniel arap Moi, having assumed the presidency when his predecessor died in 1978, had taken steps to encourage businesses to become dependent on political contacts for their access to capital. Moi, however, struggled to retain his influence over business once the financial reforms progressively adopted throughout the decade appeared to become permanent. By the country's third multiparty presidential election in 2002, several high-profile entrepreneurs abandoned the incumbent and his chosen successor in favor of an opposition candidate.

But nearly a decade of financial reform would have to pass before members of the business community would openly support the opposition despite their long-standing grievances against Moi and the ruling Kenya African National Union (KANU). Moi had sought to shore up his political base throughout the 1980s by undertaking a series of redistributive measures aimed at minimizing the influence of ethnic Kikuyu entrepreneurs who had come to dominate the economy under the presidency of Jomo Kenyatta, a Kikuyu himself and Moi's predecessor (Holmquist 2002; Widner 1992). Moi initiated this redistributive campaign by banning ethnic associations in 1980 with the intent of dismantling the Gikuyu-Embu-Meru Association (GEMA), which had originally formed to consolidate the economic power of certain Kikuyu elites (Throup 1987).[50] He then proceeded to position his own coethnic Kalenjin as intermediaries vis-à-vis

---

[47] Alex Gustave Azeebaze, "Elites Rdpc de l'Ouest à Douala: mobilisation pour un candidat absent," *Le Messager*, 30 October 2004.

[48] Virginie Gomez, "Les 25 qui font bouger le Cameroun," *L'Express*, 11 April 2005, p. 2.

[49] Joe Dinga Pefok and Mirabel Azangeh, "Biya Designated Bamilekes' Single Candidate," *The Post*, 4 October 2004.

[50] GEMA Holdings issued shares to members as a means of financing agricultural, industrial, and commercial activities of elites from Kiambu and Nakuru. GEMA, though a business association, was actively involved in politics. GEMA members Jackson Havester Angaine, James Gichuru, Njenga Karume, Kihika Kimani, and Njoroge Mungai were involved in the 1976 "Change the Constitution" movement that sought to prevent Moi's automatic succession to the presidency upon Kenyatta's death.

international capital and to promote alliances between the Kalenjin and the Asian minority concentrated in the manufacturing and wholesaling sectors (Ajulu 2002; Chege 1998; Vandenberg 2003).[51]

Partly as a consequence of Moi's actions, Kikuyu-owned businesses were among the hardest hit by the country's economic decline. High-profile entrepreneurs from this ethnic group, the country's largest, became increasingly vulnerable to bankruptcy as they lost their once privileged access to state mechanisms of support. They saw the shuttering of well-known firms among their coethnics as a reflection of Moi's intention to drive them out of business. Already squeezed by rising interest rates and reduced credit availability, they were unable to secure bailouts from the government. According to Njenga Karume, the Kikuyu entrepreneur who was the founding chairman of GEMA, "My most difficult and demanding years in business came during Moi's years in power.... Whereas well-connected individuals were getting unsecured loans from banks after 'orders from above,' I could not access any of them. I was not one of the regime's favourites and I was out in the cold" (Karume and wa Gethoi 2009, 258–259).

The financial controls available to the Kenyan government in the 1980s induced Kikuyu entrepreneurs to respond to Moi's economic restructuring by resorting to private solutions rather than collective action. Throup and Hornsby (1998, 62) note that they might have been able "to prevent the onslaught against Kikuyu capital, but by remaining silent and hoping that they could reach personal accommodations with the regime they had been humbled one by one." For his part, Njenga Karume, the former GEMA chairman, pursued a political strategy to survive commercially. Once elected to the one-party parliament, Karume asked his friend Stanley Oloitiptip, a cabinet minister and proven Moi ally, to intercede on his behalf with the president (Karume and wa Gethoi 2009, 258–259). Karume was subsequently appointed as an assistant minister in Moi's cabinet, which presumably allowed him to secure the loans he had been previously denied.[52]

But relying on political intervention was a strategy that could cut both ways. The case of Madhupaper, a paper-manufacturing firm that spawned a decade-long legal saga, is emblematic of the opportunities and risks created by politicized finance.[53] Samuel Macharia, a Kikuyu entrepreneur, founded Madhupaper in 1976 with financing from state-owned banks, the Industrial

---

[51] Kenyatta had perceived Asian entrepreneurs as an obstacle to indigenous economic expansion, while Moi saw them as allies who posed no political threat due to their minority status.

[52] Karume served as an assistant minister in various portfolios from 1979 through 1991.

[53] The Madhupaper saga was covered extensively in the local press. Not only did Macharia carry out a public campaign alleging that he was being targeted in order to favor Kenyan Asian investors, but the extent of government involvement in the Madhupaper case was also debated in parliament. See, for example, "Madhupaper Project on Stormy Seas," *Weekly Review* (Nairobi), 15 November 1985, p. 17; "The Plot Thickens," *Weekly Review* (Nairobi), 3 February 1989, p. 24; "Back to Square One," *Weekly Review* (Nairobi), 17 March 1989, p. 17; "The End of the Paper Chase?" *Weekly Review* (Nairobi), 21 July 1989, p. 25.

Development Bank and the National Bank of Kenya. Despite his firm's loss-making operations, Macharia was able to lobby the government in the following years to secure additional financing from other state-owned banks, including government backing for a loan from the World Bank's International Finance Corporation (IFC). In 1985, however, Macharia's implicit political support was abruptly terminated. This was the same year, incidentally, that Moi's government sought to dislodge the Kikuyu leader of the Kenya National Chamber of Commerce and Industry (KNCCI), as explained previously. In this case, once the government withdrew the guarantees it had offered in connection with Macharia's IFC loan, the Kenya Commercial Bank, the Kenya Commercial Finance Company, and the Kenya National Capital Corporation – all state-owned institutions – followed suit by recalling the loans they were owed by Madhupaper. The company entered into receivership after defaulting. Macharia then again sought a political solution to his financial problem by asking Joseph arap Letting, Moi's cabinet secretary and head of the civil service, to intervene in the negotiations with his creditors. But, now apparently out of favor with the regime, Macharia failed to get the favorable outcome he sought.[54]

Kenyan Business Vacillates During the Transition

The public demand for multiparty politics in 1990 may have been initiated by Kenneth Matiba and Charles Rubia, two former ministers who happened to be wealthy Kikuyu entrepreneurs,[55] but most Kikuyu entrepreneurs hesitated to support the opposition even after Moi legalized the formation of opposition parties.[56] These entrepreneurs were not only uncertain as to whether they could support the opposition without incurring reprisals; they were unsure as to which politician to endorse within the opposition. The Forum for the

---

[54] The ensuing negotiations between Macharia and his creditors resulted in a years-long civil suit that followed the country's political trajectory. In 1992, the year in which multiparty politics were legalized, Macharia filed a lawsuit against his creditors, alleging that undue political influence had been used to compel him to overpay in clearing his debts. In 2003, the year in which Kenya's first multiparty alternation occurred, the High Court found in Macharia's favor. However, in 2008, the year after Kenya's violent presidential election, the Court of Appeal reversed the High Court's decision. The Court of Appeal found that Macharia had voluntarily entered into a repayment agreement with his creditors and that there was no evidence of political compulsion. The text of the Court of Appeal's decision in *Kenya Commercial Bank Ltd. & Another vs. Samuel Kamau Macharia & 2 Others* can be found at www.kenyalaw.org.

[55] Matiba and Rubia were arrested after calling for a pro-democracy rally. The regime was probably concerned that a Kikuyu–Luo alliance might be in the making, as indicated by secret meetings Matiba and Rubia had been holding with Oginga Odinga, the long-time Luo dissident, and his son Raila Odinga, who was also arrested. The news of these arrests led to riots on 7 July 1990, the day the rally was to be held. Matiba suffered a stroke while in detention and was flown to London for hospitalization (Throup and Hornsby 1998).

[56] Section 2A, the constitutional provision establishing a one-party state, was repealed in December 1991.

Restoration of Democracy (FORD), which had been established in May 1991 as a national multiethnic pro-democracy coalition, became a registered political party in January 1992. But the power struggle that ensued within FORD in the months leading up to the December 1992 presidential election eventually split the party into rival factions. Matiba led a Kikuyu faction along with some Luhya politicians to form FORD-Asili, meaning "the original" in Swahili, while Oginga Odinga, the country's first vice-president and a longtime dissident, led a faction of his coethnic Luos, including some Luhya, to form FORD-Kenya.

The standard narrative for this moment in Kenyan politics suggests that ethnic competition and mistrust prevented Matiba and Odinga from cementing their alliance.[57] On the one hand, Kikuyus in FORD wanted one of their own to lead the coalition, but feared that politicians from other ethnic groups, mainly the Luo, would take control of the party while Matiba was recovering from a sudden stroke (Oyugi 1992). On the other hand, Odinga was the dean of the opposition by virtue of his longstanding opposition to KANU. And given his bitter experience as Kenyatta's vice president in the 1960s, Odinga had little cause to trust a power-sharing agreement from another Kikuyu president.[58] Efforts by neutral individuals, including civil society representatives, church leaders, and the U.S. ambassador, could not unite Matiba and Odinga (Hempstone 1997; Throup and Hornsby 1998).

But FORD's disintegration can also be attributed to the political reticence of the business community in 1992. Rather than using their resources to tip the balance in favor of Matiba or Odinga during the party's internal leadership battle, most entrepreneurs instead chose to abstain altogether. Their reticence may seem odd, given that "the economy was in such straits that many Kikuyu business leaders were looking for someone openly to defend their interests" (Throup and Hornsby 1998, 62). However, at the time, Moi's statist economic controls provided him with an effective punishment mechanism to discourage most entrepreneurs from donating to any opposition candidate. Those who dared to do so quickly learned their mistake. Convinced that Moi's regime tracked the banking transactions of individual businesses, one Kikuyu entrepreneur recalls,

People could be punished.... I believed in a strong opposition in 1992, so I gave some money to Jaramogi [Oginga Odinga]. He told me that he wanted to unite with the rest of the opposition. His idea was that he was the oldest so he could accommodate the rest of the opposition and they could work together to write a new constitution. I agreed with

---

[57] Kenya's presidential election rules encouraged the formation of multiethnic coalitions: a successful candidate had to win 25 percent of the vote in five of the country's eight provinces. In the early 1990s, this was a hurdle that no party besides KANU could clear.

[58] Commentators attribute Odinga's refusal to become another candidate's lieutenant to his feeling that the Kikuyu owed him a debt: he challenged British colonial authorities to release Kenyatta from prison when many other politicians would not have dared. He then helped Kenyatta attain power at the time of independence only to be later expelled from KANU and the government over their ideological differences.

that idea. But Moi found out. He rang me. He knew everything. I then had to support him, too.... I probably then gave a bit more to Moi.[59]

Moi's financial controls would have been sufficient to deter most entrepreneurs from siding with the opposition. But FORD's leadership candidates were also populists who had little appeal for most in the business community. Odinga had made a career out of criticizing the country's economic inequalities and espousing greater redistribution (Odinga 1967).[60] Matiba, being a Kikuyu entrepreneur, would have been the obvious choice as the political champion of Kikuyu business. However, he was also outspoken in his radical politics and sought to attract a mass following among poor voters. Muigai (1995, 183–184) notes that Matiba "shunned the monied and the elite and appealed directly to the urban and rural poor." From the perspective of Kikuyu business, Matiba's statements offered no assurance that he could represent or implement their preferences (Oyugi 1992).[61]

The business community may have wanted an alternation in the presidency, but they wanted it on their own terms. Contrary to a pure ethnic logic, a limited number of Kikuyu entrepreneurs were willing to split their community's vote by financing the formation of another party that would compete with Matiba's FORD-Asili.[62] The Democratic Party (DP) formed by Mwai Kibaki, Moi's vice president from 1978 to 1988 and a finance minister from 1969 to 1981, became popularly perceived as the party of those who had profited in the Kenyatta years (Throup 1993; Muigai 1995). Kibaki's principal backer, for example, was businessman Njenga Karume, the former chairman of GEMA – the very organization Moi had dismantled in 1980.

Kenya's Kikuyu Entrepreneurs are Courted by the Incumbent

Throughout the 1990s, Moi made a concerted effort to isolate Kibaki from potential Kikuyu financiers. At the same time Moi was permitting Kenya's financial liberalization to move forward, he was focused on courting Kikuyu entrepreneurs in a manner that had never been done before, precisely because he was losing the capacity to blackmail them through financial controls. Grignon et al. (2001, 19) note that in the lead-up to the 1997 elections

---

[59] Author interview, Nairobi, 8 August 2008.

[60] After being politically rehabilitated by Moi in the early 1980s, Odinga was quickly marginalized once again after making comments in reference to land grabbing during Kenyatta's tenure.

[61] See Matiba's critique of Kenyan politics and his call for a new social contract (Matiba 1993). Matiba was also a vocal critic of the Asian business minority, warning that "Asians must stop their corrupt methods now otherwise they should be packing ready to go when we take power" (Quoted in Munene 2001, 50).

[62] In the 1992 election, the Kikuyu did split their votes. Kibaki won the parliamentary constituencies in northern Kikuyuland, which include Kibaki's natal Nyeri district as well as Nyandarua and Kirinyaga districts. Kibaki also won in the neighboring Laikipia district in the Rift Valley, but he lost the southern half of Kikuyuland to Matiba, whose base was in Murang'a district. Matiba also won Kiambu district and most of Nairobi.

"DP suffered most from the divisive strategies of KANU," while Munene claims that "Kikuyu elite who had supported Kibaki in 1992 abandoned him as some of them flocked to the KANU bandwagon" (Munene 2001, 44). Moi made two distinct attempts to coopt Kibaki's potential Kikuyu financiers before the 1997 elections.

Moi sought an entente with the Kikuyu elites who had been part of GEMA, and still enjoyed considerable influence among their coethnics, by convening reconciliation talks following ethnic clashes that erupted along the Rift Valley in the aftermath of the 1992 elections (Kenya Human Rights Commission 1998; Republic of Kenya 1999). Moi had his right-hand man and long-time cabinet minister, Nicholas Biwott, lead a delegation in negotiations with Kikuyu representatives that included Njenga Karume, Kibaki's financier and GEMA's former chairman. While these were supposed to be confidence-building talks to reduce conflict among the ethnic communities in the Rift Valley, they were essentially political negotiations aimed at bringing Kikuyu elites linked to GEMA back into the ruling party fold. These negotiations unexpectedly collapsed after Kibaki's DP won a by-election in Kipipiri constituency. KANU leaders claimed that their GEMA counterparts had reneged on a promise to deliver the constituency to them (Karume and wa Gethoi 2009; Njogu 2001).

Once Moi's gambit with GEMA leaders failed, he turned his attention to Kikuyu personalities who were not affiliated with GEMA. In the run-up to the 1997 elections, he specifically encouraged the formation of the Central Province Development Support Group (CPDSG) to woo a broader range of Kikuyu elites that included businesspeople, parastatal chiefs, and civil servants. By underscoring the futility of remaining in opposition, namely, the potential loss of state contracts for individual businesses and the loss of development funds for their region, the CPDSG gave Kikuyu elites considerable incentive to support it. CPDSG consisted of prominent Kikuyu entrepreneurs led by Samuel Macharia – the owner of Madhupaper who had sought Moi's intervention in his loan negotiations with Kenya Commercial Bank (KCB) – and included entrepreneurs from a cross section of economic sectors such as Joseph Wanjui, a former chairman of the Kenya Association of Manufacturers (KAM), Chris Kirubi, the vice chairman of KAM, Stanley Githunguri, an insurance company owner and property developer, and John Ngata Kariuki, a hotelier.[63] According to one entrepreneur linked to the CPSDSG,

It was pragmatism that drove businessmen to participate in the CPDSG. Because the regime was in control of virtually everything, you had to consider how to best engage it.... You could not be antagonistic to the government if you wanted to develop and expand your business. You had to conduct diplomacy to enable your business to grow.[64]

---

[63] Some claim that these entrepreneurs were attracted to CPDSG by the opportunity to communicate directly with Moi about the need for further economic reform, but there is no evidence of their influence on subsequent policy decisions. See Warigi Gitau, "Can Kikuyu MPs Weather Political Storms?," *Daily Nation* (Nairobi), 3 January 1999.

[64] Author interview, Nairobi, 18 July 2008.

CPDSG members became directly involved in the selection of candidates for the KANU primaries leading up to the 1997 election (Munene 2001; Njogu 2001). The group's most symbolic event was a luncheon organized to raise funds for Moi's reelection campaign at the Hotel Inter-Continental on 6 December 1997, just weeks before the election (Munene 2001, 44). The approximately 500 businesspeople attending the event contributed some 100 million shillings, or about $1.6 million, to the campaign.[65]

The CPDSG was intended to have a symbolic impact, says Joseph Kamotho, the long-serving KANU secretary general who helped to coordinate the initiative at the time. A Kikuyu himself, Kamotho notes that KANU "didn't need business to help pay for the election. The bulk of the financing was not private."[66] The formation of CPDSG was instead supposed to signal to Kikuyu elites that Moi continued to influence their business prospects and should therefore remain allied to the ruling party. More concretely, obliging Kikuyu entrepreneurs to become CPDSG members ensured that their financial contributions would not go to Moi's political rivals, particularly Kibaki.

Moi was far less concerned that other opposition parties would acquire resources because most of their leaders were broke by mid-decade. Matiba's FORD-Asili was falling apart as he progressively withdrew from politics due to health reasons and declining resources. Since he was not making a run for the presidency in 1997, Matiba was no longer willing to finance FORD-Asili's parliamentary candidates. Its parliamentary seats therefore dropped from 31 to 1 after the 1997 elections. More generally, Matiba's experience served as a cautionary tale for the business community: several of his businesses allegedly began to fail under government pressure after he entered politics. Chris Kirubi, a former chairman of the Kenya Association of Manufacturers (KAM) and one of Kenya's most prominent entrepreneurs, recalls from this period:

I couldn't afford to get too involved. I have too many interests, so it was important that I remain neutral. I represent the livelihoods of many people whose salaries I pay. I would have put them in danger if I had recklessly gotten involved in politics. I would have been either successful or destroyed overnight. Look at what happened to Matiba. All his businesses – the tourism and the schools – were undermined. Government banks could be ordered by Moi to recall loans. That is why I only borrowed from international banks.[67]

A lack of financing also resulted in the breakup of FORD-Kenya. From the beginning, Oginga Odinga and his deputy, Michael Wamalwa, struggled to raise funds.[68] Odinga eventually secured two million shillings from Kamlesh Pattni,

---

[65] Bernard Namunane and David Mugonyi, "Kibaki Date to Cost Sh 1 Million a Plate," *Daily Nation* (Nairobi), 30 July 2007.

[66] Author interview, Nairobi, 18 July 2008.

[67] Author interview, Nairobi, 6 August 2008.

[68] Odinga had even approached the U.S. ambassador to Kenya for funding, though unsuccessfully (Hempstone 1997).

an Asian businessman implicated in the Goldenberg scandal that involved the highest levels of government.[69] Not coincidentally, it is at this time that FORD-Kenya began cooperating informally with KANU in parliament.[70] Odinga's party, nevertheless, split upon his death in 1994. Wamalwa was unable to secure the financing he needed to keep FORD-Kenya from breaking apart, as he fended off efforts by Odinga's son, Raila, to take over the party. The party lost over half of its MPs when Raila led its Luo members to form the National Development Party (NDP) in the run-up to the 1997 elections. Wamalwa later acknowledged that many of his party's MPs defected to Kibaki's DP because he lacked the money to pay for electoral campaigns in their constituencies, further hampering his ability to secure funding: "After 25 MPs left us on the eve of an election, to our would-be donors, it looked like the party was falling apart. As a result, they refused to give us the money."[71]

While most opposition parties were fragmenting due to the lack of resources, Kibaki's own DP unexpectedly held together through the 1997 elections.[72] Moi's cooptation of Kikuyu entrepreneurs had limited Kibaki's pool of contributions, but whatever financing was made available to the DP enabled the party to consolidate its position. In a highly fluid party system – nearly one-third of the 104 opposition parliamentarians who won seats in 1997 had started in a different party the previous year – DP's resources enabled the party to recruit and hold onto more competitive candidates (Hornsby 2001). It became the largest opposition party through the 1997 elections by attracting more veteran candidates: only 52% of its candidates were newcomers as opposed to the 70% average among other opposition parties. And these DP candidates had a higher success rate when compared to the rest of the opposition: 30% of DP candidates won in their constituencies versus an average 14% for all other opposition parties.[73]

---

[69] Pattni was the figure at the center of the Goldenberg scandal of the early 1990s. Pattni colluded with KANU politicians and government officials to embezzle billions of shillings in an export-compensation scheme for nonexistent gold exports. Estimates suggest that the scheme cost the country several percentage points of its GDP. More than 1,000 individuals were on the take, including KANU ministers and opposition politicians.

[70] When Wamalwa became FORD-Kenya chairman and leader of the Opposition upon Odinga's death, he also became chairman of the Public Accounts Committee in parliament, which was investigating the Goldenberg scandal. Wamalwa issued a report in 1995 that not only cleared Moi's government of any wrongdoing, but also claimed that Pattni was owed an additional two billion shillings (Munene 2001).

[71] Tim Wanyoni, "We Shall Agree on One Candidate to Face KANU," Interview with Michael Kijana Wamalwa, *Daily Nation* (Nairobi), 4 March 2002.

[72] Kibaki won the presidential poll in every Central Province constituency. His DP also held onto all parliamentary seats in northern Kikuyuland, but still had a harder time winning southern Kikuyu parliamentary constituencies, though the party did win the seats in the newly created Maragwa district. DP won an additional three seats outside its traditional Kikuyu–Embu–Meru constituencies: three in Coast Province and one in the Rift Valley's Maasailand.

[73] The KANU success rate was 51% (107 of 210 candidates).

Kenya's Kikuyu Entrepreneurs Defect

Incremental financial reforms adopted throughout the 1990s help to account for Kibaki's ability to progressively attract and retain supporters from the business community. Moi's need to secure additional lending from the international financial institutions had compelled him to agree to the liberalization of credit, foreign currency, and interest rates (World Bank 2003). Of course, the political impact of these reforms was not instantly felt. Businessman James Koome, a long-time backer of Kibaki, observes that DP organizers still encountered difficulties in convincing entrepreneurs to donate to the party at the time of 1997 elections.

Our network of supporters expanded, but a lot were still reluctant. Those who had become wealthy under Moi were afraid of the repercussions. Those who made money through political links were less likely to give money.[74]

The speed with which the government scaled back certain regulations – in several instances, quite literally overnight – certainly prompted the business community to question the permanence of those reforms. Since Moi was known to be an impulsive decision-maker who often contradicted his own ministers and announced policy changes off the cuff, Kenyan entrepreneurs were unlikely to respond immediately to any announced reforms by shifting their investments, economic or political.

The strongest signal that financial liberalization might endure came after the 1997 presidential election. Moi's government had been under pressure from the IMF and the World Bank since the start of decade to reduce its holdings in the main state-owned banks, Kenya Commercial Bank (KCB) and National Bank of Kenya (NBK), because they were at the center of the regime's informal system of politicized lending. As the country's largest bank, the KCB, in particular, served as a bellwether for the Kenyan business community. Moi had previously relented to IMF pressure in permitting KCB shares to be sold on the Nairobi Stock Exchange, but no divestment had changed the government's status as the bank's majority shareholder. The state's equity was slowly reduced to 80% in 1988, 70% in 1990, and 60% 1996.

But after having achieved his second reelection in December 1997, Moi authorized the government's largest divestment in banking. Reducing the state's shareholding in KCB to a minority interest was a condition set by the IMF for restarting negotiations over frozen lending. Consequently, the state reduced its holdings in the bank from 60% to 35% in April 1998.[75] The privatization

---

74 Author interview, Nairobi, 5 August 2008.

75 The flotation of the government's shares coincided with a housecleaning of KCB management, which had been implicated in a scandal involving insider loans, and a broader set of operational reforms that followed within the year. See Mbatau Wa Ngai, "KCB Still a Good Investment," *Daily Nation* (Nairobi), 29 March 1998; Mark Turner, "Kenya Reforms Win IMF Talks," *Financial Times* (London), 18 December 1999, p. 4; IMF Press Release No. 00/45, 28 July 2000.

of KCB, and the manner in which it was conducted, constituted the clear-est signal to business that the conditions for accessing finance had been fun-damentally transformed. Because the bank's stock was floated through the Nairobi Stock Exchange, the government could not simply transfer the bank to an entrepreneur friendly to the regime. KCB shares were instead acquired by the Kikuyu-dominated business community that Moi had long sought to neu-tralize through financial manipulation. In effect, the privatization of KCB, the country's largest bank, meant that Moi's government would no longer serve as the business sector's principal creditor. Only NBK remained a majority state-owned commercial bank.

The timing of KCB's privatization helps to explain why members of the business community, particularly Kikuyu entrepreneurs, proved increasingly willing to support the opposition after 1997. Under conditions of liberal-ized finance, Kibaki was able to cultivate a wider set of financiers, including former KANU supporters, in his bid to become a coalition formateur in the run-up to the 2002 presidential election. His donors included some 20 high-profile businessmen.[76] This Council of Elders, as this circle of donors became known, was chaired by Joseph Wanjui, who had been a member of the Central Province Development Support Group (CPDSG) that supported Moi in 1997. Even the CPDSG's former leader, Samuel Macharia, switched his support to Kibaki after having had his radio station periodically shut down between 1999 and 2001 for running programs that criticized corruption.[77] The chairman of the Kenyan Association of Manufacturers (KAM) in 1999–2000, Chris Kirubi, who was among the businessmen who donated to Moi's 1997 reelection cam-paign, became the single largest donor to Kibaki's 2002 campaign, reputedly contributing 12 million shillings, or about $150,000.

The most instructive vignette of the increasing freedom felt by Kenya's busi-ness community after a decade of financial liberalization concerns its response to the defection of Njenga Karume, Kibaki's long-time financier. Constitutionally barred from running in the December 2002 presidential election, Moi sought to neutralize Kikuyu elites by designating Uhuru Kenyatta as KANU's presi-dential candidate. Uhuru, the son of the country's founding president and an ethnic Kikuyu, could credibly promise that the ruling party would serve the interests of Kikuyu business (Oloo 2004).[78] Karume, who happens to be from the Kenyatta's home district of Kiambu, announced that he would support

---

[76] These include prominent businessmen Eddy Njoroge, Nathan Kang'ethe, Peter Kanyago, John Murenga, Duncan Ndegwa, and Robert Gacheche. See John Kamau, "Kitchen Cabinet Regroups," *East African Standard* (Nairobi), 13 June 2004.

[77] Macharia's backing was particularly useful, since it provided what amounted to free advertising for Kibaki and the coalition he would eventually form. See Nick Wachira, "The Unlikely Media Mogul," *East African Standard*, 21 March 2005.

[78] Having failed to win his own parliamentary constituency in 1997, Uhuru seemed to have little to recommend him as a presidential candidate. But Moi may have been grooming him for the position for some time. After the 1997 election, he appointed Uhuru to parliament as a nomi-nated MP. Moi later appointed him to the cabinet as minister of local government.

Uhuru over Kibaki in September 2002. Karume's defection, not coincidentally, occurred when he found himself in financial straits. Four months prior, in May 2002, the brewery that represented one of his largest ventures was shut down.[79] A related lawsuit that he lost two years earlier led to what Karume considered to be "the largest financial loss I had ever suffered" – a loss he attributed to political intervention (Karume and wa Gethoi 2009, 274–275). And it was under such conditions that Karume chose to return to the fold of the ruling party.

Moi most likely intended Karume's defection to initiate another realignment of Kikuyu elites, but his tactic failed to provoke its intended response. Instead, Kibaki's financiers chose to publicly state their own continued support for the DP and its candidate by publishing a paid advertisement in the *Daily Nation*, one of the country's largest circulating newspapers, just days after Karume's defection. The statement included the signatures of Duncan Ndegwa, a former central banker, James Koome, a businessman who helped to recruit other entrepreneurs to back Kibaki, and Joseph Wanjui, the businessman previously affiliated with Moi's CPDSG. Such overt refusal to politically ally with a sitting president would have been unlikely without the changes brought through financial liberalization.

CONCLUSION

The evidence presented in this chapter shows that business remains allied to the political status quo where incumbents manage to sustain the state's control over capital. This is what has occurred in Cameroon. However, in those countries obliged to undertake liberalizing reforms, incumbents have lost their capacity to punish defections through financial reprisals. Entrepreneurs in these circumstances become free to diversify their campaign contributions among parties, if not offer outright support to the opposition. This is the pattern found in Kenya.

The argument advanced here has a broader implication. Business may play an outsized role in determining the distribution of resources among political contestants, not only between incumbent and opposition, but also among opposition candidates. In this sense, business acts as a primary elector for the opposition. By concentrating resources on its favored candidate, business is able to narrow the field of potential candidates and to determine who might be most likely to become the incumbent's principal challenger, if not his eventual successor. This theme is explored in the next chapter.

---

[79] Maguta Kimemia, "Karume Loses Sh241 Million Award, *Daily Nation* (Nairobi), 12 August 2000; Muna Wahome, "High Duty and a Shrinking Market Are Beer Firm's Undoing," *Daily Nation* (Nairobi), 15 May 2002; Mwenda Njoka, "Karume's Journey – The Long Trip Back to Kanu," *East African Standard*, 8 September 2002.

7

Opposition Bargaining across Ethnic Cleavages

> No one on the basis of his own tribe will be able to be elected head of state.... Those who think that they will use only their tribes are mistaken.
>
> Omar Bongo, president of Gabon, 1993[1]

This chapter examines how the private resources of the business community can influence the process as well as the outcome of coalition bargaining among opposition politicians from different ethnic groups. Previous chapters have shown that African entrepreneurs had sufficient cause to oppose entrenched incumbents who had mismanaged their countries' economies for decades. But it was only in countries where cash-strapped leaders were obliged to adopt financial reforms that entrepreneurs were subsequently able to reconsider their political alignments. My claim is that business' campaign contributions – rather than the arrangement of electoral rules, the intensity of ethnic competition, or the intervention of civil society – determines the likelihood of successful coalition bargaining among opposition politicians, particularly when those donations are concentrated on select politicians.

The bargaining episodes that took place in the run-up to presidential elections held in Cameroon in 2004 and Kenya in 2002 are the focus of this chapter. The principal opposition parties in each country had previously insisted on competing independently. And the cost of such fragmentation had become obvious to all the parties involved: had opposition politicians been able to unite in any earlier election, they would have been assured victory. In Cameroon, "a bewildering fragmentation of the opposition set in, reducing its chances for success" (Takougang and Krieger 1998, 147). In Kenya, it could be said that "Daniel arap Moi did not really win these elections, a divided opposition lost them"

---

[1] Bongo offered this insight while campaigning for his reelection in Gabon's 1993 presidential race (Gary Strieker, "Gabon's Bongo Faces Elections Forced by Unrest," CNN, Transcript #337-3, 28 September 1993). Bongo eventually became the longest-serving head of state in Africa, having become president in 1967 and managing to win reelection through multiparty contests in 1993, 1998, and 2003.

(Grignon et al. 2001, 15). Yet, despite facing similar incentives for electoral coordination, the opposition politicians in these two countries arrived at different outcomes by their third multiparty contest. The Cameroonian opposition remained fragmented after engaging in protracted coalition negotiations, while the Kenyan opposition successfully managed to bargain themselves to a multiparty coalition with a single presidential candidate.

Informed by interviews with many of the actors directly involved in coalition negotiations in each country, I show in this chapter that the divergent outcomes in Cameroon and Kenya can be traced back to the availability of campaign resources from business. In Cameroon, continuing political influence in finance exacerbated the opposition's fragmentation. Entrepreneurs from all ethnic groups had been compelled to retain their links to the ruling party in order to stay in business – just as they had prior to the onset of multiparty politics. President Paul Biya's oil-backed regime further complicated bargaining among opposition politicians by providing public financing for political parties, thereby raising the reservation price among all politicians. Public financing, when coupled with the suppression of campaign donations from business, effectively narrowed the bargaining range in which a mutually acceptable agreement could be located among opposition politicians. As a result, a potential coalition formateur like John Fru Ndi was unable to secure the financing needed to offer upfront payments to other politicians to endorse his candidacy. The very mode of bargaining in which Fru Ndi was obliged to participate suggests that he had little financial leverage: he was forced to compete on equal footing with other politicians in an open selection process that he ultimately lost. Despite being the only opposition politician with proven national appeal, Fru Ndi remained incapable of acting as a coalition formateur who could rally the support of opposition politicians with ethno-regional bases.

In Kenya, once the ruling party could no longer mediate business' access to finance, many entrepreneurs found their favored opposition candidate in Mwai Kibaki. The former vice president and finance minister became the focal candidate for their campaign contributions not only because he is an ethnic Kikuyu, like much of the indigenous business community, but because he had also been known to be business-friendly while serving in government. Kibaki was subsequently able to assemble the resources needed to withstand cooptation and coercion from the ruling party as well as to rally other politicians around his candidacy. Having become the favored candidate of the business community, Kibaki was the only opposition politician who had the resources needed to act as a coalition formateur in the run-up to the 2002 election, offering upfront payments that would compensate other politicians for their endorsements. Kibaki's superior campaign resources enabled him to control the course of bargaining within the opposition, negotiating exclusively with a choice set of politicians with ethnic bases, all while eschewing demands from civil society to create a broad, consensus-based movement.

In what follows, I first discuss how ethnic and clientelistic factors serve as parameters for formateur selection among opposition candidates. I then examine the Cameroon and Kenya cases in turn, placing the cut and thrust of coalition bargaining into a structured comparative context. I specifically focus on how opposition politicians arranged their bargaining modalities, jockeyed for position as potential formateurs, and exercised financial leverage in their negotiations. The concluding section places these bargaining episodes within the framework of the broader argument.

ETHNICITY AND CLIENTELISM IN FORMATEUR SELECTION

The selection of an opposition coalition candidate, or formateur, is not a straightforward affair in African multiparty systems. There is usually more than one candidate who could plausibly lead an opposition coalition. Indeed, the payoffs for being a formateur are sufficiently high to attract a surplus of candidates.[2] But the opposition parties in these countries lack shared norms or established rules for selecting a formateur. Because most African executives are directly elected in presidential or semipresidential systems, there are no institutionalized procedures to follow, as would occur in parliamentary systems after elections are held. And because African parties are often the personal vehicles of their founding leaders, few parties have accepted open primaries for candidate selection. Under such conditions, it is not evident what factors structure coalition bargaining among the opposition. What attributes could an opposition politician exploit to become the focal candidate for other politicians as well as the entrepreneurs willing to finance an opposition campaign?

Examining data on the leading opposition candidates in African elections held between 1990 and 2005, I find that the parameters influencing formateur selection in parliamentary democracies – size and experience – are also at play in coalition negotiations among African opposition politicians. The literature on parliamentary coalitions has established two relevant empirical regularities concerning government formation: the largest parties are far more likely to become formateurs and parties with previous government experience are also more likely to become formateurs (Ansolabehere et al. 2005; Bäck and Dumont 2008; Diermeier and Merlo 2004; Warwick 1996).[3] Adapting the intuition from these findings to the context of African executive elections, I find that the opposition candidates who become formateurs are from ethnic groups that are more than twice the average size in the region; and those with previous government experience are also nearly twice as likely to become formateurs.

Ethnicity serves as an obvious parameter for formateur selection in Africa's multiethnic countries. Most African countries are highly diverse: the average

---

[2] If a formateur were to win the election, she would not only lead the government. Her party would most likely receive a disproportionate number of ministerial appointments (Ansolabehere et al. 2005; Baron and Ferejohn 1989; Warwick and Druckman 2001). And she could then bias government expenditures toward her supporters (Calvo and Murillo 2004; Cox and McCubbins 1986; Solé-Ollé and Sorribas-Navarro 2008; Tavits 2009).

[3] The proportional relationship between party size and portfolio share is also well established (Browne and Franklin 1973; Gamson 1961; Mershon 2001; Schofield and Laver 1985).

TABLE 7.1. *Opposition Candidate Selection and Ethnic Identity*

	Opposition candidate ethnic group (%)	Incumbent leader ethnic group (%)	Ethnic fractionalization
Opposition coalition (29)	28.1	23.9	.76
Opposition fragmentation (52)	30.6	22.2	.74
Difference	−2.5	1.7	.02
	$p = 0.64$	$p = 0.74$	$p = 0.57$

Note: The number of elections is shown in parentheses. Two-tailed difference-of-means tests are calculated from two-sample *t*-tests with equal variances.

ethnic group represents only 12% of a country's total population, and nearly two-thirds of all ethnic groups in the region account for 10% or less (Fearon 2003). As long as voting is expected to occur along ethnic lines, candidates from larger groups should be systematically favored in coalition bargaining simply because they appeal to larger blocs of voters. Opposition coalition formateurs, in fact, are from considerably larger ethnic groups. Table 7.1 shows that the opposition candidates who become formateurs are, on average, from ethnic groups that account for 28% of a country's population.[4] This suggests that opposition candidates who lead multiparty coalitions are typically emerging from a country's largest or second largest ethnic group; the regional averages are 34% and 19%, respectively.

Opposition politicians from larger ethnic groups should be more likely to become coalition formateurs, in part, because they are the most viable challengers at the national level. In a highly fragmented polity, such politicians may command the votes needed to transform a multiparty alliance that is sure to lose into a viable electoral alternative. As a result, when compared to their counterparts from smaller ethnic groups, these politicians may have an easier time securing campaign contributions from entrepreneurs as well as winning cross-ethnic endorsements. Table 7.1 shows that, regardless of whether the opposition coalesces or fragments, the leading candidate will emerge from a relatively large ethnic group. In either case, politicians and voters appear to rally around the same kind of candidate, that is, one with a relatively large demographic base.

The same ethnic dynamic appears to operate among incumbent leaders because they too tend to be from groups that are larger than the regional average. This holds true regardless of whether the opposition coalesces or not. If an

---

[4] For every election between 1990 and 2005, I used media sources and secondary materials to code the ethnicity of every opposition candidate when the opposition formed a multiparty coalition and of the leading opposition candidate (by votes) when the opposition fragmented. I repeated the exercise for incumbent candidates. I then used the ethnic group data in Fearon (2003) to estimate the sizes of their respective ethnic groups.

TABLE 7.2. *Opposition Candidate Selection and Government Experience*

	Opposition candidate served in government?		
	No	Yes	Total
Opposition coalition	11 (25%)	20 (49%)	31
Opposition fragmentation	33 (75%)	21 (51%)	54
Total	44	41	85
	$\chi^2 = 5.18, p = 0.02$		

Note: Column percentages are shown in parentheses.

incumbent's ethnic identity has any impact on opposition candidate selection, it is by inducing the selection of candidates from relatively larger groups. But, again, this tends to occur in all elections. When the opposition coalesces behind a formateur, its candidate is from a larger group in 12 of 29 elections (41%) and from the same group as the incumbent in 9 of 29 elections (31%). When the opposition fragments, the leading opposition candidate is from a larger group in 28 of 59 elections (47%) and from the same group as the incumbent in 10 of 59 elections (17%).

A candidate's experience in government, more so than ethnicity, is a criterion that shapes opposition electoral strategies. The Africanist literature has long shown that political leadership is attained by patrons who regularly distribute resources among their clients (Bayart 1989; Daloz 1999; Médard 1982). Politicians who have served in government are the best placed to accumulate the wealth needed to attain and retain leadership status. Being in government typically enables those at the highest levels to appropriate land, acquire capital for business ventures, or be placed on the boards of private firms. In this context, the challenge for opposition candidates is to signal that they are willing and able to engage in redistribution. Candidates who have previously served in government should have a special advantage in this regard.

The data confirm that opposition candidates with high-level government experience are more likely to become coalition formateurs. Table 7.2 shows that they are nearly twice as likely to lead an opposition coalition than politicians with no government experience.[5] While 20 of 41 (49%) former government officials have organized multiethnic coalitions around their candidacies, only 11 of 44 (25%) opposition politicians with no such experience have managed to do the same. This is a statistically significant difference.

Former government officials may end up leading nearly two-thirds of all opposition coalitions because they face lower transaction costs in negotiating cross-ethnic endorsements. On the one hand, these candidates may be able

---

[5] I code former heads of state, ministers, and assistant ministers as having had previous government experience.

to raise more funds by exploiting relationships cultivated during their time in office. They can lobby for campaign donations among the entrepreneurs with whom they have successfully engaged in a quid pro quo in the past. Entrepreneurs who become wealthy through contracts or privileges secured with the aid of former government officials would have an incentive to invest in their return to power. On the other hand, these candidates may be able to leverage their record in office to lower the costs associated with securing political endorsements. Less risk should be associated with former government officials when compared with those who have had no opportunity to demonstrate how they would behave in power, especially in the redistribution of resources vis-à-vis other groups. And less risk should translate into less costly upfront payments for endorsements from other politicians.

The narratives presented for Cameroon and Kenya show that ethnic identity and government experience did, to some extent, influence the bargaining among opposition politicians. The failed presumptive coalition formateur in Cameroon, John Fru Ndi, lacked both of these qualities, making him a less compelling candidate for the rest of the opposition. The successful coalition formateur in Kenya, Mwai Kibaki, possessed both: he was a member of the country's largest ethnic group and had proven his ability to mobilize that electoral bloc; he had been a long-serving cabinet minister who had extensive connections in government, business, and the bureaucracy. However, these factors alone are insufficient to account for the outcomes in these cases. What mattered was the willingness of entrepreneurs to financially support a candidate in opposition. In Cameroon, the business class remained aligned with the ruling party, so no opposition politician could secure the resources needed to purchase cross-ethnic endorsements. In Kenya, the support of the business class enabled Kibaki to become a formateur by securing key endorsements and strategic withdrawals from politicians who represented other ethnic constituencies.

THE BARGAINING NARRATIVE IN CAMEROON

The failure of opposition politicians to coordinate in the run-up to Cameroon's 2004 presidential election is conventionally attributed to the country's deep ethnic divisions. In the view of Nyamnjoh (1999, 104), one of the country's most informed scholars, "If the opposition has stayed divided, unable to agree on a common strategy or a consensual candidate, the ethnic factor of mutual distrust and suspicion is largely to blame." While ethnic considerations surely influenced coalition negotiations among opposition politicians, I argue that their repeated bargaining failures have not been due to irreconcilable group interests. I claim that opposition politicians have been unable to arrive at mutually agreeable electoral bargains because they lack the funds needed to make those agreements palatable. Put simply, without the financial backing of Bamileke businessmen, no Cameroonian politician has been able to accumulate the kind of campaign war chest needed to act as a coalition formateur, offering upfront payments to compensate other politicians for their cross-ethnic endorsements.

That compensation is needed to make politicians indifferent between running on their own and endorsing the candidacy of a rival candidate.

The case study presented here demonstrates that the lack of financing from business, rather than ethnic divisions, shaped the coalition bargaining among opposition politicians. I show that, in the bargaining that ensued in anticipation of the 2004 presidential election, the ethnic identities of the competing candidates were secondary to their campaign resources. With Bamileke entrepreneurs having sealed their alliance with the ruling party by the mid-1990s, John Fru Ndi, the presumed leader of the opposition, lost much of his luster as it became apparent that he could not finance a national campaign on his own. Indeed, Fru Ndi failed to become a formateur once members of the opposition's protocoalition concluded that other candidates, regardless of their ethnicity, had greater potential for raising campaign funds. Sanda Oumarou, a Fulbe Muslim banker, became contender for coalition leadership by subsidizing many of its campaign activities. Coalition members even sought to recruit Edouard Akame Mfoumou, President Paul Biya's onetime ally as well as his coethnic, as a potential candidate because of his considerable wealth. The opposition's protocoalition then settled on Adamou Ndam Njoya, a respected politician from the small Bamoun minority, because of his prospective fundraising ability among the Cameroonian diaspora. These developments are discussed further below, as I examine how opposition politicians structured their bargaining modalities, jockeyed for position, and considered their financial options.

Bargaining Modalities

Opposition coordination became a possibility when Fru Ndi and Ndam Njoya, the country's leading opposition politicians, publicly announced their intention to field a unity candidate one year ahead of the October 2004 presidential election. Representing a potential Francophone-Anglophone coalition, they issued a joint declaration on 20 August 2003 to "solemnly commit, individually and collectively, to the people of Cameroon and the friends of Cameroon, to nominate a single opposition candidate to the 2004 presidential election."[6] Their Coalition pour la Réconciliation et la Reconstruction Nationale (CRRN) was officially launched on 12 November 2003 with the adoption of a common platform endorsed by five parties: Fru Ndi's Social Democratic Front (SDF), Ndam Njoya's Union Démocratique Camerounaise (UDC), Marcel Yondo's Mouvement pour la Libération et la Démocratie au Cameroun (MLDC), Aaron Mukuri Maka's Mouvement pour la Démocratie et le Progrès (MDP), and Antar Gassagaye's Union pour la République (UPR).[7]

---

[6] "Présidentielle 2004: les leaders de l'opposition pour un candidat unique," *Agence France Presse*, 22 August 2003.

[7] An opposition grouping, the Front des Forces Alternatives (FFA), was established earlier, in March 2003, among more radical parties based in Douala; however, these were all minor parties with no parliamentary representation and little potential for national impact. Their coalition efforts also came to naught. I do not discuss their efforts here.

Although opposition politicians claimed that a common platform had to be established before they could agree on a unity candidate, it was clear from the outset that they had no obvious basis for selecting such a candidate. In the year leading up to the presidential election, the CRRN mainly served as a vehicle for promoting the notion of a unity candidate among voters. Meanwhile, behind closed doors, opposition politicians sought among themselves a consensus on the modalities for selecting a candidate. The subsequent bargaining was characterized by features that speak to the general lack of resources among these opposition politicians: little discretion was exercised in limiting coalition membership and a national tour-qua-contest became an improvised mechanism for selecting a candidate.

Opposition bargaining occurred among a relatively large set of politicians, none of which had the means to dictate the terms of the negotiations. The CRRN's membership expanded in its first few months to include actors representing a cross section of the country's major ethno-regional groups. Fru Ndi, a Christian Anglophone from North West Province, and Ndam Njoya, a Muslim Francophone from West Province, were joined by Fulbe politicians Sanda Oumarou of the Action pour le Redressement National (ARN), which was mainly based in Adamawa Province, and Issa Tchiroma Bakary of La Dynamique des Mémorandistes du Grand Nord.[8] A year earlier, the publication of a "Grand North Memorandum," which Tchiroma helped to write and Sanda endorsed, cataloged discrimination against the region and was widely seen as signaling the formation of a new regional party that might once again split the opposition vote. However, the addition of these two Fulbe politicians to the CRRN in February 2004 was interpreted as an auspicious sign for the opposition's electoral coordination, reflecting a union of western and northern politicians against the incumbent's southern-based regime.

But in expanding its membership, the CRRN was also becoming a motley assortment of former ministers, veteran oppositionists, and occasional defectors. No politician or party looking to join the CRRN was rejected.[9] It was unclear why Fru Ndi or Ndam Njoya would give standing to bargaining partners whose potential contribution in terms of resources or votes was questionable. At least half of those who joined the opposition coalition had previously served in Biya's government at some point since the return of multiparty politics. Tchiroma himself broke with the Union Nationale pour la Démocratie et le Progrès (UNDP) when it was the largest opposition party in the National Assembly in order to become a transport minister in Biya's government in 1992.[10] Célestin Bedzigui, an ethnic Beti who led the tiny Parti de l'Alliance

---

[8] Issa Tchiroma was technically a member of Bello Bouba Maigari's UNDP, but had been suspended from the party for one year as a result of perennial leadership conflicts.

[9] Author interviews, Yaounde, 26 March 2006; 29 March 2006.

[10] Tchiroma's political trajectory is another example that neither past repression nor ethnic rivalry is an impediment to political cooperation. Biya's government imprisoned Tchiroma after the 1984 coup attempt led by Ahidjo's Fulbe allies although he had no connection to the failed putsch.

Libérale (PAL), traded an endorsement for Biya's 1992 reelection in exchange for the directorship of a state-owned company.[11] Antar Gassagaye, a politician from Far North Province, became a secretary of state in Biya's cabinet under similar conditions. Henri Hogbe Nlend, an ethnic Bassa leader of one faction of the fissiparous Union des Populations du Cameroun (UPC), was made a science minister after running against Biya in the otherwise boycotted presidential election of 1997.

Because no opposition politician had the financial resources to act as a coalition formateur – to effectively buy the support of others – the continual addition of new members may have served to offset the lack of trust among these politicians.[12] If some members were coopted by the ruling party, enough of the others would remain to rally around a unity candidacy. Fru Ndi repeatedly offered public assurances that all CRRN members would respect the choice of coalition candidate. At the first CRRN rally in Douala, the country's economic capital, on 13 March 2004, Fru Ndi walked onto the stage with a child in hand and went on to warn that a traitor to the opposition coalition would "drink the blood" of that child. Yet, Ndam Njoya admitted at a press conference after the same rally, "We cannot guarantee the nondefection of members, but if that occurs, we will do everything possible so that the majority continues on with the struggle."[13]

Interviews with coalition members suggest that the CRRN turned a national tour designed to promote the coalition into an informal primary because no opposition politician had the resources to impose himself as a coalition formateur.[14] The opposition had not been able to agree to a selection mechanism between November 2003, when the CRRN was officially launched, and March 2004, when its national tour was inaugurated. Therefore, over the following six months, CRRN members had the opportunity to display their financing and mobilizing capacities through rallies organized in each of Cameroon's ten provinces. Party leaders had an opportunity to publicly demonstrate their voter appeal by having their supporters turn out at each venue with placards in hand. And because CRRN members were responsible for sponsoring different stages of the tour, they had the opportunity to signal to their peers that they could underwrite a national campaign. While Fru Ndi's SDF exhibited greater

---

[11] Several scholars have used Bedzigui's political career as an example of how ethnicity can be leveraged for personal advantage. Bedzigui has used the novelty of being an ethnic Beti in opposition in order to gain either political appointments or to forge new alliances. See Monga (2000).

[12] Individual politicians have consistently pursued their personal advantage at key moments when the opposition as a whole could have gained. In 1992, when Dakolé Daïssala's Mouvement Démocratique pour la Défense de la République (MDR) could have helped create an opposition-controlled National Assembly, he instead chose to trade his six parliamentary seats for ministerial posts in Biya's government (Socpa 2000). In 1997, when Fru Ndi's SDF became the largest legislative opposition party, he sidelined the smaller opposition parties in negotiating leadership posts in the National Assembly with the ruling party.

[13] Roland Tsapi, "L'opposition fait sa rentrée," *Le Messager*, 15 March 2004, p. 3.

[14] Author interviews, Yaounde, 28 March 2006; 7 April 2006.

ability in mobilizing its supporters at various locations, none of the presumed frontrunners proved to have the capacity to independently shoulder the costs of campaigning, often leaving unpaid bills along the tour's route. The CRRN's financial accounts indicate that no party was able to fully pay for its allocated share of expenses.

Candidate Jockeying

Because no opposition politician had become a focal candidate for business' campaign donations, none enjoyed an advantage over his peers when coalition negotiations were initiated, or managed to gain one as they proceeded. The CRRN's formation was, of course, motivated by each politician's desire to use the coalition to compensate for his own weaknesses. In this respect, it was understood that a united front between Fru Ndi and Ndam Njoya, who were seen as "radically different and completely complementary,"[15] could present a real challenge to Biya's reelection, though individually they would have a negligible chance. Fru Ndi, a charismatic populist, had proven his wide appeal in the first multiparty election of 1992 despite not being able to speak French, the country's dominant language.[16] But his reputation had suffered since then: electoral support for his SDF had waned in subsequent elections as continuous intraparty squabbles hinted at a leader who lacked the wherewithal to hold his party together.[17] In fact, Fru Ndi had been unable to prevent SDF parliamentarians from holding individual consultations with members of the regime in the run-up to the 2004 election.[18] For his part, Ndam Njoya maintained a national reputation as a reformer.[19] He, however, never proved that his electoral appeal could be expanded beyond the urban intellectuals who made up his party or his small ethnic enclave of Noun Division in West Province, where he served as mayor of Foumban. Further complicating the negotiations, Sanda Oumarou, a former minister with a career in banking,[20] emerged as a viable challenger to

---

[15] Francois Soudan and Alex Siewe, "Comment l'opposition s'est suicidée," *Jeune Afrique L'Intelligent*, 30 September 2004.

[16] Fru Ndi enjoyed early strong support in the Anglophone provinces of North West and South West along with the Francophone provinces of Littoral and West, winning 36% of the vote to the incumbent's 40%.

[17] The SDF's legislative seat share was nearly halved from the 1997 to the 2002 legislative elections. In 1998, ten of the SDF's 43 MPs resigned, claiming that Fru Ndi managed the SDF in a tribalistic and autocratic manner. In 2002, 19 of the SDF's 22 seats were from North West Province, reducing it to the status of a regional party.

[18] Author interview, Yaounde, 28 March 2006.

[19] Ndam Njoya is the son of Arouna Njoya, who assisted Ahidjo in orchestrating the federation of the two Cameroons, and a cousin of the Sultan of Foumban. Ndam Njoya himself served in Ahidjo's government from 1975 to 1982, rising from vice minister to minister. His reform efforts as a minister of education gave him a reputation for integrity and honesty. But as a candidate in the 1992 presidential election, Ndam Njoya came in fourth with 3.6% of the vote.

[20] Sanda Oumarou was also seen as a modernizer during his tenure as telecommunications minister, overseeing the postal system's computerization and the introduction of the first mobile

the two opposition veterans largely because he proved willing to pay for nearly two-thirds of the costs associated with the CRRN national tour.[21]

Unable to reach agreement on a coalition candidate by the summer of 2004, the potential candidates chose to leave the decision to a yet-to-be-named selection committee. Here, Fru Ndi's SDF managed to secure a numerical advantage in its representation on the committees that were subsequently formed. On 18 August 2004, a five-person team, four of whom were SDF representatives, announced the 15 criteria to be used in choosing the unity coalition candidate if opposition party leaders failed to arrive at a consensus. Most of the criteria required subjective evaluations of each candidate's personal leadership qualities.[22]

To further strengthen his position, and possibly signal his willingness to go it alone if not selected as the coalition candidate, Fru Ndi organized a party congress for his SDF just days before the CRRN candidate selection committee was to meet. The SDF party congress was held at Bamenda, the capital of North West Province, and on 11 September 2004 it declared Fru Ndi its presidential candidate after he easily defeated two challengers.

What Fru Ndi did not anticipate was that CRRN members would quietly seek an alternative to the set of candidates already available to them.[23] In the weeks prior to the selection of a unity candidate, Sindjoun Pokam, a Bamileke intellectual and civil society representative to the CRRN, had begun recruiting Edouard Akame Mfoumou, the then head of the national airline, as a possible opposition coalition candidate.[24] Pokam reasoned that Akame Mfoumou, a former minister of defense and finance, brought together the qualities that other opposition candidates lacked.[25] As an ethnic Beti from the president's South Province and a member of the ruling party's central committee, he had the capacity to split the regime's support among both elites and voters. What

---

telephone network. He previously had a career in banking, serving as the deputy director of Bank of America Cameroon as well as the director of research and credit at the Cameroon Development Bank. He resumed this career when he left the government, becoming the director general of Amity Bank.

[21] Author interview, Yaounde, 7 April 2006.

[22] The 15 criteria required a candidate to have a commitment to the rigorous implementation of the coalition platform; have proven communication skills; have an established international reputation; be financially solvent; have a love of country; be in good mental and physical health; be honest and deliberate; be open to dialogue and teamwork; have an incorruptible personal and professional life; be brave and combative; have a proven strong personality; be popular within the country; have a demonstrated and unwavering commitment to change; have proven managerial skill; and be tolerant and inspire confidence.

[23] Marcel Yondo, leader of the small MLDC, was also a candidate, but he was never in serious contention.

[24] Venant Mboua and Jacques Doo Bell, "Candidat unique: blocages à la coalition," *Le Messager*, 15 September 2004; "Présidentielle 2004: l'opposition peine à designer un candidat unique," *Agence France Presse*, 15 September 2004; Richard Touna, "Tractations: Akame Mfoumou à l'épreuve du consensus," *Le Messager*, 16 September 2004; Jean Baptiste Ketchateng, "Célestin Bedzigui: Je ne suis pas une taupe," *Mutations*, 5 October 2004.

[25] Author interview, Yaounde, 5 April 2006.

is more, Akame Mfoumou had reputedly become extremely wealthy through his years of government service, meaning that he could independently finance a national campaign. Pokam was also betting on Akame Mfoumou having the motivation to break with the ruling party, since Biya had dismissed him from his ministerial post in 2001, presumably for becoming a potential threat. Akame Mfoumou had begun to develop his own clientelistic network and was seen by many as too overt in his ambition to succeed the president.

Akame Mfoumou's last-minute candidacy was serious enough that other CRRN members – Issa Tchiroma, Célestin Bedzigui, and Antar Gassagaye – went to meet with him to lobby for his candidacy. Akame Mfoumou remained noncommittal, asking them to first seek a consensus within the coalition.[26] If Akame Mfoumou was playing coy, it remained unclear to what purpose. The CRRN selection committee agreed that he could be considered a candidate as long as he personally presented an application along with a copy of his resignation letter from the ruling party. But it is at this time – precisely as Biya was returning to Cameroon from a holiday in France – that Akame Mfoumou suddenly cut off communication with all CRRN members. He disappeared from Yaounde and could no longer be reached by telephone. Akame Mfoumou later claimed, in an interview with the government's *Cameroon Tribune*, that he had kept Biya informed of his contacts with the opposition, making it clear to the president that for "nothing in the world could I go to the other side to contest his candidacy."[27] But according to Pokam and others, Akame Mfoumou withdrew from consideration because he had been threatened by the regime.[28]

The CRRN selection committee began its formal deliberations for the selection of the opposition's coalition candidate on 13 September 2004. This left less than two days to designate the candidate because nominations to the Ministry of Territorial Administration, which approves all nominations, were due on 15 September 2004. The committee's eleven members chose to proceed by awarding a point for each of the fifteen selection criteria on the basis of consensus.[29] Because a single committee member could effectively veto the allocation of a point to any of the contenders for the nomination, Fru Ndi was afforded a significant advantage in this respect. Four of the eleven committee members were from his own SDF. Yet, nearing midnight on 15 September, the selection

---

[26] Author interviews, Yaounde, 26 March 2006; 5 April 2006.

[27] Essama Essomba, "'Je dois tout au président Biya,'" *Cameroon Tribune*, 20 September 2004, p. 7.

[28] Akame Mfoumou, in his public affirmation of allegiance to Biya, perhaps protested too strongly: "My fidelity and my loyalty towards the head of state are unwavering. I have already emphasized it: I owe him everything. And I insist in saying, as was said by Christ in the Gospel, that it is not those who say 'Lord, Lord,' but those who do what the Lord wants that are loyal to Him. It is therefore not enough to say, 'Mr. President we are with you.' That, we all say. To this needs to be added concrete actions and results, which further reinforces the strength of our regime." See Essama Essomba, "'Je dois tout au président Biya,'" *Cameroon Tribune*, 20 September 2004, p. 7.

[29] The selection committee was composed of Issa Tchiroma Bakary, chairman, Mukury Maka (MDP), Antar Gassagaye (UPR), Jean Pahaï (PPC), Henri Hogbe Nlend (UPC), Théophile Yimgaing Moyo (UDC), Sindjoun Pokam (civil society representative), Tazoacha Asonganyi (SDF), Pierre Mouafo (SDF), Pascal Zamboue (SDF), and Bebbe Njoh (SDF).

committee announced that Ndam Njoya had been designated as the coalition candidate with fifteen total points. Sanda Oumarou placed second with twelve points; Fru Ndi earned eleven points; and Marcel Yondo ten points.[30] Ndam Njoya was subsequently introduced as the opposition coalition candidate at a press conference, soon after which he left for France to cultivate diplomatic contacts and meet with the Cameroonian diaspora.[31]

Fru Ndi publicly withdrew from the CRRN on the same day Ndam Njoya's candidacy was announced. Ndam Njoya and other CRRN members attempted to reach an accord with Fru Ndi after the latter indicated that he was open to dialogue.[32] Ndam Njoya offered Fru Ndi a choice among the most important cabinet portfolios for his SDF, including the premiership for himself.[33] But even mediation efforts led by Cardinal Tumi, the Archbishop of Douala and a longtime critic of Biya's regime, failed to reconcile the two sides. Fru Ndi announced his definite withdrawal from the CRRN on 22 September 2004, once again enabling the incumbent to compete against a fragmented opposition. Biya was reelected on 11 October 2004 with 71% of the vote.

Financial Leverage

Opposition politicians and informed commentators have attributed the CRRN's fractured denouement to a variety of causes. One common explanation involves manipulation by the ruling party, which allegedly orchestrated the CRRN's implosion by infiltrating it through agents acting on its behalf, namely, Issa Tchiroma, Antar Gassagaye, and Célestin Bedzigui.[34] Fru Ndi himself cried foul, claiming that Tchiroma, the selection committee chairman, had manipulated the procedures as well as the votes within the committee. But such accusations flew both ways. Commenting on Fru Ndi's defection from the CRRN, Tchiroma alluded to rumors about Fru Ndi's own dealings with the ruling party: "A man is credible when he keeps his commitments. What happened today had been long predicted by the national press, which knew better than we did."[35]

But intricate plots that might have been concocted by the ruling party are not necessary to account for the CRRN's fragmentation. This outcome

---

[30] Fru Ndi lost four points in the following areas: being able to communicate; being open to dialogue and teamwork; having proven management skills; being tolerant and inspiring confidence.

[31] Sanda Oumarou became the coalition's campaign director.

[32] Venant Mboua, "L'opposition divisée: Fru Ndi et Tchiroma se dechirent," *Le Messager*, 17 September 2004.

[33] Alex Gustave Azebaze, "Comment Fru Ndi a été récalé," *Le Messager*, 16 September 2004.

[34] For an example of this argument, see Jean Takougang, "La candidature d'Akame Mfoumou ou l'histoire insolite d'une Coalition noyautée," *Le Messager*, 29 September 2004, p. 11. Another common claim is that opposition politicians engage in coalition bargaining as a ruse. They raise their own profiles by doing so and thereby negotiate their cooptation into the regime.

[35] Quoted in Francis Ampère Simo, "Retour sur 'la nuit des longs couteaux,'" *Le Messager*, 17 September 2004.

could have been predicted more directly by the opposition's lack of campaign funding from business. It is apparent that Fru Ndi, the putative leader of the opposition, did not have the resources required to become a coalition formateur. SDF representatives as well as CRRN partners agree that Fru Ndi lacked the wherewithal to secure the endorsements of his counterparts.[36] Fru Ndi did have access to some resources, including contributions from other SDF representatives and party dues from SDF members. However, these funds remained limited and had declined over time (Krieger 2008). Fru Ndi simply did not have enough resources with which to compensate other politicians for their endorsements. Had he the funds to offer upfront payments to other opposition politicians, he never would have submitted to the CRRN's informal primary or point-based selection process. He most likely would have narrowed his set of bargaining partners and taken the lead in setting more concrete terms for their negotiations.

The role of money in coalition bargaining was, paradoxically, exacerbated by the availability of state subsidies. Cameroon's public finance law, which distributes approximately $1 million among political parties every year, played a critical role in raising the cost of securing cross-ethnic endorsements.[37] Although significant arrears occur because funds are not disbursed in a timely manner, their distribution provides a guide to the financial position of Fru Ndi relative to other potential opposition candidates. Table 7.3 shows that the large part of public financing, approximately 64%, is allocated to Biya's Rassemblement Démocratique du Peuple Camerounais (RDPC).[38] Fru Ndi's SDF receives about 18%, or about half of what the opposition as a whole receives. The next closest opposition party, Ndam Njoya's UDC, receives just 13% of what the SDF alone collects.[39]

While Fru Ndi controlled the lion's share of public financing available to the opposition, it proved insufficient to keep his own party from fragmenting. A continuous stream of defections since the early 1990s indicates either that the public funds allocated to the SDF were inadequate to sustain a party with national ambitions or that they were not being redistributed within the party. After the 2002 legislative elections, the SDF was weakened by the resignations of former parliamentarians and party officials, including the party's chairman in Central Province, where Bamileke voters provided the party's

---

[36] Author interviews, Yaounde, 26 March 2006; 28 March 2006.

[37] Law No. 2000/15 of 19 December 2000 provides 500 million CFA francs annually for the public financing of parties. Half of the total is allocated based on legislative seat share; the other half is allocated based on vote share to every party receiving at least five percent of the vote in one constituency. Presidential Decree No. 2001/205 of 8 October 2001 established a commission to regulate the use of these public monies by requiring each party to submit an accounting of their expenses. This provision, however, has not been enforced.

[38] The figures in Table 7.3 are from Thierry Ngogang, "Fru Ndi, Bello, Ndam Njoya, Doumba... passent à la caisse," *Mutations*, 5 April 2004, p. 4.

[39] Among the parties represented in the legislature, only the SDF and UDC are in opposition. Both the UNDP and the UPC form part of the presidential majority.

TABLE 7.3. *Annual Public Financing for Political Parties in Cameroon*

Party	Seat share ($)	Vote share ($)	Total ($)
RDPC	414,924	224,803	639,727
SDF	61,264	115,439	176,703
UDC	13,924	9,114	23,037
UNDP	2,785	88,098	90,883
UPC	8,354	18,227	26,581
MDR		9,114	9,114
ANDP		6,076	6,076
MDP		6,076	6,076
PPC		3,038	3,038
ADD		3,038	3,038
MP		3,038	3,038
UFDC		3,038	3,038
La Nationale		3,038	3,038
POPC		3,038	3,038
AMEC		3,038	3,038
MLDC		3,038	3,038
Total			1,002,500

Note: Figures are in U.S. dollars using the conversion rate on 22 January 2004.
Seat and vote shares are based on the 2002 legislative election. Party acronyms:
Rassemblement Démocratique du Peuple Camerounais (RDPC); Social Democratic
Front (SDF); Union Démocratique du Cameroun (UDC); Union Nationale pour
la Démocratie et le Progrès (UNDP); Union des Populations du Cameroun (UPC);
Mouvement pour la Défense de la République (MDR); Alliance Nationale pour la
Démocratie et le Progrès (ANDP); Mouvement pour la Démocratie et le Progrès
(MDP); Parti Progressiste Camerounais (PPC); Alliance pour la Démocratie et
le Développement (ADD); Mouvement Progressiste (MP); Union des Forces
Démocratiques du Cameroun (UFDC); Parti des Ouvriers et Paysans Camerounais
(POPC); Action pour la Méritocratie et l'Egalité des Chances (AMEC); Mouvement
pour la Libération et le Développement du Cameroun (MLDC). *Source:* Thierry
Ngogang, "Fru Ndi, Bello, Ndam Njoya, Doumba...passent à la caisse," *Mutations*,
5 April 2004, p. 4.

electoral base in and around Yaounde, the national capital. In the run-up to
the 2004 election, complaints over the manner in which Fru Ndi allocated
posts within the SDF, including its parliamentary delegation and provincial
chapters, revealed an ongoing crisis within the party.[40] Perhaps more revealing
is that, during the process for selecting the CRRN candidate, Fru Ndi's own
lieutenants did not act to protect him. Since SDF representatives made up four
of the eleven members on the selection committee – and points were awarded
to each candidate on the basis of consensus among committee members – they
could have acted as a veto to ensure their party chairman came out ahead. Even
after Fru Ndi decided to leave the CRRN, the former SDF mayor of a Douala

[40] Alex Gustave Azebaze, "Fru Ndi affronte ses pairs fondateurs," *Le Messager*, 2 April 2004, p. 3.

TABLE 7.4. *Public Financing for Cameroon's Presidential Candidates in 2004*

Candidate	Pre-election distribution			Post-election	
	Equal ($)	Seats ($)	Subtotal ($)	Distribution ($)	Total ($)
Paul Biya	30,625	405,611	436,236	695,016	1,131,252
John Fru Ndi	30,625	59,889	90,514	170,520	261,034
Adamou Ndam Njoya	30,625	13,611	44,236	43,806	88,042
13 other candidates	398,125	10,889	409,014	70,658	479,672
Total	490,000	490,000	980,000	980,000	1,960,000

Note: Figures are in U.S. dollars using the conversion rate on 1 October 2004. Seat shares are based on the 2002 legislative election and were distributed before the election. The post-election distribution was based on vote shares from the 2004 election.
Source: Republic of Cameroon National Elections Observatory, "General Report on the Conduct of the Presidential Election of 11 October 2004," Yaounde, 18 July 2005.

borough, Jean-Paul Lozenou Nana, a Bamileke, broke with Fru Ndi's party to support the rump opposition coalition.

Compounding the lack of electoral funding from business, which made Fru Ndi too poor to compensate other opposition politicians for their endorsements, the public financing of presidential candidates also made it too costly for Fru Ndi to step down in favor of any other politician. It also made his endorsement too expensive for any other politician to obtain. As shown in Table 7.4, nearly $2 million in public funds were distributed among all registered presidential candidates in 2004. Half of this money was allocated prior to the election based on a formula that gave each candidate an equal share plus a supplemental share based on each party's representation in the legislature; the other half was allocated based on vote shares after the election.[41]

The information in Table 7.4 can be used to calculate a pre-electoral reservation price for each opposition candidate. Each candidate knew with certainty what sum would be received before the election, as shown in the pre-election subtotals: $90,514 for Fru Ndi, $44,236 for Ndam Njoya, and $36,898, on average, for other minor candidates. Since a candidate who did not run on his own party ticket would forfeit his share, the tradeoff between running independently and endorsing another candidate was knowable and quantifiable for each candidate.

[41] The public finance law provides for one billion CFA francs to be divided for the presidential election: 250 million CFA francs to be divided equally among the political parties nominating candidates; 250 million CFA francs divided among parties in the National Assembly according to their seat share; and 500 million CFA francs to be shared in proportion to their presidential vote share. The first half is distributed 15 days before the election, which is when the campaign legally opens. The figures are from Republic of Cameroon National Elections Observatory, "General Report on the Conduct of the Presidential Election of 11 October 2004," Yaounde, 18 July 2005.

The distribution of public financing suggests why Fru Ndi left the CRRN after Ndam Njoya was selected as its candidate. Fru Ndi expected to receive twice as much public financing as Ndam Njoya. Without the support of private financing from business, it was impossible for the Ndam Njoya to muster the nearly $91,000 it would have taken to make Fru Ndi indifferent between staying in the CRRN versus running independently. But this is a conservative estimate. If Fru Ndi had calculated his reservation price using his estimated vote share, the cost of securing his endorsement would have more than doubled. But not only did Ndam Njoya lack the funds needed to compensate Fru Ndi for his endorsement; he did not have enough to hold on to even minor politicians. Two weeks after Ndam Njoya became the CRRN candidate, Antar Gassagaye (UPR) defected to Biya's electoral coalition when he could not secure any financial reward from the opposition coalition leader.[42] When Gassagaye announced his defection in a 5 p.m. radio broadcast, he claimed – perhaps, from his perspective, somewhat honestly – that opposition politicians had defeated their own cause through "selfishness." He stated,

This decision is very important, and we have come to it because the objectives of the coalition could not be achieved due to the predominance of selfishness.... Therefore, we could no longer see the purpose of remaining in the coalition and we call on our activists to vote usefully, that is to say, to vote for President Paul Biya.[43]

Ndam Njoya's subsequent election campaign was austere. According to the CRRN's budget, over 85% of the $44,236 received in public financing before the election went to costs such as transport, printing, and other basic services.[44] Ndam Njoya simply did not have the means to secure Fru Ndi's or any other politician's endorsement.

THE BARGAINING NARRATIVE IN KENYA

The emergence of a multiethnic opposition coalition during Kenya's 2002 presidential election surprised politicians and commentators alike. Opposition politicians had discussed the possibility of forming such a coalition in the 1992 and 1997 elections, but they never managed to resolve the central question of who would be the coalition candidate. Personal ambitions and ethnic concerns seemed to interact to produce perpetual division. As Brown (2001, 729) noted the year before the 2002 election, "Every candidate desired the presidency – where power is highly concentrated – for himself and none would settle for the vice-presidency or the promise of a ministerial appointment that could be rescinded at any time." Nevertheless, the very same set of actors who had vied for power separately in 1997 – Mwai Kibaki of the Democratic Party (DP),

---

[42] Author interview, Yaounde, 7 April 2006.
[43] "Antar Gassagaye quitte la Coalition et rejoint Biya," *Agence France Presse*, 1 October 2004.
[44] See also Thierry Ndong, "Ouverture de campagne: La Coalition fait la politique de ses moyens," *Le Messager*, 27 September 2004.

Michael Kijana Wamalwa of FORD-Kenya, and Charity Ngilu of the Social Democratic Party (SDP) – were able to arrive at a mutually agreeable bargain in the run-up to the 2002 election. This difference, I claim, can be attributed to the increased campaign financing made available to Kibaki from the business sector as a result of extensive financial liberalization by the end of the 1990s. Kibaki was able to use those resources to offer upfront payments to Wamalwa and Ngilu, making a power-sharing agreement more attractive to both even if they knew it might not be honored after the election.

The Kenyan case study presented here shows that Kibaki, having secured the backing of Kikuyu businessmen as campaign donors, was able to drive the bargaining process as a coalition formateur. The evidence suggests that his financial resources gave him the leverage necessary to restrict his negotiating partners only to those actors who could deliver large enough ethnic constituencies to challenge the ruling party at the national level. This effectively meant sidelining many of the civil society organizations that had lobbied for a broad-based coalition aimed at reforming the political system *in toto*. What is more, Kibaki had the financial wherewithal to fend off a credible challenge from Simeon Nyachae, a former finance minister and a respected member of parliament, who had sought to position himself as a compromise candidate. I discuss these developments below by examining the bargaining modalities among opposition politicians, their jockeying for the coalition candidacy, and their respective financial resources.

Bargaining Modalities

The opposition's likely presidential contenders – Kibaki, Wamalwa, Ngilu, and Nyachae – began holding informal talks about the formation of an opposition coalition two years in advance of the December 2002 election.[45] While consultations among all the possible candidates occurred with growing formality and frequency, they took on added urgency once Moi, in anticipation of the upcoming election, appointed one of his long-time critics, Raila Odinga, to his cabinet in June 2001. Through that appointment, Moi was able to signal his continued ability to coopt individuals from the opposition's ranks. In this context, Kibaki, the official leader of the Opposition in the National Assembly, was arguably its most influential member. But that alone would have been insufficient to give him a free hand in shaping the course of coalition bargaining.[46] It was with the

---

[45] In December 2000, Nyachae was already publicly stating, "We have sat together to negotiate how we shall go about this issue, and once we conclude our talks, we shall come out in public and tell people the way forward." See Peter Angwenyi, "Nyachae Discloses Anti-Kanu Strategy," *Daily Nation* (Nairobi), 2 December 2000.

[46] Kibaki's meeting with the other two opposition party leaders occurred only days after Moi formalized his working relationship with Raila Odinga's NDP by appointing Raila to the cabinet. See Macharia Gaitho, "DP's Game Plan Ahead of Polls," *Daily Nation* (Nairobi), 21 June 2001; Ayub Savula, "FORD K, DP and NPK in Merger Plan, Says Wamalwa," *The East African Standard* (Nairobi), 26 November 2001.

backing of his political financiers that Kibaki was able to make overtures to his opposition counterparts while simultaneously ensuring, over the following year, that the modalities of bargaining reflected his interests: limiting actual negotiations to a small set of actors and selecting a candidate through backroom negotiations rather than an open primary.

The opposition coalition that Kibaki ultimately led in 2002 has often been portrayed as a broad-based union of political parties and civil society organizations. The country's religious and professional associations – by surviving outside the ruling party's patronage system – had become the main champions of democratic reform throughout the 1990s. And the formation of an opposition coalition was widely seen as an integral part of that reform agenda (Kennedy and Kibara 2003; Mutunga 1999). Democracy activists therefore played a visible role in lobbying opposition politicians to coalesce, convening multiparty talks, and lending their popular legitimacy to the single candidate initiative. Kivutha Kibwana, co-convener of the National Convention Executive Council (NCEC) that was originally founded to mobilize mass support for constitutional reform, announced at a press conference that his organization would "formally engage all the key opposition alliances in dialogue with a view to creating bridges for greater unity."[47] Willy Mutunga, the executive director of the Kenya Human Rights Commission, acted as chairman of a council made up of opposition party and civil society representatives to produce a memorandum of understanding laying out the strategy for the elections.[48] On 12 February 2002, Kibaki, Wamalwa, and Ngilu publicly endorsed that memorandum, binding them to form the National Alliance for Change (NAC) behind a common candidate for the presidential election.[49]

The opposition bargaining over a presidential candidate, however, was eventually limited to a small set of actors – the candidates themselves or their surrogates. Civil society activists had long intended for an opposition coalition to serve as a vehicle for broader constitutional reform (Mutunga 2002), but the politicians themselves were focused on maximizing their electoral fortunes. Civil society leaders were therefore increasingly sidelined as coalition deliberations progressed.[50] Although the NAC memorandum of understanding signed in February 2002 had committed the parties to an open and transparent nomination process, by July 2002, Kibaki, Wamalwa, and Ngilu were negotiating

---

[47] Eliud Miring'uh, "NCEC in Bid to Unite Opposition," *The East African Standard* (Nairobi), 12 February 2002.

[48] Claire Gatheru, "Three Parties And NCEC to Sign Poll Deal," *Daily Nation* (Nairobi), 6 February 2002; Robert Oduol, "The Troubled Search for Joint Opposition Platform," *Daily Nation* (Nairobi), 3 February 2002.

[49] The document had no legal value, so the move was mainly a signal to politicians and voters rather than an actual guarantee to one another. A measure approximating mutual assurance could be found in the joint proposal sent to the Constitution of Kenya Review Commission in March 2002. Their recommendations included the creation of a prime minister post to be appointed by the president.

[50] Author interviews, Nairobi, 10 September 2004; 12 September 2004; 25 September 2004.

the top posts among themselves behind closed doors.[51] Representatives of the main candidates formed "the committee of 12" to negotiate the distribution of posts that would be available after the election to the exclusion of the junior members in their protocoalition, including the civil society organizations and smaller political parties.[52]

Kibaki's backroom deals cost him the support of civil society groups. The NCEC, a movement for which constitutional reform was a priority, withdrew its support from the NAC in March 2002 for having drawn up constitutional proposals without consulting them.[53] In October 2002, when Kibaki announced that he agreed with Moi's decision to hold elections under the existing constitution, civil society leaders openly criticized him. Willy Mutunga, who withdrew from the NAC at the time, called for a religious leader to be supported as head of a transitional government rather than Kibaki or any other opposition politician.[54]

The division between activists and politicians was not new, of course. It was reminiscent of the 1997 crisis in which Moi was able to win the support of opposition politicians in creating the Inter-Party Parliamentary Group (IPPG) talks aimed at keeping the constitutional review process within the National Assembly rather than creating a society-based constitutional convention. This time, however, it was Kibaki who managed to offer other politicians the incentives necessary to ignore the pressure from civil society. By forestalling constitutional reform, he was able to protect his role as coalition formateur, since section 15 of the former Kenyan constitution empowered a president to appoint members of the government – the vice president and cabinet ministers – without regard to partisan affiliation and without need for legislative confirmation.[55]

Kibaki would not have been able to restrict the set of actors involved in coalition negotiations were it not for his financial resources. Wamalwa and Ngilu would have preferred allowing civil society representatives to participate in their negotiations, since it would have effectively given them additional votes in the candidate selection process. It is quite likely that an open process would have given them an advantage over Kibaki, who had often been depicted by democracy activists as a latecomer to their movement and a hesitant reformer. Instead, Kibaki's resources gave him the leverage needed

---

[51] The NAC retreat held at the Aberdares Country Club on 7–9 July 2002 was mainly restricted to MPs.

[52] The committee included Njenga Karume, one of Kibaki's financiers. See Fred Oluoch, "Royal Opposition: Big Three 'Stealing' NAC Nominations," *Daily Nation* (Nairobi), 30 July 2002; Robert Oduol, "Kibaki 'King' in Opposition Alliance's Power Gambit, *Daily Nation* (Nairobi), 1 April 2002.

[53] Eliud Miring'uh, "Blow for Alliance as NCEC Withdraws Support," *The East African Standard* (Nairobi), 7 March 2002.

[54] Biketi Kikechi, "Ufungamano Slams NAK Boss over Remark on Polls," *The East African Standard* (Nairobi), 9 October 2002.

[55] The country's original 1963 constitution was replaced by a new constitution in 2010.

to assemble an opposition coalition through dyadic deals rather than an open primary process.

Candidate Jockeying

The essential composition for a viable opposition coalition in Kenya had been known since 2000, but its exact formulation remained in doubt for most of the period leading up to the December 2002 election. Such a coalition would include some combination of Kibaki, Wamalwa, Ngilu, and Nyachae, since the combined vote shares of their ethnic constituencies would equal, if not surpass, the ruling party's electoral base. But Kibaki faced considerable competition for coalition leadership from Nyachae, a former finance minister who was widely known to have considerable business holdings.[56] Having taken over the leadership of the moribund FORD-People – effectively buying a party – Nyachae, an ethnic Kisii, went on to position himself as the alternative to the ethnic Kikuyu presidency that Kibaki represented, and which many Kenyans feared.[57]

Nyachae actively competed with Kibaki in making a bid for the support of Wamalwa and Ngilu. Although he had been invited to participate in the "breakfast meetings" held among the other three candidates throughout much of 2001, Nyachae refused to attend, preferring to meet with each separately.[58] Criticizing Kibaki's dominance of the NAC, Nyachae proposed the creation of an opposition movement that was more inclusive of civil society and small parties as well as more focused on proposing a reform agenda.[59] He then proceeded to announce the formation of the Kenya People's Coalition (KPC) as such a movement, positioning it as a rival to the Kibaki-dominated NAC.[60]

Nyachae sought to outmaneuver Kibaki by forcing him into an open contest. Looking to cultivate the support of civil society and politicians from smaller ethnic groups, he advocated the selection of a candidate through a primary in which either party delegates or voters determined the choice.[61] Nyachae pitched

---

[56] Nyachae left the cabinet in 1999 after being demoted from the finance portfolio to industrial development, a move prompted by his anticorruption and reform measures. He was subsequently forced out as the KANU chairman in Kisii.

[57] Kenyatta, the country's first president, was a Kikuyu and favored his own group in the distribution of economic and political resources. Some saw a Kibaki presidency as a return to the status quo ante.

[58] Njeri Rugene, "MP Upsets Shaky Opposition Unity Plans," *Daily Nation* (Nairobi), 4 November 2001; Macharia Gaitho, "Nyachae's Presidential Gameplan Unfolds Three Days before Ford People Nominated Him," *Daily Nation* (Nairobi), 10 December 2001.

[59] Gitau Warigi, "The Ghost of 1997 Failure," *Daily Nation* (Nairobi), 13 January 2002.

[60] The KPC was launched as a pact with Paul Muite's Safina Party. See Njeri Rugene, "Nyachae-Muite Seal Surprise Poll Pact," *Daily Nation* (Nairobi), 1 February 2002.

[61] Macharia Gaitho, "Nyachae's Presidential Gameplan Unfolds Three Days before Ford People Nominated Him," Daily Nation (Nairobi), 10 December 2001; Robert Oduol, "Parliamentary Nominations Promise a Great Test," *Daily Nation* (Nairobi), 25 February 2002; Peter Atsiaya and Hilton Otenyo, "Ford People Boss Blocking Opposition Unity, Says Wamalwa," *The East African Standard* (Nairobi), 20 May 2002.

his proposal by casting himself as more democratic and less chauvinistic than Kibaki:

Are we really being honest when four politicians sit together to negotiate on who is to be president? Who has given us this mandate? The key thing here should be inclusivity and wide consultations. Otherwise, we remain divided.... The truth is that these people [party leaders] are prisoners of their own communities.[62]

Nyachae expanded this strategy by offering a package of reforms, including an interim constitution that would require a winning candidate to win at least 50% of the vote in a run-off system.[63]

Although Nyachae's personal resources allowed him to credibly vie for the coalition's candidacy, they were insufficient to enable him to overcome Kibaki's perceived advantage, as both political analysts and Nyachae's own campaign staff confirm.[64] Moreover, the relatively small size of Nyachae's ethnic group – about 5% of the population – raised doubts about his ability to pull together a sufficient number of votes to bring about an alternation in power. This was a fact recognized by other opposition politicians and the entrepreneurs who funded them.

Within the Kibaki-dominated NAC, Wamalwa capitalized on the same latent anti-Kikuyu sentiment that Nyachae played on by repeatedly threatening to pull out of the opposition coalition if Kibaki were selected as its candidate. Just prior to the announcement of the NAC, in February 2002, Wamalwa floated the notion of Kibaki stepping down in his favor, noting that a Kikuyu had already been president and that "Kenyans feel that a Luhya should succeed President Moi as the chief executive of the land on an Opposition party's ticket."[65] A week later, Wamalwa threatened not to sign onto the NAC if Njenga Karume, one of Kibaki's principal financiers, did not recant a statement asserting that only Kibaki could become the opposition's presidential candidate.[66] Wamalwa continued making such threats over several months of negotiations,[67] though it is unclear whether their purpose was to assure him

[62] Njeri Rugene, "MP Upsets Shaky Opposition Unity Plans," *Daily Nation* (Nairobi), 4 November 2001.

[63] Njeri Rugene, "Minimum Reforms in Opposition Unity Plan," *Daily Nation* (Nairobi), 10 February 2002.

[64] Author interviews, Nairobi, 9 September 2004; 24 September 2004.

[65] Robert Wafula, "Stop Dreaming of the Presidency, Wamalwa Tells DP Leader," *Daily Nation* (Nairobi), 4 February 2002. Wamalwa later retracted his statements. See Judith Akolo, "I Did Not Rule DP Out of Race, Declares Wamalwa," *The East African Standard* (Nairobi), 5 February 2002; Claire Gatheru, Mugumo Muhene, and Muniu Riunge, "Wamalwa: My Stand On Presidential Poll," *Daily Nation* (Nairobi), 5 February 2002.

[66] Mburu Mwangi, "New Blow to Opposition Unity," *Daily Nation* (Nairobi), 11 February 2002.

[67] In July 2002 – four months after Wamalwa had committed to the selection of a single candidate – his surrogates were still suggesting that Kibaki, being Kikuyu, would not be acceptable. See Ben Agina, Martin Mutua, and Ayub Savula, "'Big 3' Act to Seal Cracks in National Alliance for Change," *The East African Standard* (Nairobi), 24 July 2002.

the presidential nomination or simply to bid up his value as a member of the coalition. In either case, he remained in the NAC despite his public misgivings of supporting a Kikuyu candidate.

Financial Leverage

Kibaki and his allies, though negotiating for nearly two years, had put off selecting a candidate for fear that any one of their slate would then be coopted by Moi.[68] On 18 September 2002, some three months before the election, Kibaki was finally announced as the presidential candidate of the National Alliance Party of Kenya (NAK).[69] Wamalwa was designated as the coalition's candidate for vice president and Ngilu as the candidate for prime minister. These nominations, while reflecting the outcome of the bargaining among the politicians, were power-sharing promises rather than an enforceable pact. Because the Kenyan constitution at the time allowed the president to appoint the vice president of his choice, Wamalwa could not be guaranteed that Kibaki would actually do so if he were sworn in. The same applied to Ngilu, since she was promised a position that would be created under a draft constitution still under review. How did these candidates come to such a power-sharing agreement? Why would Wamalwa and Ngilu accept such terms when they would be required to deliver the votes of their coethnics without any guarantee of participation in a post-election government?

The answer to both questions can be attributed to Kibaki's financial leverage, that is, the support offered by his donors from the business community. By 2002, Kibaki had the financial backing to mount a credible challenge to the ruling party. According to one party leader who was involved in the coalition negotiations, "Only Kibaki could marshal the resources needed for a national election. There were many rich people in his community who would help him."[70] Kibaki used those resources in bargaining with Wamalwa and Ngilu, neither of whom could compete with him in attracting campaign financing.

There is no direct evidence for the amount of electoral funds under the control of opposition party leaders, but a proxy might be found in their pattern of Harambee donations. Meaning "let's pull together" in Swahili, Harambee rallies were institutionalized by the country's first president in the 1960s as a self-help scheme to collect funds for community development projects. Over time, however, Harambee rallies acquired a political significance as politicians used them to ostentatiously signal their ability and willingness to provide a community with resources (Widner 1992). And the donations distributed by opposition politicians at such events often come from the resources made available

---

[68] This delaying tactic was also used in Cameroon's opposition in 2004.

[69] NAK was the acronym added to Ngilu's NPK. This move was a necessary legal fiction because Kenya's electoral rules had no provision for coalitions; there was no legal mechanism for multiple parties to endorse a common candidate.

[70] Author interview, Nairobi, 29 July 2008.

to them by their supporters in business. In this context, the data collected on Harambee donations by the Kenya chapter of Transparency International can be disaggregated to assess the relative financial position of the contenders for opposition coalition leadership – Kibaki's DP, Wamalwa's FORD-Kenya, Ngilu's SDP, and Nyachae's FORD-People.[71]

Figures 7.1 and 7.2 show that Harambee donations made in 2000–2002 by individuals affiliated with Kibaki's DP far exceeded, both in financial and geographic terms, the donations made by those associated with other opposition parties. Figure 7.1 indicates that the donations made by DP affiliates more than equaled the donations of all other opposition parties combined, that is, about $100,000.[72] Moreover, Figure 7.2 shows that DP also had a greater geographic reach than any other opposition party. It made donations in 62 constituencies, that is, 30% of the country's 210 constituencies. FORD-Kenya made the next largest distribution with 37 constituencies, or 18% of the total.

While all parties made Harambee donations across a range of ethnic constituencies, DP appears to have the most varied portfolio, if simply because it had the most to give.[73] Opposition parties, on average, channeled two-thirds of their donations to constituencies found within their own ethnic bases. However, Kibaki's DP was not only the largest donor to Kikuyu constituencies, but also the largest opposition contributor to Mijikenda constituencies in Coast Province and minority-populated constituencies in Rift Valley and Eastern Provinces. It provided nearly a quarter of opposition donations to Luhya constituencies. Kibaki's DP could also afford to make donations to constituencies controlled by other parties, possibly as a means of luring candidates or votes in those constituencies. Nearly a third of DP donations went to constituencies controlled by the ruling party.

The Harambee data indicate that Kibaki could easily outspend his rivals in reaching out to a cross section of Kenyan politicians. In this respect, the entrepreneurs who financed Kibaki's electioneering were also instrumental in undertaking negotiations with local opinion leaders who influenced how their communities voted. In certain cases, some of the businessmen negotiating on Kibaki's behalf clinched the most important endorsements. For example, at a later stage of the process, James Koome, a Nairobi-based businessman who formed part of Kibaki's campaign team, was sent to the capital of Nyanza

---

[71] There are 3,191 observations in Transparency International – Kenya's Harambee data set. Each observation includes details such as the donor's name, the amount of the donation, the donor's party affiliation, and the constituency in which the Harambee was held. After deleting cases with no identifiable party or constituency, the sample is reduced to 1,127 observations.

[72] I exclude Raila Odinga's NDP from these calculations. Since Raila began cooperating with Moi in 1998 and joined the cabinet in 2001, it is reasonable to assume that a good part of the money used by Raila for Harambee donations was coming from the state. Based on the distribution of donations made by the NDP in 2000–2002, it does appear that the party was able to significantly increase the amount it distributed in the year after Raila became minister of energy on 11 June 2001. I estimate this bonus to be approximately $38,000.

[73] I coded each constituency by the ethnicity of its MP.

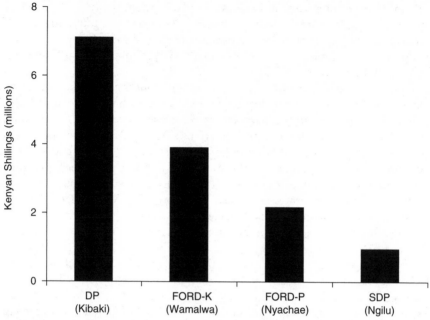

FIGURE 7.1. Total Harambee donations by Kenyan opposition parties, 2000–2002.
Source: Transparency International – Kenya.

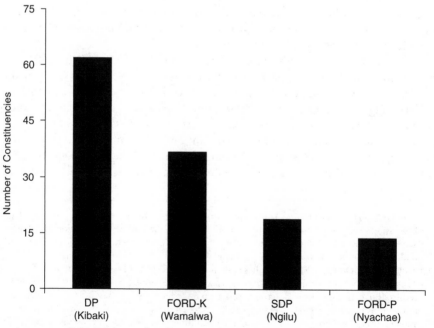

FIGURE 7.2. Distribution of Harambee donations by Kenyan opposition parties, 2000–2002.
Source: Transparency International – Kenya.

Province to help secure an endorsement from Raila Odinga, who had earlier joined the ruling party and was about to defect back to the opposition. Given the political animosity that had developed over the years between the Luo and Kikuyu ethnic groups – Raila's father, Oginga Odinga, was forced out of the vice presidency by Kenyatta, an ethnic Kikuyu – it was vital to ensure that other communal leaders would support Raila's endorsement of Kibaki. Otherwise, it was unlikely that Raila would agree to support him. Koome, who happens to be an ethnic Meru, was sent to smooth over the negotiations with leaders of Raila's ethnic group. He recalls,

I myself traveled to Kisumu to meet with the Luo Council of Elders. They didn't want to meet with a Kikuyu. I had a twelve-hour meeting to convince them to support the coalition. I gave them assurances that the "betrayal" would not be repeated. It was the only way Raila could join.[74]

What made Kibaki's negotiations easier was the fact that most other opposition party leaders, including Ngilu and Wamalwa, had been financially exhausted from competing in previous elections. Ngilu reportedly raised only some 10 million shillings ($158,000) for her presidential bid in the 1997 race, which was insufficient to pay for her own national campaign and subsidize the campaigns of the 103 parliamentary candidates who ran on her Social Democratic Party (SDP) ticket.[75] Although Ngilu proved in 1997 that she could command a significant vote share from her coethnic Kambas, a vital electoral bloc at the national level, she lacked the means to ensure her continued influence over the SDP itself.

By 2000, Ngilu's rivals within the SDP, including Apollo Njonjo, its secretary-general, and Peter Anyang' Nyong'o, a veteran pro-democracy campaigner, had managed to block the renewal of her candidacy. They did so by revising the party constitution to require all presidential and parliamentary candidates to have a university degree, which Ngilu lacked.[76] Since she would need to control a party to continue bargaining with Kibaki and Wamalwa over the formation of a coalition, Ngilu left the SDP and created the National Party of Kenya (NPK), taking with her four other MPs.

In announcing the launch of the NPK at Nairobi's Holiday Inn, in June 2001,[77] Ngilu acknowledged public reservations about the formation of a new party in an already crowded field: "The question will be asked why we are forming yet another political party when we are also calling for unity of political parties."[78] She justified her move by declaring that its principal objective would be to form part of a post-Moi government of national unity. Knowing

---

[74] Author interview, Nairobi, 5 August 2008.

[75] John Githongo, "What Happened to the Ngilu Campaign Wave?," *The East African Standard* (Nairobi), 8 January 1998.

[76] Peter Munaita, "Prospect of a United Opposition after Moi's Exit Haunts Kanu," *The East African* (Nairobi), 25 January 2001.

[77] The NPK was officially registered as a political party on 15 March 2001.

[78] Odhiambo Orlale, "Ngilu Says No to Moi," *Daily Nation* (Nairobi), 25 June 2001.

her own financial limitations, Ngilu signaled that she was willing to negotiate on the terms:

The era of alliances is here with us. We are into the era of issue-oriented politics and political parties sharing the same ideology and politics will surely merge. But before that happens, we cannot close the door to the formation of new political parties with a vision for this nation.[79]

Wamalwa's financial situation was worse than Ngilu's. He publicly acknowledged that his FORD-Kenya had competed in the 1997 elections "without a shilling."

Our situation was so bad that I was not even able to travel to Mombasa [Kenya's second largest city] during the campaigns. I was grounded in my house...while Raila Odinga, Charity Ngilu and Mwai Kibaki hopped from one town to another by plane or helicopter.[80]

Wamalwa, nevertheless, managed to win 48% of the vote in Western Province, largely among his Luhya coethnics. But the effort nearly ruined him financially because, like many Kenyan politicians, he had taken out several loans to finance his campaign. Having accrued some 34 million shillings ($440,000) in debt, Wamalwa had three cases pending in bankruptcy court by early 2002.

Were the court to declare him insolvent, Wamalwa would have been disqualified from the 2002 elections because Kenyan law prohibits a bankrupt person from voting or holding a public office. The court made such a move on 7 February 2002 by issuing a receivership order against Wamalwa for failing to pay a 3.6 million shilling loan with a 20% annual interest rate.[81] However, somewhat surprisingly, Wamalwa was able to deposit a check for 600,000 shillings on 13 February 2002 to earn a temporary reprieve from the court. Perhaps it was not coincidental that he managed to make that deposit just one day after participating along with Kibaki in the public unveiling of the NAC, which suggests that quid pro quo was involved in their negotiations. A month later, Wamalwa announced that he felt "quite sure that by the end of May [2002], I'll

---

[79] Ibid.

[80] Tim Wanyoni, "We shall agree on one candidate to face KANU," Interview with Michael Kijana Wamalwa, *Daily Nation* (Nairobi), 4 March 2002. Wamalwa's deputy Musikari Kombo has further noted that financing the 1997 campaign "was a struggle. His [Wamalwa's] friends borrowed. We even sold some of our assets. That is why Wamalwa's presidential campaign was really underfunded" (quoted in David Mugonyi, "How Donations to Politicians Oil the Wheels of Corruption," *Daily Nation* [Nairobi], 24 April 2006).

[81] For details on Wamalwa's bankruptcy travails, see David Mugonyi, "Wamalwa's Sh34m Debt to Be Cleared By Taxpayers," *Daily Nation* (Nairobi), 11 March 2004; Grace Muiruri, "Ford Boss Debt Case Goes to Full Hearing," *The East African Standard* (Nairobi), 23 May 2002; Tony Kago, "Wamalwa Back to Brink of Bankruptcy, *Daily Nation* (Nairobi), 20 March 2002; Tony Kago, "Wamalwa Escapes Bankruptcy," *Daily Nation* (Nairobi), 13 February 2002; Tony Kago, "Presidential Hopeful Faces Bankruptcy," *Daily Nation* (Nairobi), 7 February 2002; Maguta Kimemia, "Wamalwa Has a Week to Pay Sh1.6m Debt," *Daily Nation* (Nairobi), 25 January 2002.

be as clean as a new pin."[82] Politicians involved in brokering the negotiations between Kibaki and Wamalwa, including a government minister, confirm that financial transfers helped to seal their agreement. Wamalwa agreed to endorse Kibaki in exchange for the vice presidency as long as Kibaki's campaign also paid for his outstanding debts as well as his home in one of Nairobi's most exclusive neighborhoods.[83]

Wamalwa returned to Western Province to rally his coethnics in support of Kibaki. Because Luhya politicians had over the years promoted the idea of having one of their own assume the presidency, this was not an easy task. Now seeking to persuade their base to support an opposition coalition under the leadership of another ethnic group's politician, Wamalwa and members of his FORD-K had to traverse the region to portray themselves as advancing Luhya communal interest through Kibaki's candidacy, stressing that they were more likely to be represented at the highest levels of government by joining forces with other groups. Soita Shitanda, a parliamentarian in Wamalwa's party, perfectly summed up this logic to a mass rally in Kakamega, the capital of Western Province: "Express it by show of hands that we are in FORD-Kenya and through it in NAK. We would wish Wamalwa to be President of Kenya, but we love victory more. We want to be part of the winning team more than producing a president" (quoted in Katumanga 2005, 215). At the same rally, Wamalwa publicly reaffirmed his support for Kibaki by declaring him an elder of the Luhya, dressing him in the colobus monkey skin used to symbolize leadership status within their community.[84]

Once Kibaki secured the endorsements of Wamalwa and Ngilu, it was Moi's own coalition that began to fall apart. Moi had previously sought to shore up support for the Kenya African National Union (KANU) by appointing Raila Odinga, an ethnic Luo opposition politician, to his cabinet in June 2001 and then folding Raila's NDP into KANU in March 2002.[85] Moi, who was constitutionally barred from seeking a third term, then designated Uhuru Kenyatta, an ethnic Kikuyu and the founding president's son, as KANU's presidential candidate in July 2002. Moi's plan, however, was undermined when his other would-be successors within KANU responded by forming an anti-Uhuru faction, the Rainbow Alliance.[86]

---

[82] Quoted in Tim Wanyoni, "We shall agree on one candidate to face KANU," Interview with Michael Kijana Wamalwa, *Daily Nation* (Nairobi), 4 March 2002.

[83] Author interviews, Nairobi, 15 July 2008; 29 July 2008.

[84] Katumanga (2005) provides a detailed analysis of the cultural norms and cues activated by Wamalwa and other politicians in this event.

[85] At that time, Moi appointed four new party vice chairmen to signal his potential successors: Uhuru Kenyatta (Kikuyu), Musalia Mudavadi (Luhya), Kalonzo Musyoka (Kamba), and Noah Katan Ngala (Mijikenda).

[86] After failing to win his own parliamentary constituency in 1997, Uhuru seemed to have little to recommend him as a presidential candidate. However, Moi may have been grooming him for the position for some time. After the 1997 election, he appointed Uhuru to the National Assembly as a nominated MP. Moi later appointed him to the cabinet as minister of local government.

After failing to resolve their conflict with Moi over the selection of a KANU presidential candidate, the Rainbow Alliance defected on 18 October 2002 – one month after Kibaki's coalition had been formally announced – and entered the Liberal Democratic Party (LDP), a defunct but registered political party. Ten days later, the LDP joined with NAK, Kibaki's alliance, to form an expanded coalition known as the National Rainbow Coalition (NARC).[87] While the two sides signed a memorandum of understanding in October 2002 that specified an equal division of cabinet positions between NAK and LDP, neither the presidential or vice presidential nominations were altered. Only Ngilu's position of prime minister was transferred to Raila Odinga.[88]

The question remains whether Kibaki's successful coordination of the opposition ultimately depended on Moi's inability to seek a third term. The claim would be that, had Moi himself been competing, the opposition would have fragmented either because he would have been perceived as undefeatable or would have coopted key opposition politicians. But, in either case, the counterfactual scenario is unlikely to have prevented an opposition coalition from being formed. While Moi purposefully remained vague about his intent to step down until his final year in office – hardliners within the ruling party had been hinting otherwise – the entrepreneurs who could finance the opposition had been distancing themselves from the incumbent well before he designated a successor. Businessmen such as Joe Wanjui and Samuel Macharia, who had supported Moi in 1997, had already switched to Kibaki in the lead-up to 2002. It was the support of such entrepreneurs that permitted Kibaki to shape the course of opposition bargaining throughout 2001–2002 despite the uncertainty over Moi's candidacy.

Even if Moi himself was not competing, he had sufficient cause to believe that only a KANU successor could ensure his immunity from prosecution after leaving office. The considerable wealth that Moi had accumulated during his years in office, coupled with the human rights violations committed by members of his government, left him vulnerable to prosecution, as many in the opposition publicly espoused (Wolf 2006).[89] Moi's imposition of Uhuru

---

[87] Talks between the two sides had been going on even before Kibaki's official candidacy had been announced in September. Ngilu and Raila represented their respective sides in those negotiations.

[88] According to the agreement specified in the memorandum between NAK and LDP, the latter was supposed to receive 13 ministers in a 22-member cabinet because Kibaki's NAK held the presidency. This agreement, however, was not completely honored in the first post-election cabinet appointed by Kibaki: LDP received 9 ministerial appointments, while NAK received 16: 12 for Kibaki's DP, 3 for Wamalwa's FORD-K, and 1 for Ngilu's NPK. Assistant ministers were more equitably divided: LDP was given 11 and NAK was given 10: 7 for DP, 2 for FORD-K, and 1 for NPK. Appointments to Kibaki's cabinet were also regionally balanced: Central Province received 5 ministers, Eastern Province 5, Western Province 5, Rift Valley 4, Nyanza 3, Coast 2, and 1 each for North East Province and Nairobi.

[89] See also Willy Mutunga's interview in Njonjo Kihuria, "Moi Succession: We Should Make These Demands," *The East African Standard* (Nairobi). 28 September 2002.

Kenyatta as the KANU presidential candidate suggests not only that he was personally invested in the campaign, but also that he was actively looking to divide the Kikuyu. But, as members of Moi's cabinet acknowledge, he no longer had the instruments necessary to repeat his earlier electoral successes, regardless of whether he himself were the ruling party's candidate.[90] Moi had lost control of the means by which to blackmail the business community. And that was the key to opposition coordination in Kenya.

CONCLUSION

This chapter has shown how the availability of campaign resources among opposition candidates influences coalition bargaining across ethnic cleavages. The Cameroon and Kenya case studies demonstrate that opposition politicians are more than willing to strike cross-cleavage bargains, even when it calls for endorsing politicians from groups that might be popularly perceived in competitive terms. The divergent outcomes in these cases were not determined by differences in levels of ethnic conflict, but by whether opposition politicians could secure the funding necessary to compensate their potential coalition partners.

In Cameroon, politicians from a cross section of ethnic constituencies – identities reinforced by Anglophone versus Francophone linguistic traditions – made a concerted effort to coalesce in the run-up to the 2004 presidential election. Interethnic animosity did not prevent them from forging such an alliance. It was the lack of support from a cowed business community. Delayed financial reform obliged the country's entrepreneurs to ally with the long-ruling incumbent. As a consequence, no opposition politician could obtain the campaign financing needed to act as a coalition formateur. None had the funds needed to manage the bargaining process and pay for the endorsements that would deliver blocs of ethnic votes. Compounding the lack of private campaign financing, the public financing of party campaigns further narrowed the range in which opposition politicians could locate a mutually agreeable bargain. Cameroon's opposition therefore entered the country's third multiparty presidential election as fragmented as before.

In Kenya, progressive financial reforms had stripped the incumbent of the instruments needed to induce the political loyalty of business. Entrepreneurs were therefore free to diversify their political contributions by the country's 2002 presidential election. The availability of private campaign financing enabled Mwai Kibaki to emerge as a coalition formateur. Bankrolled by prominent entrepreneurs, he was able to compensate his opposition counterparts for their endorsements and withdrawals. In this respect, Kibaki was an unlikely coalition candidate: he belonged to the very ethnic group that politicians from other groups had long criticized for dominating the country's government and

---

[90] Author interview, Nairobi, 30 September 2004.

economy. Yet, these same politicians chose to rally around Kibaki's candidacy by the country's third multiparty presidential election. They did so, in part, because Kibaki had the wherewithal to structure the bargaining process among the opposition, negotiating exclusively with a choice set of politicians while ignoring demands from civil society to pursue a broader reform agenda.

8

Multiethnic Opposition Coalitions in African Elections

> If the opposition can present a single candidate ... then we will have a good chance of winning because you cannot cheat a whole nation for long.
>
> Edem Kodjo, opposition presidential candidate in Togo, 2003[1]

The argument developed through the previous chapters attributes opposition behavior in Africa's multiparty elections to the state control of capital. My general claim is that the liberalization of finance enables opposition politicians to pursue a pecuniary coalition-building strategy by using the resources of business to secure cross-ethnic endorsements. I have provided both qualitative and quantitative evidence at each link of the causal chain to explain the conditions under which incumbents relinquish their control over the financial sector; business chooses to defect from the incumbent regime in support of the opposition; and opposition politicians successfully bargain across ethnic cleavages to form electoral alliances.

In this chapter, I now seek to establish whether the outcomes traced through the cases of Cameroon and Kenya are consistent with the electoral strategies pursued by opposition politicians across the region. I test my argument with a sample of all African countries that held executive elections between 1990 and 2005. The indicators that were examined in previous chapters to assess the politicization of finance – the total number of commercial banks (Chapter 4), the availability of credit to the private sector (Chapter 5), and the tenure of

---

[1] Kodjo, a former secretary general of the Organization of African Unity (OAU), was one of six opposition candidates who competed in Togo's 2003 presidential election against Gnassingbé Eyadéma, the country's ruler since 1967. Togo's main opposition parties had been collaborating under the umbrella of a protocoalition, the Coalition des Forces Démocratiques (CFD), but ultimately chose to field individual candidates in 2003 after failing to agree on a consensus candidate. Certain Togolese politicians refused to work with Kodjo himself, who had fractured an earlier opposition alliance by accepting the premiership in Eyadéma's government after legislative elections in 1994. See "La Cour constitutionnelle rejette le recours d'Olympio," *UN Integrated Regional Information Networks*, 8 May 2003; Ebow Godwin, "Opposition Split as Presidential Polls Approach," *Inter Press Service*, 6 May 1998.

the chamber of commerce president (Chapter 6) – are used here as explanatory variables. Through this empirical analysis, I show that the state control of
capital significantly affects the likelihood of multiethnic opposition coalitions
being formed for executive elections. The ability of entrepreneurs to diversify their campaign contributions under conditions of financial liberalization
appears to account for much of the variation in opposition coalition building
across countries and within countries across time. Indeed, the empirical results
show that the variables linked to the openness of the financial system are more
consistent predictors of opposition behavior in Africa's multiparty systems
than either electoral rules or ethnic cleavages.

The rest of this chapter is organized as follows. I continue in the next section by discussing the identification of multiethnic opposition coalitions in
African countries. I describe the measures for the hypotheses regarding private
resources as well as alternative explanations concerning patronage, ethnicity,
institutions, and the quality of democracy. I then proceed with the quantitative
analysis to assess the extent to which the explanatory variables conform to
theoretical predictions. I conclude by discussing how these results affect our
understanding of interethnic bargaining in contemporary African politics.

THE IDENTIFICATION OF MULTIETHNIC OPPOSITION COALITIONS

Multiethnic opposition coalitions are identified in each election through observable coding rules. First, the opposition coalition endorses a single candidate for
executive office. This is straightforward. A coalition's designated candidate for
the presidency, or the premiership in a parliamentary system, must be publicly
announced and agreed to by the parties to the coalition.

Second, the opposition coalition is multiethnic. A coalition must represent
more than one ethnic group or region. The ethnic and regional makeup of a
coalition is determined by the identity of the coalition candidate and the other
party leaders supporting him or her. For example, the opposition National
Rainbow Coalition (NARC) that came together for the 2002 presidential election in Kenya could be easily identified as a multiethnic electoral alliance.
NARC presidential candidate Mwai Kibaki is an ethnic Kikuyu who was supported by Kijana Wamalwa, a Luhya, Charity Ngilu, a Kamba, and eventually
Raila Odinga, a Luo.

Third, the opposition coalition is pre-electoral. Multiple opposition politicians or parties must endorse a single candidate prior to the election in a plurality system or the first round in a runoff system. This rule excludes instances of
first-round promises for a second-round endorsement or instances of second-
round endorsements that were not preceded by any first-round negotiations.[2]

---

[2] This eliminates a total of six cases that occurred in countries with runoff systems. There were
four instances in which opposition parties agreed prior to the first round to endorse their best-
placed finisher for the second round: Central African Republic 1999, Chad 2001, Guinea 1998,
and Niger 1993. However, only the presidential election in Niger actually went to a second

The purpose of such a rule is to distinguish bargaining that entails upfront and verifiable costs for politicians in the form of strategic candidate withdrawals from promises that do not require commitments to be honored in advance.

Opposition coalitions are further restricted to those electoral alliances that are made up of politically relevant actors. The political relevance of the participating parties is established through parliamentary representation or through expert assessments found in country case studies. Expert assessments are particularly important in coding the first post-transition elections, since parliamentary history could not be used in such instances to assess the relative weight of the parties. This restriction serves to eliminate potential false positives, that is, opposition coalitions formed by "hopeless" or "briefcase" parties. Coalition bargaining is nearly costless for such parties because none of the participants is independently a viable candidate whose participation might affect the outcome of the election. For example, in Angola, the five-party Democratic Angola Coalition (DAC) that was formed during the 1992 presidential election is not counted as an instance of opposition coordination because the Union for the Total Independence of Angola (UNITA) refused to join. All other participants in the DAC were minor parties with no known political influence.

Based on this identification of multiethnic opposition coalitions, Figure 8.1 shows that politicians have regularly coordinated their electoral efforts across ethnic cleavages since the region's second multiparty era began. There are 32 opposition coalitions among the 85 contested executive elections (38%) held across the region between 1990 and 2005.[3] This rate, at first glance, is considerably lower than what is found among parliamentary democracies. Golder (2006) shows that parties have formed pre-electoral coalitions in 66% of the elections held in 23 advanced parliamentary democracies between 1946 and 2002. However, the coalition-building rate among Africa's opposition parties is, in fact, higher than one might expect based on institutional or historical context. First, the majority of executive elections in Africa are conducted under presidential systems – 42 of 49 countries in Sub-Saharan Africa hold presidential elections – and there is no institutional requirement that a multiparty coalition be formed in order to win an office that is ultimately held by a single individual. Second, the majority of executive elections in Africa are conducted under conditions that are biased in favor of incumbents – Lindberg (2006) finds that only 56% of elections in the region could be classified as free and fair – so opposition politicians in the region must contend with greater hurdles in coalition-building than what would be typically expected in established democracies.

round. There were two other instances in which opposition parties endorsed a candidate in the second round without any first-round commitments being made: Niger 1999 and Sierra Leone 1996.

[3] A total of 99 executive elections were held between 1990 and 2005. The opposition boycotted 14 of those elections, which are excluded from the sample under analysis. An electoral boycott does require coordination among opposition parties; however, for party leaders, it does not entail the same cost as a coalition, namely, withdrawing in favor of another candidate.

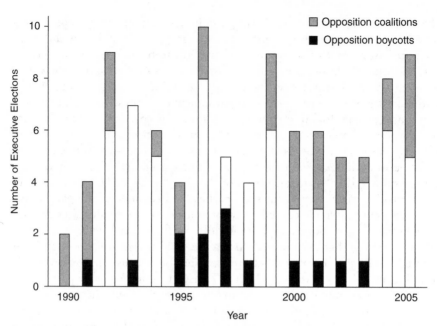

FIGURE 8.1. Opposition coalitions in contested executive elections, 1990–2005.
Source: Calculations based on author's database.

Figure 8.1 shows the number of multiethnic opposition coalitions as a share of the total number of elections in that time period. What is immediately striking is the absence of a time trend in the data: there is no continuous increase or decrease in the incidence of opposition electoral coordination over time. The ratio of opposition coalitions is 50% for the 26 elections held between 1990 and 1994. This ratio falls to 32% for the 24 elections held in 1995–1999, but then rises to 44% for the 35 elections held in 2000–2005.[4] More critically, these opposition coalitions are substantively important, accounting for over half of executive turnover – 15 of 27 cases – seen in the same time period. The opposition coalitions identified for each election are listed in Appendix D.

I separately confirm that this coding of the dependent variable – the formation of a multiethnic opposition coalition – reflects actual political alignments by comparing it against the total number of presidential candidates registered for an election as well as the effective number of presidential candidates resulting from that election. If the opposition coalitions identified here are being formed through the coordination of endorsements across ethnic lines, then one would expect to find fewer candidates in these elections when compared with those where no such endorsements are made. The data corroborate this observable implication. There are, on average, two fewer presidential

---

[4] Only in three of the 16 years under review were no opposition coalitions formed: 1993, 1997, and 1998.

candidates registered for elections in which pre-electoral opposition coalitions are formed: 6.3 versus 8.3 candidates. The difference in means between these two samples is statistically significant in a one-tailed test ($p = 0.0411$). The effective number of candidates also declines in elections with pre-electoral opposition coalitions: 2.47 versus 2.95 candidates. The difference in means between these two samples just misses standard statistical significance in a one-tailed test ($p = 0.0572$).

HYPOTHESES AND MEASURES

This book attributes the formation of multiethnic opposition coalitions to the business sector's relative autonomy from state-controlled capital, but the comparativist and Africanist literatures also present unambiguous expectations about the impact of other institutional, political, and sociological factors on the electoral behavior of politicians. I summarize here the relevant explanations, providing falsifiable hypotheses along with a description of the variables used in the analysis. While these hypotheses offer distinct causal mechanisms, they are not necessarily mutually exclusive. All could be influencing the likelihood of opposition coalition formation on some level. The empirical analysis that follows will enable us to assess each mechanism's plausibility as well as to gauge its explanatory power when compared with the alternatives.

The Financial Autonomy of Business

This book began from the premise that coalition bargaining in Africa's inchoate multiparty systems suffers from a credible commitment problem: it requires trading a promise of future power-sharing for electoral support tangibly demonstrated today. Unless a coalition formateur can make a self-binding commitment to that promise before the election is held, her partners have reason to fear that, were the coalition to win, the formateur could maximize her own welfare by reneging. The formateur can easily and unilaterally renegotiate the pre-electoral bargain once in office; she can choose to give less than what was promised or nothing at all. This would leave the opposition politician who devoted time and energy to getting the formateur elected with no pay-off.[5] Lacking some enforceable means for honoring the pre-electoral bargain, such a politician may therefore choose to reject power-sharing promises from a potential formateur.

---

[5] Consider that this opposition politician, in choosing to support another, might open herself up to another form of risk. Politicians, even those from small ethnic groups, run for the presidency not because they believe they can win, but because it enhances their status among constituents as players on the national scene who can potentially negotiate their way into the government. Not running for office – to stand down in favor of another candidate – exposes a politician to the risk of losing that leadership status, since another coethnic might choose to vie for the presidency and thereby usurp her mantle. In the worst of all possible scenarios, this opposition politician backs a losing coalition candidate and loses control of her ethnic constituency to a rival.

I argue that opposition politicians in African countries have sought to alleviate the credible commitment problem through the distribution of private resources, which, in poor countries, must largely come from the business community. If greater financial freedom permits entrepreneurs to identify their interests separately from those of the incumbent, and thereby encourages them to diversify their campaign donations, then the resources available to the opposition should be expected to rise. The opposition politician bankrolled by business is better positioned to become a coalition formateur because she can give other politicians upfront payments that compensate them *ex ante* for the possibility that power-sharing promises may not be honored *ex post*. These payments can range from subsidies for a politician's electioneering in a particular constituency to direct cash payments made to a party leader.

The ability of a coalition formateur to offer such bargains on a national scale will critically depend on the financial autonomy of business. As explained in previous chapters, this is problematic in much of Africa because statist controls have historically enabled incumbents to use the threat of reprisals to induce the cooperation of business. Opposition coalitions are therefore most likely to emerge in liberalized financial systems in which the flow of private resources does not depend on the discretion of government officials. This leads to the first hypothesis.

H_1: *Greater financial autonomy for business should be associated with an increased likelihood of multiethnic opposition coalition formation.*

To test H_1, which represents this book's principal argument, the dependent variables examined in previous chapters are now employed as explanatory variables at this point in the analysis: the total number of commercial banks, the availability of credit to the private sector, and the tenure of the chamber of commerce president. These variables serve as indicators of the broader conceptual variable, the dependence of business on state-controlled capital. Greater political control over finance capital in African countries has historically been associated with restricted access, while financial liberalization has led to the loosening of that control. The evidence presented in Chapter 4 demonstrated that post-independence presidents sought to neutralize the mobilization of opposition by limiting capital accumulation among rival groups, which meant restricting the number of commercial banks. This was a legacy that persisted across time. In this respect, countries with a larger number of banks are expected to show a greater incidence of multiethnic opposition coalition building.

Chapter 5 showed that leaders of resource-poor countries were more likely to adopt financial reforms, including the relaxation of capital controls, while those with larger patronage-based coalitions were less likely to adopt such measures. It further confirmed that the countries that undergo financial liberalization subsequently show statistically significant higher levels of credit provision to the private sector. According to Beck et al. (1999), private credit as a share of GDP provides a measure of the extent to which financial intermediaries channel savings to investors. Higher levels of private credit provision are therefore expected to increase the likelihood of multiethnic opposition coalition formation.

Chapter 6 established that the tenure of chamber of commerce presidents is significantly shaped by the extent of capital controls rather than solely by the legal model governing the chamber's organization. Business communities dependent on the state for access to capital appear more likely to support longer presidencies in the chamber of commerce in order to cultivate political connections. Countries with shorter tenures, reflecting business' relative independence from the state, are therefore expected to have a greater likelihood of multiethnic opposition coalition formation. In the analysis, the tenure of the chamber president is also interacted with the chamber's legal framework, since the autonomy of business should be more pronounced when business is self-organizing under the private law model.

GDP growth averaged over a five-year period is added to the models to control for the general availability of private resources. Entrepreneurs may be less willing to finance the opposition in difficult times, and, conversely, more willing in periods of growth. In effect, this measure of growth could reflect the opposition's liquidity constraint. An increase in GDP growth should increase the probability of multiethnic opposition coalition building either by increasing the number of entrepreneurs willing to make political contributions or by increasing the average size of those contributions. For the analysis, GDP growth is averaged over the five-year period prior to an election.

Attributing opposition coalition building to economic growth may seem to contradict the established empirical findings linking incumbent reelection to economic performance (Kramer 1971; Nannestad and Paldam 1994; Powell and Whitten 1993). An alternative explanation for the emergence of a multiethnic opposition coalition could be stated in terms of the classic economic vote function: voters are satisfied with the incumbent's management of a growing economy, so they are more likely to reelect him. Recognizing that the incumbent is now in a stronger electoral position, opposition politicians would respond by coalescing. In the context of Africa, however, opposition strategies are unlikely to be induced by the fear that economic growth will favor the incumbent at the polls.[6] According to the Afrobarometer surveys conducted in 12 countries in the region, two-thirds of respondents typically rate their economies negatively. And most respondents largely believe their personal living standards have been falling over time (Bratton and Cho 2006).

Patronage Politics

The centralized and personalized control of patronage in the hands of the incumbent is generally believed to make multiethnic opposition coalitions

---

[6] The Afrobarometer surveys were conducted in 12 African countries in three rounds between 1999 and 2006. The surveys pose a standard set of questions in local languages with a randomly selected, nationally representative sample size of 1,200 respondents in each country.

unlikely. Because the distribution of state resources occurs at the executive's discretion – all clientelistic networks ultimately have their source at the state's apex – political actors come to depend on the incumbent's largesse for the means to maintain their own leadership positions (Chabal and Daloz 1999; van de Walle 2007). The incumbent's singular control of patronage resources means that alternative coalitions to the one in power are unlikely to be formed. As long as the incumbent possesses the means with which to selectively purchase the support or the silence of rivals, opposition politicians have an incentive to focus their coalition-building efforts with the incumbent rather than each other.

The patronage literature generally depicts opposition bargaining as a prisoner's dilemma: bargaining among opposition politicians breaks down because each politician seeks to maximize his own payoff by negotiating him or herself into the incumbent's patronage network rather than bargaining with his or her opposition counterparts. To accomplish this, incumbents merely need to extend their clientelistic networks to bring "into their ranks the hungriest of their 'opponents' to help put a modern veneer on the status quo" (Monga 1997, 169). The repeated entry of opposition leaders into the governments of their rivals – as has occurred in Cameroon, Gabon, Kenya, and Senegal – underscores their tenuous autonomy vis-à-vis the executive's patronage.

H_2: *Greater access to patronage resources should enable incumbents to lower the likelihood of multiethnic opposition coalition formation.*

While all African incumbents have expansive powers and share the same incentive to hold onto power, what distinguishes them is their abilities to deploy patronage resources. In other words, incumbents are distinguished by their constraints, not their inclinations to use patronage. Government expenditure as a percentage of GDP is used as a rough proxy for incumbent patronage resources. The more a government involves itself in economic activities, the more leverage it can exercise over business. A greater state presence in the economy should lead entrepreneurs to deprive the opposition of resources, leaving those politicians more vulnerable to cooptation by the incumbent. This variable is therefore expected to have a negative impact on the formation of multiethnic opposition coalitions.

Those incumbents who can exploit rents from oil or aid are better placed to demobilize the opposition through cooptation. In Sao Tome e Principe, for example, the discovery of significant offshore oil deposits altered the balance between government and opposition parties. No party had managed to simultaneously control the executive and legislative branches between 1994 and 2001. But between the July 2001 presidential election and March 2002 parliamentary election, the country's political parties signed a pact for the formation of a government of national unity. Commentators noted that "nobody wanted to be outside the government when the first petrodollars arrived" (Deegan 2003, 5).

The incumbent's resource rents are captured through a dummy variable for countries in which oil represents over one third of merchandise exports. Ross (1999), later amended by Dunning (2008), has shown that natural resource dependence can impede the development of democracy in poorer states. Since incumbents who can tap into oil rents have deeper pockets than their counterparts in nonoil states, they should be more likely to coopt opposition politicians and thereby reduce the likelihood of their coordination. Jensen and Wantchekon (2004) have corroborated this finding with data on Africa.[7] There are 12 established oil-producing states in the region; two others, Mauritania and Sao Tome e Principe, are new producers; 17 others have negotiated either concessions or ongoing explorations.[8]

Aid as a percentage of GDP is used to capture the possibility that incumbents who can exploit external revenue sources have a greater capacity to coopt their opposition. Incumbents whose income is not tied to the productivity of the domestic economy may engage in greater predation (Bates 2001; Knack 2001), enabling them to present opposition politicians with more attractive offers. The expected effect of aid on multiethnic opposition coalition building is thus expected to be negative.

Political Institutions

The comparative literature has consistently shown that politicians' choices over strategies are greatly influenced by the institutional context in which they compete for power. We should expect to find that different electoral rules and power-sharing arrangements will affect the likelihood of multiethnic opposition coalition formation, particularly for executive elections. Cox (1997) hypothesizes that linkage – the ability of parties to coordinate nationally across electoral districts – depends on the strength of electoral rules. The incentives to coalesce are expected to be higher in a plurality system because weaker candidates will be induced to ally with the two most viable candidates. And they should decrease under a runoff system, since it becomes more difficult for politicians to determine whether they can benefit from strategic voting under such a system. However, using a sample of African cases, van de Walle (2006) finds that the two-round majority system is associated with greater opposition coalition building in Africa. In this view, opposition politicians are able to use the first round to gauge their respective levels of support and then unite as they move into the second round. He notes that 11 of 18 cases of opposition victory in the region have occurred in countries with runoff systems.

[7] None of these works explicitly links resource rents to the cooptation of elites. Their analyses focus instead on the relationship between the ruling regime and the general population, explaining how rents could be employed to win voter support or repress groups. Jensen and Wantchekon (2004, 821) do note that "incumbents may simply use the natural resource rents to buy off the opposition."

[8] See Philippe Perdrix, "De nouveaux eldorados," *Jeune Afrique/L'Intelligent*, 25 December 2005, pp. 83–85.

Empirical studies of African elections raise doubts about the extent to which institutional variables may drive the bargaining among opposition politicians. While the literature on electoral rules has established that the number of parties is correlated with the strength of electoral rules, Golder and Wantchekon (2004) find that the number of parties is not necessarily higher under more permissive electoral rules. They reason that the lack of experience with electoral institutions in the region, coupled with the geographic concentration of ethnic groups, may account for a larger number of parties, regardless of electoral rules. Dominant party systems have emerged in countries using both first-past-the-post and proportional representation systems (Mozaffar 2002; Rakner and Svasand 2002; van Cranenburgh 2003). Nevertheless, the received wisdom on electoral rules offers a clear hypothesis.

H_3: *Plurality rules should increase the likelihood of multiethnic opposition coalition formation.*

A dichotomous variable indicates whether a country's executive elections are held under a runoff system. According to H_3, the likelihood of multiethnic opposition coalition formation should be lower in runoff systems because opposition politicians will want to put off negotiations until after the first round in order to engage in bargaining that is backed with information about their respective vote shares.

A relevant control in this context is democratic experience. Corroborating Golder and Wantchekon's intuition, Kuenzi and Lambright (2001) find a divergence in party system institutionalization between those countries with established multipartism and newer democracies. Lindberg (2006) argues that elections have a "self-reinforcing power," finding that repeated elections improve a country's level of democracy, whether measured in terms of fair elections or civil liberties. And all the cases of opposition victory in van de Walle's (2006) study of opposition coalitions occurred in countries considered free or partly free according to Freedom House. I therefore control for a country's democratic experience with a simple count of previous multiparty elections. The likelihood of a multiethnic opposition coalition forming is expected to be greater as politicians adapt to the exigencies of electoral competition under relatively open conditions.

H_4: *Greater democratic experience should increase the likelihood of multiethnic opposition coalition formation.*

Three sources of data provide measures to control for the quality of democracy. The Polity score from the Polity IV Project (Marshall and Jaggers 2009) provides an aggregate measure for the institutionalization of democratic and authoritarian tendencies within the political system. Opposition coordination should be less likely to occur in countries with lower Polity scores. The Cingranelli and Richards (2007) human rights data set provides an alternative empowerment index, which is a composite measure of government respect for basic freedoms of association, participation, and speech. Additionally, since a regime's authoritarian instruments are more likely to be activated in the service of an entrenched ruler, a dichotomous measure is used to control for whether the incumbent is running for reelection.

Ethnic Cleavages

The fragmentation of opposition parties in African countries could be attributed to the ethnic heterogeneity of their societies. Because multiparty competition is considered a zero-sum game, the selection of one ethnic group's candidate could be perceived as making that group better off at the expense of others. A more nuanced version of this argument suggests that heterogeneity itself is not the problem. It is the very ethnic nature of political mobilization that discourages political compromise. Because parties in multiethnic societies can most easily mobilize mass support by advancing communal appeals, candidates end up competing for votes among coethnics by seeking to outbid each other in championing the interests of their particular group within the broader political arena (Horowitz 1985; Rabushka and Shepsle 1972). The demands articulated by ethnic parties thus become increasingly extreme, making political compromise more difficult as competing ethnic interests become irreconcilable. In Kenya, for example, it has been argued that "[t]he fragmentation of the opposition along ethnic lines is one of the main reasons why Moi ... survived two multiparty elections" (Carey 2002, 59).

H_5: *Increasing heterogeneity should decrease the likelihood of multiethnic opposition coalition formation.*

Some scholars suggest that achieving compromise is particularly difficult when the social structure is polarized. Control of the state becomes vital to each group's future if all sides believe that the eventual political victor will have no incentive to share power or distribute resources, creating the fear of permanent political exclusion. Lijphart (1977) finds democracy most at risk of breakdown when "there are two major segmental parties, two stable alliance parties, or a majority party confronting two or more smaller parties." According to Horowitz (1985), ethnic conflict arises when "a few groups are so large that their interactions are a constant theme of politics at the center." Empirical studies suggest that the relationship between ethnic heterogeneity and political compromise is nonlinear. Collier (1998) finds that politics are most likely to turn violent in societies found at a middle range of ethnic diversity; highly diverse societies are found to be even less conflict-prone than relatively homogeneous societies. Similarly, Bates (1999b) finds that violence rises when one ethnic group approaches half or more of the total population, suggesting that the fear of permanent political exclusion may encourage other groups to turn to violence as a political strategy. These insights suggest that that bargaining across polarized cleavages makes compromise more difficult.

H_6: *Ethnic polarization should decrease the likelihood of multiethnic opposition coalition formation.*

I use Fearon's (2003) ethnic fractionalization index to capture the potential number of social cleavages that might be politically activated in a country. Following the original ethno-linguistic fractionalization index (Atlas Narodov Mira 1964), this measure offers a statistic for the likelihood that two people chosen at random will be from different ethnic groups. A higher ethnic fractionalization score is expected, according to H_5, to be associated with a lower likelihood of opposition coalition formation.

For the purposes of H_6, I use Reynal-Querol's (2002) measure of ethnic polarization. This index attains a maximum value of 1 when society is divided into two equal-sized groups and a minimum value of 0 either when the society is completely homogenous or every person belongs to a different group. Increasing polarization is expected to decrease the likelihood of opposition coalition formation.

EXPLAINING THE FORMATION OF MULTIETHNIC OPPOSITION COALITIONS

I estimate a binomial logistic regression model to assess whether my theory of pecuniary coalition building can account for the variation across African countries. The units of analysis are executive elections held between 1990 and 2005.[9] Recall how multiethnic opposition coalitions are identified for each election: a coalition endorses a single candidate for executive office; a coalition represents more than one ethnic group or region; a coalition is formed prior to the election in a plurality system or the first round in a runoff system. This information is used to code the dependent variable dichotomously: 1 if a subset of opposition parties competed as a multiethnic coalition for an executive election; 0 if no such coalition was formed. The model includes explanatory variables intended to test competing theories associated with financial controls, political patronage, ethnic cleavages, and electoral institutions. The description, measurement, and source of all variables are listed in Appendix C. All explanatory variables are lagged in the analysis. The elections in the sample are listed in Appendix D along with their respective multiethnic opposition coalitions.

Table 8.1 reports the results from the binomial logistic analysis of multiethnic opposition coalition formation. The results are shown in log-odds units,

---

[9] I examine only elections in which more than one candidate was permitted to run for office. This sample of executive elections includes parliamentary races from Botswana, Ethiopia, Mauritius, and South Africa. I reason that these cases should be counted as executive elections, since each party's candidate for prime minister or president is known before the time of election. Moreover, in these countries, the powers of the prime ministers (Ethiopia and Mauritius) or the presidents elected by parliament (Botswana and South Africa) are as expansive as those of their counterparts in presidential systems.

TABLE 8.1. *The Determinants of Opposition Coalition Formation*

	Model 1	Model 2	Model 3
Number of commercial banks	0.098**		
	(0.050)		
Private credit provision, % GDP		0.065**	
		(0.032)	
Private law chamber of commerce			3.228***
			(1.028)
Tenure of chamber president			0.211**
			(0.100)
Private law chamber × tenure			-0.482***
			(0.156)
GDP growth, 5-year average	0.298***	0.383***	0.340**
	(0.112)	(0.122)	(0.150)
GDP per capita, log	0.576	-0.213	0.388
	(0.354)	(0.560)	(0.580)
Polity score	-0.079	-0.075	-0.005
	(0.059)	(0.059)	(0.065)
Runoff system	0.162	0.005	0.319
	(0.748)	(0.651)	(0.976)
Ethnic fractionalization	1.403	1.528	3.118
	(1.870)	(2.168)	(2.902)
Government expenditure, % GDP	-0.114**	-0.116**	0.012
	(0.050)	(0.058)	(0.143)
Oil exporter	-3.159**	-0.734	-2.836
	(1.323)	(1.841)	(3.212)
Constant	-5.104*	-1.030	-7.921
	(2.683)	(3.415)	(6.908)
Observations	76	76	61
Log likelihood	-40.64	-40.24	-29.35
Pseudo R^2	0.1957	0.2036	0.2890

(continued)

TABLE 8.1. *(continued)*

	Model 4	Model 5	Model 6	Model 7	Model 8	Model 9	Model 10
Private credit provision, % GDP	0.048**	0.062***	0.059***	0.048**	0.062***	0.067***	0.0615***
	(0.020)	(0.019)	(0.019)	(0.019)	(0.019)	(0.019)	(0.019)
GDP growth, 5-year average	0.310***	0.317***	0.309***	0.281**	0.320***	0.356***	0.338***
	(0.105)	(0.117)	(0.120)	(0.117)	(0.117)	(0.136)	(0.127)
Government expenditure, % GDP	−0.130***	−0.124**	−0.119**	−0.122**	−0.123**	−0.087	−0.126**
	(0.047)	(0.056)	(0.058)	(0.049)	(0.056)	(0.059)	(0.058)
Number of previous multiparty elections		0.150	0.125	0.016	0.147	0.254	0.129
		(0.169)	(0.174)	(0.159)	(0.168)	(0.196)	(0.183)
Opposition coalition in previous election		1.393*	1.384	0.760	1.400	0.900	1.584*
		(0.839)	(0.871)	(0.701)	(0.854)	(0.903)	(0.962)
Regime years		−0.000	0.002	0.018	−0.000	−0.009	0.018
		(0.026)	(0.028)	(0.024)	(0.026)	(0.027)	(0.027)
Polity score		−0.143**	−0.143**		−0.145**	−0.146**	−0.156**
		(0.062)	(0.062)		(0.064)	(0.063)	(0.071)
Foreign aid, % GDP			−0.005				
			(0.023)				
Oil exporter			−0.936				
			(1.423)				
Empowerment index				−0.083			
				(0.142)			
Incumbent competes in election					−0.152		
					(0.777)		

	(1)	(2)	(3)	(4)	(5)	(6)	(7)
Ethnic polarization						−3.514* (2.010)	
Incumbent from plurality group							−1.980* (1.060)
Constant	−0.452 (0.678)	−1.300 (0.944)	−1.163 (1.146)	−0.444 (1.046)	−1.207 (1.072)	0.036 (1.257)	0.504 (0.756)
Observations	76	76	76	76	76	72	73
Log likelihood	−42.02	−38.84	−38.53	−40.76	−38.81	−36.06	−35.51
Pseudo R^2	0.168	0.231	0.237	0.193	0.232	0.257	0.262

Notes: The dependent variable is the formation of a multiethnic opposition coalition. All independent variables are lagged. Robust standard errors are in parentheses. *** $p < 0.01$, ** $p < 0.05$, * $p < 0.10$, two-tailed tests.

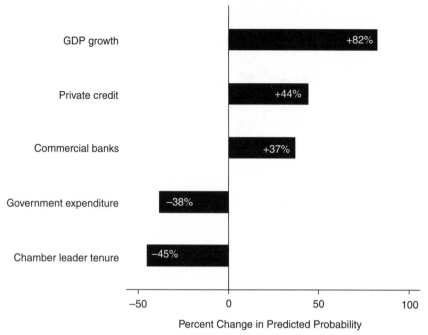

FIGURE 8.2. Determinants of opposition coalition formation.
Note: Each bar represents the percentage change in the predicted probability of a multi-ethnic opposition coalition being formed when the corresponding independent variable increases by one standard deviation from the regional mean, *ceteris paribus.*

which are difficult to interpret directly. I convert them into predicted probabilities to provide a more intuitive discussion of how each independent variable affects the likelihood that a multiethnic opposition coalition will emerge. Models 1 through 3 in Table 8.1 present a base model specification with alternating measures for the financial autonomy of business – the number of commercial banks, private credit provision, and the tenure of the chamber of commerce president interacted with the chamber's legal framework.

All model specifications in Table 8.1 provide support for H_1: the likelihood of a multiethnic opposition coalition being formed significantly increases with the financial autonomy of business. The log odds reported for the indicators of business' financial autonomy all have their expected sign and are significantly different from zero. Figure 8.2 summarizes the findings in terms of the percentage change in the predicted probability of a multiethnic opposition coalition forming when each of the main independent variables increases by one standard deviation from the regional mean, holding all other variables constant. Taken together, these findings corroborate the book's broader claim that the resources of business are critical for the electoral coordination of opposition politicians across ethnic cleavages in African countries. Coalition formateurs are far more likely to successfully conclude electoral bargains when they have

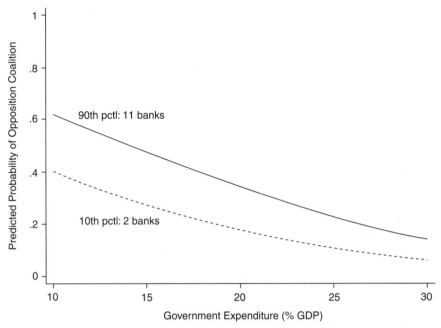

FIGURE 8.3. Predicted probability of opposition coalition and commercial banking access.

the resources with which to provide upfront payments that compensate opposition politicians for their endorsements.

Chapter 4 established that African leaders sought to repress commercial banking when their coethnics were not from cash crop–growing regions, fearing that capital accumulation in such areas could be used to organize challenges to their authority. Model 1 in Table 8.1 employs the number of commercial banks as a measure of the relative freedom of business to access banking. This version of the model correctly classifies 70% of the outcomes. Suggesting that the early strategy of African leaders has had a long-lasting impact on opposition coordination, this explanatory variable has the predicted positive sign and attains the 0.05 significance level. Expanding the number of commercial banks from the regional mean by one standard deviation, from six to twelve banks, would be expected to increase the predicted probability of opposition coalition formation from 0.38 to 0.52, holding all other variables at their mean values and dummy variables at their modal values.[10] Based on the estimates from Model 1, Figure 8.3 illustrates how expanding the commercial banking sector from the 10th to the 90th percentile increases the likelihood of opposition politicians

[10] The simulated values were generated through the Clarify program (Tomz et al. 2001). The independent variables in Model 1 are set at the mean or modal values reported in Appendix C: commercial banks = 6, GDP growth = 2.9, GDP per capita = 5.9, Polity = –2.9, runoff system = 1, ethnic fractionalization = 0.73, government expenditure = 14.6, and oil exporter = 0.

forming a multiethnic coalition. Figure 8.3 also shows that such an expansion would help to offset the disadvantages faced by the opposition at higher levels of government expenditure, which I discuss further below.

The case of Botswana provides a concrete example of how banking might reflect the financial dependence of business. Although Botswana is often lauded as democratic exemplar when contrasted with other African countries, the persistent fragmentation found among opposition parties in that country might be linked to the ruling party's powerful influence over business. The Botswana Democratic Party (BDP) has been able to remain in office without interruption since 1966 partly because opposition parties have been unable to secure support from business. Using rents from diamond mining, the BDP has managed to augment its financial influence without having to undertake strategies usually employed in other African countries, that is, nationalizing commercial banks, making equity investments in them, or imposing burdensome administrative controls. Instead, it has used private-sector development schemes to allocate credit on a political basis (Danevad 1995; Good 1994; Molutsi 2004; Tsie 1996), while restricting entry into the banking sector to a relatively small number of institutions, none of which is locally owned (Harvey 1998). The country has had only four commercial banks, on average, since 1985 despite enjoying a nearly continuous economic expansion during that time period.[11]

Botswana's business community cannot afford to support the opposition without putting its connections with the BDP – and its main links to financing – at risk. This is why, during the 2004 parliamentary elections, the ruling party could announce that it had received approximately half a million dollars from the business community, while opposition candidates were forced to run self-financed campaigns (Molomo and Sebudubedu 2005).[12] David Magang, a BDP member of parliament from 1979 to 2002 and a minister under two presidents, is explicit about this relationship in his autobiography: "the opposition has always been at a disadvantage, primarily because they lack the requisite resources to mount a campaign on the same footing as that of the ruling BDP.... For example, it is no secret that the BDP enjoys substantial financial support from certain corporate heavyweights with huge foreign investment (the party's sources of external funding, though acknowledged, are a closely guarded secret known only to the president and the party treasurer)" (Magang 2008, 460–461).

Although politics and business are inextricably linked in all countries, the near total allegiance of business to Botswana's ruling party is suggestive of a

---

[11] Author's calculation based on entries in annual volumes of *Africa South of the Sahara* (Europa Publications Limited 1971–2006).

[12] The BDP raised a similar amount from undisclosed sources for the 1999 elections (Somolekae 2005). Also, in 2004, Satar Dada, an appointed MP and one of Botswana's richest men, provided the BDP with 57 new vehicles for the election campaign. Dada is the owner of the local Toyota and Land Rover franchises, while Land Rover also happens to be the vehicle of choice for the Botswana Defense Forces (Good and Taylor 2006).

deep-rooted dynamic aimed at sustaining the status quo.[13] When Mbiganyi Charles Tibone retired from his position as chairman of Barclays Bank, the country's largest bank, he was elected to parliament as a member of BDP in the 2004 elections and quickly appointed as the minister for minerals, energy, and water.[14] That same year, Neo Moroka, a former president of the Botswana Confederation of Commerce and Manpower (BOCCIM) who made his early career at Barclays Bank, left his position as managing director of British Petroleum Botswana to become an elected member of parliament for the BDP and was subsequently appointed trade minister.

Chapter 5 showed that private credit provision has been higher in African countries that liberalized the financial sector. In Table 8.1, Model 2 uses private credit provision as an alternate measure for business' access to capital. The estimated effects of private credit provision also corroborate the theory of pecuniary coalition building (H_1). This specification of the model correctly classifies 71% of outcomes. The results in Model 2 suggest that increasing the provision of private credit from the regional mean by one standard deviation, from 13.4% to 22.9%, would increase the predicted probability of multiethnic opposition coalition formation from 0.34 to 0.49, holding all other variables at their mean or modal values.[15] Figure 8.4 uses the estimates from Model 2 to illustrate how raising the level of private credit provision from the 10th to the 90th percentile would increase the predicted probability of opposition politicians coalescing, offsetting the advantage that incumbents might gain through government expenditure.

Gabon, where the opposition has remained divided, provides an example of how the supply of credit underpins the business community's allegiance to the ruling party. President Omar Bongo, who made no secret of using his country's oil revenue to sustain a patronage-based regime (Bongo and Routier 2001),[16] aggressively used public resources to bring government and business into a tight embrace while he was in power between 1967 and 2009. The integration of the president's family members and regime allies into Gabonese commerce

---

[13] Opposition parties publicly complained when Barclays' managing director in Botswana, Thulisizwe Johnson, who also happens to be the vice president of the BOCCIM, actively campaigned for the BDP during the 2009 elections. See Lekopanye Mooketsi, "Opposition Attack Barclays Chief for Supporting BDP," *Mmegi/The Reporter* (Botswana), 17 August 2009.

[14] Conflicts inevitably arise when business and politics are combined. Botswana's former president, Festus Mogae, has sued Mbiganyi Charles Tibone in court under allegations of investment fraud. See Gideon Nkala, "Trade Secrets Spilled in Tibone/Mogae Case," *Mmegi/The Reporter* (Botswana), 11 July 2008; Isaiah Morewagae, "Big Shots Trade Accusations in Court," *Mmegi/The Reporter* (Botswana), 29 July 2009.

[15] The independent variables in Model 2 are set at the mean or modal values reported in Appendix C: private credit = 13.4, GDP growth = 2.9, GDP per capita = 5.9, Polity = −2.9, runoff system = 1, ethnic fractionalization = 0.73, government expenditure = 14.6, and oil exporter = 0.

[16] See also "Interview with Gabonese President Bongo on Situation in Gabon, CAR," *Radio France Internationale*, Paris, 29 October 2003; Xan Rice, "Papa Bongo's 40 Years in Power," *The Guardian* (London), 5 May 2008, p. 15.

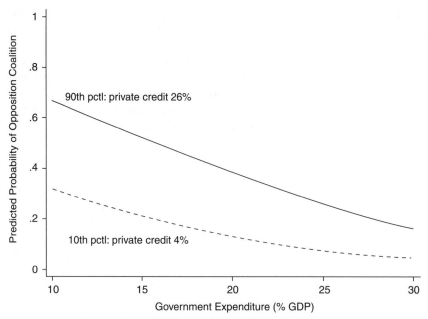

FIGURE 8.4. Predicted probability of opposition coalition and private credit provision.

is especially apparent in the area of finance.[17] BGFI Bank, for example, is the country's leading commercial bank precisely because it is considered "the regime's financial control tower"[18] or "the president's bank."[19] Prominent local entrepreneurs control the bank's shares in partnership with the president's relatives and other members of the ruling party.[20] BGFI's president, Patrice Otha, simultaneously served as Bongo's deputy chief of staff, while BGFI's managing director, Henri Claude Oyima, is a Bongo relative who also served as his informal financial advisor, all while being president of the Confédération Patronale Gabonaise, the country's employers' association.[21]

The overlapping membership in Gabon's political and financial circles mirrors the state's continued influence over access to private credit. Following the collapse of oil prices in the mid-1980s, the role of the state in mediating that

[17] Philippe Perdrix, "Comment gérer l'après-Bongo," *Jeune Afrique*, 16 July 2009.

[18] "Omar Bongo se blinde d'avocats," *La Lettre du Continent*, 26 March 2009.

[19] "Recherche président désespérément," *Jeune Afrique*, 16 July 2009.

[20] "BGFIBank, un établissement en or à Libreville," *La Lettre du Continent*, 14 June 2001; "Ces discrètes petites banques d'affaires," *La Lettre du Continent*, 9 November 2006; "BGFIBank, nouveau jackpot en 2007," *La Lettre du Continent*, 19 June 2008; "Qui va hériter de la cagnotte en or?," *La Lettre du Continent*, 25 June 2009.

[21] "Mobilisation générale au palais," *La Lettre du Continent*, 21 April 2005; "Qui sont 'les indéboulonnables'?," *La Lettre du Continent*, 8 November 2007.

access was magnified as the number of commercial banks was halved and the provision of private credit collapsed. During the 1990s, precisely when opposition politicians would need to turn to business for campaign contributions, Gabonese entrepreneurs found that their access to credit was increasingly limited, and if they wanted continued access to that financing, they would more than likely have to deal with a bank connected to the state. Between 1990 and 2000, the state held equity stakes in four of the country's six commercial banks with an average of 25.9%.[22] Such a figure underestimates the government's actual influence in banking because the state has tended to take equity shares in the country's largest banks, often retaining close ties with their management. Etienne Mouvagha Tchioba, for example, is the long-time president of Banque Internationale pour le Commerce et l'Industrie du Gabon, a bank which is at least 25% state-owned and one of the country's largest. Mouvagha Tchioba is a former government minister who left the ruling party in the 1990s to start his own party, though he continued to consider himself part of the presidential majority allied to the president. After Bongo's death in 2009, he formally rejoined the ruling party now led by Ali Bongo Ondimba, Bongo's son. Under such conditions, with the country's principal banks so clearly linked to the regime, few in the business community would be willing to put their credit lines in jeopardy to support any opposition candidate.

Chapter 6 established that the business community adapts its organization, as reflected in the chamber of commerce, to prevailing conditions in finance. The tenure of the chamber of commerce president was shown to be systematically longer under stricter financial controls. In Table 8.1, Model 3 employs this proxy for business autonomy by including the number of years served by the chamber president, a dummy variable for countries with private law chambers, and an interaction between the two. This specification of the model correctly classifies 75% of outcomes, though with a smaller sample due to missing observations. Again, the results corroborate the expectations of pecuniary coalition building.

Model 3 suggests that the impact of the chamber president's tenure depends on the legal framework governing the organization of business. The three variables together indicate that longer tenures lower the likelihood of multiethnic opposition coalition formation only under private law chambers. When the tenure of a private law chamber president is extended by one standard deviation, from the regional mean of 4.6 years to 8.6 years, the predicted probability falls from 0.53 to 0.29, holding all other variables at their mean and modal values.[23]

---

[22] Author's calculation based on entries in annual volumes of *Africa South of the Sahara* (Europa Publications Limited 1971–2006).

[23] The independent variables in Model 3 are set at the mean or modal values reported in Appendix C: chamber leader tenure = 4.6, GDP growth = 2.9, GDP per capita = 5.9, Polity = −2.9, runoff system = 1, ethnic fractionalization = 0.73, government expenditure = 14.6, and oil exporter = 0.

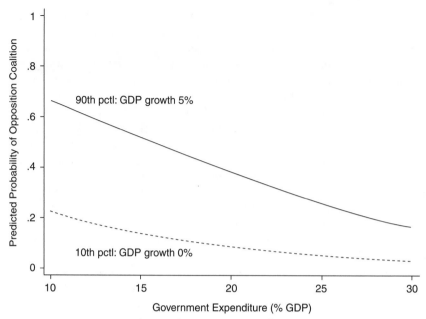

FIGURE 8.5. Predicted probability of opposition coalition and GDP growth.

All model specifications in Table 8.1 show that GDP growth, possibly reflecting liquidity within the business community, has a positive impact on multiethnic opposition coalition building, as illustrated in Figure 8.5. The estimated log odds from Model 2 indicate that doubling average growth from 3% to 6%, a one standard deviation increase from the regional mean, would also nearly double the predicted probability of opposition coalition formation from 0.34 to 0.62, holding all other variables at their mean and modal values. The estimated effects of economic growth on the opposition's electoral coordination reinforce a pattern from the data. Multiethnic opposition coalitions were forged in African countries where economic growth was a full percentage point higher, on average, than the sample mean. Only one of the 32 opposition coalitions in the sample coincides with economic decline: Liberia in 2005.

The variables used to proxy for the influence of patronage in Table 8.1 are government expenditure, oil production, and foreign aid. These variables generally move in the expected negative direction, but they perform inconsistently in support of H_2: a greater capacity for patronage distribution should be systematically associated with opposition fragmentation. Most models show that higher levels of government expenditure will lower the likelihood of multiethnic opposition coalition formation, as illustrated in Figures 8.3 through 8.5. According to Model 2, a one standard deviation increase in government expenditure from the regional mean, a move from 14.6% to 21.1% of GDP, would reduce the predicted probability from 0.34 to 0.21, holding all other variables at their mean or modal values.[24] This finding confirms the general intuition among Africanist scholars that incumbents manipulate the distribution of state resources in order to reinforce their hold on power. More specifically, in the context of this study, the finding suggests that opposition politicians are less likely to secure the support of business as the state's presence in the economy increases.

The variables for foreign aid and oil exporters, shown in Model 6, are statistically indistinguishable from zero. Other patronage measures that failed to attain statistical significance, though not reported here, include the number of cabinet ministers, aid per capita, and a dummy variable for mineral exporters. It may be the case that the lack of statistical significance is due to the quality of the measures employed in the analysis; they may not adequately capture the mechanism by which incumbents exercise their influence on the opposition. Alternatively, the impact of certain variables may be operating through the indicators for business' financial autonomy. Oil exporters, for example, were shown in Chapter 5 to have significantly lower levels of private credit provision.

The institutional variables generally fail to show any consistent impact on the ability of opposition politicians to form multiethnic coalitions. Contrary to the expectation in H_3, the effect of the runoff system is statistically indistinguishable from zero. This variable fails to achieve statistical significance in Models 1 through 3. The empirical record indicates that opposition parties are somewhat more likely to endorse a single coalition candidate when competing under plurality systems than runoff systems, though this difference is not statistically significant. There are 11 instances of opposition coalitions among the 26 elections held under plurality rules (42%). In runoff systems, opposition coalitions were formed before the first round in 21 of 59 elections (36%). This number is surprisingly high, given that the runoff system is thought to encourage politicians to adopt a wait-and-see approach, as they use their first-round votes to bargain with whomever moves into the second round. But the logic of delaying coalition bargaining until after first-round may be influenced by the fact that opposition politicians also understand the incumbent's motivation to avoid a runoff – precisely because it creates a focal candidate for the opposition. While two-thirds of the sample holds elections under a runoff system, only 20 of 59 executive elections, or slightly over one-third of such elections, required a runoff between 1990 and 2005.

There is no systematic evidence to support the argument of H_4 that opposition politicians are more likely to form alliances under more established or more practiced democracy. The emergence of multiethnic opposition coalitions does not appear to be associated with democratic experience or the quality of democracy. As shown in Models 5 through 10, the log odds on the number of

---

[24] The independent variables in Model 2 are set at the mean or modal values reported in Appendix C: private credit = 13.4, GDP growth = 2.9, GDP per capita = 5.9, Polity = −2.9, runoff system = 1, ethnic fractionalization = 0.73, government expenditure = 14.6, and oil exporter = 0.

previous multiparty elections, as a control for democratic experience, indicate that the likelihood of a multiethnic opposition coalition being formed increases as more elections are held. However, this variable is statistically indistinguishable from zero in all models.

Table 8.1 shows that the conventional indices for the quality of democracy often fail to attain standard levels of statistical significance. The Polity score does not attain statistical significance in Models 1 through 3. And when it does, as in Models 5 through 10, the Polity score moves against the direction expected by H_4, suggesting that opposition coalitions are more likely to emerge under more authoritarian conditions. A plausible interpretation for this result is that opposition politicians may seek to coalesce when they suspect the incumbent will use fraud or some extralegal means to stay in office.[25] But an alternate measure, the CIRI empowerment index, shows no such relationship.[26] Neither does the incumbent's personal participation in the election appear to affect the likelihood of the opposition coalescing, as shown in Model 8. It may be that these measures are too crude to show any effect on opposition behavior. However, this institutional nonresult is consistent with previous work indicating that the patterns in Africa's multiparty politics are not yet fully consistent with institutional theories. One way to read this nonresult is that perhaps formal institutions will not have their predicted effects until politicians enter into stable coordination equilibria in whatever form that may be.

The impact of ethnic cleavages on multiethnic opposition coalition formation is similarly ambiguous. Contradicting the logic of H_5, the estimated log odds on the Fearon (2003) measure of ethnic fractionalization in Models 1 through 3 indicate that greater social diversity is associated with a higher likelihood of opposition coalition formation. But this measure does not attain statistical significance.[27] There are two possible explanations for the apparent lack of influence by ethnic cleavages. One is that the impact of those cleavages may be more difficult to gauge because the distribution of fractionalization scores for African countries is highly skewed, regardless of which index is employed; nearly all African countries appear in the upper quartile when compared across regions. Another factor is the changing nature of political mobilization as a result of ongoing institutional reform. Opposition coalition building may be a national-level game among politicians with identity-based constituencies, but the very basis of those constituencies may be shifting over

[25] But pure coercion is unlikely to be the story. Though not reported here, the models in Table 8.1 were tested with alternate measures for state-related violence. None demonstrated a discernible effect on multiethnic opposition coalition formation. The tested controls included the incumbent's military background, the level of military spending, coup experience, civil war experience, and the CIRI measures for state-sponsored coercion – torture, extrajudicial killing, political imprisonment, and disappearance.

[26] The Freedom House index, as an alternate democracy measure, failed to attain statistical significance.

[27] The results remain the same when the Posner (2004) measure for politically relevant ethnic groups is substituted for the Fearon (2003) index.

time as institutional reforms begin to influence the incentives that politicians have to build minimum-winning coalitions (Posner 2005).

Providing support for H_6, the Reynal-Querol (2002) measure of ethnic polarization attains statistical significance at conventional levels and in the hypothesized direction. Since the literature suggests that ethnic polarization increases the likelihood of conflict, multiethnic opposition coalition building is expected to be less likely in countries where the two largest groups are nearly equally sized versus countries where the population is made up of multiple groups of various sizes. Model 9 shows that greater polarization lowers the likelihood of a multiethnic opposition coalition being formed. The statistical significance of this variable, however, depends on what other controls are added to the model.

The incumbent's potential vote share appears to have no impact on multiethnic opposition coalition building. If the incumbent's own ethnic base of support is sufficiently large, opposition politicians might see little point in forming a coalition that would be a sure loser. But, in Model 10, the dummy variable indicating that an incumbent is from a plurality ethnic group does not attain statistical significance. In fact, the empirical record shows that an incumbent's ethnic membership appears to have little influence on the opposition's electoral calculus: when the incumbent is from the plurality, 38% of those cases have opposition coalitions; when the incumbent is not from the plurality, 35% of the cases have coalitions.[28]

Corroborating this finding, the incumbent's past electoral performance appears to have no relationship with the likelihood of multiethnic opposition coalition formation. The vote share data on 44 relevant African executive elections shows that the incumbent's previous vote share is 54% when the opposition coalesces versus 56% when they fragment. This is not a statistically significant difference. While this suggests that an incumbent's electoral strength has no bearing on the opposition's own coalition bargaining, this is unlikely to be the case. Given the controversy that typically accompanies vote counting in African elections – consider recent elections in Kenya and Zimbabwe – what is more plausible is that opposition politicians do not take the election results as an accurate or reliable measure of the incumbent's true electoral appeal.

CONCLUSION

This chapter has presented cross-national evidence that multiethnic opposition coalition formation in African countries is not merely conditioned by ethnic diversity or experience with electoral institutions. While opposition politicians

---

[28] I also calculated Londregan et al.'s (1995) measure for ethnic size dominance for each incumbent. The measure is a modified Herfindahl index in which the numerator is the population share of the politician's ethnic group. The values fall between 0 and 1 as the relative size of the incumbent's ethnic group increases. However, this measure also failed to attain statistical significance.

certainly must overcome bargaining problems that originate in the complex nature of their societies, the findings from this analysis suggest that a large part of the electoral coordination problem is a resource story. It is the financial autonomy of business – as proxied by the number of commercial banks, the level of private credit provision, and the tenure of the chamber of commerce president – that significantly affects the opposition's ability to secure the resources needed to negotiate cross-ethnic endorsements through upfront payments. Otherwise, when incumbents can prevent business from financing their rivals, it becomes more difficult for the opposition to coalesce behind a candidate who can offer only uncertain promises about post-election power sharing.

The results from this chapter pose a challenge for political scientists who study the role of ethnicity in electoral politics. Although scholarly and journalistic accounts of African elections often suggest that the mobilization of ethnicity hinders democratization, the analysis presented here suggests that neither diversity nor polarization has a definitive impact on one vital aspect of electoral democracy – bargaining across social cleavages. My argument is built on the observation that successful coalition bargaining in African countries hinges on the ability of politicians to deliver blocs of their coethnics' votes. Yet, we still know relatively little about the mechanisms through which politicians are able to create those blocs and leverage them in political negotiations. Future research on voter mobilization and party development in multiethnic societies would greatly benefit from a sharper focus on the kind of political bargaining that routinely occurs between representatives of different ethnic constituencies.

9

Democratic Consolidation in Africa

> My model is Washington. Just look at the example he gave us. After leading his country to independence ... he retired with the decision of seeing his successors develop his work. What more beautiful fate could I wish?
>
> Félix Houphouët-Boigny, president of Côte d'Ivoire, 1963[1]

This book is motivated by a substantive question: Under what conditions can politicians from different ethnic groups agree to share power? This is a question that must be addressed if we believe that interethnic cooperation is needed for democracy to survive in multiethnic polities. The answer, however, is not obvious. The violent breakdown of democracy can be readily attributed to enduring ethnic antagonisms or irreconcilable ethnic preferences. A popular book on the subject is unequivocal in stating that "the global spread of markets and democracy is a principal, aggravating cause of group hatred and ethnic violence throughout the non-Western world" (Chua 2004, 9). Journalistic accounts routinely pass off election crises in African countries as the product of "atavistic tribal rivalry,"[2] as in Côte d'Ivoire, "an atavistic vein of tribal tension,"[3] as in Kenya, or to "murderous ethnic rivalries,"[4] as in Madagascar.

While it may seem intuitive that groups fearing an uncertain political future might resort to extraconstitutional means to pursue their collective interests, the recent findings from political science on the relationship between ethnic mobilization and democratic consolidation are ambiguous. Scholars have shown that ethnic identities, when interacting with democratic institutions, can result in a wide range of political strategies (Chandra 2004b; Ferree 2010; Posner 2005). Some studies show that political violence is more likely to occur with

---

[1] Quoted in Woronoff (1972, 292). Houphouët-Boigny did not retire after leading his country to independence in 1960. Instead, he stayed on as Côte d'Ivoire's president until his death in 1993.

[2] "Carnage in Ivory Coast," editorial, *The Times* (London), 9 April 2011.

[3] Jeffrey Gettleman, "Disputed Vote Plunges Kenya into Bloodshed," *New York Times*, 31 December 2007.

[4] James Lamont, "Two Presidents in One Island Reopen Murderous Rivalries," *Financial Times* (London), 15 May 2002.

the initial democratization of multiethnic states (Ellingsen 2000; Mousseau 2001), while others find that ethnic-based parties can help to stabilize multiethnic democracies (Birnir 2007; Chandra 2004a).

I contribute to our understanding of democratic consolidation in multiethnic societies by examining interethnic coalition building among opposition politicians in African countries. Incumbent regimes in Africa solve the leadership and redistributive issues entailed by coalition formation with relative ease, since a president can mix the coercion needed to eliminate rivals with the cooptation needed to induce the support of select ethnic groups. But opposition parties face considerable uncertainty in resolving these issues. It is neither evident which candidate should lead a multiethnic coalition nor it is apparent how offices and resources should be divided among coalition members. My findings suggest that economic liberalization has advanced the cause of electoral democracy in Africa by reducing the uncertainty associated with these aspects of opposition coalition bargaining. By tracing the impact of financial reforms on the behavior of entrepreneurs and politicians, I show how the free flow of campaign resources enables opposition candidates to pursue a pecuniary coalition-building strategy. Cross-ethnic endorsements secured through upfront payments can transform one ethnic group's aspirant into a nationally competitive coalition formateur. In this regard, ethnicity matters insofar as it structures how the constituencies of politicians are organized and mobilized. But I demonstrate that these ethnic cleavages pose little obstacle to power sharing between the representatives of different groups.

In this concluding chapter, I briefly revisit the causal explanation before pointing to limitations that may provide avenues for continuing inquiry in this area. I then expand on the argument's contributions to, and implications for, the broader comparative study of economic and political reform.

THE EXPLANATION RESTATED

I have sought to parse the challenges to multiethnic opposition coalition building in African countries by examining the influence of one of the factors most often cited by the politicians I have interviewed in Cameroon, Ethiopia, Kenya, and Senegal – and that would be money. The argument I have subsequently developed in this book might strike some readers as a gross oversimplification. It seems to downplay the fact that ethnicity suffuses politics in many of the countries where democratization has stalled. How can the distribution of money among select politicians mollify collective concerns? For other readers, the argument is simply uninformative. It seems to overplay a constraint that is faced wherever politicians must compete to win office. Why should the lack of money be any more constraining for African opposition politicians than for their counterparts in other parts of the world?

My response to both concerns starts from an uncontroversial premise: political coalitions have been negotiated through the allocation of resources in Africa's patronage-based regimes since independence (Bratton and van de

Walle 1997; Jackson and Rosberg 1982; Lemarchand 1972). While the collective mobilization that has occurred in the pursuit of those resources has often taken an undeniably ethnic form, the underlying logic has been redistributive. African politicians have proven time and again that they can negotiate political bargains that bridge cleavages so long as they are then able to deliver resources to their coethnic constituents. Politicians have an incentive to strike such bargains because their own leadership positions are based, in large part, on that redistribution (Chabal and Daloz 1999; van de Walle 2007; Wantchekon 2003).

These redistributive dynamics have, since the return to multipartism, created both opportunities and constraints for African politicians. On the one hand, the singular importance of resources means that political negotiations lend themselves to solutions that are tangible and divisible. Politicians are undoubtedly more likely to join coalitions that will provide them the resources to secure their leadership positions among their coethnics today as well as permit them to continue cultivating that relationship tomorrow. On the other hand, these redistributive dynamics make coalition building a resource-intensive strategy that not all politicians can afford to undertake. African incumbents can satisfy the demands of their coalition partners by diverting state funds to them prior to an election and promising to appoint them to offices that can be used to channel public resources to their constituents after the election. And it is in this respect that opposition politicians are at a disadvantage.

Coalition bargaining among African opposition politicians breaks down because they are unable to meet pre- or post-election resource demands. The only thing cash-strapped opposition formateurs can offer in exchange for the cross-ethnic endorsements of their potential partners is the promise, should they win the election, of an appointment to a desirable office. This is an unattractive bargain from the perspective of the potential partner. She would be expected expend her own resources to shore up her own leadership position while simultaneously campaigning among her coethnics on behalf of the formateur. All of this would have to be done without any guaranteed compensation. At the same time, she would have to accept the considerable risk associated with the formateur's power-sharing promise, that is, the high probability attached to losing against the incumbent and the non-negligible probability that the formateur may renege on his or her bargain if the opposition coalition does win.

I argue that money is especially important for opposition politicians in Africa because it enables them to satisfy the resource requirements of coalition bargaining. An opposition formateur with access to private resources can make a power-sharing bargain more attractive to potential partners by offering upfront payments. A payment is used to compensate a coalition partner for withdrawing from the race and endorsing the formateur before the election. Moreover, a payment serves as a signaling device that communicates the formateur's intention of fulfilling power-sharing promises after the election. In effect, by posting a bond with coalition partners, the formateur is making an investment that makes his or her electoral cooperation credible. This logic suggests that opposition coalition negotiations are more likely to be successfully concluded when a formateur can afford to pay for cross-ethnic endorsements.

I demonstrate in this book that an opposition formateur's capacity to undertake a pecuniary coalition-building strategy has been constrained by the historically intertwined relationship between the state and capital. Opposition coherence, according to my view, depends on the relative autonomy of business from state-controlled capital. Private resources only become available to the opposition as incumbents are forced to relinquish the instruments that have been used to manipulate capital for political gain since the time of independence. I therefore hypothesize that multiethnic opposition coalitions should form more frequently in African countries where financial systems have been liberalized.

To corroborate my theory of pecuniary coalition formation, I provide evidence for the four interlocking parts of the causal mechanism. I first establish that the intensity of the financial controls imposed soon after independence in African countries depended on the nature of the constituency supporting a country's founding leader. Second, I show that the liberalization of finance in African countries is related to the business–state relationship imposed by founding leaders at independence as well as the resource rents available to the regime in power. Third, I demonstrate that business responds to changing regulatory conditions in finance by realigning politically, supporting opposition politicians when they no longer fear reprisals by a government that mediates their access to financial markets. Finally, I show how, under conditions of liberalized finance, an opposition coalition formateur bankrolled by business can offer power-sharing promises coupled with upfront payments to secure cross-ethnic endorsements.

As I seek to explain how the access to capital can influence the interaction among politicians and entrepreneurs from different ethnic groups, I do not claim that financial liberalization will lead to political change in axiomatic fashion. The relationship I posit is probabilistic. And, as examined here, it has limitations that merit further investigation by other scholars.

One limitation concerns the behavior of entrepreneurs as actors in the reform process. This is a limitation that is especially pertinent to the growing study of electoral authoritarianism. Just as investors face uncertainty regarding the security of their investments where property rights are poorly defined, entrepreneurs who seek to diversify their campaign contributions in hybrid regimes, which combine democratic and authoritarian traits, face uncertainty regarding their safety when the reform process remains incomplete. I do not explicitly address whether a specific reform is necessary for a regime's economic allies to resolve the uncertainty surrounding defection. Nor do I specify whether actors from certain economic sectors are more likely to defect in response to the signals from reform. In the case of Kenya, I suggest that, beyond the continuous implementation of financial reforms over an eight-year period, the privatization of the country's largest commercial bank provided business as a whole with an observable bellwether of the incumbent's capacity to impose sanctions. It remains to be shown more systematically how the level of uncertainty over reform implementation influences the political decisions of economic actors in authoritarian regimes, particularly when mistakes can be costly.

Ethiopia provides a relevant example. The ruling Ethiopian People's Revolutionary Democratic Front (EPRDF) enacted considerable economic and financial reforms in the run-up to the 2005 parliamentary elections, including the licensing of six privately owned indigenous banks in a banking system that had been completely state-owned. Under these conditions, some members of the business community saw increasing scope to maneuver politically. One popular opposition leader, Berhanu Nega, himself an economist and entrepreneur, sought to exploit this growing freedom by adapting an American fundraising practice. He hosted a fundraising dinner, at about $100 per plate, to collect the funds needed to build a coalition among opposition politicians representing a cross section of Ethiopia's ethnic groups.[5] But some 800 of the 1,000 entrepreneurs who made contributions to the opposition coalition ultimately decided not to attend the event. Their absence signaled at that point that much of the business community feared repercussions would be exacted if they publicly diversified their campaign contributions.[6]

The EPRDF may have permitted privately owned banks to enter the financial sector, but it had also refused to privatize the state-owned Commercial Bank of Ethiopia, which controls up to 70% of the market, or to permit the entry of foreign-owned banks ("From the Bullet to the Bank Account" 2006; Harvey 1996; International Monetary Fund 2005b). This may explain why the EPRDF's own campaign received active support from forty of the country's most prominent entrepreneurs, who formed a committee to raise among themselves three million birr, or about $345,000, as well as to orchestrate a meeting of some 3,000 businesspeople to publicly endorse the reelection of the incumbent prime minister, Meles Zenawi.[7]

Another limitation of my argument concerns the level of electoral coordination. I show that upfront payments can help to secure cross-ethnic endorsements in patronage-based polities. But I only ask whether a politician from one ethnic group supports the candidate from another group. This is a dichotomous coding of the dependent variable, which means that I do not account for the potentially broader variation in electoral coordination. For example, I do not explain why opposition politicians choose to form multiparty coalitions rather than merge their regional parties into a single national party. This may

---

[5] The opposition also sought to raise funds among the Ethiopian diaspora, which is mainly found in the United States. The leading opposition coalition, the Coalition for Unity and Democracy (CUD), raised approximately $100,000 in the months leading up to the 2005 election. Author interviews, Washington, DC, 20 December 2008; Oakland, CA, 8 August 2008.

[6] Most of those who made donations to the opposition coalition insisted that their donations be anonymous.

[7] Tamrat G. Giorgis, "Meles Promises Stability, Continuity, Predictability," *Fortune* (Addis Ababa), 8 May 2005.

be an area where identities can matter. It remains to be shown to what extent and in what ways cleavages might affect this outcome.

Ethiopia again serves as an example. In the lead-up to the 2005 parliamentary elections, an ethnic Oromo opposition leader, Merera Gudina, rejected a proposal to merge his own Oromo National Congress (ONC) with the All Ethiopia Unity Party (AEUP) led by Hailu Shawel, an ethnic Amhara opposition politician. Merera was willing to join a multiparty coalition, but he would not become a lieutenant in a single party that combined the country's two largest ethnic groups. While this bargain would have provided him with more resources than he could have ever secured independently, Merera also faced a historical constraint. Oromo elites had, over the previous fifty years, honed a political narrative emphasizing their exploitation under Amhara rule in the formation of the modern Ethiopian state. From Merera's perspective, to become an officer in an Amhara-run party would have signaled to his own base that he no longer represented their interests.

But ethnic cleavages can be flexible in other ways that our current understanding of electoral politics in multiethnic societies cannot accommodate. Although Merera would not fold his party under the umbrella of another ethnic group, he was still willing to take their money. Merera's party has, over the years, attracted financial support mainly from Amharas in the United States. This ethnic diaspora has been willing to provide funding to the party of another ethnic group because its leader advocates a position that complements their own. Some Oromo politicians demand outright secession from Ethiopia, but Merera has staked a position in favor of regional autonomy for his coethnics within a federal state. He thus represents an Oromo politician with whom Amharas, who tend to favor a unitary Ethiopian state, can reach a political compromise.

IMPLICATIONS FOR ECONOMIC REFORM

The findings associated with the pecuniary theory developed in this book contradict commonly held notions regarding economic reform's impact on the democratization process. It has been argued over the past two decades that the economic liberalization promoted by the international financial institutions has undermined democracy and sparked conflict in developing countries. According to this view, the policies associated with the Washington Consensus have reinforced the position of rapacious elites while marginalizing the poor. These outcomes are thought to prove wrong the supposed positive relationship between free markets and open politics.

The argument claiming that economic reforms have undercut democratic norms largely centers on the role played by the International Monetary Fund (IMF) and the World Bank as policy advisors and donor representatives. The accountability mechanism associated with democracy is subverted, the argument goes, by the very fact that nonelected external institutions can impose policies on unwilling populations. Participation in structural adjustment programs makes governments accountable to those institutions rather than to their own citizens (Mkandawire 1992, 1999a). The conditionalities that governments must follow result in antidemocratic behavior. Governments are not only obliged to limit their intervention in the economy, but they are also forced to resist the demands from voters for policies aimed at ameliorating poverty and inequality (Abrahamsen 2000; Ferguson 2006).

The argument attributing violent conflict to economic reform appears in a range of versions. One claims that the adoption of structural adjustment programs weakens the capacity of governments to supply the social services needed to meet basic human needs. This hollowing out of the state apparatus through austerity measures exacerbates socioeconomic disparities between groups, which, in turn, leads to violent conflict (Adekanye 1995; Stewart 2008). In the case of Rwanda, Chossudovsky (1997) argues that the 1994 genocide was precipitated by IMF and World Bank policies that triggered an economic crisis and robbed the state of the instruments needed to cushion the resulting social costs. In other versions of the argument, the state is not a helpless bystander; it is empowered to actively commit violence. The enactment of liberalization either provokes conflict between winners and losers to the point at which one will use the state to repress the other (Chua 2004) or requires the state to repress whatever protests erupt in response to unpopular policies (Abouharb and Cingranelli 2006; Bussmann et al. 2005). In the case of Rwanda, Storey (2001) claims that support provided under World Bank programs strengthened a government that would then go on to orchestrate a genocide.

The detractors of economic liberalization must be taken seriously due to the *prima facie* plausibility and the social relevance of their arguments. But the evidence presented in this book challenges the causal inferences drawn from previous research. The political patterns I am able to associate with financial reforms are inconsistent with the expectations raised by liberalization's detractors. First, I show that the representatives of different ethnic groups, each of which is differently affected by liberalization, are more likely to cooperate where financial reforms have been implemented to a greater degree. This pattern of behavior should not be observed, especially concerning something as consequential as leadership selection, if reform is exacerbating tensions between groups, as is often claimed. Second, I demonstrate that the coordination of electoral opposition against entrenched incumbents is more likely to occur where financial reforms have been implemented to a greater degree. This outcome suggests that reform can induce greater accountability by incumbents over the longer term by facilitating the emergence of real electoral competition in countries where none existed previously. This too is inconsistent with the claim that economic liberalization has ultimately diminished the prospects for democratization.

Much remains unknown about the reciprocal relationship between economic reform and political change in societies governed by hybrid regimes – a sample that includes most African countries. While we should expect economic performance to matter for the consolidation of democracy (Haggard and Kaufman 1995; Przeworski 1991), the pecuniary theory advanced in this book implies that the actual design of economic institutions is particularly important in multiethnic societies. Economic design, in this sense, means more than the choice between statism and laissez-fairism. It entails determining how policies ranging from investment to taxation affect the incentives for elites to cooperate across ethnic cleavages that represent distinct economic interests. Just as Lijphart (1969, 1977) argues that particular types of political institutions are more likely to stabilize democracy in multiethnic societies, one might speculate that certain economic arrangements are more likely to foster the interethnic accommodation needed for stable democracy. But what are those economic arrangements? Under what conditions will they satisfy the interests of elites and the communal groups they organize? Will those arrangements necessarily generate the development needed to promote popular support for democracy? These are questions that remain to be explored.

Their answers will be of special relevance to the long-term democratization and development of African countries. Political scientists produced a large literature on economic reform in African countries throughout the 1990s (e.g., Callaghy and Ravenhill 1993; Sandbrook 1993; van de Walle 2001; Widner 1994); however, their attention to this subject seems to have since waned. Ironically, this occurred when the region exhibited greater cross-national variation in economic policies than at any other time since independence. Many countries retain policies hostile to private enterprise, but several others have pursued policies that promote private investment. The pecuniary theory advanced in this book would suggest that such outcomes are linked to the political behavior of elites. In other words, improved business-related policies might be the payoff to elites for bankrolling the formation of multiethnic opposition coalitions. Elites could be immediately rewarded if their coalition wins. But, even if their coalition loses, the increased competition produced by the opposition's electoral coordination might induce the incumbent to produce better policies.

Figure 9.1 corroborates this intuition. It shows that opposition outcomes can be mapped onto the variation in business-related policies in African countries. Using data from the World Bank's Doing Business Project (2011), the panels in Figure 9.1 indicate that the countries where multiethnic opposition coalitions were formed in 1990–2005 went on to create a friendlier business environment between 2006 and 2010. Wherever opposition parties managed to coalesce, business would later face an appreciably lower administrative burden in terms of paying taxes or completing trade procedures. The change associated with opposition coordination is greater than the change brought about by alternation alone.

Development scholars and practitioners need to examine the potential impact of electoral coordination on Africa's economic development. This would be a marked departure from at least one influential strand of development thinking

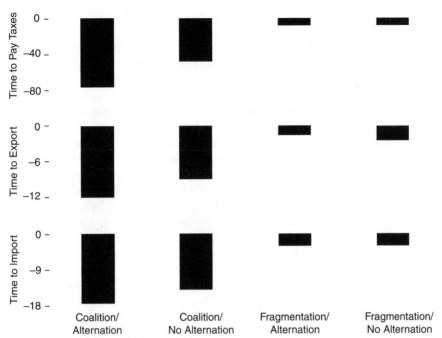

FIGURE 9.1. Opposition outcomes and business payoffs. Note: The panels show how countries that varied in opposition outcomes in 1990–2005 subsequently exhibited different rates of change in the conduct of essential business-related transactions. The bars represent the average annual change between 2006 and 2010 in the number of hours required to pay taxes; the number of days required to complete exporting procedures; and the number of days required to complete importing procedures.

Source: World Bank's *Doing Business Report* (2011).

that emphasizes the primacy of bureaucratic autonomy. Based on the example of successful industrializers in East Asia and elsewhere, this view suggests that better economic outcomes are more likely to be produced where politically insulated government agencies are staffed with competent bureaucrats who understand local conditions (Evans 1995) and who are able to guide judicious state interventions in the market (Wade 1990). However, the lesson from this book would be that economic policymaking in African countries would benefit from greater rather than less exposure to politics. A more productive relationship between state and business is unlikely to emerge in Africa's multiethnic societies until ethnic-based opposition parties can routinely coordinate their challenges to incumbents. Otherwise, incumbents who face a fragmented opposition need not fear losing power, which, in turn, means they have little incentive to craft better policy, build a more efficient bureaucracy, or restrict the abuse of scarce public resources. Such outcomes would be as welcomed by poor citizens as by wealthy elites.

IMPLICATIONS FOR POLITICAL REFORM

I contribute to democratic theorizing in this book by developing a model in which the access to capital shapes electoral coordination. The explanation I offer suggests that neither civil society nor electoral systems are as important as the control of capital for promoting the emergence of coherent opposition in multiethnic societies with developing economies. My argument, in this respect, provides no innovation. It builds on a version of democratic theory that has long posited a relationship between modernization and democratization (Boix and Stokes 2003; Burkhart and Lewis-Beck 1994; Jackman 1973; Lipset 1959; Przeworski et al. 2000). What my argument does offer is a precise causal mechanism that highlights the role of elites and the importance of resources in electoral coordination where democratic institutions have yet to be consolidated.

My depiction of the constraints faced by the opposition in Africa's patronage-based polities indicates that coordination among elites from different ethnic groups is highly sensitive to the dispersal of economic power. These elites are unable to coordinate because incumbents have been able to use statist policies to discriminate among them. Reforms that diffuse the access to capital generate new opportunities for their coordination. In this sense, financial liberalization may provide a "coordination device" – in Weingast's terms (1997) – through which elites can reach consensus on the proper limits to executive power.

This account of elite participation in multiethnic opposition coalition building extends insights from earlier scholarship on the role of elites in the democratization process (Dahl 1971; Moore 1966; O'Donnell and Schmitter 1986; Przeworski 1991; Rustow 1970). However, the interpretation I offer is at odds with models in which elites grudgingly accept democracy as a second-best solution for controlling the masses. Elites are often depicted as reluctant democratizers, seeking to block mass participation in politics due to their fears over redistribution (Acemoglu and Robinson 2006; O'Donnell 1973; Rueschemeyer et al. 1992). But my own reading of the African record suggests that, when neither political liberties nor property rights are fully respected, elites fear expropriation from above more so than redistributive claims from below. Given the conditions found in most patronage-based polities, elites have an incentive to invest in the formation of a coherent electoral opposition that can act as a check on government and ensure favorable policies.

While my focus in this book is on contemporary African cases, the pecuniary theory I have developed travels well beyond this region. Its generalizability permits an application to cases in other parts of the world as well the reappraisal of historic cases. To be consistent with my argument, it would have to be shown in any given case that greater access to capital enabled elites to support the emergence of a coherent electoral opposition, whether as a multiparty coalition or a broad-based national party.

Consider the paradigmatic British case. Although that country's eighteenth-century politics is often depicted as a two-party rivalry between Whigs and Tories, no coordinated opposition existed in parliament for most of the period between the Glorious Revolution and the Reform Act of 1832. An organized opposition was considered illegal up through the end of the seventeenth century. It would take another century for the notion of opposition to the monarch's government to gain legitimacy (Foord 1965). Partisan identities certainly did exist, but political alliances were based on social and family networks among politicians who sought favors through government (Namier 1929). The rise and fall of opposition reflected the ability of the monarch and his ministers to use royal patronage to neutralize challengers (Plumb 1967).[8] Opposition in this period was "a thing of shreds and patches" (Owen 1957, 4). The Tories, while retaining their ideological position (Colley 1985), effectively ceased to exist as a coherent political grouping when many were absorbed into government during what has been called the Whig Oligarchy of 1714–1760; the Whigs themselves were divided into rival factions during this time (O'Gorman 1975).

Parliamentary opposition did increase with George III's accession to the throne in 1760, but the new monarch soon managed, like his predecessors, to assert his predominance over the political scene through patronage. He could prevent the various factions from coordinating against him through economic inducements, including financing the election of parliamentary allies through the crown's personal fund (Evans 1985; Foord 1947).[9] That the House of Commons lacked a coherent opposition by the start of the nineteenth century is evident in the appeal made during the 1802 parliamentary election by *The Morning Chronicle*, a Whig-affiliated paper, for an opposition that would be "so near to the power of Government as to be an effectual check upon them ... an active, honest, constitutional opposition, which should have influence to prevent encroachments on the great charter of our liberties" (quoted in O'Gorman 1982, 67).

While the House of Commons was populated by fluid factions rather than stable parties for much of the eighteenth century, my claim would be that, at a time when partisan identity influenced commercial and financial relationships (Carruthers 1996; Stasavage 2007), the increasing openness of finance in Britain had a concomitant impact on the electoral coordination of opposition politicians. The "financial revolution" that marked the beginning of that century served not only to constrain government spending (Dickson 1967; North and Weingast 1989), but also spurred innovations in the financial system that led to the growth of credit facilities and merchant banking (Anderson 1970; Chapman 1984; Pressnell 1956). These developments in finance would have enabled the main opposition in parliament, the Rockingham Whigs, to

---

[8] The crown preserved its prerogative to choose ministers, as stipulated in the Revolution Settlement of 1689, regardless of their ability to win majorities in the House of Commons.

[9] Only about 30% of parliamentary seats were contested between the Glorious Revolution and the 1832 reforms. Yet, in the 1784 general election, George III's election funding helped to defeat some 90 sitting MPs, a striking figure at a time when most MPs were returned unopposed as the nominees of aristocratic families or the crown. (Evans 1985). See von den Steinen's (1972) study of the Buckinghamshire election for an illustration of the role of money in eighteenth-century campaigns.

create a common party fund to complement their incipient organizational efforts (Ginter 1966). Raised among private donors, this party fund permitted opposition leaders to offset the Crown's use of secret service accounts to finance the reelection of its preferred ministers (Namier 1929). In this way, the opposition was able to expand the range of contestation across constituencies by coordinating the nominations of new candidates and subsidizing their campaigns.[10] The opposition thus managed to consolidate its position in the 1790 election, absorbing smaller factions and stabilizing its numbers in the House of Commons (O'Gorman 1982, 20). For the first time, the Crown failed to increase its allies in the House of Commons, as had occurred in every previous eighteenth century election.

My pecuniary theory can also be applied to reinterpret the emergence of coherent opposition in the early American republic. It is well known that the founding fathers considered parties to be a destabilizing force that had to be actively discouraged, if not repressed (Hofstadter 1969; Lipset 1967). Less recognized is the fact that, during much of the first half of the nineteenth century, U.S. presidents often managed to amalgamate whatever fragmented opposition they faced into their own governing majorities. This partly explains why Tocqueville focused on the role of civil society, rather than political parties, in sustaining American democracy. When he visited the United States in 1831 – two years after Andrew Jackson won the presidency as the candidate of the Democratic Party organized by Martin Van Buren – Tocqueville (1988, 178) described the American political scene in terms that would be familiar to students of today's hybrid regimes: "It sometimes happens in a nation where opinions are divided that the balance between parties breaks down and one of them acquires an irresistible preponderance. It breaks all obstacles, crushes its adversary, and exploits the whole of society for its own benefit."

The Democrats' electoral advantage was eroded over time as their rivals adopted the same party-building strategy. The initial success of Van Buren's party could be attributed to a strategy that accommodated sectional differences (Aldrich 1995), but I would point to the fact that the emergence of such parties followed the country's financial revolution.[11] It is in the 1820s, when the elements of a modern financial system were established (Rousseau and Sylla 2005; Sylla 1998), that Van Buren is able to build the first modern political party to challenge the patronage-based factions that controlled New York state government. The coherence of his party was achieved, in part, with the support of business. According to Cole (1984, 94), Van Buren and his partisan allies

[10] The cost of running for parliament in the eighteenth century dissuaded most prospective candidates. For a description of the role played by money in a constituency election, see Smith's (1969) study of Yorkshire elections from that period. Namier (1929, 49) notes that "Government itself encouraged merchants to undertake constituencies which were too costly for the ordinary run of candidates, and used contracts to indemnify them for their election expenses."

[11] There were only three banks in the United States in 1789. Following the financial reforms pursued by Alexander Hamilton in the 1790s, that number expanded by 28 in the 1790s and an additional 73 in the following decade (van Fenstermaker 1965).

"realized that the political parties needed machinery and that money and jobs fueled such machinery." Since the booming economy of the early nineteenth century had made the control of credit increasingly profitable, Van Buren's allies specifically sought to cultivate the support of merchants and bankers by strategically allocating bank charters, which had to be granted through legislative act, on a partisan basis. The former would have access to the credit often denied by Federalist-controlled banks (Sellers 1991, 46), while the latter would be ensured larger rents through restrictions on entry (Benson 1961; Bodenhorn 2003; Hammond 1957).[12]

With access to the private resources provided by business, Van Buren could build his party by channeling funds to the campaigns of his party's candidates in competitive districts. Seavoy (1982, 60) goes so far as to claim that the manipulation of bank charters enabled Van Buren "to weld an alliance of factions into a disciplined party." That other politicians sought to imitate this party-building strategy is evident in the increasing politicization seen among New York's business community in subsequent elections, including defections between parties (Gatell 1967). More generally, I speculate that a relationship could be established between the open access to finance, as gauged by the adoption of liberalized banking entry laws, and levels of party competition across American states. Political factions that gained control of state capitals could impose limits on banking entry to create privileges that aligned commercial interests with those of the governing coalition. The Southern states that restricted entry into banking and undertook extensive state intervention in the sector eventually became *de facto* one-party states. By contrast, the New England and Midwestern states that adopted liberalized bank chartering became the most politically competitive states (Bodenhorn 2003; Wallis 2008).

A fragmented opposition eventually coalesced into national parties in the British and American cases after each experienced a financial revolution, but the pecuniary theory of this book does not imply that opposition coordination must necessarily take such a form. In this respect, electoral rules and social heterogeneity do matter (Cox 1997; Mozaffar et al. 2003; Ordeshook and Shvetsova 1994). But an implication deduced from the pecuniary theory suggests that opposition politicians in multiethnic, patronage-based polities will have an incentive to continue mobilizing their constituents along ethnic lines. Greater financial liberalization should be expected to encourage politicians to cement their control over ethnic constituencies because it will determine their ability to attract campaign funding from entrepreneurs as well as their ability to strike bargains with other politicians. In short, politicians will continue to organize along ethnic lines as long as they can secure the additional payoff from acting as brokers for their coethnics' votes.

This ethnic partisanship is conventionally perceived as an obstacle to democratization. The fear is that ethnic voting will lead to permanent majorities and

---

[12] The legislative majority required to grant a bank charter was raised to two-thirds after Van Buren's allies achieved control of the legislature in the 1820 election.

minorities, creating conditions in which certain groups perceive violence as their only recourse for acquiring power. Yet, the political constraints imposed by ethnic voting should not be exaggerated. The politicians who make appeals on the basis of ethnicity also understand the fundamental problem of multiparty competition – they know that they must secure the support of other groups if they are to win or hold onto power. The African cases examined in this book indicate that most politicians are pragmatic in leveraging their ethnic constituencies in exchange for access to power. Recall that even in the case of failed opposition coordination, in Cameroon, politicians were actively searching for a candidate around whom they could rally, regardless of ethnicity. What proved decisive in that case was the lack of resources, not the extent of ethnic partisanship.

A related implication from the pecuniary theory is that, under liberalized finance, multiethnic coalitions will become increasingly fluid. The availability of funding does not predict the creation of stable legislative majorities, since politicians can always be bid away through promises and payments. In the African cases, for example, it did not take long for the multiethnic opposition coalitions that formed in Senegal in 2000 and in Kenya in 2002 to fall apart and lead to new configurations in subsequent elections. Although opposition politicians in both countries chose to come together to bring about a transition in power, they also chose to retain their individual party labels rather than to form a single party under their coalition formateur.

This depiction of fluid coalitions among ethnic-based parties does not approximate the idealized democracy that many would like to see emerge in African countries. But the normatively desirable outcomes associated with democracy may not necessarily require the dissolution of ethnic parties into national parties founded on ideology. What is necessary is their coordination. It is the ability of ethnic parties to coalesce for electoral and legislative ends that will ensure that the political arena remains open. For example, while turnover in power is expected to enhance the quality of democracy in countries where multiparty competition is still new, it is less obvious that a losing opposition coalition can do the same. Consider the patterns in Figure 9.2, which compares the levels of democracy among African countries with no turnover in the executive between 1990 and 2005. Figure 9.2 shows the distinct trend lines in the average Polity score for countries where the opposition remains fragmented versus countries where the opposition coalesces but does not win. Although the average Polity score declines in both sets of countries with every year that an election approaches, the two diverge from the election year onwards. Democratic practices appear to deteriorate in countries where the opposition has been unable to build electoral alliances, while those rights are preserved where the opposition manages to coordinate – despite losing the election.

The patterns shown in Figure 9.2 suggest that opposition coalitions may play a vital role consolidating democracy in African countries. Nevertheless, scholars and policymakers concerned by party instability have argued for using institutional reforms to induce politicians to form stronger national parties. In

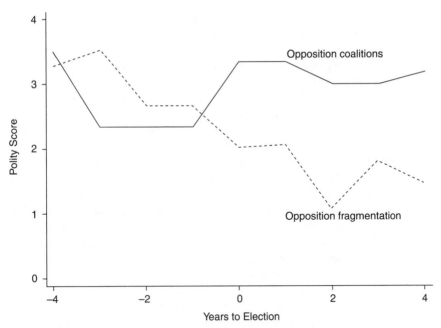

FIGURE 9.2. The quality of democracy without alternation.
Source: Polity IV Project.

the area of campaign finance, for instance, African countries remain largely
unregulated: few countries have clear rules for party revenues and expenditures; and those that do rarely enforce them. The adoption of public finance has
therefore become an increasingly popular reform among democracy promoters
in the region. Parties must be provided with a minimal level of financial support
in order to guarantee their critical role in sustaining democracy. Otherwise, the
argument goes, their organizations will lack the resources needed to compete
effectively and their party leaders will remain beholden to private interests.

The insights from the pecuniary theory suggest that such a policy prescrip-
tion may be ineffectual, if not wrongheaded. It remains unclear what impact
public funding might have on party building in countries dominated by patronage politics. In such a context, public financing alone will not ensure that parties have a more level playing field, better represent their constituencies, or are
more insulated from special interests. Opposition party leaders might instead
be induced to serve the interests of the very government that provides them
with those resources. The adoption of public finance requires the consent of
the incumbent, so any reform could be manipulated to lock in a ruling party's
advantage. Among the African countries that provide direct public financing
to parties – about a quarter of the region – nearly all have a two-thirds legislative majority. And the distribution of legislative seats is used to calculate party
allocations in most cases. In fact, countries with direct public party financing
are associated a larger incumbent vote share on average: 64% in countries with

public financing versus 56% in countries with none. Countries with public financing are neither more likely to produce opposition coalitions or alternations in power.[13]

The stricter regulation of campaign finance, contrary to its intended effect, may actually help to ensure the opposition's fragmentation. Under the restricted access to private resources that already prevails in most African countries, any move to require the reporting of private donations would serve to stem the flow of donations to opposition parties. Entrepreneurs would interpret such reporting requirements as being aimed at them rather than the parties themselves. Being put on such a list would signal their defection and reprisals from the incumbent would soon follow. This has been the concern in Tanzania. The Election Expenses Act of 2010 may allow individuals to make unlimited contributions to any candidate or party, but it also requires all such donors to be identified. Given the political dominance of the ruling Chama Cha Mapinduzi (CCM), including the politicized connections that still influence economic opportunities, opposition politicians complain that the reporting requirement will discourage their potential donors.[14] This problem would remain even if stricter regulation were coupled with public finance. As shown in the case study of Cameroon, public finance made opposition coordination more difficult by effectively bidding up the value of each opposition politician – often beyond his actual electoral weight. Anyone who sought to be a coalition formateur had to offer his counterparts a much higher proposal in order to secure their endorsement. That became nearly impossible under the financial control retained by the incumbent.

The findings of this book make clear that resources play a critical role in facilitating electoral coordination in Africa's inchoate multiparty systems. But across the region there have been too few resources for the opposition. This fact should lead us to reconsider reforms ostensibly aimed at limiting the corrupting influence of money in politics. Much remains unknown about the results that such reforms might produce. They may well exaggerate the already asymmetric capacities of incumbent and opposition parties. The impact of these reforms should be gauged by whether they would facilitate or hinder cross-cleavage bargaining among opposition politicians. The consolidation of democracy in Africa over the long term is unlikely to occur without that kind of cooperation.

---

[13] My calculations are based on information compiled by the Ace Electoral Knowledge Network (http://aceproject.org).

[14] "Democracy and Governance Assessment of Tanzania: Final Report," United States Agency for International Development (USAID), June 2010; "Statement of the National Democratic Institute (NDI) Pre-Election Delegation to Tanzania's October 2010 Elections," National Democratic Institute (NDI), 21 May 2010.

Appendix A

Commercial Banking Sector Size and Multiethnic Opposition Coalitions in Africa

Country	Number of Banks			Number of	
	1985	Trendline (1985–2000)	2000	Elections	Coalitions
Nigeria	28		40	2	1
Kenya	14		26	3	1
Côte d'Ivoire	19		17	3	1
Ghana	8		13	3	1
Uganda	7		12	2	2
Mauritius	3		11	4	4
Mozambique	1		11	3	2
Zambia	7		10	3	1
Senegal	9		9	2	1
Benin	1		8	3	2
Burkina Faso	2		8	3	0
Cameroon	10		8	3	0
Guinea	3		8	3	0
Tanzania	3		8	3	2
Ethiopia	2		7	3	1

(*continued*)

Country	Number of Banks			Number of	
	1985	Trendline (1985–2000)	2000	Elections	Coalitions
Gabon	11		6	3	0
Gambia	5		6	3	1
Madagascar	2		6	3	2
Malawi	3		6	3	2
Mali	4		6	3	2
Mauritania	5		6	3	2
Niger	6		6	4	0
Togo	7		5	4	1
Botswana	3		4	3	0
Congo Republic	3		4	2	0
Sierra Leone	5		4	2	0
Central African Republic	4		3	3	0
Chad	4		3	2	0
Guinea-Bissau	1		3	3	0

Note: The number of elections and opposition coalitions is for the 1990–2005 period.

Appendix B

Sources on Commodity Exports and Ethnic Production by Country

Country	Commodities	Sources
Benin	Palm kernels	Wartena (2006); Williams (1969)
Botswana	Cattle meat, game meat	Good (1992); Moroke et al. (2008)
Burkina Faso	Cotton, shea nuts	Saul (1986); Schwartz (1996)
Burundi	Coffee, cotton	Burundi (1970); Weinstein (1974)
Cameroon	Cocoa, coffee	Joseph (1977); Monga (2001)
Central African Republic	Cotton, coffee	Melly (2002); Thompson and Adloff (1960)
Chad	Cotton, millet	Lemarchand (1980); Thompson and Adloff (1960)
Congo, Republic	Sugar, palm kernels	Gauze (1973); Thompson and Adloff (1960)
Côte d'Ivoire	Coffee, cocoa	Boone (2003); Woods (2003)
Gabon	Cocoa, coffee	Chamberlain (1978); Wunder (2003)
Gambia	Groundnuts	Carney and Watts (1991); Mwakikagile (2010)
Ghana	Cocoa	Allman (1993); Osei-Kwame and Taylor (1984)
Kenya	Coffee, tea	Bates (1989); Throup and Hornsby (1998)
Madagascar	Coffee, vanilla	Jackson (1971); Thompson and Adloff (1965); Wilson (1992)
Malawi	Tobacco, tea	Power (2010); Vaughan (2007)
Mali	Groundnuts, cotton	Benjaminsen (2001); Jolly and Gadbois (1996)
Mauritius	Sugar	Brautigam (1997)
Niger	Groundnuts, millet	Collins (1976)

Country	Commodities	Sources
Nigeria	Cocoa, groundnuts	Bascom (1969); Berry (1975); Hogendorn (1978); Yusuf (1975)
Rwanda	Coffee	Pottier (1993); Verwimp (2003)
Senegal	Groundnuts	Boone (2003); Cruise O'Brien (1971)
Sierra Leone	Palm kernels	Howard (1976); Lynn (1997)
Tanzania	Sisal, cotton	Hyden (1980); Wisjen and Tanner (2002)
Togo	Cocoa, coffee	Amenumey (1989)
Uganda	Coffee, cotton	Jorgensen (1981); Richards et al. (1973)
Zambia	Tobacco	Kanduza (1983); Lombard and Tweedie (1974)

Appendix C

Variables: Definitions, Sources, and Summary Statistics

Variable	Definition	Source	Mean	SD	Min	Max
Banking crisis in previous 5 years	Dichotomous variable indicates whether a systemic banking crisis occurred in previous 5 years	Laeven and Valencia (2008)	0.136		0	1
British colony	Dichotomous variable indicates former British colony	Europa Publications (1971–2006)	0.353		0	1
Cabinet size	Total number of cabinet ministers	Arriola (2009)	21.524	6.849	8	52
Capital liberalization	Index measures regulatory restrictions on international financial transactions, including current account transactions, capital account transactions, and the surrender of export proceeds	Chinn and Ito (2008)	−0.707	0.922	−2	3
Currency crisis in previous 5 years	Dichotomous variable indicates whether a currency crisis occurred in the previous 5 years	Laeven and Valencia (2008)	0.197		0	1
Debt crisis in previous 5 years	Dichotomous variable indicates whether a debt crisis occurred in the previous 5 years	Laeven and Valencia (2008)	0.089		0	1

Variable	Definition	Source	Mean	SD	Min	Max
Debt service, % GDP	The sum of principal repayments and interest paid in foreign currency on long-term debt, interest paid on short-term debt, and repayments to the IMF	World Bank (2009)	4.832	5.005	0	80.757
Empowerment index	Index measures respect for the freedom of movement, speech, political participation, and workers' rights	Cingranelli and Richards (2007)	6.071	2.260	1	10
Ethnic fractionalization	Herfindahl concentration index measuring ethnolinguistic diversity	Fearon (2003)	0.728	0.179	0.18	0.95
Ethnic polarization	Index of polarization using distribution of groups	Reynal-Querol (2002)	0.567	0.176	0.017	0.843
Europeans in 1950, log	Estimated European population in African colonies for the 1940–1950 period	Dotson and Dotson (1969); Trewartha and Zelinsky (1954)	8.309	1.429	5.704	11.219
Exporter constituency	Dichotomous variable indicates if the ethnic group of country's founding leader cultivates a major cash crop	Constructed with data from FAO and sources listed in Appendix B	0.407		0	1
Exports, % GDP	Exports of goods and services as a share of GDP	World Bank (2009)	27.893	17.127	2.525	89.624
Fixed exchange rate	Dichotomous variable indicates fixed exchange rate regime	Reinhart and Rogoff (2004)	0.468		0	1
Foreign aid, % GDP	Net disbursements of grants and loans made on concessional terms by donor agencies as a share of GDP	World Bank (2009)	12.376	11.653	-0.278	95.556

(continued)

Variable	Definition	Source	Mean	SD	Min	Max
GDP growth, 5-year average	Annual real GDP change averaged over previous 5 years	World Bank (2009)	2.878	3.152	−16.394	8.527
GDP per capita, log	GDP per capita (constant 2000 US$)	World Bank (2009)	5.881	0.835	4.035	8.951
Government expenditure, % GDP	Annual expenditure for purchases of goods and services by all levels of government, excluding most parastatals, as a share of GDP	World Bank (2009)	14.581	6.523	6.167	45.263
Incumbent competes in election	Dichotomous variable indicates whether incumbent seeks reelection	Constructed from media sources and case studies	0.779		0	1
Incumbent from plurality	Dichotomous variable indicates incumbent is from country's largest ethnic group	Constructed from country case studies	0.368		0	1
Landlocked country	Dichotomous variable indicates if a country has no sea coast	Europa Publications (1971–2006)	0.344		0	1
Leader years in power	Number of years national leader has held executive office	Europa Publications (1971–2006)	9.912	7.884	0	44
Loan amount, log	World Bank loan amount in U.S. dollars	Dollar and Svensson (2000)	4.104	0.798	1.609	6.215
Manufacturing, % GDP	Manufacturing as a share of GDP	World Bank (2009)	10.300	5.308	1.873	37.163
Mineral exporter	Dichotomous variable indicates mineral exports represent over one-third or more of merchandise exports	World Bank (2009)	0.212		0	1
Number of commercial banks	Total number of commercial banks in a country-year	Constructed with data from Europa Publications (1971–2006)	6.038	6.251	1	53

Variable	Definition	Source	Mean	SD	Min	Max
Number of coups	Total number of successful coups	McGowan (2003)	1.592	1.853	0	6
Number of previous multiparty elections	Number of previous multiparty executive elections	Constructed from Lindberg (2006) and country case studies	1.475	1.918	0	9
Oil exporter	Dichotomous variable indicates fuel exports represent over one-third or more of merchandise exports	World Bank (2009)	0.137		0	1
Opposition coalition	Dichotomous variable indicates if two or more opposition parties formed a coalition for an election held in 1990–2005	Constructed from domestic and foreign media sources for the one-year period leading up to the election.	0.323		0	1
Polity score	Index for the democratic and autocratic characteristics of a state's institutions: political participation, executive recruitment, and executive constraints	Marshall and Jaggers (2009)	−2.861	5.784	−9	10
Population, log	Total country population	World Bank (2009)	15.595	1.124	13.090	18.743
Private credit provision	Private credit provided by deposit money banks as a share of GDP	Beck et al. (1999)	13.414	9.476	1.102	57.216
Private law chamber of commerce	Dichotomous variable indicates if chamber of commerce is organized under the private law model	Fedotov (2007); Pilgrim and Meier (1995)	0.563		0	1
Regime years	Number of years incumbent regime has been in power	Constructed with data from Europa Publications (1971–2006)	16.737	12.974	0	45

(continued)

Variable	Definition	Source	Mean	SD	Min	Max
Runoff system	Dichotomous variable indicates two-round runoff system in executive elections	Nohlen et al. (1999)	0.707		0	1
Settler mortality, log	Death rate per 1,000 soldiers in the nineteenth century	Acemoglu et al. (2001)	5.902	0.912	3.417	7.986
Tenure of chamber president	Years chamber of commerce president has been in office	Constructed with data from Europa Publications (1971–2006)	4.556	3.988	1	23

Appendix D

Multiethnic Opposition Coalitions in Africa, 1990–2005

Country	Year	Coalition	Parties	Boycott	Turnover
Angola	1992	No		No	No
Benin	1991	Yes	Mouvement pour la Démocratie et le Progrès Social (MDPS), Union Démocratique des Forces du Progrès (UFDP), Union pour la Liberté et le Développement (ULD), Union pour le Triomphe du Renouveau Démocratique (UTRD)	No	Yes
Benin	1996	Yes	Front d'Action pour le Rénouveau et le Développement (FARD-Alafia), Notre Cause Commune (NCC), Rassemblement des Démocrates Libéraux pour la Reconstruction Nationale (RDL-Vivoten)	No	Yes
Benin	2001	No		Yes	No
Botswana	1994	No		No	No
Botswana	1999	No		No	No
Botswana	2004	No		No	No
Burkina Faso	1991	No		Yes	No
Burkina Faso	1998	No		Yes	No

(continued)

Country	Year	Coalition	Parties	Boycott	Turnover
Burkina Faso	2005	No		No	No
Burundi	1993	No		No	Yes
Cameroon	1992	No		No	No
Cameroon	1997	No		Yes	No
Cameroon	2004	No		No	No
Central African Republic	1993	No		No	Yes
Central African Republic	1999	No		No	No
Central African Republic	2005	No		No	No
Chad	1996	No		No	No
Chad	2001	No		No	No
Congo	1992	No		No	Yes
Congo	2002	No		No	No
Côte d'Ivoire	1990	Yes	Front Populaire Ivoirien (FPI), Parti Ivoirien des Travailleurs (PIT), Parti Socialiste Ivoirien (PSI), Union des Socio-Démocrates (USD)	No	No
Côte d'Ivoire	1995	No		Yes	No
Côte d'Ivoire	2000	No		Yes	Yes
Ethiopia	1995	No		Yes	No
Ethiopia	2000	No		No	No
Ethiopia	2005	Yes	All Ethiopia Unity Party (AEUP), Coalition for United and Democracy (CUD), Ethiopian Democratic League (EDL), Rainbow Ethiopia – Movement for Democracy and Social Justice, United Ethiopian Democratic Party (UEDP-Medhin); Council of Alternative Forces for Peace and Democracy in Ethiopia (CAFPDE), Oromo National Congress (ONC), Southern Ethiopia Peoples' Democratic Coalition (SEPDC), United Ethiopian Democratic Forces (UEDF)	No	No

Country	Year	Coalition	Parties	Boycott	Turnover
Gabon	1993	No		No	No
Gabon	1998	No		No	No
Gabon	2005	No		No	No
Gambia	1992	No		No	No
Gambia	1996	No		No	No
Gambia	2001	Yes	Gambia People's Party (GPP), People's Progressive Party (PPP), United Democratic Party (UDP)	No	No
Ghana	1992	No		No	No
Ghana	1996	Yes	New Patriotic Party (NPP), People's Convention Party (PCP)	No	No
Ghana	2000	No		No	Yes
Ghana	2004	No		No	No
Guinea	1993	No		No	No
Guinea	1998	No		No	No
Guinea	2003	No		Yes	No
Guinea-Bissau	1994	No		No	No
Guinea-Bissau	1999	No		No	Yes
Guinea-Bissau	2005	No		No	Yes
Kenya	1992	No		No	No
Kenya	1997	No		No	No
Kenya	2002	Yes	Democratic Party (DP), Forum for the Restoration of Democracy-Kenya (FORD-K), Liberal Democratic Party (LDP), National Party of Kenya (NPK), National Rainbow Coalition (NARC)	No	Yes
Liberia	1997	No		No	Yes
Liberia	2005	Yes	Liberia First Group (LFG), United Party (UP)	No	Yes
Madagascar	1992	Yes	Forces Vives Rasalama (FVR), Union Nationale pour le Développement et la Démocratie	No	Yes
Madagascar	1996	No		No	Yes

(*continued*)

Country	Year	Coalition	Parties	Boycott	Turnover
Madagascar	2001	Yes	Groupe de Réflexion et d'Action pour le Développement (GRAD-Iloafo), Mpitolona ho amin'ny Fandrosoan'i Madagasikara (MFM), Rénaissance du Parti Social Démocratique (RPSD), Tiako-i-Madagasikara (TIM)	No	Yes
Malawi	1994	Yes	Congress for the Second Republic (CSR), Malawi Democratic Union (MDU), United Democratic Front (UDF), United Front for Multi-Party Democracy (UFMD)	No	Yes
Malawi	1999	Yes	Alliance for Democracy (AFORD), Malawi Congress Party (MCP)	No	No
Malawi	2004	No		No	No
Mali	1992	Yes	Association Démocratique pour le Mali – Parti Africain pour la Solidarité et la Justice (ADEMA-PASJ)	No	Yes
Mali	1997	No		Yes	No
Mali	2002	Yes	Bloc pour la Démocratie et l'Intégration Africaine (BDIA-Faso Jigi), Mouvement pour la Démocratie et le Changement (MDC), Mouvement pour l'Indépendance, la Renaissance et l'Intégration Africaine (MIRIA), Parti de la Solidarité et du Progrès (PSP), Union Soudanaise-Rassemblement Démocratique Africain (US-RDA)	No	Yes

Country	Year	Coalition	Parties	Boycott	Turnover
Mauritania	1992	Yes	El Hor (EH), Mouvement Démocrates Indépendents (MDI), Mouvement National Démocratique (MND), Parti Mauritanien pour Renouveau (PMR), Union des Forces Démocratiques (UFD)	No	No
Mauritania	1997	No		Yes	No
Mauritania	2003	Yes	Alliance pour la Justice et la Démocratie (AJD), Coalition pour une Alternance Pacifique (CAP), Mouvement pour la Citoyenneté et la Démocratie (MCD), Parti pour la Liberté l'Egalité et la Justice (PLEJ), Union des Forces de Progrès (UFP)	No	No
Mauritius	1991	Yes	Parti Mauricien Social Démocrate (PMSD), Parti Travailliste (PTr)	No	No
Mauritius	1995	Yes	Mouvement Militant Mauricien (MMM), Parti Travailliste (PTr)	No	Yes
Mauritius	2000	Yes	Mouvement Militant Mauricien (MMM), Militant Socialist Movement (MSM)	No	Yes
Mauritius	2005	Yes	Mouvement Militant Socialiste Mauricien (MMSM), Parti Mauricien Xavier-Luc Duval (PMXD), Parti Travailliste (PTr)	No	Yes
Mozambique	1994	No		No	No
Mozambique	1999	Yes	Aliança Independente de Moçambique (ALIMO), Frente de Ação Patriotica (FAP), Frente Democrática Unida (FDU), Frente Unida	No	No

(*continued*)

Country	Year	Coalition	Parties	Boycott	Turnover
			de Moçambique (FUMO), Movimento Nacionalista Moçambicano (MONAMO), Partido de Convenção Nacional (PCN), Partido para o Progresso do Povo de Moçambique (PPPM), Partido Renovador Democrático (PRD), Partido de Unidade Nacional (PUN), Resistência Nacional Moçambicana (RENAMO), União Nacional Moçambicana (UNAMO)		
Mozambique	2004	Yes	Aliança Independente de Moçambique (ALIMO), Frente de Ação Patriotica (FAP), Frente Democrática Unida (FDU), Frente Unida de Moçambique (FUMO), Movimento Nacionalista Moçambicano (MONAMO), Partido de Convenção Nacional (PCN), Partido Ecologista de Moçambique (PEMO), Partido para o Progresso do Povo de Moçambique (PPPM), Partido Renovador Democrático (PRD), Partido de Unidade Nacional (PUN), Resistência Nacional Moçambicana (RENAMO)	No	No
Namibia	1994	No		No	No
Namibia	1999	No		No	No
Namibia	2004	No		No	No
Niger	1993	No		No	Yes
Niger	1996	No		No	No
Niger	1999	No		No	Yes
Niger	2004	No		No	No

Country	Year	Coalition	Parties	Boycott	Turnover
Nigeria	1999	Yes	Alliance for Democracy (AD), All People's Party (APP)	No	Yes
Nigeria	2003	No		No	No
Rwanda	2003	No		No	No
Senegal	1993	No		No	No
Senegal	2000	Yes	Action pour le Développement National (ADN), And-Jëf/ Parti Africain pour la Démocratie et le Socialisme (AJ-PADS), Ligue Démocratique/Mouvement pour le Parti du Travail (LD-MPT), Mouvement pour le Socialisme et l'Unité (MSU), Parti Démocratique Sénégalais (PDS), Parti de l'Indépendance et du Travail (PIT), Union Démocratique pour le Fédéralisme (UDF-Mboolomi)	No	Yes
Sierra Leone	1996	No		No	Yes
Sierra Leone	2002	No		No	No
South Africa	1994	No		No	Yes
South Africa	1999	No		No	No
South Africa	2004	Yes	Democratic Alliance (DA), Inkatha Freedom Party (IFP)	No	No
Tanzania	1995	Yes	Chama Cha Demokrasia na Maendeleo (CHADEMA), National Convention for Construction and Reform (NCCR-Mageuzi), Tanzania Labour Party (TLP)	No	No
Tanzania	2000	Yes	Chama Cha Demokrasia na Maendeleo (CHADEMA), Civic United Front (CUF)	No	No

(*continued*)

Country	Year	Coalition	Parties	Boycott	Turnover
Tanzania	2005	No		No	No
Togo	1993	No		Yes	No
Togo	1998	No		No	No
Togo	2003	No		No	No
Togo	2005	Yes	Alliance pour la Démocratie et le Développement Intégral (ADDI), Comité d'Action pour le Renouveau (CAR), Convention Démocratique des Peuples Africains (CDPA), Pacte Socialiste pour le Renouveau (PSR), Union pour la Démocratie et la Solidarité (UDS-Togo), Union des Forces de Changement (UFC)	No	No
Uganda	1996	Yes	Democratic Party (DP), National Liberation Party (NLP), Uganda People's Congress (UPC)	No	No
Uganda	2001	Yes	Democratic Party (DP), Elect Kizza Besigye Task Force	No	No
Zambia	1991	Yes	Movement for Multiparty Democracy (MMD)	No	Yes
Zambia	1996	No		Yes	No
Zambia	2001	No		No	No
Zimbabwe	1990	Yes	Conservative Alliance of Zimbabwe (CAZ), Zimbabwe Unity Movement (ZUM)	No	No
Zimbabwe	1996	No		Yes	No
Zimbabwe	2002	No		No	No

References

Abiad, Abdul, and Ashoka Mody. 2005. "Financial Reform: What Shakes It? What Shapes It?" *American Economic Review* 95 (1): 66–88.

Abouharb, M. Rodwan, and David L. Cingranelli. 2006. "The Human Rights Effects of World Bank Structural Adjustment, 1981–2000." *International Studies Quarterly* 50: 233–62.

Abrahamsen, Rita. 2000. *Disciplining Democracy: Development Discourse and Good Governance in Africa*. London: Zed Books.

Abramowitz, Alan. 1988. "Explaining Senate Election Outcomes." *American Political Science Review* 82 (June): 385–403.

Acemoglu, Daron, Simon Johnson, and James A. Robinson. 2001. "The Colonial Origins of Comparative Development: An Empirical Investigation." *American Economic Review* 91 (5): 1369–401.

Acemoglu, Daron, and James A. Robinson. 2006. *Economic Origins of Dictatorship and Democracy*. New York: Cambridge University Press.

Ackrill, Margaret, and Leslie Hannah. 2001. *Barclays: The Business of Banking, 1690–1996*. New York: Cambridge University Press.

Adekanye, J. 'Bayo. 1995. "Structural Adjustment, Democratization and Rising Ethnic Tensions in Africa." *Development and Change* 26: 355–74.

Ajulu, Rok. 2002. "Politicised Ethnicity, Competitive Politics and Conflict in Kenya: A Historical Perspective." *African Studies* 61 (2): 251–68.

Aldrich, John H. 1995. *Why Parties? The Origin and Transformation of Political Parties in America*. Chicago, Ill.: University of Chicago Press.

Alibert, J., and J.-E. Sathoud. 1975. "The Activities of Commercial Banks in French-Speaking African States." *Journal of African Law* 19 (1–2): 36–51.

Allman, Jean Marie. 1993. *The Quills of the Porcupine: Asante Nationalism in an Emergent Ghana*. Madison: University of Wisconsin Press.

Amenumey, D.E.K. 1989. *The Ewe Unification Movement: A Political History*. Accra: Ghana University Press.

Amin, Samir. 1969. *Le Monde des Affaires Sénégalais*. Paris: Éditions de Minuit.

Amorim Neto, Octavio, and Gary Cox. 1997. "Electoral Institutions, Cleavage Structures, and the Number of Parties." *American Journal of Political Science* 41: 149–74.

Amselle, Jean-Loup. 1977. *Les Negociants de la Savane: Histoire et Organisation Sociale des Kooroko*. Paris: Editions Anthropos.

Anderson, B.L. 1970. "Money and the Structure of Credit in the Eighteenth Century." *Business History* 12 (2): 85–101.

Anderson, Benedict. 1983. *Imagined Communities: Reflections on the Origin and Spread of Nationalism*, 2nd ed. New York: Verso.

Ansolabehere, Stephen, and Alan S. Gerber. 1994. "The Mismeasure of Campaign Spending: Evidence from the 1990 U.S. House Elections." *Journal of Politics* 56 (4): 1106–18.

Ansolabehere, Stephen, James M. Snyder, Jr., Aaron B. Strauss, and Michael M. Ting. 2005. "Voting Weights and Formateur Advantages in the Formation of Coalition Governments." *American Journal of Political Science* 49 (3): 550–63.

Apter, David E. 1961. *The Political Kingdom in Uganda: A Study in Bureaucratic Nationalism*. Princeton, N.J.: Princeton University Press.

——— 1964a. "Ghana." In *Political Parties and National Integration in Tropical Africa*, ed. J.E. Coleman and C.G. Rosberg. Berkeley: University of California Press.

——— 1964b. "Some Reflections on the Role of a Political Opposition in New Nations." In *Independent Black Africa: The Politics of Freedom*, ed. W.J. Hanna. Chicago, Ill.: Rand McNally.

Arrighi, Giovanni, and John S. Saul. 1968. "Socialism and Economic Development in Tropical Africa." *Journal of Modern African Studies* 6 (2): 141–69.

Arriola, Leonardo R. 2009. "Patronage and Political Stability in Africa." *Comparative Political Studies* 42 (10): 1339–62.

Atangana, Martin-René. 1998. *Capitalisme et Nationalisme au Cameroun: Au Lendemain de la Seconde Guerre Mondiale 1946–1956*. Paris: Université de Paris I, Panthéon-Sorbonne.

Austen, Ralph A. 1987. *African Economic History: Internal Development and External Dependency*. London: James Currey.

Austin, Dennis. 1964. *Politics in Ghana, 1946–1960*. New York: Oxford University Press.

Austin, Gareth, and Chibuike Ugochukwu Uche. 2007. "Collusion and the Competition in Colonial Economies: Banking in British West Africa, 1916–1960." *Business History Review* 81 (Spring): 1–26.

Azam, Jean-Paul. 2005. "The Paradox of Power Reconsidered: A Theory of Political Regimes in Africa." *Journal of African Economies* 15 (1): 26–58.

Azikiwe, Nnamdi. 1961. *Zik: A Selection from the Speeches of Nnamdi Azikiwe*. London: Cambridge University Press.

Bäck, Hanna, and Patrick Dumont. 2008. "Making the First Move: A Two-Stage Analysis of the Role of Formateurs in Parliamentary Government Formation." *Public Choice* 135 (3–4): 353–73.

Baron, David P., and John A. Ferejohn. 1989. "Bargaining in Legislatures." *American Political Science Review* 83 (4): 1181–206.

Bascom, William Russell. 1969. *The Yoruba of Southwestern Nigeria*. New York: Holt, Rinehart and Winston.

Basedau, Matthias, Gero Erdmann, and Andreas Mehler, eds. 2007. *Votes, Money and Violence: Political Parties and Elections in Sub-Saharan Africa*. Uppsala: Nordic Africa Institute.

Bates, Robert H. 1981. *Markets and States in Tropical Africa*. Berkeley: University of California Press.

——— 1983. "The Commercialization of Agriculture and the Rise of Rural Political Protest." In *Essays on the Political Economy of Rural Africa*. Berkeley: University of California Press.

1989. *Beyond the Miracle of the Market: The Political Economy of Agrarian Development in Kenya*. New York: Cambridge University Press.

1999a. "The Economic Bases of Democratization." In *State, Conflict, and Democracy in Africa*, ed. R. Joseph. Boulder, Colo.: Lynne Rienner.

1999b. "Ethnicity, Capital Formation, and Conflict." Working Paper Series 99–11, Weatherhead Center for International Affairs, Harvard University, December 1999.

2001. *Prosperity and Violence: The Political Economy of Development*. New York: W.W. Norton.

Bates, Robert H., and Anne O. Krueger, eds. 1993. *Political and Economic Interactions in Economic Policy Reform: Evidence from Eight Countries*. Cambridge, Mass.: Blackwell.

Bates, Robert H., David L. Epstein, Daniel C. Esty, Jack A. Goldstone, Ted Robert Gurr, Barbara Harff, Colin H. Kahl, Marc Levy, Monty G. Marshall, Pamela T. Surko, Jr., John C. Ulfelder, and Alan N. Unger. 2000. "State Failure Task Force Report: Phase III Findings." McLean, Va.: Science Applications International Corporation (SAIC).

Bauer, P.T. 1954a. "Origins of the Statutory Export Monopolies of British West Africa." *Business History Review* 28 (3): 197–213.

1954b. *West African Trade: A Study of Competition, Oligopoly and Monopoly in a Changing Economy*. Cambridge: Cambridge University Press.

1975. "British Colonial Africa: Economic Retrospect and Aftermath." In *Colonialism in Africa, 1870–1960*, ed. L.H. Gann and P. Duignan. London: Cambridge University Press.

Baumgartner, Frank R., and Beth L. Leech. 1998. *Basic Interests: The Importance of Groups in Politics and Political Science*. Princeton, N.J.: Princeton University Press.

2001. "Interest Niches and Policy Bandwagons: Patterns of Interest Group Involvement in National Politics." *Journal of Politics* 63 (4): 1191–213.

Bayart, Jean François. 1989. *L'Etat en Afrique: Politique du Ventre*. Paris: Fayard.

Baylies, Carolyn, and Morris Szeftel. 1984. "The Rise to Political Prominence of the Zambian Business Class." In *The Dynamics of the One-Party State in Zambia*, ed. C. Gertzel, C. Baylies, and M. Szeftel. Manchester: Manchester University Press.

Beck, Linda J. 2008. *Brokering Democracy in Africa: The Rise of Clientelist Democracy in Senegal*. New York: Palgrave Macmillan.

Beck, Thorsten, Asli Demirguc-Kunt, and Ross Levine. 1999. "A New Database on Financial Development and Structure." Policy Research Working Paper 2146. Development Research Group, World Bank, Washington, D.C.

Beck, Thorsten, Asli Demirguc-Kunt, and Vojislav Maksimovic. 2004. "Bank Competition and Access to Finance: International Evidence." *Journal of Money, Credit and Banking* 36 (3): 627–48.

Benjaminsen, Tor A. 2001. "The Population-Agriculture-Environment Nexus in the Malian Cotton Zone." *Global Environmental Change* 11: 283–95.

Benson, Lee. 1961. *The Concept of Jacksonian Democracy: New York as a Test Case*. Princeton, N.J.: Princeton University Press.

Berman, Bruce J., and Colin Leys, eds. 1994. *African Capitalists in African Development*. Boulder, Colo.: Lynne Rienner.

Berman, Bruce J., Dickson Eyoh, and Will Kymlicka. 2004. "Ethnicity and the Politics of Democratic Nation-Building in Africa." In *Ethnicity and Democracy in Africa*, ed. B. Berman, D. Eyoh, and W. Kymlicka. Oxford: James Currey.

Berry, Sara. 1975. *Cocoa, Custom, and Socio-Economic Change in Rural Western Nigeria*. Oxford: Clarendon Press.

2009. "Property, Authority and Citizenship: Land Claims, Politics and the Dynamics of Social Division in West Africa." *Development and Change* 40 (1): 23–45.

Berthelemy, Jean-Claude. 1997. "From Financial Repression to Liberalization: The Senegalese Experience." In *Experiences with Financial Liberalization*, ed. K.L. Gupta. Boston: Kluwer.

Beveridge, Andrew A., and Anthony Oberschall. 1979. *African Businessmen and Development in Zambia*. Princeton, N.J.: Princeton University Press.

Bienen, Henry. 1967. "What Does Political Development Mean in Africa?" *World Politics* 20 (1): 128–41.

1970. *Tanzania: Party Transformation and Economic Development*, 2nd ed. Princeton, N.J.: Princeton University Press.

1974. *Kenya: The Politics of Participation and Control*. Princeton, N.J.: Princeton University Press.

Bienen, Henry, and Jeffrey Herbst. 1996. "The Relationship between Political and Economic Reform in Africa." *Comparative Politics* 29 (1): 23–42.

Birnir, Jóhanna Kristín. 2007. *Ethnicity and Electoral Politics*. New York: Cambridge University Press.

Block, Fred. 1977. "The Ruling Class Does Not Rule: Notes on the Marxist Theory of the State." *Socialist Revolution* 7 (33): 6–27.

Bodenhorn, Howard. 2003. *State Banking in Early America: A New Economic History*. New York: Oxford University Press.

Bogaards, Mathijs. 2004. "Counting Parties and Identifying Dominant Party Systems in Africa." *European Journal of Political Research* 43: 173–97.

Boix, Carles. 2003. *Democracy and Redistribution*. New York: Cambridge University Press.

Boix, Carles, and Susan C. Stokes. 2003. "Endogenous Democratization." *World Politics* 55 (4): 517–49.

Bongo, Omar, and Airy Routier. 2001. *Blanc comme Nègre: Entretiens avec Airy Routier*. Paris: Grasset.

Boone, Catherine. 1990. "The Making of a Rentier Class: Wealth Accumulation and Political Control in Senegal." *Journal of Development Studies* 26 (3): 425–49.

1992. *Merchant Capital and the Roots of State Power in Senegal 1930–1985*. New York: Cambridge University Press.

1993. "Commerce in Côte d'Ivoire: Ivoirianisation without Ivoirian Traders." *Journal of Modern African Studies* 31 (1): 67–92.

2003. *Political Topographies of the African State: Territorial Authority and Institutional Choice*. New York: Cambridge University Press.

2005. "State, Capital, and the Politics of Banking Reform in Sub-Saharan Africa." *Comparative Politics* 37 (4): 401–20.

2009. "Electoral Populism Where Property Rights Are Weak: Land Politics in Contemporary Sub-Saharan Africa." *Comparative Politics* 41 (2): 183–201.

Box-Steffensmeier, Janet M., and Christopher J.W. Zorn. 2001. "Duration Models and Proportional Hazards in Political Science." *American Journal of Political Science* 45 (4): 972–88.

Brachet, Christian. 2008. "Banking Supervision in the CFA Franc Countries." In *Small States, Smart Solutions: Improving Connectivity and Increasing the Effectiveness of Public Services*, ed. E.M. Favaro. Washington, D.C.: World Bank.

Brambor, Thomas, William Roberts Clark, and Matt Golder. 2006. "Are African Party Systems Different?" *Electoral Studies* 20: 1–9.

Bratton, Michael, and Wonbin Cho. 2006. "Where Is Africa Going? Views from Below. A Compendium of Trends in Public Opinion in 12 African Countries, 1999–2006." Afrobarometer Working Paper No. 60. East Lansing, MI: Afrobarometer.

Bratton, Michael, Robert Mattes, and Emmanuel Gyimah-Boadi. 2005. *Public Opinion, Democracy, and Market Reform in Africa.* New York: Cambridge University Press.

Bratton, Michael, and Daniel N. Posner. 1999. "A First Look at Second Elections in Africa, with Illustrations from Zambia." In *State, Conflict, and Democracy in Africa,* ed. R. Joseph. Boulder, Colo.: Lynne Rienner.

Bratton, Michael, and Nicolas van de Walle. 1997. *Democratic Experiments in Africa: Regime Transitions in Comparative Perspective.* New York: Cambridge University Press.

Brautigam, Deborah. 1997. "Institutions, Economic Reform, and Democratic Consolidation in Mauritius." *Comparative Politics* 30 (1): 45–62.

—— 1999. "The 'Mauritius Miracle': Democracy, Institutions, and Economic Policy." In *State, Conflict, and Democracy in Africa,* ed. R. Joseph. Boulder, Colo.: Lynne Rienner.

Brautigam, Deborah, Lise Rakner, and Scott Taylor. 2002. "Business Associations and Growth Coalitions in Sub-Saharan Africa." *Journal of Modern African Studies* 40 (4): 519–47.

Brenner, G.A., H. Fouda, and J.M. Toulouse. 1990. "Les Tontines et la Création d'Entreprises au Cameroun." In *L'Entreprenueriat en Afrique Francophone,* ed. Hénault and M'Rabet. Paris: AUPELF-UREF John Libbey Eurotext.

Brown, Stephen. 2001. "Authoritarian Leaders and Multiparty Elections in Africa: How Foreign Donors Help to Keep Kenya's Daniel arap Moi in Power." *Third World Quarterly* 22 (5): 725–39.

Brownbridge, Martin. 1998. "Government Policies and Development of Banking in Kenya." In *Banking in Africa: The Impact of Financial Sector Reform since Independence,* ed. M. Brownbridge and C. Harvey. Trenton, N.J.: Africa World Press.

Brownbridge, Martin, and Charles Harvey, eds. 1998. *Banking in Africa: The Impact of Financial Sector Reform since Independence.* Trenton, N.J.: Africa World Press.

Browne, Eric C., and Mark N. Franklin. 1973. "Aspects of Coalition Payoffs in European Parliamentary Democracies." *American Political Science Review* 67 (2): 453–69.

Burkhart, Ross E., and Michael S. Lewis-Beck. 1994. "Comparative Democracy: The Economic Development Thesis." *American Political Science Review* 88 (4): 903–10.

"Burundi: Political and Ethnic Powderkeg." 1970. *Africa Report* 15 (8): 18–20.

Bussmann, Margit, Gerald Schneider, and Nina Wiesehomeier. 2005. "Foreign Economic Liberalization and Peace: The Case of Sub-Saharan Africa." *European Journal of International Relations* 11 (4): 551–79.

Bustin, Edouard. 1963. "The Congo." In *Five African States: Responses to Diversity,* ed. G.M. Carter. Ithaca, N.Y.: Cornell University Press.

Callaghy, Thomas M. 1984. *The State-Society Struggle: Zaire in Comparative Perspective.* New York: Columbia University Press.

Callaghy, Thomas M., and John Ravenhill, eds. 1993. *Hemmed In: Responses to Africa's Economic Decline.* New York: Columbia University Press.

Calvo, Ernesto, and Maria Victoria Murillo. 2004. "Who Delivers? Partisan Clients in the Argentine Electoral Market." *American Journal of Political Science* 48 (4): 742–57.

Cammett, Melani Claire. 2007. *Globalization and Business Politics in Arab North Africa*. New York: Cambridge University Press.

Carey, Sabine C. 2002. "A Comparative Analysis of Political Parties in Kenya, Zambia, and the Democratic Republic of Congo." *Democratization* 9 (3): 53–71.

Carney, Judith, and Michael Watts. 1991. "Disciplining Women? Rice, Mechanization, and the Evolution of Mandinka Gender Relations in Senegambia." *Signs* 16 (4): 651–81.

Carruthers, Bruce G. 1996. *City of Capital: Politics and Markets in the English Financial Revolution*. Princeton, N.J.: Princeton University Press.

Carter, Gwendolen M. 1960. "The Opposition in Ghana." In *Independence for Africa*. New York: Praeger.

Chabal, Patrick, and Jean-Pascal Daloz. 1999. *Africa Works: Disorder as Political Instrument*. Oxford: James Currey.

Chamberlain, Christopher. 1978. "The Migration of the Fang into Central Gabon during the Nineteenth Century: A New Interpretation." *International Journal of African Historical Studies* 11 (3): 429–56.

Chandra, Kanchan. 2004a. "Ethnic Parties and Democratic Stability." *Perspectives on Politics* 3 (2): 235–52.

2004b. *Why Ethnic Parties Succeed: Patronage and Ethnic Head Counts in India*. New York: Cambridge University Press.

Chapman, Stanley. 1984. *The Rise of Merchant Banking*. London: Taylor & Francis.

Chaudhry, Kiren A. 1994. "Economic Liberalization and the Lineages of the Rentier State." *Comparative Politics* 27 (1): 1–25.

1997. *The Price of Wealth: Economies and Institutions in the Middle East*. Ithaca, N.Y.: Cornell University Press.

Chege, Michael. 1998. "Introducing Race as a Variable into the Political Economy of Kenya Debate: An Incendiary Idea." *African Affairs* 97 (387): 209–30.

Cheserem, Micah. 2006. *The Will to Succeed: An Autobiography*. Nairobi: Jomo Kenyatta Foundation.

Chhibber, Pradeep, and Ken Kollman. 2004. *The Formation of National Party Systems: Federalism and Party Competition in Britain, Canada, India and the United States*. Princeton, N.J.: Princeton University Press.

Chinn, Menzie D., and Hiro Ito. 2008. "A New Measure of Financial Openness." *Journal of Comparative Policy Analysis* 10 (3): 309–22.

Chossudovsky, Michel. 1997. *The Globalisation of Poverty: Impacts of IMF and World Bank Reforms*. London: Zed Books.

Chua, Amy. 2004. *World on Fire: How Exporting Free Market Democracy Breeds Ethnic Hatred and Global Instability*. New York: Anchor Books.

Cingranelli, David L., and David L. Richards. 2007. "The Cingranelli-Richards (CIRI) Human Rights Dataset."

Clark, John F., and David E. Gardinier, eds. 1997. *Political Reform in Francophone Africa*. Boulder, Colo.: Westview Press.

Clough, Paul, and Gavin Williams. 1987. "Decoding Berg: The World Bank in Rural Northern Nigeria." In *State, Oil, & Agriculture in Nigeria*, ed. M.J. Watts. Berkeley, Calif.: Institute of International Studies.

Cohen, Andrew. 2008. "Business and Decolonisation in Central Africa Reconsidered." *Journal of Imperial and Commonwealth History* 36 (4): 641–58.

Cole, Donald B. 1984. *Martin Van Buren and the American Political System*. Princeton, N.J.: Princeton University Press.

Coleman, James S. 1954. "Nationalism in Tropical Africa." *American Political Science Review* 48 (2): 404–26.

Coleman, James S., and Carl G. Rosberg, eds. 1964. *Political Parties and National Integration in Tropical Africa*. Berkeley: University of California Press.

Coleman, William D. 1990. "State Traditions and Comprehensive Business Associations: A Comparative Structural Analysis." *Political Studies* 38 (2): 231–52.

Colley, Linda. 1985. *In Defiance of Oligarchy: The Tory Party 1714–60*. New York: Cambridge University Press.

Collier, David, and Ruth Berins Collier. 1979. "Inducements versus Constraints: Disaggregating 'Corporatism.'" *American Political Science Review* 73 (4): 967–86.

Collier, Paul. 1991. "Africa's External Relations: 1960–90." *African Affairs* 90 (360): 339–56.

——— 1998. "The Political Economy of Ethnicity." Paper prepared for the Annual World Bank Conference on Development Economics, Washington, D.C., April 20–21, 1998.

Collier, Ruth Berins. 1982. *Regimes in Tropical Africa: Changing Forms of Supremacy, 1945–1975*. Berkeley: University of California Press.

Collins, John Davison. 1976. "The Clandestine Movement of Groundnuts across the Niger-Nigeria Boundary." *Canadian Journal of African Studies* 10 (2): 259–78.

Coquery-Vidrovitch, Catherine. 1977. "Mutation de l'Impérialisme Colonial Français dans les Années 30." *African Economic History* (4): 103–52.

Cossé, Stéphane. 2006. "Strengthening Transparency in the Oil Sector in Cameroon: Why Does It Matter?" IMF Policy Discussion Paper PDP/06/2. Washington, D.C.: International Monetary Fund.

Cowen, Michael, and Kabiru Kinyanjui. 1977. *Some Problems of Capital and Class in Kenya*. Nairobi: Institute for Development Studies, University of Nairobi.

Cox, Gary, and Mathew D. McCubbins. 1986. "Electoral Politics as a Redistributive Game." *Journal of Politics* 48 (2): 370–89.

Cox, Gary W. 1997. *Making Votes Count: Strategic Coordination in the World's Electoral Systems*. Cambridge: Cambridge University Press.

——— 1999. "Electoral Rules and Electoral Coordination." *Annual Review of Political Science* 2: 145–61.

——— 2005. "Electoral Institutions and Political Competition: Coordination, Persuasion and Mobilization." In *Handbook of New Institutional Economics*, ed. C. Ménard and M.M. Shirley. Dordrecht, Netherlands: Springer.

Crick, Wilfred F., ed. 1965. *Commonwealth Banking Systems*. Oxford: Clarendon Press.

Crook, Richard C. 1997. "Winning Coalitions and Ethno-Regional Politics: The Failure of the Opposition in the 1990 and 1995 Elections in Côte d'Ivoire." *African Affairs* 96 (383): 215–42.

Cruise O'Brien, Donal B. 1971. *The Mourides of Senegal: The Political and Economic Organization of an Islamic Brotherhood*. Oxford: Clarendon Press.

——— 1998. "The Shadow-Politics of Wolofisation." *Journal of Modern African Studies* 36 (1): 25–46.

Dahl, Robert A. 1971. *Polyarchy: Participation and Opposition.* New Haven, Conn.: Yale University Press.

Daloz, Jean-Pascal, ed. 1999. *Le (non-) renouvellement des élites en Afrique subsaharienne.* Bordeaux: Centre d'Étude d'Afrique Noire.

Danevad, Andreas. 1995. "Responsiveness in Botswana Politics: Do Elections Matter?" *Journal of Modern African Studies* 33 (3): 381–402.

de Miras, Claude. 1982. "L'Entrepreneur ivoirien ou une bourgeoisie privée de son état." In *État et Bourgeoisie en Côte d'Ivoire*, ed. Y.A. Fauré and J.-F. Médard. Paris: Karthala.

Decker, Stephanie. 2005. "Decolonising Barclays Bank DCO? Corporate Africanisation in Nigeria, 1945–69." *Journal of Imperial and Commonwealth History* 33 (3): 419–40.

Deegan, Heather. 2003. "Elections in Africa – The Past Ten Years. Briefing Paper No. 2." London: The Royal Institute of International Affairs.

Diamond, Larry. 1987. "Class Formation in the Swollen African State." *Journal of Modern African Studies* 25 (4): 567–96.

1996. "Is the Third Wave Over?" *Journal of Democracy* 7 (3): 20–37.

Dickson, P.G.M. 1967. *The Financial Revolution in England.* London: Macmillan.

Diermeier, Daniel, and Antonio Merlo. 2004. "An Empirical Investigation of Coalition Bargaining Procedures." *Journal of Public Economics* 88: 783–97.

Doe, Lubin. 1995. "Managing Cameroon's Banking Sector – In and Out of Crisis – The Role of the Government." *African Development Review* 7 (1): 103–66.

Dollar, David, and Jakob Svensson. 2000. "What Explains the Success or Failure of Structural Adjustment Programmes?" *Economic Journal* 110 (466): 894–917.

Dongmo, Jean Louis. 1981. *Le Dynamisme Bamiléké (Cameroun).* Vol. II. Yaounde: Centre d'édition et de production pour l'enseignement et la recherche.

Dotson, Floyd, and Lillian O. Dotson. 1969. "The Economic Role of Non-Indigenous Ethnic Minorities in Colonial Africa." In *Colonialism in Africa, 1870–1960*, ed. L.H. Gann and P. Duignan. London: Cambridge University Press.

Downs, Anthony. 1957. *An Economic Theory of Democracy.* New York: Harper and Row.

Dunning, Thad. 2008. *Crude Democracy: Natural Resource Wealth and Political Regimes.* New York: Cambridge University Press.

Duverger, Maurice. 1954. *Political Parties.* New York: Wiley.

Eagles, Munroe. 1993. "Money and Votes in Canada – Campaign Spending and Parliamentary Election Outcomes, 1984 and 1988." *Canadian Public Policy-Analyse de Politiques* 19 (4): 432–49.

Easterly, William. 2005. "What Did Structural Adjustment Adjust? The Association of Policies and Growth with Repeated IMF and World Bank Adjustment Loans." *Journal of Development Economics* 76: 1–22.

Easterly, William, and Ross Levine. 1997. "Africa's Growth Tragedy: Policies and Ethnic Divisions." *Quarterly Journal of Economics* 112 (November): 1203–50.

Economic Commission for Africa. 2004. *Land Tenure Systems and their Impacts on Food Security and Sustainable Development in Africa.* Addis Ababa: Economic Commission for Africa.

Economist Intelligence Unit. 2000. *Country Profile: Kenya.* London: Economist Intelligence Unit.

Ekeh, Peter P. 1975. "Colonialism and the Two Publics in Africa: A Theoretical Statement." *Comparative Studies in Society and History* 17 (1): 91–112.

Ellingsen, Tanja. 2000. "Colorful Community or Ethnic Witches' Brew?: Multiethnicity and Domestic Conflict during and after the Cold War." *Journal of Conflict Resolution* 44 (2): 228–49.

Engberg, Holger L. 1965. "Commercial Banking in East Africa, 1950–63." *Journal of Modern African Studies* 3 (2): 175–200.

1973. "The Operations Account System in French-Speaking Africa." *Journal of Modern African Studies* 11 (4): 537–45.

Engberg, Holger L., and William A. Hance. 1969. "Growth and Dispersion of Branch Banking in Tropical Africa, 1950–1964." *Economic Geography* 45 (3): 195–208.

Epstein, David L., Robert H. Bates, Jack A. Goldstone, Ida Kristensen, and Sharyn O'Halloran. 2006. "Democratic Transitions." *American Journal of Political Science* 50 (3): 551–69.

Erickson, Robert S., and Thomas R. Palfrey. 1998. "Campaign Spending and Incumbency: An Alternative Simultaneous Equations Approach." *Journal of Politics* 60 (2): 355–73.

2000. "Equilibria in Campaign Spending Games: Theory and Data." *American Political Science Review* 94 (3): 595–609.

Esseks, John D. 1971. "Political Independence and Economic Decolonization: The Case of Ghana under Nkrumah." *Western Political Quarterly* 24 (1): 59–64.

Europa Publications Limited. 1971–2006. *Africa South of the Sahara*. London: Europa Publications.

Evans, Eric J. 1985. *Political Parties in Britain, 1783–1867*. London: Methuen.

Evans, Peter B. 1995. *Embedded Autonomy: States and Industrial Transformation*. Princeton, N.J.: Princeton University Press.

Eyoh, Dickson. 1998. "Through the Prism of a Local Tragedy: Political Liberalisation, Regionalism and Elite Struggles for Power in Cameroon." *Africa: Journal of the International African Institute* 68 (3): 338–59.

Ezé-Ezé, Donatien. 2001. "La structure bancaire dans le processus de financement de l'économie camerounaise." *Afrique et développement* 26 (3 & 4): 1–26.

Fauré, Yves A., and Jean-François Médard. 1982. *Etat et Bourgeoisie en Côte d'Ivoire*. Paris: Karthala.

Fearon, James D. 2003. "Ethnic and Cultural Diversity by Country." *Journal of Economic Growth* 8: 195–222.

Fedotov, Victor I. 2007. "Organizational and Legal Models of Chambers." Washington, D.C.: Center for International Private Enterprise.

Ferguson, James. 2006. *Global Shadows: Africa in the Neoliberal World Order*. Durham, N.C.: Duke University Press.

Ferree, Karen E. 2004. "The Micro-Foundations of Ethnic Voting: Evidence from South Africa." Afrobarometer Working Paper No. 40. East Lansing, MI.

2010. *Framing the Race in South Africa: The Political Origins of Racial Census Elections*. New York: Cambridge University Press.

Fieldhouse, D.K. 1986. *Black Africa 1945–1980*. London: Allen & Unwin.

Fish, M. Steven. 2005. *Democracy Derailed in Russia: The Failure of Open Politics*. New York: Cambridge University Press.

Fish, M. Steven, and Robin S. Brooks. 2004. "Does Diversity Hurt Democracy?" *Journal of Democracy* 15 (1): 154–66.

Fish, M. Steven, and Matthew Kroenig. 2009. *The Handbook of National Legislatures: A Global Survey*. New York: Cambridge University Press.

Foord, Archibald S. 1947. "The Waning of 'The Influence of the Crown.'" *The English Historical Review* 62 (245): 484–507.

Forrest, Tom. 1994. *The Advance of African Capital: The Growth of Nigerian Private Enterprise*. Charlottesville: University Press of Virginia.

Fotso, Victor. 1979. *Tout pour la Gloire de mon Pays*. Yaounde: CEPER.

Fourchard, Laurent. 2003. "Propriétaires et Commerçants Africains à Ouagadougou et à Bobo-Dioulasso (Haute-Volta), fin 19ème siècle–1960." *Journal of African History* 44 (3): 433–61.

Freund, Bill. 1984. *The Making of Contemporary Africa: The Development of African Society since 1800*. London: Macmillan.

Frieden, Jeffrey. 1991. *Debt, Development, and Democracy: Modern Political Economy and Latin America, 1965–1985*. Princeton, N.J.: Princeton University Press.

"From the Bullet to the Bank Account. The Economic Empire of the Ethiopian People's Revolutionary Democratic Front (EPRDF). A Preliminary Assessment." 2006.

Fry, Richard. 1976. *Bankers in West Africa: The Story of the Bank of British West Africa Limited*. London: Hutchinson Benham.

Gabriel, Jürg Martin. 1999. "Cameroon's Neopatrimonial Dilemma." *Journal of Contemporary African Studies* 17 (2): 173–96.

Gamson, William A. 1961. "A Theory of Coalition Formation." *American Sociological Review* 26 (3): 373–82.

Gandhi, Jennifer, and Ellen Lust-Okar. 2009. "Elections under Authoritarianism." *Annual Review of Political Science* 12 (403–422).

Gandhi, Jennifer, and Adam Przeworski. 2006. "Cooperation, Cooptation, and Rebellion under Dictatorship." *Economics and Politics* 18 (1): 1–26.

Gann, Lewis H., and Peter Duignan, eds. 1975. *Colonialism in Africa, 1870–1960*. Vol. 4. The Economics of Colonialism. London: Cambridge University Press.

Gatell, Frank Otto. 1967. "Money and Party in Jacksonian America: A Quantitative Look at New York City's Men of Quality." *Political Science Quarterly* 82 (2): 235–52.

Gauze, Rene. 1973. *The Politics of Congo-Brazzaville*. Translated by Virginia Thompson and Richard Adloff. Stanford, Calif.: Stanford University Press.

Gelbard, Enrique A., and Sergio Pereira Leite. 1999. "Measuring Financial Development in Sub-Saharan Africa." WP/99/105. Washington, D.C.: International Monetary Fund.

Gellner, Ernest. 1983. *Nations and Nationalism*. Ithaca, N.Y.: Cornell University Press.

Gerber, Alan S. 1998. "Estimating the Effect of Campaign Spending on Election Outcomes Using Instrumental Variables." *American Political Science Review* 92 (June): 401–11.

———. 2004. "Does Campaign Spending Work?: Field Experiments Provide Evidence and Suggest New Theory." *American Behavioral Scientist* 47 (5): 541–74.

Gerschenberg, Irving. 1972. "Banking in Uganda since Independence." *Economic Development and Cultural Change* 20 (3): 504–23.

Gertzel, Cherry. 1962. "Relations Between African and European Traders in the Niger Delta 1880–1896." *Journal of African History* 3 (2): 361–6.

Ginter, Donald E. 1966. "The Financing of the Whig Party Organization, 1783–1793." *The American Historical Review* 71 (2): 421–40.

Golder, Matt, and Leonard Wantchekon. 2004. "Africa: Dictatorial and Democratic Electoral Systems since 1946." In *Handbook of Electoral System Choice*, ed. J. Colomer. London: Palgrave.

Golder, Sona N. 2006. *The Logic of Pre-Electoral Coalition Formation.* Columbus: Ohio State University Press.

Goldsmith, Arthur A. 2002. "Business Associations and Better Governance in Africa." *Public Administration and Development* 22: 39–49.

Good, Kenneth. 1992. "Interpreting the Exceptionality of Botswana." *Journal of Modern African Studies* 30 (1): 69–95.

——— 1994. "Corruption and Mismanagement in Botswana: A Best-Case Example?" *Journal of Modern African Studies* 32 (3): 499–521.

Good, Kenneth, and Ian Taylor. 2006. "Unpacking the 'Model': Presidential Succession in Botswana." In *Legacies of Power: Leadership Change and Former Presidents in African Politics,* ed. R. Southall and H. Melber. Uppsala: Nordic Africa Institute.

Green, Donald P., and Jonathan S. Krasno. 1988. "Salvation for the Spendthrift Incumbent: Re-estimating the Effects of Campaign Spending in House Elections." *American Journal of Political Science* 32 (November): 884–907.

Green, Matthew N. 2008. "The 2006 Race for Democratic Majority Leader: Money, Policy, and Personal Loyalty" *PS* (January): 63–7.

Gregory, Robert G. 1993. *Quest for Equality: Asian Politics in East Africa, 1900–1967.* New Delhi: Orient Longman.

Grignon, Francois, Marcel Rutten, and Alamin Mazrui. 2001. "Observing and Analysing the 1997 General Elections: An Introduction." In *Out for the Count: The 1997 General Elections and Prospects for Democracy in Kenya,* ed. M. Rutten, A. Mazrui and F. Grignon. Kampala: Fountain Publishers.

Gros, Jean-Germain. 1995. "The Hard Lessons of Cameroon." *Journal of Democracy* 6 (3): 112–27.

Grosh, Barbara. 1990. "Parastatal-Led Development: The Financial Sector in Kenya, 1971–1987." *African Development Review* 2 (2): 27–48.

Gulde, Anne-Marie, and Catherine Pattillo. 2006. "Financial Sector Reform in Sub-Saharan Africa." *The Journal of Social, Political and Economic Studies* 31 (2): 133–42.

Gulde, Anne-Marie, Catherine Patillo, Jakob Christensen, Kevin Carey, and Smita Wagh. 2006. *Sub-Saharan Africa Financial Sector Challenges.* Washington, D.C.: International Monetary Fund.

Haber, Stephen, Douglass C. North, and Barry R. Weingast, eds. 2008. *Political Institutions and Financial Development.* Stanford, Calif.: Stanford University Press.

Haggard, Stephan, and Robert R. Kaufman. 1995. *The Political Economy of Democratic Transitions.* Princeton, N.J.: Princeton University Press.

Hammond, Bray. 1957. *Banks and Politics in America: From the Revolution to the Civil War.* Princeton, N.J.: Princeton University Press.

Handley, Antoinette. 2008. *Business and the State in Africa: Economic Policy-Making in the Neo-Liberal Era.* New York: Cambridge University Press.

Hargreaves, John D. 1982. "Toward the Transfer of Power in British West Africa." In *The Transfer of Power in Africa,* ed. P. Gifford and W.R. Louis. New Haven, Conn.: Yale University Press.

Harneit-Sievers, Axel. 1995. "African Business, 'Economic Nationalism,' and British Colonial Policy: Southern Nigeria, 1935–1954." *African Economic History* (23): 79–128.

Hart, David M. 2004. "'Business' Is Not an Interest Group: On the Study of Companies in American National Politics." *Annual Review of Political Science* 7: 47–69.

Hart, Elizabeth, and E. Gyimah-Boadi. 2000. *Business Associations in Ghana's Economic and Political Transition*. Accra: Center for Democracy and Development.

Harvey, Charles. 1996. "Banking Reform in Ethiopia." IDS Working Paper 37. Brighton: Institute of Development Studies.

——. 1998. "Banking Policy in Botswana: Orthodox but Untypical." In *Banking in Africa: The Impact of Financial Sector Reform since Independence*, ed. M. Brownbridge and C. Harvey. Trenton, N.J.: Africa World Press.

Heberlig, Eric, Marc Hetherington, and Bruce Larson. 2006. "The Price of Leadership: Campaign Money and the Polarization of Congressional Parties." *Journal of Politics* 68 (4): 992–1005.

Heilbrunn, John R. 1997. "Commerce, Politics, and Business Associations in Benin and Togo." *Comparative Politics* 29 (4): 473–92.

Hempstone, Smith. 1997. *Rogue Ambassador: An African Memoir*. Sewanee, Tenn.: University of the South Press.

Herbst, Jeffrey. 1990. "The Structural Adjustment of Politics in Africa." *World Development* 18 (7): 949–58.

Hicken, Allen, and Heather Stoll. 2008. "Electoral Rules and the Size of the Prize: How Political Institutions Shape Presidential Party Systems." *Journal of Politics* 70 (4): 1109–27.

Himbara, David. 1994. *Kenyan Capitalists, the State, and Development*. Boulder, Colo.: Lynne Rienner.

Hiscox, Michael J. 2002. *International Trade & Political Conflict: Commerce, Coalitions, and Mobility*. Princeton, N.J.: Princeton University Press.

Hodgkin, Thomas. 1957. *Nationalism in Colonial Africa*. New York: New York University Press.

——. 1961. *African Political Parties*. London: Penguin.

Hofstadter, Richard. 1969. *The Idea of a Party System: The Rise of Legitimate Opposition in the United States, 1780–1840*. Berkeley: University of California Press.

Hogendorn, Jan S. 1978. *Nigerian Groundnut Exports: Origins and Early Development*. Zaria: Ahmadu Bello University Press.

Holmquist, Frank W. 2002. "Business and Politics in Kenya in the 1990s. Occasional Paper." Copenhagen: Centre of African Studies, University of Copenhagen.

Holmquist, Frank W., Frederick S. Weaver, and Michael D. Ford. 1994. "The Structural Development of Kenya's Political Economy." *African Studies Review* 37 (1): 69–105.

Honohan, Patrick, and Thorsten Beck. 2007. *Making Finance Work for Africa*. Washington, D.C.: World Bank.

Hopkins, A.G. 1966. "Economic Aspects of Political Movements in Nigeria and in the Gold Coast 1918–1939." *Journal of African History* 8 (1): 133–52.

——. 1987. "Big Business in African Studies." *Journal of African History* 28 (1): 119–40.

Hornsby, Charles. 2001. "Election Day and the Results." In *Out for the Count: The 1997 General Elections and Prospects for Democracy in Kenya*, ed. M. Rutten, A. Mazrui, and F. Grignon. Kampala: Fountain Publishers.

Horowitz, Donald L. 1985. *Ethnic Groups in Conflict*, 2nd ed. Berkeley: University of California Press.

Howard, Allen M. 1976. "The Relevance of Spatial Analysis for African Economic History: The Sierra Leone–Guinea System." *Journal of African History* 17 (3): 365–88.

Howard, Marc Morje, and Philip G. Roessler. 2006. "Liberalizing Electoral Outcomes in Competitive Authoritarian Regimes." *American Journal of Political Science* 50 (2): 365–81.

Humphreys, Macartan, and Robert H. Bates. 2005. "Political Institutions and Economic Policies: Lessons from Africa." *British Journal of Political Science* 35: 403–28.

Hunter, Guy. 1962. *The New Societies of Tropical Africa.* New York: Praeger.

Huntington, Samuel. 1991. *The Third Wave: Democratization in the Late Twentieth Century.* Norman: University of Oklahoma Press.

Hyden, Goran. 1983. "Problems and Prospects of State Coherence." In *State Versus Ethnic Claims: African Policy Dilemmas,* ed. D. Rothchild and V.A. Olorunsola. Boulder, Colo.: Westview Press.

1980. *Beyond Ujamaa in Tanzania: Underdevelopment and an Uncaptured Peasantry.* Berkeley: University of California Press.

Iliffe, John. 1983. *The Emergence of African Capitalism.* Minneapolis: University of Minnesota Press.

International Monetary Fund. 1996. "IMF Approves Three-Year Loan for Kenya under the ESAF." Press Release No. 96/21, 26 April. Washington, D.C.: International Monetary Fund.

2000. "Cameroon: Preliminary Document on the Enhanced Initiative for Heavily Indebted Poor Countries." Washington, D.C.: International Monetary Fund.

2002. "Kenya: Selected Issues and Statistical Appendix." IMF Country Report No. 02/84. Washington, D.C.: International Monetary Fund.

2005a. "Cameroon: Ex Post Assessment of Longer-Term Program Engagement." IMF Country Report No. 05/189. Washington, D.C.: International Monetary Fund.

2005b. "The Federal Democratic Republic of Ethiopia: Ex Post Assessment of Long-Term Fund Engagement." IMF Country Report No. 05/26. Washington, D.C.: International Monetary Fund.

2008. "Kenya: Ex Post Assessment of Longer-Term Program Engagement." IMF Country Report No. 08/338. Washington, D.C.: International Monetary Fund.

Jackman, Robert W. 1973. "On the Relationship of Economic Development to Political Performance." *American Journal of Political Science* 17 (3): 611–21.

Jackson, R.T. 1971. "Agricultural Development in the Malagasy Republic." *East African Geographical Review* 9: 69–78.

Jackson, Robert H., and Carl G. Rosberg. 1982. *Personal Rule in Black Africa.* Berkeley: University of California Press.

Jacobson, Gary C. 1978. "The Effects of Campaign Spending in Congressional Elections." *American Political Science Review* 72 (2): 469–91.

1990. "The Effects of Campaign Spending in House Elections: New Evidence for Old Arguments." *American Journal of Political Science* 34 (2): 334–62.

Jayne, T.S., Takashi Yamano, Michael Weber, David Tschirley, Rui Benfica, Anthony Chapoto, and Ballard Zulu. 2003. "Smallholder Income and Land Distribution in Africa: Implications for Poverty Reduction Strategies." *Food Policy* 28: 253–75.

Jensen, Nathan, and Leonard Wantchekon. 2004. "Resource Wealth and Political Regimes in Africa." *Comparative Political Studies* 37 (7): 816–41.

Jewsiewicki, B. 1977. "The Great Depression and the Making of the Colonial Economic System in the Belgian Congo." *African Economic History* 4 (Fall): 153–76.

Johnston, Ronald J., Charles J. Pattie, and Lucy C. Johnston. 1989. "The Impact of Constituency Spending on the Result of the 1987 British General Election." *Electoral Studies* 8 (2): 143–55.

Joireman, Sandra Fullerton. 1997. "Opposition Politics and Ethnicity in Ethiopia: We Will All Go Down Together." *Journal of Modern African Studies* 35 (3): 387–407.

Jolly, Curtis M., and Millie Gadbois. 1996. "The Effect of Animal Traction on Labour Productivity and Food Self-Sufficiency: The Case of Mali." *Agricultural Systems* 51 (4): 453–67.

Jorgensen, Jan Jelmert. 1981. *Uganda: A Modern History*. London: Helm.

Joseph, Richard A. 1977. *Radical Nationalism in Cameroun: Social Origins of the U.P.C. Rebellion*. Oxford: Clarendon Press.

———. 1984. "Class, State and Prebendal Politics in Nigeria." In *State and Class in Africa*, ed. N. Kasfir. London: Frank Cass.

Jua, Nantang. 1990. "Economic Management in Neo-Colonial States: A Case Study of Cameroon." Research Report no. 38. Leiden: African Sudies Centre.

———. 1993. "State, Oil and Accumulation." In *Itinéraires d'Accumulation au Cameroun*, ed. P. Geschiere and P. Konings. Paris: Karthala.

Kahler, Miles. 1981. "Political Regime and Economic Actors: The Response of Firms to the End of Colonial Rule." *World Politics* 33 (3): 383–412.

Kamgna, Séverin Yves, and Leonnel Dimou. 2008. "Efficacité technique des banques de la CEMAC." MPRA Paper No. 9603.

Kanduza, Ackson. 1983. "The Tobacco Industry in Northern Rhodesia, 1912–1938." *International Journal of African Historical Studies* 16 (2): 201–29.

Kanogo, Tabitha. 1987. *Squatters & the Roots of Mau Mau*. Nairobi: East African Publishers.

Karl, Terry L. 1990. "The Dilemmas of Democratization in Latin America." *Comparative Politics* 23 (1): 1–21.

———. 1995. "The Hybrid Regimes of Central America." *Journal of Democracy* 6: 72–87.

———. 1997. *The Paradox of Plenty: Oil Booms and Petro-States*. Berkeley: University of California Press.

Karlan, Pamela S. 1994. "Not by Money but by Virtue Won? Vote Trafficking and the Voting Rights System." *Virginia Law Review* 80 (7): 1455–75.

Karume, Njenga, and Mutu wa Gethoi. 2009. *Beyond Expectations: From Charcoal to Gold*. Nairobi: Kenway.

Kasara, Kimuli. 2007. "Tax Me If You Can: Ethnic Geography, Democracy, and the Taxation of Agriculture in Africa." *American Political Science Review* 101 (1): 159–72.

Katumanga, Musambayi. 2005. "Constructing the Abaluhya Unity." In *The Moi Succession*, ed. H. Maupeu, M. Katumanga, and W. Mitullah. Nairobi: Transafrica Press.

Katzin, Margaret. 1964. "The Role of the Small Entrepreneur." In *Economic Transition in Africa*, ed. M.J. Herskovits and M. Harwitz. Evanston, Ill.: Northwestern University Press.

Kaunda, Kenneth. 1968. *Zambia's Economic Reforms: The Mulungushi Declaration*. Lusaka: Government Printer.

Kennedy, Masime, and Gichira Kibara. 2003. "Regime Transitions and the Institutionalization of Democracy in Kenya: The December 2002 Elections and Beyond." *The East African Journal of Human Rights and Democracy* 1 (1): 13–29.

Kennedy, Paul. 1988. *African Capitalism: The Struggle for Ascendency*. New York: Cambridge University Press.

———. 1994. "Political Barriers to African Capitalism." *Journal of Modern African Studies* 32 (2): 191–213.

Kenya Human Rights Commission. 1998. *Killing the Vote: State Sponsored Violence and Flawed Elections in Kenya*. Nairobi: Kenya Human Rights Commission.

Keynes, John Maynard. 1964. *The General Theory of Employment, Interest, and Money*. New York: Harvest.

Khadiagala, Gilbert M., and Michael G. Schatzberg. 1987. "The Kenyan Bourgeoisie, External Capital, and the State: An Introduction." In *The Political Economy of Kenya*, ed. M.G. Schatzberg. New York: Praeger.

Kilby, Peter. 1969. *Industrialization in an Open Economy: Nigeria 1945–66*. Cambridge: Cambridge University Press.

Kilson, Martin L. 1958. "Nationalism and Social Classes in British West Africa." *Journal of Politics* 20 (2): 368–87.

⸺ 1963. "Authoritarian and Single-Party Tendencies in African Politics." *World Politics* 15 (2): 262–94.

⸺ 1964. "Sierra Leone." In *Political Parties and National Integration in Tropical Africa*, ed. J. Coleman and C.G. Rosberg. Berkeley: University of California Press.

⸺ 1970. "The Emergent Elites of Black Africa, 1900 to 1960." In *Colonialism in Africa, 1870–1960*, ed. L.H. Gann and P. Duignan. Cambridge: Cambridge University Press.

Kipkorir, B.E. 2009. *Descent from Cherang'any Hills: Memoirs of a Reluctant Academic*. Nairobi: Macmillan Kenya.

Kitching, G.N. 1980. *Class and Economic Change in Kenya: The Making of an African Petite Bourgeoisie, 1905–1970*. New Haven, Conn.: Yale University Press.

Kitschelt, Herbert, and Steven I. Wilkinson, eds. 2007. *Patrons, Clients, and Policies: Patterns of Democratic Accountability and Political Competition*. New York: Cambridge University Press.

Knack, Stephen. 2001. "Aid Dependence and the Quality of Governance: Cross-Country Empirical Tests." *Southern Economic Journal* 68 (2): 310–29.

Kobou, Georges, Dominique Njinkeu, and Bruno Powo Fosso. 2008. "The Political Economy of Cameroon's Post-Independence Growth Experience." In *The Political Economy of Economic Growth in Africa, 1960–2000*, ed. B.J. Ndulu, S.A. O'Connell, J.-P. Azam, R.H. Bates, A.K. Fosu, J.W. Gunning, and D. Njinkeu. New York: Cambridge University Press.

Kofele-Kale, Ndiva. 1986. "Ethnicity, Regionalism, and Political Power: A Post-Mortem of Ahidjo's Cameroon." In *The Political Economy of Cameroon*, ed. M.G. Schatzberg and I.W. Zartman. New York: Praeger.

⸺ 1987. "Class, Status, and Power in Postreunification Cameroon: The Rise of an Anglophone Bourgeoisie, 1961–1980." In *Studies in Power and Class in Africa*, ed. I.L. Markovitz. New York: Oxford University Press.

Konings, Piet. 1996. "The Post-Colonial State and Economic and Political Reforms in Cameroon." In *Liberalization in the Developing World: Institutional and Economic Changes in Latin America, Africa, and Asia*, ed. A.E. Fernández Jilberto and A. Mommen. New York: Routledge.

⸺ 2004. "Opposition and Social-Democratic Change in Africa: The Social Democratic Front in Cameroon." *Commonwealth and Comparative Politics* 42 (3): 289–311.

⸺ 2007. "The Neoliberalising African State and Private Capital Accumulation: The Case of Cameroon." In *Big Business and Economic Development: Conglomerates and Economic Groups in Developing Countries and Transition Economies under Globalisation*, ed. A.E. Fernández Jilberto and B. Hogenboom. London: Routledge.

Kramer, Gerald H. 1971. "Short-Term Fluctuations in U.S. Voting Behavior, 1896–1964." *American Political Science Review* 65 (65): 131–43.

Kraus, Jon. 2002. "Capital, Power and Business Associations in the African Political Economy: A Tale of Two Countries, Ghana and Nigeria." *Journal of Modern African Studies* 40 (3): 395–436.

Krieger, Milton. 1994. "Cameroon's Democratic Crossroads, 1990–4." *Journal of Modern African Studies* 32 (4): 605–28.

   2008. *Cameroon's Social Democratic Front: Its History and Prospects as an Opposition Political Party (1990–2011).* Bamenda: Langaa RPCIG.

Krueger, Anne O. 1993. *Political Economy of Policy Reform in Developing Countries.* Cambridge, Mass.: MIT Press.

Kuenzi, Michelle, and Gina Lambright. 2001. "Party System Institutionalization in 30 African Countries." *Party Politics* 7 (4): 437–68.

Kuisel, Richard F. 1983. *Capitalism and the State in Modern France.* Cambridge: Cambridge University Press.

La Porta, Rafael, Florencio Lopez-de-Silanes, and Andrei Shleifer. 2002. "Government Ownership of Banks." *The Journal of Finance* 62 (1): 265–301.

La Porta, Rafael, Florencio Lopez-de-Silanes, Andrei Shleifer, and Robert W. Vishny. 1998. "Law and Finance." *Journal of Political Economy* 106 (6): 1113–55.

Laeven, Luc, and Fabian Valencia. 2008. "Systemic Banking Crises: A New Database." IMF Working Paper No. 08/224.

Laver, Michael, and Norman Schofield. 1990. *Multiparty Government: The Politics of Coalition in Europe.* Ann Arbor: The University of Michigan Press.

Laver, Michael, and Kenneth A. Shepsle. 1990. "Coalitions and Cabinet Government." *American Political Science Review* 84 (3): 873–90.

Le Vine, Victor T. 1968. "Political Elite Recruitment and Political Structure in French-Speaking Africa." *Cahiers d'Etudes Africaines* 8 (31): 369–89.

   1971. *The Cameroon Federal Republic.* Ithaca, N.Y.: Cornell University Press.

   1986. "Leadership and Regime Changes in Perspective." In *The Political Economy of Cameroon,* ed. M.G. Schatzberg and I.W. Zartman. New York: Praeger.

LeBas, Adrienne. 2006. "Polarization as Craft: Explaining Party Formation and State Violence in Zimbabwe." *Comparative Politics* 38 (4): 419–38.

Leblang, David A. 1997. "Domestic and Systemic Determinants of Capital Controls in the Developed and Developing World." *International Studies Quarterly* 41 (3): 435–54.

Lemarchand, Rene. 1964. *Political Awakening in the Belgian Congo.* Berkeley: University of California Press.

   1972. "Political Clientelism and Ethnicity in Tropical Africa: Competing Solidarities in Nation-Building." *American Political Science Review* 66 (1): 68–90.

   1980. "The Politics of Sara Ethnicity: A Note on the Origins of the Civil War in Chad." *Cahiers d'Études Africaines* 20 (80): 449–71.

Leonard, David K., and Scott Straus. 2003. *Africa's Stalled Development: International Causes & Cures.* Boulder, Colo.: Lynne Rienner.

Levi, Margaret. 1988. *Of Rule and Revenue.* Berkeley: University of California Press.

Levitsky, Steven, and Lucan A. Way. 2002. "The Rise of Competitive Authoritarianism." *Journal of Democracy* 13 (2): 51–65.

Levitt, Steven D. 1994. "Using Repeat Challengers to Estimate the Effect of Campaign Spending on Election Outcomes in U.S. House Elections." *Journal of Political Economy* 102 (4): 777–98.

Lewis, Arthur. 1965. *Politics in West Africa*. London: George Allen & Unwin.

Lewis, Peter. 1996. "Economic Reform and Political Transition in Africa: The Quest for a Politics of Development." *World Politics* 49 (1): 92–129.

Leys, Colin. 1974. *Underdevelopment in Kenya: The Political Economy of Neo-Colonialism*. London: Heinemann.

———. 1978. "Capital Accumulation, Class Formation, and Dependency: The Significance of the Kenyan Case." In *The Socialist Register, 1978*, ed. R. Miliband and J. Saville. New York: Monthly Review Press.

———. 1982. "Accumulation, Class Formation and Dependency: Kenya." In *Industry and Accumulation in Africa*, ed. M. Fransman. London: Heinemann.

Lijphart, Arend. 1969. "Consociational Democracy." *World Politics* 21 (2): 207–25.

———. 1977. *Democracy in Plural Societies*. New Haven, Conn.: Yale University Press.

Lindberg, Staffan I. 2006. *Democracy and Elections in Africa*. Baltimore, Md.: Johns Hopkins University Press.

Lindblom, Charles E. 1977. *Politics and Markets*. New York: Basic Books.

Lipset, Seymour M. 1959. "Some Social Requisites of Democracy: Economic Development and Political Legitimacy." *American Political Science Review* 53 (1): 69–105.

———. 1967. *The First New Nation*. Garden City, N.Y.: Doubleday.

———. 2000. "The Indispensability of Political Parties." *Journal of Democracy* 11 (1): 48–55.

Lipset, Seymour M., and Stein Rokkan, eds. 1967. *Party Systems and Voter Alignments*. New York: Free Press.

Lloyd, P.C. 1966. Introduction to *The New Elites of Tropical Africa*, ed. P.C. Lloyd. London: Oxford University Press.

Loimeier, Roman. 1997. *Islamic Reform and Political Change in Northern Nigeria*. Evanston, Ill.: Northwestern University Press.

Lombard, C. Stephen, and Alex H.C. Tweedie. 1974. *Agriculture in Zambia since Independence*. Lusaka: Institute for African Studies, University of Zambia.

Londregan, John, Henry Bienen, and Nicolas van de Walle. 1995. "Ethnicity and Leadership Succession in Africa." *International Studies Quarterly* 39: 1–25.

Lonsdale, John. 1968. "Some Origins of Nationalism in East Africa." *Journal of African History* 9 (1): 119–46.

Lust-Okar, Ellen. 2005. *Structuring Conflict in the Arab World: Incumbents, Opponents, and Institutions*. New York: Cambridge University Press.

Lynn, Martin. 1997. *Commerce and Economic Change in West Africa: The Palm Oil Trade in the Nineteenth Century*. New York: Cambridge University Press.

MacGaffey, Janet. 1987. *Entrepreneurs and Parasites: The Struggle for Indigenous Capitalism in Zaire*. Cambridge: Cambridge University Press.

Magaloni, Beatriz. 2006. *Voting for Autocracy: Hegemonic Party Survival and its Demise in Mexico*. New York: Cambridge University Press.

Magang, David. 2008. *The Magic of Perseverance: The Autobiography of David Magang*. Cape Town: Centre for Advanced Studies of African Societies.

Mamdani, Mahmood. 1976. *Politics and Class Formation in Uganda*. New York: Monthly Review Press.

Mann, Gregory, and Jane I. Guyer. 1999. "Imposing a Guide on the Indigène: The Fifty Year Experience of the Sociétés de Prèvoyance in French West and Equatorial Africa." In *Credit, Currencies and Culture: African Financial Institutions in Historical Perspective*, ed. E. Stiansen and J.I. Guyer. Uppsala: Nordic Africa Institute.

Manning, Carrie. 2005. "Assessing African Party Systems after the Third Wave." *Party Politics* 11 (6): 707–27.

Mansfield, Edward, and Jack Snyder. 1995. "Democratization and War." *Foreign Affairs* 74: 79–97.

Markovitz, Irving L. 1977. *Power and Class in Africa*. Englewood Cliffs, N.J.: Prentice-Hall.

——— ed. 1987. *Studies in Power and Class in Africa*. New York: Oxford University Press.

Marris, Peter, and Anthony Somerset. 1971. *African Businessmen: A Study of Entrepreneurship and Development in Kenya*. London: Routledge and Kegan Paul.

Marsden, Keith. 1990. "African Entrepreneurs: Pioneers of Development." International Finance Corporation Discussion Paper No. 009. Washington, D.C.: World Bank.

Marshall, Monty G., and Keith Jaggers. 2009. "Polity IV Project." University of Maryland, College Park.

Martin, Guy. 1995. "Continuity and Change in Franco-African Relations." *Journal of Modern African Studies* 33 (1): 1–20.

Martin, Lanny W., and Georg Vanberg. 2003. "Wasting Time? The Impact of Ideology and Size on Delay in Coalition Formation." *British Journal of Political Science* 33 (2): 323–32.

Marty, Marianne. 2002. "Mauritania: Political Parties, Neo-patrimonialism, and Democracy." *Democratization* 9 (3): 92–108.

Masson, Paul R., and Catherine Patillo. 2005. *The Monetary Geography of Africa*. Washington, D.C.: Brookings Institution Press.

Matiba, Kenneth S.N. 1993. *Kenya: Return to Reason*. Nairobi: Kalamka Ltd.

Maxon, Robert M. 1992. "The Colonial Financial System." In *An Economic History of Kenya*, ed. W.R. Ochieng' and R.M. Maxon. Nairobi: East African Educational Publishers.

Mazrui, Ali A., and Michael Tidy. 1984. *Nationalism and New States in Africa*. London: Heinemann.

Mbembe, Achille. 1993. "Épilogue: Crise de légitimité, restauration autoritaire et déliquescence de l'État." In *Itinéraires d'Accumulation au Cameroun*, ed. P. Geschiere and P. Konings. Paris: Karthala.

M'bokolo, Elikia. 1982. "French Colonial Policy in Equatorial Africa in the 1940s and 1950s." In *The Transfer of Power in Africa*, ed. P. Gifford and W.R. Louis. New Haven: Yale University Press.

McCracken, John. 1998. "Blantyre Transformed: Class, Conflict and Nationalism in Urban Malawi." *Journal of African History* 39: 247–69.

McGowan, Patrick J. 2003. "African Military Coups d'Etat, 1956–2001: Frequency, Trends and Distribution." *Journal of Modern African Studies* 41 (3): 339–70.

McGowan, Patrick J., and H.K.M. Wacirah. 1974. "The Evolution of Tanzanian Political Leadership." *African Studies Review* 17 (1): 179–204.

McKinnon, Ronald. 1973. *Money and Capital in Economic Development*. Washington, D.C.: Brookings Institution.

McMann, Kelly M. 2006. *Economic Autonomy and Democracy: Hybrid Regimes in Russia and Kyrgyzstan*. New York: Cambridge University Press.

McWilliam, M.D. 1962. "Banking in Kenya, 1950–1960." *East African Economics Review* 9 (1): 16–40.

Médard, Jean-François. 1982. "The Underdeveloped State in Tropical Africa: Political Clientelism or Neo-Patrimonialism." In *Private Patronage and Public Power: Political Clientelism in the Modern State*, ed. C. Clapham. London: Frances Pinter.

Mehran, Hassanali, Piero Ugolini, Jean Philippe Briffaux, George Iden, Tonny Lybek, Stephen Swaray, and Peter Hayward. 1998. *Financial Sector Development in Sub-Saharan African Countries*. Washington, D.C.: International Monetary Fund.

Melly, Paul. 2002. "Central African Republic – Uncertain Prospects." Writenet Paper No. 14/2001. UNHCR Emergency and Security Service.

Mendy, Marcel. 2001. *Wade et le Sopi: La longue marche*. Vol. 1. Versailles: Les classiques africains.

Meredith, David. 1986. "State Controlled Marketing and Economic 'Development': The Case of the West African Produce Board." *The Economic History Review* 39 (1): 77–91.

Mershon, Carol. 2001. "Contending Models of Portfolio Allocation and Office Payoffs to Party Factions: Italy, 1963–79." *American Journal of Political Science* 45 (2): 277–93.

Michels, Robert. 1962. *Political Parties: A Sociological Study of the Oligarchical Tendencies of Modern Democracy*. Translated by E. Paul and C. Paul. New York: Free Press.

Mittelman, James H. 1978. "Underdevelopment and Nationalisation: Banking in Tanzania." *Journal of Modern African Studies* 16 (4): 597–617.

Mkandawire, Thandika. 1992. "The Political Economy of Development with a Democratic Face." In *Africa's Recovery in the 1990s*, ed. G.A. Cornia, R. van der Hoeven and T. Mkandawire. New York: St. Martin's Press.

1999a. "Crisis Management and the Making of 'Choiceless Democracies'." In *State, Conflict, and Democracy in Africa*, ed. R. Joseph. Boulder, Colo.: Lynne Rienner.

1999b. "The Political Economy of Financial Reform in Africa." *Journal of International Development* 11: 321–42.

Molomo, Mpho, and Wilford Molefe. 2005. "Voters and Electoral Performance of Political Parties in Botswana." In *40 Years of Democracy in Botswana, 1965–2005*, ed. Z. Maundeni. Gaborone: Mmegi.

Molomo, Mpho, and David Sebudubedu. 2005. "Funding of Political Parties: Levelling the Political Playing Field." In *40 Years of Democracy in Botswana, 1965–2005*, ed. Z. Maundeni. Gaborone: Mmegi.

Molutsi, Patrick. 2004. "Botswana: The Path to Democracy and Development." In *Democratic Reform in Africa*, ed. E. Gyimah-Boadi. Boulder, Colo.: Lynne Rienner.

Monga, Celestin. 1997. "Eight Problems with African Politics." *Journal of Democracy* 8 (3): 156–70.

Monga, Yvette. 2000. "'Au village!': Space, Culture, and Politics in Cameroon." *Cahiers d'Études Africaines* XL-4 (160): 723–49.

2001. "The Politics of Identity Negotiation in Cameroon." *International Negotiation* 6: 199–228.

Moore, Barrington. 1966. *Social Origins of Dictatorship and Democracy*. Boston: Beacon Press.

Morgenthau, Ruth Schachter. 1964. *Political Parties in French-Speaking West Africa*. London: Oxford University Press.

Moroke, T.S., E.N. Makhwaje, and A. Abdullahi. 2008. "Agricultural Policy Development: Effect on Agricultural Production in Botswana." In *Land and Water*

Management in Southern Africa: Towards Sustainable Agriculture, eds. Calvin Nhira et al. Pretoria: The Africa Institute of South Africa.

Mouiche, Ibrahim. 2005. *Autorités Traditionnelles et Démocratisation au Cameroun: Entre Centralité de l'Etat et Logiques de Terroir.* Berlin: LIT Verlag.

Mousseau, Demet Yalcin. 2001. "Democratizing with Ethnic Divisions: A Source of Conflict?" *Journal of Peace Research* 38 (5): 547–67.

Mozaffar, Shaheen. 2002. "Patterns of Electoral Governance in Africa's Emerging Democracies." *International Political Science Review* 23 (1): 85–101.

Mozaffar, Shaheen, and James R. Scarritt. 2005. "The Puzzle of African Party Systems." *Party Politics* 11 (4): 399–421.

Mozaffar, Shaheen, James R. Scarritt, and Glen Galaich. 2003. "Electoral Institutions, Ethnopolitical Cleavages and Party Systems in Africa's Emerging Democracies." *American Political Science Review* 97 (3): 391–406.

Muigai, Githu. 1995. "Ethnicity and the Renewal of Competitive Politics in Kenya." In *Ethnic Conflict and Democratization in Africa*, ed. H. Glickman. Atlanta, Ga.: African Studies Association Press.

Munene, Macharia. 2001. *The Politics of Transition in Kenya: 1995–1998.* Nairobi: Quest & Insight.

Mutunga, Willy. 1999. *Constitution-Making from the Middle: Civil Society and Transition Politics in Kenya, 1992–1997.* Nairobi: SAREAT.

——— 2002. "The Unfolding Political Alliances and their Implications for Kenya's Transition." In *Building an Open Society: The Politics of Transition in Kenya*, ed. L.M. Mute, W. Kioko, and K. Akivaga. Nairobi: Claripress.

Mwakikagile, Godfrey. 2010. *Ethnic Diversity and Integration in the Gambia: The Land, the People, and the Culture.* Dar es Salaam: Continental Press.

Myerson, Roger B. 2008. "The Autocrat's Credibility Problem and Foundations of the Constitutional State." *American Political Science Review* 102 (1): 125–39.

Mylonas, Harris, and Nasos Roussias. 2007. "When Do Votes Count?: Regime Type, Electoral Conduct, and Political Competition in Africa." *Comparative Political Studies* 41 (11): 1466–91.

Namier, Lewis. 1929. *The Structure of Politics at the Accession of George III.* London: Macmillan.

Nannestad, Peter, and Martin Paldam. 1994. "The VP Function: A Survey of the Literature on Vote and Popularity Functions after 25 Years." *Public Choice* 79 (3–4): 213–45.

Nasibi, Rueben Indiatsi. 1992. "Financial Institutions and Monetary Policy in Post-Independence Kenya." In *An Economic History of Kenya*, ed. W.R. Ochieng' and R.M. Maxon. Nairobi: East African Educational Publishers.

Ndegwa, Stephen N. 2001. "A Decade of Democracy in Africa." *African and Asian Studies* 36 (1): 1–16.

Ndongko, Wilfred A. 1986. *Economic Management in Cameroon: Policies and Performance.* Leiden: African Studies Centre.

Newlyn, W.T., and D.C. Rowan. 1954. *Money and Banking in British Colonial Africa.* Oxford: Clarendon Press.

Ngayap, Pierre Flambeau. 1983. *Cameroun, qui gouverne? De Ahidjo à Biya: l'héritage et l'enjeu.* Paris: Harmattan.

——— 1999. *L'Opposition au Cameroun: Les années de braise.* Paris: L'Harmattan.

Ngwasiri, C.N. 1989. "The Effect of Legislation on Foreign Investment – The Case of Cameroon." *Journal of African Law* 33 (2): 192–204.

Njogu, Kimani. 2001. "The Culture of Politics and Ethnic Nationalism." In *Out for the Count: The 1997 General Elections and Prospects for Democracy in Kenya*, ed. M. Rutten, A. Mazrui, and F. Grignon. Kampala: Fountain Publishers.

Nohlen, Dieter, Michael Krennerich, and Bernhard Thibaut, eds. 1999. *Elections in Africa: A Data Handbook*. New York: Oxford University Press.

Norris, Pippa, and Robert Mattes. 2003. "Does Ethnicity Determine Support for the Governing Party?" Afrobarometer Working Paper No. 26. East Lansing, Mich.

North, Douglass C., and Barry R. Weingast. 1989. "Constitutions and Commitment: The Evolution of Institutions Governing Public Choice in Seventeenth-Century England." *Journal of Economic History* XLIX (4): 803–32.

Nuembissi Kom, Paul. 2007. "Elites Urbaines et Politique Locale au Cameroun: Le Cas de Bayangam," MA Thesis, Faculté des Science Juridiques et Politiques, Université de Yaoundé II.

Nugent, Paul. 2007. "Banknotes and Symbolic Capital: Ghana's Election under the Fourth Republic." In *Votes, Money and Violence: Political Parties and Elections in Sub-Saharan Africa*, ed. M. Basedau, G. Erdmann, and A. Mehler. Uppsala: Nordic Africa Institute.

Nwabughuogu, Anthony I. 1982. "From Wealthy Entrepreneurs to Petty Traders: The Decline of African Middlemen in Eastern Nigeria, 1900–1950." *Journal of African History* 23 (3): 365–79.

Nyamnjoh, Francis B. 1999. "Cameroon: A Country United by Ethnic Ambition and Difference." *African Affairs* 98 (390): 101–18.

Nyangira, Nicholas. 1987. "Ethnicity, Class, and Politics in Kenya." In *The Political Economy of Kenya*, ed. M.G. Schatzberg. New York: Praeger.

Nyang'oro, Julius E., and Timothy M. Shaw, eds. 1989. *Corporatism in Africa: Comparative Analysis and Practice*. Boulder, Colo.: Westview Press.

Nyerere, Julius K. 1967. *Freedom and Unity: A Selection from Writings and Speeches, 1952–1965*. London: Oxford University Press.

O'Brien, F.S., and Terry C.I. Ryan. 2001. "Kenya." In *Aid and Reform in Africa: Lessons from Ten Case Studies*, ed. S. Devarajan, D. Dollar, and T. Holmgren. Washington, D.C.: World Bank.

Ochieng', William R. 1989. "Independent Kenya, 1963–1986." In *A Modern History of Kenya*, ed. W.R. Ochieng'. Nairobi: Evans Brothers.

Odinga, Oginga. 1967. *Not Yet Uhuru: The Autobiography of Oginga Odinga*. London: Heinemann.

O'Donnell, Guillermo. 1973. *Modernization and Bureaucratic Authoritarianism: Studies in South American Politics*. Berkeley: University of California.

——— 1996. "Illusions about Consolidation." *Journal of Democracy* 7 (2): 34–51.

O'Donnell, Guillermo, and Philippe C. Schmitter. 1986. *Transitions from Authoritarian Rule: Tentative Conclusions about Uncertain Democracies*. Baltimore, Md.: Johns Hopkins University Press.

O'Gorman, Frank. 1975. *The Rise of Party in England: The Rockingham Whigs, 1760–82*. London: George Allen & Unwin.

——— 1982. *The Emergence of the British Two-Party System, 1760–1832*. London: Edward Arnold.

Oloo, Adams G.R. 2004. "Money and Politics: The Case of Party Nominations in Kenya." Unpublished manuscript. Department of Political Science and Public Administration, University of Nairobi.

Olson, Mancur. 1982. *The Rise and Decline of Nations: Economic Growth, Stagflation, and Social Rigidities*. New Haven, Conn.: Yale University Press.

Olukoshi, Adebayo O., ed. 1998. *The Politics of Opposition in Contemporary Africa*. Uppsala: Nordic Africa Institute.

Ordeshook, Peter, and Olga Shvetsova. 1994. "Ethnic Heterogeneity, District Magnitude, and the Number of Parties." *American Journal of Political Science* 38 (1): 100–23.

Osaghae, Eghosa. 1999. "Democratization in Sub-Saharan Africa: Faltering Prospects, New Hopes." *Journal of Contemporary African Studies* 17 (1): 5–28.

Osei-Kwame, Peter, and Peter J. Taylor. 1984. "A Politics of Failure: The Political Geography of Ghanaian Elections, 1954–1979." *Annals of the Association of American Geographers* 74 (4): 574–89.

Ottaway, Marina. 1999. "Ethnic Politics in Africa: Change and Continuity." In *State, Conflict, and Democracy in Africa*, ed. R. Joseph. Boulder, Colo.: Lynne Rienner.

Owen, John B. 1957. *The Rise of the Pelhams*. New York: Barnes & Noble.

Owona Nguini, Mathias Eric. 1996. "L'Etat et les milieux d'affaires au Cameroun: autoritarisme, ajustement au marché et démocratie." *Polis* 2 (2).

Oyugi, Walter O. 1992. "Ethnicity in the Electoral Process: The 1992 General Elections in Kenya." *African Journal of Political Science* 2 (1): 41–69.

Palda, Filip, and Kristian Palda. 1998. "The Impact of Campaign Expenditures on Political Competition in the French Legislative Elections of 1993." *Public Choice* 94 (1–2): 157–74.

Pedler, Frederick. 1975. "British Planning and Private Enterprise in Colonial Africa." In *Colonialism in Africa, 1870–1960*, ed. L.H. Gann and P. Duignan. London: Cambridge University Press.

Pempel, T.J., ed. 1990. *Uncommon Democracies: The One-Party Dominant Regimes*. Ithaca, N.Y.: Cornell University Press.

Person, Yves. 1982. "French West Africa and Decolonization." In *The Transfer of Power in Africa*, ed. P. Gifford and W.R. Louis. New Haven, Conn.: Yale University Press.

Pilgrim, Markus, and Ralf Meier. 1995. "National Chambers of Commerce: A Primer on the Organization and Role of Chamber Systems." Washington, D.C.: Center for International and Private Enterprise

Pill, Huw, and Mahmood Pradhan. 1995. "Financial Indicators and Financial Change in Africa and Asia." IMF Working Paper 95/123. Washington, D.C.: International Monetary Fund.

Pitcher, M. Anne. 2004. "Conditions, Commitments, and the Politics of Restructuring in Africa." *Comparative Politics* 36 (4): 379–98.

Plumb, J.H. 1967. *The Origins of Political Stability, England, 1675–1725*. Boston: Houghton Mifflin.

Popiel, Paul A. 1994. "Financial Systems in Sub-Saharan Africa: A Comparative Study." World Bank Discussion Paper No. 260. Washington, D.C.: World Bank.

Posner, Daniel N. 1995. "Malawi's New Dawn." *Journal of Democracy* 6 (1): 131–45.

——— 2004. "Measuring Ethnic Fractionalization in Africa." *American Journal of Political Science* 48 (4): 849–63.

——— 2005. *Institutions and Ethnic Politics in Africa*. New York: Cambridge University Press.

Pottier, Johan. 1993. "Taking Stock: Food Marketing Reform in Rwanda, 1982–89." *African Affairs* 92 (366): 5–30.

Powell, G. Bingham, and Guy D. Whitten. 1993. "A Cross-National Analysis of Economic Voting: Taking Account of the Political Context." *American Journal of Political Science* 37 (2): 391–414.

Power, Joey. 2010. *Political Culture and Nationalism in Malawi: Building Kwacha.* Rochester, N.Y.: University of Rochester Press.

Pratt, Cranford. 1982. "Colonial Governments and the Transfer of Power in East Africa." In *The Transfer of Power in Africa*, ed. P. Gifford and W.R. Louis. New Haven, Conn.: Yale University Press.

Pressnell, L.S. 1956. *Country Banking in the Industrial Revolution.* Oxford: Oxford University Press.

Przeworski, Adam. 1991. *Democracy and the Market: Political and Economic Reforms in Eastern Europe and Latin America.* New York: Cambridge University Press.

1999. "Minimalist Conception of Democracy: A Defense." In *Democracy's Value*, ed. I. Shapiro and C. Hacker-Cordon. Cambridge: Cambridge University Press.

Przeworski, Adam, Michael E. Alvarez, Jose Antonio Cheibub, and Fernando Limongi. 2000. *Democracy and Development: Political Institutions and Well-Being in the World, 1950–1990.* New York: Cambridge University Press.

Przeworski, Adam, and Michael Wallerstein. 1982. "The Structure of Class Conflict in Democratic Capitalist Societies." *American Political Science Review* 76 (2): 215–38.

Quinn, John J. 1999. "The Managerial Bourgeoisie: Capital Accumulation, Development and Democracy." In *Postimperialism and World Politics*, ed. R.L. Sklar and D. Becker. Westport, Conn.: Praeger.

Rabushka, Alvin, and Kenneth A. Shepsle. 1972. *Politics in Plural Societies.* Columbus, Ohio: Merrill.

Radnitz, Scott. 2010. *Weapons of the Wealthy: Predatory Regimes and Elite-Led Protests in Central Asia.* Ithaca, N.Y.: Cornell University Press.

Rakner, Lise. 2001. "The Pluralist Paradox: The Decline of Economic Interest Groups in Zambia in the 1990s." *Development and Change* 32: 521–43.

Rakner, Lise, and Lars Svasand. 2002. *Multiparty Elections in Africa's New Democracies.* Bergen: Chr. Michelsen Institute.

Rakner, Lise, and Nicolas van de Walle. 2009. "Opposition Weakness in Africa." *Journal of Democracy* 20 (3): 108–21.

Rand McNally and Company. 1945–1965. *Rand McNally International Bankers Directory.* Chicago: Rand McNally.

Rapley, John. 1993. *Ivoirien Capitalism: African Entrepreneurs in Côte d'Ivoire.* Boulder, Colo.: Lynne Rienner.

Rathbone, Richard. 1973. "Business in Politics: Party Struggle in Ghana, 1949–57." *Journal of Development Studies* 9 (3): 391–401.

Reinhart, Carmen M., and Kenneth S. Rogoff. 2004. "The Modern History of Exchange Rate Arrangements: A Reinterpretation." *Quarterly Journal of Economics* 119 (1): 1–48.

Reinhart, Carmen M., and Ioannis Tokatlidis. 2000. "Financial Liberalization: The African Experience." Paper prepared for the African Economic Research Consortium Workshop, Nairobi, Kenya, 2–7 December 2000.

Republic of Kenya. 1999. "Report of the Judicial Commission Appointed to Inquire into Tribal Clashes in Kenya." The Commissions of Inquiry Act, Cap. 102. Nairobi: Government Printer.

2005. "Report of the Judicial Commission of Inquiry into the Goldenberg Affair." Nairobi: Government Printer.

Reynal-Querol, Marta. 2002. "Ethnicity, Political Systems, and Civil Wars." *Journal of Conflict Resolution* 46 (1): 29–54.

Reynolds, Andrew. 1995. "Constitutional Engineering in Southern Africa." *Journal of Democracy* 6 (2): 86–99.

Rich, Jeremy M. 2007. *A Workman is Worthy of His Meat: Food and Colonialism in the Gabon Estuary*. Lincoln: University of Nebraska Press.

Richards, Audrey I., Ford Sturrock, and Jean M. Fortt, eds. 1973. *Subsistence to Commercial Farming in Present-Day Buganda: An Economic and Anthropological Survey*. Cambridge: Cambridge University Press.

Riker, William H. 1962. *The Theory of Political Coalitions*. New Haven, Conn.: Yale University Press.

———. 1982a. *Liberalism Against Populism: A Confrontation Between the Theory of Democracy and the Theory of Social Choice*. Prospect Heights, Ill.: Waveland Press.

———. 1982b. "The Two-Party System and Duverger's Law: An Essay on the History of Political Science." *American Political Science Review* 76: 753–66.

Rogowski, Ronald. 1989. *Commerce and Coalitions: How Trade Affects Domestic Political Alignments*. Princeton, N.J.: Princeton University Press.

Root, Hilton L. 1994. *The Fountain of Privilege: Political Foundations of Markets in Old Regime France and England*. Berkeley: University of California Press.

Ross, Michael L. 1999. "Does Oil Hinder Democracy?" *World Politics* 53 (April): 325–61.

Rotberg, Robert I. 1965. *The Rise of Nationalism in Central Africa: The Making of Malawi and Zambia, 1873–1964*. London: Oxford University Press.

Rothchild, Donald, and Victor A. Olorunsola. 1983. "Managing Competing State and Ethnic Claims." In *State Versus Ethnic Claims: African Policy Dilemmas*, ed. D. Rothchild and V.A. Olorunsola. Boulder, Colo.: Westview Press.

Rousseau, Peter L., and Richard Sylla. 2005. "Emerging Financial Markets and Early U.S. Growth." *Explorations in Economic History* 42: 1–26.

Rouyer, Alwyn R. 1975. "Political Recruitment and Political Change in Kenya." *Journal of Developing Areas* 9 (4): 539–62.

Rueschemeyer, Dietrich, Evelyne Huber Stephens, and John D. Stephens. 1992. *Capitalist Development and Democracy*. Chicago, Ill.: University of Chicago Press.

Rustow, Dankwart A. 1970. "Transitions to Democracy: Toward a Dynamic Model." *Comparative Politics* 2 (3): 337–64.

Sabato, Larry, and Glenn Simpson. 1996. *Dirty Little Secrets: The Persistence of Corruption in American Politics*. New York: Random House.

Sandbrook, Richard. 1985. *The Politics of Africa's Economic Stagnation*. Cambridge: Cambridge University Press.

———. 1993. *The Politics of Africa's Economic Recovery*. New York: Cambridge University Press.

Saul, Mahir. 1986. "Development of the Grain Market and Merchants in Burkina Faso." *Journal of Modern African Studies* 24 (1): 127–53.

Scarritt, James R. 2006. "The Strategic Choice of Multiethnic Parties in Zambia's Dominant and Personalist Party System." *Commonwealth and Comparative Politics* 44 (2): 234–56.

Scarritt, James R., and Shaheen Mozaffar. 1999. "The Specification of Ethnic Cleavages and Ethnopolitical Groups for the Analysis of Democratic Competition in Africa." *Nationalism and Ethnic Politics* 5 (Spring): 82–117.

Schachter, Ruth. 1961. "Single-Party Systems in West Africa." *American Political Science Review* 55 (2): 294–307.

Schaffer, Frederic C. 1998. *Democracy in Translation: Understanding Politics in an Unfamiliar Culture*. Ithaca, N.Y.: Cornell University Press.

Schatz, Sayre P. 1977. *Nigerian Capitalism*. Berkeley: University of California Press.

Schatzberg, Michael G. 2001. *Political Legitimacy in Middle Africa*. Bloomington: Indiana University Press.

Schedler, Andreas. 2002. "Elections without Democracy: The Menu of Manipulation." *Journal of Democracy* 13 (2): 36–50.

ed. 2006. *Electoral Authoritarianism: The Dynamics of Unfree Competition*. Boulder, Colo.: Lynne Rienner.

Scheiner, Ethan. 2006. *Democracy Without Competition in Japan: Opposition Failure in a One-Party Dominant State*. New York: Cambridge University Press.

Schmitter, Philippe C., and Terry L. Karl. 1996. "What Democracy Is ... and Is Not." In *The Global Resurgence of Democracy*, ed. L. Diamond and M. Plattner. Baltimore, Md.: Johns Hopkins University Press.

Schneider, Ben Ross. 2002. "Why Is Mexican Business So Organized?" *Latin American Research Review* 37 (1): 77–118.

2004. *Business Politics and the State in Twentieth-Century Latin America*. New York: Cambridge University Press.

Schofield, Norman, and Michael Laver. 1985. "Bargaining Theory and Portfolio Payoffs in European Coalition Governments 1945–1983." *British Journal of Political Science* 15 (2): 143–64.

Schumpeter, Joseph A. 1942. *Capitalism, Socialism and Democracy*. New York: Harper & Row.

Schwartz, Alfred. 1996. "Attitudes to Cotton Growing in Burkina Faso: Different Farmers, Different Behaviours." In *Economics of Agricultural Policies in Developing Countries*, eds. Michel Benoît-Cattin et al. Paris: Editions de la Revue Française d'Economie.

Seavoy, Ronald E. 1982. *The Origins of the American Business Corporation, 1784–1855*. Wesport, Conn.: Greenwood Press.

Sebudubedu, David, and Bertha Z. Osei-Hwedie. 2010. "In Permanent Opposition: Botswana's Other Political Parties." *South African Journal of International Affairs* 17 (1): 85–102.

Seck, Diery, and Yasim H. El Nil. 1993. "Financial Liberalization in Africa." *World Development* 21 (11): 1867–81.

Sellers, Charles. 1991. *The Market Revolution: Jacksonian America, 1815–1846*. New York: Oxford University Press.

Sender, John, and Sheila Smith. 1986. *The Development of Capitalism in Africa*. London: Methuen.

Shaw, Edward. 1973. *Financial Deepening in Economic Development*. New York: Oxford University Press.

Shaw, Timothy M. 1982. "Beyond Neo-Colonialism: Varieties of Corporatism in Africa." *Journal of Modern African Studies* 20 (June): 239–61.

Shenton, Robert W. 1986. *The Development of Capitalism in Northern Nigeria*. Toronto: University of Toronto Press.

Shepsle, Kenneth A. 1991. "Discretion, Institutions, and the Problem of Government Commitment." In *Social Theory for a Changing Society*, ed. P. Bourdieu and J.S. Coleman. Boulder, Colo.: Westview Press.

Shils, Edward. 1971. "Opposition in the New States of Asia and Africa: The Situation of Opposition Parties in the New States." In *Studies in Opposition*, ed. R. Barker. London: Macmillan.

Shin, Myungsoon, Youngjae Jin, Donald A. Gross, and Kihong Eom. 2005. "Money Matters in Party-Centered Politics: Campaign Spending in Korean Congressional Elections." *Electoral Studies* 24 (1): 85–101.

Sindjoun, Luc. 1998. "La Politique d'Affection en Afrique Noire: Société de Parenté, 'Société d'Etat' et Libéralisation Politique au Cameroun." Occasional Paper Series 2 (1). Harare: African Association of Political Science.

Sklar, Richard L. 1963. *Nigerian Political Parties: Power in an Emergent African Nation.* Princeton, N.J.: Princeton University Press.

———. 1979. "The Nature of Class Domination in Africa." *Journal of Modern African Studies* 17 (4): 531–52.

Smith, Mark A. 2000. *American Business and Political Power.* Chicago, Ill.: University of Chicago Press.

Smith, Robert Worthington. 1969. "Political Organization and Canvassing: Yorkshire Elections before the Reform Bill." *American Historical Review* 74 (5): 1538–60.

Snyder, Frank Gregory. 1965. *One-Party Government in Mali: Transition toward Control.* New Haven, Conn.: Yale University Press.

Snyder, Jack. 2000. *From Voting to Violence: Democratization and Nationalist Conflict.* New York: Norton.

Socpa, Antoine. 2000. "Les dons dans le jeu électoral au Cameroun" *Cahiers d'Études Africaines* 40 (157): 91–108.

Solé-Ollé, Albert, and Pilar Sorribas-Navarro. 2008. "The Effects of Partisan Alignment on the Allocation of Intergovernmental Transfers: Differences-in-Differences Estimates for Spain." *Journal of Public Economics* 92 (12): 2302–19.

Somolekae, Gloria. 2005. "Political Parties in Botswana." EISA Research Report No. 27. Johannesburg.

Stasavage, David. 1997. "The CFA Franc Zone and Fiscal Discipline." *Journal of African Economies* 6 (1): 132–67.

———. 2003. *The Political Economy of a Common Currency: The CFA Franc Zone Since 1945.* London: Ashgate.

———. 2007. "Partisan Politics and Public Debt: The Importance of the 'Whig Supremacy' for Britain's Financial Revolution." *European Review of Economic History* 11 (1): 123–53.

State Geological Committee of the Soviet Union. 1964. *Atlas Narodov Mira.* Moscow: Miklukho-Maklai Ethnological Institute, Department of Geodesy and Cartography, State Geological Committee of the Soviet Union.

Stewart, Frances, ed. 2008. *Horizontal Inequalities and Conflict: Understanding Group Violence in Multi-Ethnic Societies.* New York: Palgrave Macmillan.

Stockwell, Sarah. 2000. *The Business of Decolonization: British Business Strategies in the Gold Coast.* New York: Oxford University Press.

Stone, Randall W. 2004. "The Political Economy of IMF Lending in Africa." *American Political Science Review* 98 (4): 577–91.

Stoner-Weiss, Kathryn. 1997. *Local Heroes: The Political Economy of Russian Regional Governance.* Princeton, N.J.: Princeton University Press.

Storey, Andy. 2001. "Structural Adjustment, State Power & Genocide: The World Bank & Rwanda." *Review of African Political Economy* 28 (89): 365–85.

Swainson, Nicola. 1980. *The Development of Corporate Capitalism in Kenya, 1918–77.* Berkeley: University of California Press.

Sylla, Richard. 1998. "U.S. Security Markets and the Banking System, 1790–1840." *Federal Reserve Bank of St. Louis Review* 80 (3): 83–98.

Sylvester, Christine. 1990. "Unities and Disunities in Zimbabwe's 1990 Election." *Journal of Modern African Studies* 28 (3): 375–400.

Takougang, Joseph. 2003. "The 2002 Legislative Election in Cameroon: A Retrospective on Cameroon's Stalled Democracy Movement." *Journal of Modern African Studies* 41 (3): 421–35.

Takougang, Joseph, and Milton Krieger. 1998. *African State and Society in the 1990s: Cameroon's Political Crossroads.* Boulder, Colo.: Westview Press.

Tamba, Isaac, and Louise Tchambane Djine. 1995. "De la crise à la réforme des institutions bancaires africaines: le cas du Cameroun." *Tiers-Monde* 36 (144): 813–35.

Tangri, Roger K. 1999. *The Politics of Patronage in Africa: Parastatals, Privatization, and Private Enterprise.* Oxford: James Currey.

Tavits, Margit. 2009. "Geographically Targeted Spending: Exploring the Electoral Strategies of Incumbent Governments." *European Political Science Review* 1 (1): 103–23.

Taylor, Scott D. 2007. *Business and the State in Southern Africa: The Politics of Economic Reform.* Boulder, Colo.: Lynne Rienner.

Temu, Andrew E., and Jean M. Due. 2000. "The Business Environment in Tanzania after Socialism: Challenges of Reforming Banks, Parastatals, Taxation and the Civil Service." *Journal of Modern African Studies* 38 (4): 683–712.

Thiam, Habib. 2001. *Par devoir et par amitié.* Paris: Rocher.

Thioub, Ibrahima, Momar-Coumba Diop, and Catherine Boone. 1998. "Economic Liberalization in Senegal: Shifting Politics of Indigenous Business Interests." *African Studies Review* 41 (2): 63–89.

Thompson, Virginia, and Richard Adloff. 1960. *The Emerging States in French Equatorial Africa.* Stanford, Calif.: Stanford University Press.

1965. *The Malagasy Republic.* Stanford, Calif.: Stanford University Press.

1975. "French Economic Policy in Tropical Africa." In *Colonialism in Africa, 1870–1960,* ed. L.H. Gann and P. Duignan. London: Cambridge University Press.

Throup, David W. 1987. "The Construction and Destruction of the Kenyatta State." In *The Political Economy of Kenya,* ed. M.G. Schatzberg. New York: Praeger.

1993. "Elections and Political Legitimacy in Kenya." *Africa: Journal of the International African Institute* 63 (3): 371–96.

Throup, David W., and Charles Hornsby. 1998. *Multi-Party Politics in Kenya: The Kenyatta and Moi States and the Triumph of the System in the 1992 Election.* Oxford: James Currey.

Tilly, Charles. 1992. *Coercion, Capital, and European States, AD 990–1992.* Cambridge, Mass.: Blackwell.

Tocqueville, Alexis de. 1988. *Democracy in America.* Translated by G. Lawrence. New York: Harper & Row.

Tomz, Michael, Jason Wittenberg, and Gary King. 2001. "CLARIFY: Software for Interpreting and Presenting Statistical Results." Cambridge, Mass.: Harvard University Press.

Trewartha, Glenn T., and Wilbur Zelinsky. 1954. "Population Patterns in Tropical Africa." *Annals of the Associations of American Geographers* 44 (2): 135–62.

Tsie, Balefi. 1996. "The Political Context of Botswana's Development Performance." *Journal of Southern African Studies* 22 (4): 599–616.

Uche, Chibuike Ugochukwu. 1997. "Banking 'Scandal' in a British West African Colony: The Politics of the African Continental Bank Crisis." *Financial History Review* 4 (1): 51–68.

———. 1998. "Accounting and Control in Barclays Bank (DCO): The Lending to Africans Episode." *Accounting, Business and Financial History* 8 (3): 239–60.

———. 1999. "Foreign Banks, Africans, and Credit in Colonial Nigeria, c. 1890–1912." *Economic History Review* 52 (4): 669–91.

———. 2003. "Credit for Africans: The Demand for a 'National Bank' in the Gold Coast Colony." *Financial History Review* 10: 75–90.

UNCTAD. 1999. *African Development in a Comparative Perspective*. Trenton, N.J.: Africa World Press.

van Cranenburgh, Oda. 2003. "Power and Competition: The Institutional Context of African Multi-Party Politics." In *African Political Parties: Evolution, Institutionalisation and Governance*, ed. M.A.M. Salih. London: Pluto Press.

van de Walle, Nicolas. 1991. "The Decline of the Franc Zone: Monetary Politics in Francophone Africa." *African Affairs* 90 (360): 383–405.

———. 1993. "The Politics of Nonreform in Cameroon." In *Hemmed In: Responses to Africa's Economic Decline*, ed. T.M. Callaghy and J. Ravenhill. New York: Columbia University Press.

———. 2001. *African Economies and the Politics of Permanent Crisis, 1979–1999*. New York: Cambridge University Press.

———. 2003. "Presidentialism and Clientelism in Africa's Emerging Party Systems." *Journal of Modern African Studies* 41 (2): 297–321.

———. 2006. "Tipping Games: When Do Opposition Parties Coalesce?" In *Electoral Authoritarianism: The Dynamics of Unfree Competition*, ed. A. Schedler. Boulder: Lynne Rienner.

———. 2007. "Meet the New Boss, Same as the Old Boss? The Evolution of Political Clientelism in Africa." In *Patrons, Clients, and Policies: Patterns of Democratic Accountability and Political Competition*, ed. H. Kitschelt and S.I. Wilkinson. New York: Cambridge University Press.

———. 2009. "The Institutional Origins of Inequality in Sub-Saharan Africa." *Annual Review of Political Science* 12: 307–27.

van Fenstermaker, J. 1965. *The Development of American Commercial Banking: 1782–1837*. Kent, Ohio: Kent State University Press.

Vandenberg, Paul. 2003. "Ethno-Sectoral Cleavages and Economic Development: Reflections on the Second Kenya Debate." *Journal of Modern African Studies* 41 (3): 437–55.

Vander Weyer, Martin. 2000. *Falling Eagle: The Decline of Barclays Bank*. London: Weidenfeld & Nicolson.

Vaughan, Megan. 2007. *The Story of an African Famine: Gender and Famine in Twentieth-Century Malawi*. New York: Cambridge University Press.

Verschave, François-Xavier. 2000. *Noir silence: Qui arrêtera la Françafrique?* Paris: Les Arènes.

Verwimp, Philip. 2003. "The Political Economy of Coffee, Dictatorship, and Genocide." *European Journal of Political Economy* 19: 161–81.

Villalón, Leonardo A., and Peter VonDoepp, eds. 2005. *The Fate of Africa's Democratic Experiments: Elites and Institutions.* Bloomington: Indiana University Press.

von den Steinen, Karl. 1972. "The Fabric of Interest in the County: The Buckinghamshire Election of 1784." *Albion* 4 (4): 206–18.

Wade, Robert. 1990. *Governing the Market: Economic Theory and the Role of Government in East Asian Industrialization.* Princeton, N.J.: Princeton University Press.

Wallerstein, Immanuel. 1961. "What Happened to the Opposition?" *West Africa*, 25 November.

⸻ 1970. "The Colonial Era in Africa: Changes in the Social Structure." In *Colonialism in Africa, 1870–1960*, ed. L. H. Gann and P. Duignan. Cambridge: Cambridge University Press.

Wallis, John Joseph. 2008. "Answering Mary Shirley's Question, or What Can the World Bank Learn from American History?" In *Political Institutions and Financial Development*, ed. S. Haber, D.C. North, and B.R. Weingast. Stanford, Calif.: Stanford University Press.

Wantchekon, Leonard. 2003. "Clientelism and Voting Behavior: Evidence from a Field Experiment in Benin." *World Politics* 55 (April): 399–422.

Warnier, Jean-Pierre. 1993. *L'Esprit d'Entreprise au Cameroun.* Paris: Editions Karthala.

Wartena, Dorothea. 2006. "Styles of Making a Living and Ecological Change on the Fon and Adja Plateaux in South Bénin, ca. 1600–1990." Unpublished Ph.D. thesis, Wageningen Universiteit.

Warwick, Paul V. 1996. "Coalition Government Membership in West European Parliamentary Democracies." *British Journal of Political Science* 26 (4): 471–99.

Warwick, Paul V., and James N. Druckman. 2001. "Portfolio Salience and the Proportionality of Payoffs in Coalition Governments." *British Journal of Political Science* 31 (4): 627–49.

Weingast, Barry R. 1997. "The Political Foundation of Democracy and the Rule of Law." *American Political Science Review* 91 (2): 245–63.

Weinstein, Warren. 1974. "Ethnicity and Conflict Regulation: The 1972 Burundi Revolt." *Africa Spectrum* 9 (1): 42–49.

Were, Maureen, Rose Ngugi, and Phyllis Makau. 2006. "Understanding the Reform Process in Kenya." In *Understanding Economic Reforms in Africa: A Tale of Seven Nations*, ed. J. Mensah. Basingstoke: Palgrave Macmillan.

Wickins, Peter Lionel. 1986. *Africa 1880–1980: An Economic History.* Capetown: Oxford University Press.

Widner, Jennifer A. 1992. *The Rise of a Party-State in Kenya: From "Harambee!" to "Nyayo!"* Berkeley: University of California Press.

⸻ 1997. "Political Parties and Civil Societies in Sub-Saharan Africa." In *Democracy in Africa: The Hard Road Ahead*, ed. M. Ottaway. Boulder, Colo.: Lynne Rienner.

Widner, Jennifer A., ed. 1994. *Economic Change and Political Liberalization in Sub-Saharan Africa.* Baltimore, Md.: Johns Hopkins University Press.

Williams, Llewelyn. 1969. "Forest and Agricultural Resources of Dahomey, West Africa." *Economic Botany* 23 (4): 352–72.

Williamson, John. 1993. "Democracy and the Washington Consensus." *World Development* 21 (8): 1329–36.

⸻ ed. 1994. *The Political Economy of Policy Reform.* Washington, D.C.: Institute for International Economics.

Wilson, Ernest J. 1990. "Strategies of State Control of the Economy: Nationalization and Indigenization in Africa." *Comparative Politics* 22 (4): 401–19.

Wilson, J.S.G. 1957. *French Banking Structure and Credit Policy.* London: G. Bell and Sons.

Wilson, Peter J. 1992. *Freedom by a Hair's Breadth: Tsimihety in Madagascar.* Ann Arbor: University of Michigan Press.

Wisjen, Frans J.S., and Ralph E.S. Tanner. 2002. *"I Am Just a Sukuma": Globalization and Identity Construction in Northwest.* Amsterdam: Rodopi.

Wolf, Thomas P. 2006. "Immunity or Accountability? Daniel Toroitich arap Moi: Kenya's First Retired President." In *Legacies of Power: Leadership Change and Former Presidents in African Politics,* ed. R. Southall and H. Melber. Uppsala: Nordic Africa Institute.

Woods, Dwayne. 2003. "The Tragedy of the Cocoa Pod: Rent-seeking, Land and Ethnic Conflict in Ivory Coast." *Journal of Modern African Studies* 41 (4): 641–55.

World Bank. 1963. *The Economic Development of Kenya.* Baltimore: Johns Hopkins Press.

—— 1981. *Accelerated Development for Sub-Saharan Africa: An Agenda for Action.* Washington, D.C.: World Bank.

—— 1996. "Republic of Cameroon. The Challenge: Harnessing Unrealized Potential. A Private Sector Assessment." Report No. 13955-CM. Washington, D.C.: World Bank.

—— 1997. "Adjustment Lending in Sub-Saharan Africa: An Update." Report No. 16594. Washington, D.C.: World Bank.

—— 2000. "Kenya: Country Assistance Evaluation." Report No. 21409. Operations Evaluation Department. Washington, D.C.: World Bank.

—— 2001. "Cameroon: Country Assistance Evaluation." Report No. 21788. Operations Evaluation Department. Washington, D.C.: World Bank.

—— 2003. "Kenya: A Policy Agenda to Restore Growth." Report No. 25840-KE. Poverty Reduction and Economic Management 2. Country Department AFC05. Africa Region. Washington, D.C.: World Bank.

—— 2005. "Doing Business in 2006. Sub-Saharan Africa Regional Report." Washington, D.C.: World Bank.

—— 2009. "World Development Indicators." Washington, D.C.: World Bank.

—— 2011. "Doing Business 2011: Making a Difference for Entrepreneurs." Washington, D.C.: World Bank.

Woronoff, Jon. 1972. *West African Wager: Houphouet versus Nkrumah.* Metuchen, N.J.: Scarecrow Press.

Wunder, Sven. 2003. "When the Dutch Disease Met the French Connection: Oil, Macroeconomics and Forests in Gabon." Report for the CIFOR-CARPE-USAID project on "The Impact of Macroeconomic and Agricultural Policies on Forest Conditions in Gabon." Bogor, Indonesia: Center for International Forestry Research.

Young, Crawford. 1986. "Zaire and Cameroon." In *Politics and Government in African States, 1960–1985,* ed. P. Duignan and R.H. Jackson. Stanford, Calif.: Hoover Institution Press.

Yusuf, Ahmed Beita. 1975. "Capital Formation and Management among the Muslim Hausa Traders of Kano, Nigeria." *Africa* 45 (2): 167–82.

Zakaria, Fareed. 1997. "The Rise of Illiberal Democracy." *Foreign Affairs* 76 (6): 22–43.

Zolberg, Aristide. 1966. *Creating Political Order: The Party-States of West Africa.* Chicago, Ill.: Rand McNally.

1969. *One-Party Government in the Ivory Coast.* Princeton, N.J.: Princeton University Press.

Zysman, John. 1983. *Governments, Markets, and Growth: Financial Systems and the Politics of Industrial Change.* Ithaca, N.Y.: Cornell University Press.

Index

Other Books in the Series (*continued from page iii*)